DK PUBLISHING, INC.

MILLENNIUM
FAMILY
ENCYCLOPEDIA

Shipping signal *see* FLAGS

Zambian bank note *see* MONEY

1970s platform shoes *see* CLOTHES AND FASHION

Colt Peacemaker *see* WEAPONS

Postage stamps *see* STAMPS AND POSTAL SERVICES

Yu'pik family, Alaska *see* ARCTIC OCEAN

Straw boater *see* SAILING AND OTHER WATER SPORTS

King and Queen *see* CHESS

Picture book *see* CHILDREN'S LITERATURE

Tenor horn *see* MUSICAL INSTRUMENTS

Gecko *see* LIZARDS

Honey fungus *see* MUSHROOMS

Durian fruit *see* FRUITS AND SEEDS

Goose eggs *see* EGGS

Monarch butterfly *see* EVOLUTION

Clown fish *see* ECOLOGY

Horsefly *see* INSECTS

Duckling *see* DUCKS, GEESE, AND SWANS

Bloodhound *see* DOGS

Chemical reactions *see* CHEMISTRY

Lightbulb *see* INVENTIONS

Ethane molecule *see* ATOMS AND MOLECULES

Personal stereo *see* RADIO

Hubble space telescope *see* SPACE EXPLORATION

Mobile phone *see* TELEPHONES

SLR camera *see* CAMERAS

DNA double helix *see* GENETICS

Jaguar XK120 *see* CARS AND TRUCKS

Flint arrowhead *see* STONE AGE

Amulet *see* EGYPT, ANCIENT

Board Game *see* VIKINGS

Clasp *see* CHINA, HISTORY OF

Throwing dice *see* ROMAN EMPIRE

Ceremonial dress *see* NORTH AMERICA, HISTORY OF

Thumbscrew *see* WITCHES AND WITCHCRAFT

Ancient coins *see* SUMERIANS

Portable sextant *see* EXPLORATION

Dagger *see* WEAPONS

Sabaton *see* ARMS AND ARMOR

MILLENNIUM
FAMILY
ENCYCLOPEDIA

VOLUME 1

Aboriginal Australians
to
Cities

DK PUBLISHING, INC.

A DK PUBLISHING BOOK

Senior Editor Jayne Parsons **Senior Art Editor** Gill Shaw

Project Editors
Marian Broderick, Gill Cooling, Maggie Crowley, Hazel Egerton, Cynthia O'Neill, Veronica Pennycook, Louise Pritchard, Steve Setford, Jackie Wilson

Project Art Editors
Jane Felstead, Martyn Foote, Neville Graham, Jamie Hanson, Christopher Howson, Jill Plank, Floyd Sayers, Jane Tetzlaff, Ann Thompson

Editors
Rachel Beaugié, Nic Kynaston, Sarah Levete, Karen O'Brien, Linda Sonntag

Art Editors
Tina Borg, Diane Clouting, Tory Gordon-Harris

DTP Designers
Andrew O'Brien, Cordelia Springer

Managing Editor Ann Kramer **Managing Art Editor** Peter Bailey

Senior DTP Designer Mathew Birch

Picture Research Jo Walton, Kate Duncan, Liz Moore

DK Picture Library Ola Rudowska, Melanie Simmonds

Country pages by PAGE*One*: Bob Gordon, Helen Parker, Thomas Keenes, Sarah Watson, Chris Clark

Cartographers Peter Winfield, James Anderson

Research Robert Graham, Angela Koo

Editorial Assistants Sarah-Louise Reed, Nichola Roberts

Production Louise Barratt, Charlotte Traill

First American Edition, 1997
2 4 6 8 10 9 7 5 3 1

Published in the United States by DK Publishing, Inc., 95 Madison Avenue, New York, New York 10016
Visit us on the World Wide Web at http://www.dk.com

Copyright 1997 © Dorling Kindersley Ltd., London

A catalog record is available from the Library of Congress.

ISBN 0-7894-2216-6

Color reproduction by Colourscan, Singapore
Printed and bound in Italy by A. Mondadori Editore, Verona

CONTRIBUTORS AND CONSULTANTS

Simon Adams BSc MSc
Historian and writer

Norman Barrett MA
Sports writer and consultant

Dr Martin R. Bates BSc, PhD
Institute of Archaeology
University of London

David Burnie BSc
Science and natural history writer

Jack Challoner BSc, ARCS, PGCE
Science writer, formerly with the Education
Unit, Science Museum, London

Julie Childs BSc
Zoologist and natural history writer,
former Head of Public Affairs, Zoological
Society of London

Neil Clark BSc
Paleontologist, Hunterian Museum and
University of Glasgow

Paul Collins MA
Institute of Archaeology
University College, London

Dr Gordon Daniels
Reader in History,
University of Sheffield

Veronica Doubleday
Lecturer, Historical and Critical Studies,
University of Brighton

John Farndon
Writer and consultant

Roger Few BA
Author on natural history and the
environment

Theresa Greenaway BSc, ARCS
Botanist and natural history writer

Frances Halpin BSc
Science consultant and teacher at
Royal Russell School

Dr Austen Ivereigh D Phil
Lecturer in Latin American History
University of Leeds

Robin Kerrod FRAS
Science writer and consultant

Bruce P. Lenman
Professor of Modern History
University of St Andrews

Nicky Levell
Curator Collections History,
The Horniman Museum

John E. Llewellyn-Jones BSc
Zoologist and botanist; writer and lecturer

Miranda MacQuitty BSc, PhD
Zoologist and natural history writer

Kevin McRae
Writer and consultant

Haydn Middleton MA
Historian and author

Mark O'Shea BSc, FRGS
Curator of Reptiles, West Midland Safari
Park; tropical herpetologist and zoologist;
natural history author

Chris Oxlade BSc
Writer and consultant, specializing in
science and technology

Douglas Palmer BSc, PhD
Writer, lecturer, and Open University tutor
specializing in palaeobiology

Steve Parker BSc
Zoologist, science writer, and scientific
fellow of the Zoological Society

Tom Parsons MA
Art historian and writer

James Pickford BA
Writer and Electronic editor FT Mastering

Richard Platt BA
Writer and consultant

Matthew Robertson
Senior invertebrate keeper, Bristol Zoo

Theodore Rowland-Entwistle BA, FRCS
Writer and consultant

Noel Simon
Member emiritus of the Species Survival
Commission of IUCN; original compiler
mammalia volume, Red Data Book

Carole Stott BA, FRAS
Astronomy and Space writer;
formerly Head of the Old Royal
Observatory, Greenwich, London

Jonathon Stroud BA
Writer and consultant: Literature

Barbara Taylor BSc
Environmental scientist and natural
history writer

Louise Tythacott
Writer and consultant: Southeast Asia

Richard Walker BSc PhD
Human biology and natural history writer

Marcus Weeks B Mus
Composer and writer

Philip Wilkinson MA
Historian and writer

Elizabeth Wyse BA
Writer and consultant

Dorling Kindersley Cartography
in conjunction with leading
cartographic consultants, embassies,
and consulates

LIST OF MAIN ENTRIES
See index for further topics

COMPARATIVE PLANET SIZES Figures refer to planet diameters

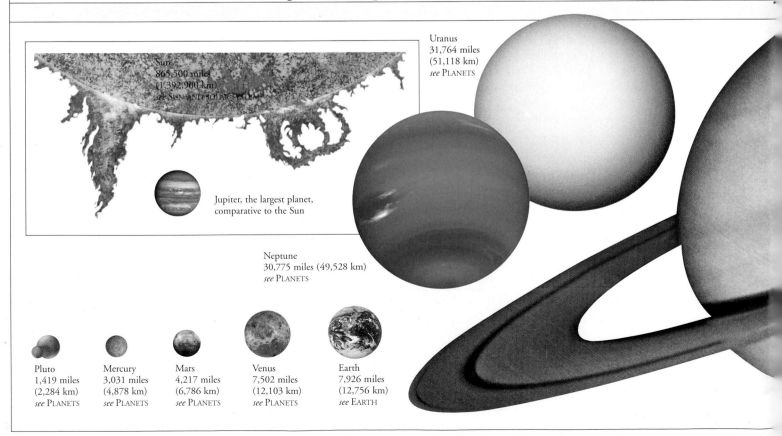

Sun
865,500 miles
(1,392,900 km)
see Sun and solar system

Jupiter, the largest planet,
comparative to the Sun

Uranus
31,764 miles
(51,118 km)
see Planets

Neptune
30,775 miles (49,528 km)
see Planets

Pluto
1,419 miles
(2,284 km)
see Planets

Mercury
3,031 miles
(4,878 km)
see Planets

Mars
4,217 miles
(6,786 km)
see Planets

Venus
7,502 miles
(12,103 km)
see Planets

Earth
7,926 miles
(12,756 km)
see Earth

Saturn
74,901 miles
(120,536 km)
see PLANETS

Jupiter
88,850 miles
(142,984 km)
see PLANETS

HOW TO USE THIS ENCYCLOPEDIA

THE FOLLOWING PAGES WILL HELP YOU get the most out of your copy of the *DK Millennium Family Encyclopedia*. The encyclopedia consists of five volumes. Volumes 1–4 contain nearly 700 main entries organized alphabetically, from Aboriginal Australians to Zoos. To find the entry you want, simply turn to the correct letter of the alphabet.

If you cannot find the topic you want, then turn to Volume 5. This volume includes an index and a gazetteer for the whole encyclopedia, which will direct you right to the page you need. In addition, Volume 5 contains hundreds of reference charts, fact boxes, lists, and tables to supplement the information provided on the main entry pages.

MEASUREMENTS AND ABBREVIATIONS

Most measurements are supplied in both imperial and metric units. Some of the most common abbreviations used in the encyclopedia are shown below in **bold** type.

°C = degrees Celsius
°F = degrees Fahrenheit
K = degrees kelvin
mm = millimeter; **cm** = centimeter
m = meter; **km** = kilometer
in = inch; **ft** = foot; **yd** = yard
g = gram; **kg** = kilogram
oz = ounce; **lb** = pound
ml = milliliter; **l** = liter
pt = pint; **gal** = gallon
sq km (**km²**) = square kilometer
sq ft (**ft²**)= square foot
kmh = kilometers per hour
mph = miles per hour
mya = million years ago
BC = before Christ
AD = anno Domini (refers to any date after the birth of Christ)
c. = circa (about)
b. = born; **d.** = died; **r.** = reigned

THE PAGE LAYOUT
The pages in this encyclopedia have been carefully planned to make each subject as accessible as possible. Main entries are broken down into a hierarchy of information – from a general introduction to more specific individual topics.

Alphabet locators
Letter flashes help you find your way quickly around the encyclopedia.

Subentries
Subentries provide important additional information and expand on points made in the introduction.

This subentry explains how rainbows are caused by raindrops in the air.

Diagrams
Clear diagrams help explain complex processes and scientific concepts.

The diagram here shows how a raindrop splits sunlight into its constituent colors.

Introduction
Clear introductions are the starting point for each entry. The introduction defines and provides an overview of each subject.

In the main entry on COLOR, the introduction explains that colors are different forms of light, and that sunlight contains light of many different colors.

ct as rudders.

Strong chest muscles pull down the wings.

Penguin rises through the water to break through the surface.

Huddling reduces heat loss.

emperor penguins carry chicks around on their feet.

KING PENGUIN

SCIENTIFIC NAME *Aptenodytes patagonica*

ORDER Sphenisciformes

FAMILY Spheniscidae

DISTRIBUTION Islands and ocean north of Antarctica

HABITAT Coasts and open sea

DIET Fish and squid

SIZE Length, including tail 95 cm (37.5 in)

LIFESPAN About 20 years

Natural history data boxes
On the natural history pages, data boxes summarize essential information about a key animal featured in the entry. The box contains information about the animal's size, diet, habitat, lifespan, distribution, and scientific name.

This data box gives you key facts about the King Penguin.

COLLEGES see SCHOOLS AND COLLEGES • COLOMBIA see SOUTH AMERICA, NORTHERN

COLOR

A WORLD WITHOUT COLOR would be dull and uninspiring. Color is a form of light. Light is made up of electromagnetic waves of varying lengths. The human eye detects these different wavelengths and sees them as different colors. White light – like that from the Sun – is a mixture of all the different wavelengths. Objects look colored because they emit or reflect only certain wavelengths of light.

White light spectrum
Passing white light through a transparent triangular block called a prism separates the different wavelengths of light. The prism refracts (bends) each wavelength by a different amount, forming a band of colors called a white light spectrum, or visible spectrum. The seven main colors are red, orange, yellow, green, blue, indigo, and violet. Red has the longest wavelength and violet the shortest. Here, a convex lens combines the colors back into white light.

Rainbow
If it rains on a sunny day, you may well see a rainbow if you stand with your back to the Sun. A rainbow is a curved white light spectrum that forms when light is reflected and refracted by raindrops in the sky.

A rainbow at dawn

How a rainbow forms
The white sunlight passes through a raindrop, the raindrop acts like a tiny prism, refracting the light and splitting it up into its separate colors. The colors fan out and emerge as a spectrum. A rainbow is made up of spectra from millions of raindrops.

Sunlight
Colors refract again.
Spectrum
Light refracts.
Colors reflect off back surface.

Color and temperature
Objects at room temperature emit (give out) electromagnetic waves, but these waves are too long for human eyes to see. Heating an object, such as this steel bar, makes the waves short enough to be seen, and the bar begins to glow. As the bar's temperature rises, it glows with different colors.

Steel bar at 1,170°F (630°C)

Steel bar at 2,790°F (1,530°C)

Spectroscope
An instrument called a spectroscope is used to analyze the light emitted by hot substances. Inside the spectroscope, a prism or diffraction grating (a glass slide scored with fine lines) splits light from a glowing substance into its component wavelengths.

Light source
Diffraction grating

Cone cells
At the back of the eye are special cells called cones that enable humans to see colors. There are three types of cones, called red, green, and blue cones. Each type of cone is sensitive to a different range of light wavelengths. White light stimulates all three types of cones.

Emission spectrum
Each chemical element gives out a unique range of light wavelengths when heated. Seen through a spectroscope, these wavelengths appear as a set of bright lines on a dark background. This is the element's emission spectrum. A compound's emission spectrum is a combination of spectra from the elements that make up the compound.

Emission spectrum of a sodium flame

Sodium flame

Cone cells

Sensitivity of red cones
Sensitivity of green cones
Sensitivity of blue cones
Visible spectrum

Sensitivity of cone cells in the human eye

Glowing white
Glowing red
Visible spectrum

Red hot and white hot
As the steel bar gets hotter, it emits more and more of the visible spectrum. At about 1,170°F (630°C), it is "red hot" and emits light from the red end of the spectrum. At about 2,790°F (1,530°C), the "white hot" bar has the entire white light spectrum.

Hot stars
The color of a star gives a clue to its age. To the naked eye, most stars look white, but their true colors can be seen through a telescope. Young stars are hot and glow with white light. Older stars are relatively cool and glow red or orange.

A cluster of young stars

Joseph von Fraunhofer
The German physicist Joseph von Fraunhofer (1787–1826) became interested in the nature of light while training as a mirror maker and lens polisher. His training enabled him to make spectroscopes of great precision. From 1814–17, he used them to make the first scientific study of the Sun's emission spectrum.

Munsell color system
Describing colors exactly using words alone is not easy. To avoid confusion, manufacturing industries use standard color-identification systems. The Munsell system is used to specify colors for dyes and pigments. It defines a color by its value (brightness), its chroma (strength), and its hue (position in the spectrum).

Color matching systems
Graphic designers use swatches of color cards to match the colors in their work with those available from printers. The designer supplies the printer with the reference number of the color, so the printer knows exactly what is wanted.

Each color has a reference number.

226

Biography boxes
Most main entry pages have biography boxes that tell you about key people who have contributed to our knowledge of the subject. The encyclopedia also has single-page entries on the life and work of more than 50 major historical figures.

This biography box describes the work of the physicist Joseph von Fraunhofer.

Headings
The topic headings enable you to see at-a-glance which subjects are covered within the main entry.

The heading Color matching systems refers to the way designers use reference numbers to match the colors on their work to the colors of printers' inks.

Labels
Labels help identify images.

INDEX

Volume 5 contains an index and a gazetteer. The index, which comes first, lists all the topics mentioned in the encyclopedia and the pages on which they can be found. The gazetteer follows on, with references to help you find all the features included on the maps.

- page numbers in **bold** type (eg Knights and heraldry **495-6**) show that the subject is a main A–Z entry in Volumes 1–4.
- page numbers in plain type (eg armour 69) send you to sub-entries, text references, and the reference section.
- grid references (eg Cremona Italy 475 C3) are letter-number combinations that locate features on maps.

This two-page entry discusses the main types of primates.

MONKEYS AND OTHER PRIMATES

Running head

There is an A–Z running head at the top of most pages to help you find important topics that are not main entries within the encyclopedia.

The running head on PRINTING tells you that although there is no main entry on primates, you can find the topic in MONKEYS AND OTHER PRIMATES.

Illustrations

Each main entry is heavily illustrated with models, photographs, and artworks, adding a vibrant layer of visual information to the page.

This annotation tells you how different colors can be produced by mixing red, green, and blue light.

Annotation

The illustrations are comprehensively annotated to draw attention to details of particular interest and to explain complex points.

COLOR

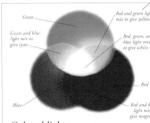

Colored lights

Different amounts of red, green, and blue light can be mixed to form light of any other color. This process is called color addition. Unlike paints, red, green, and blue are the primary colors of light. Equal amounts of any two primary colors give a secondary color (yellow, cyan, or magenta). When all three primaries are mixed in equal amounts, white light is produced.

Pigments

A pigment is a chemical that absorbs only certain colors from white light. This process is called color subtraction. Yellow, magenta, and cyan are primary pigments. Each absorbs one of the primary colors of light and reflects the other two. For example, a yellow pigment absorbs blue light but reflects green and red, which mix to give yellow. An equal mix of all three pigments absorbs all the colors from white light, giving black.

Color printing
To print a color picture, three single-color images are printed on top of each other – one in cyan, one in magenta, and one in yellow. Each picture is made up of tiny colored dots. The dots overlap and reflect the wavelengths of light to give all the other colors required. A black image is then added to make the picture sharper.

Picture is made up of tiny ink dots.

Mixing paints
Paints are pigments mixed with water or oil. Any color except white can be made by mixing the three primary pigments. Mixing paints has the effect of evenly mixing the pigments, and absorbing more of the white light spectrum.

Color television
The principle of adding colored lights is used in color television. The screen is covered with tiny strips that glow with red, green, or blue. They are so small that, at normal viewing distance, the human eye mixes the light coming from them. By adjusting the intensity of these three colors, the sensation of any other color is produced.

Image is formed by tiny glowing strips.

Painting with dots
"Pointillism" is a style of painting in which an artist uses thousands of tiny colored dots to build up a picture. When viewed close up, the colors of the individual dots are clearly visible. Like the colored strips on a television screen, the dots are too small to be seen from farther away. When viewed from a distance, the dots seem to merge, giving areas a single color.

Scattering and interference

Two other processes, called scattering and interference, can remove colors from the spectrum. Interference occurs when light from two sources meets and combines. In scattering, some parts of the spectrum are briefly absorbed by particles of matter and then radiated out again in all directions.

Blue sky
Sunlight includes all the colors of the spectrum. The sky appears blue during the day because air molecules in the atmosphere scatter light from the blue end of the spectrum in all directions.

Soap bubble
When white light strikes a soap bubble, it reflects off both the inner and outer surfaces of the bubble. The reflected light rays interfere, canceling out some colors but making others appear bright.

Interference creates a pattern of bright colors and dark bands.

Using interference
Stress is a force that can stretch or bend objects. Engineers shine plastic models of their designs to test their ability to withstand stress. The plastic molecules make the light rays split up and interfere. The interference patterns show the points of greatest stress.

High stress

Thomas Young
The English doctor and physicist Thomas Young (1773–1829) carried out many experiments to prove that light travels in waves. He realized that colors are light waves of different lengths and that interference colors occur where light waves meet and combine. Young also investigated color vision. In 1801, he proposed that the human eye contains three types of color sensors (now called cone cells), sensitive to blue, red, and green light.

Reflecting colors

Objects have color only when light falls upon them, because colors do not exist in total darkness. An object that appears one color in white light may look different when illuminated by colored light. The yellow pot in this sequence of pictures appears yellow only in white light.

White light
The yellow pot reflects the red and green parts of the white light spectrum, but absorbs the blue part.

Red light
The yellow pot reflects red light, and therefore appears red when illuminated by red light.

Green light
When illuminated by green light, the yellow pigment reflects the green light and appears green.

Blue light
When only blue light is available, the yellow pot absorbs the blue light, making it look black.

| FIND OUT MORE | DYES AND PAINTS | EYES AND VISION | LIGHT | PHOTOGRAPHY | PRINTING | TELEVISION |

227

Find out more

The Find Out More lines at the end of each entry direct you to other relevant main entries in the encyclopedia. Using the Find Out More lines can help you understand an entry in its wider context.

On COLOR, the Find Out More line directs you to the entry on PRINTING, where there is a detailed explanation of the color printing process and how printing presses work.

PRINTING

PRINTING's Find Out More line sends you to CHINA, HISTORY OF, which lists ancient Chinese inventions, including printing.

Timelines

An entry may include a timeline that gives the dates of key events in the history or development of the subject.

The PRINTING timeline stretches from the printing of the first books in ancient China to the computerization of modern printing.

COLLECTION PAGES

There are more than 70 pages of photographic collections, which follow main entries and provide a visual guide to the subject. They are organized under clear headings.

CHINA, HISTORY OF

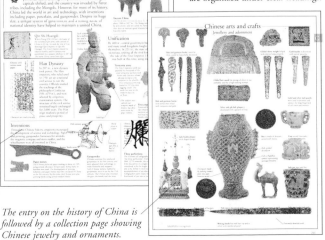

The entry on the history of China is followed by a collection page showing Chinese jewelry and ornaments.

CONTINENT AND COUNTRY PAGES

The Encyclopedia contains entries on all the world's continents and countries, each containing a detailed map. Continent entries focus on the physical geography of the region; country entries provide information about the society and economy of the country. Below is the single-page entry on the Netherlands

The country's flag appears by its name.

Locator map

A small map in the top left-hand corner of the page shows you where the region lies within a continent or in relation to the rest of the world.

Map of Netherlands' position in Europe.

The introduction defines the region and provides an overview to the entry.

Compass points north

Scale bar

Scale bar and compass

Each map has a scale bar that shows how distances on the map relate to actual miles and kilometers. The compass shows you which direction on the map is north (N).

Grid reference

The numbers and letters around the map help you find all the places listed in the index.

The index gives Amsterdam's grid reference as C4, so you can find it on the map by locating the third square along (C) and the fourth square down (4).

Population density

A population density diagram shows how many people there are to every square mile or square kilometer.

The Netherlands is a very densely populated country

KEY TO MAP

——— International border	Lake	● Capital city
····· Disputed border	Seasonal lake	◎ Major town
——— Road	∿ River	● Minor town
——— Railroad	——— Canal	▲ Spot height (feet)
✈ International airport	⊢ Waterfall	▼ Spot depth (feet)

Country file

On each country page there is a fact box containing key details about the country, such as its population, capital city, area, currency, political system, and main language and religion. Other categories of information include:

Literacy – the percentage of people over 15 years old who can read and write.
People per doctor – a rough guide to the availability of medical facilities.
Life expectancy – how long an average person can expect to live.

Climate

A climate diagram gives details of rainfall levels and temperatures in the country, region, or continent.

Average summer temperature
Average winter temperature
Average rainfall

Single country's average in capital city

Average summer temperature
Average winter temperature
Average rainfall

Regional average is the average of all capital cities on map

Concise explanation of the country's main physical characteristics.

Land use

The land-use diagram tells you how much of the country's total land area is taken up by, for example, woodland, agriculture, and urban developments such as villages, towns, and cities.

Most of the land in the Netherlands is used for farming.

Urban/rural split

A small diagram shows the percentage of people living in urban (built-up) areas and rural (country) areas.

The majority of people in the Netherlands live in urban areas.

NETBALL see BALL GAMES

NETHERLANDS

ALSO CALLED HOLLAND, the Netherlands straddles the deltas of five major rivers in northwest Europe. The Dutch people say they created their own country because they have reclaimed about one-third of the land from sea or marshland by enclosing the area with earth barriers, or dikes, and draining the water from it. Despite being one of the most densely populated countries in the world, the Netherlands enjoys high living standards. Amsterdam is the official capital, although the government is based at The Hague.

NETHERLANDS FACTS
CAPITAL CITY Amsterdam (seat of government The Hague)
AREA 37,330 sq km (14,413 sq miles)
POPULATION 15,612,000
MAJOR RELIGION Christian
CURRENCY Guilder
LIFE EXPECTANCY 78 years
PEOPLE PER DOCTOR 410
GOVERNMENT Multi-party democracy
ADULT LITERACY 99%

Physical features
The Netherlands is mainly flat, with 27 per cent of the land below sea level, and protected from the sea by natural sand dunes along the coast, and by artificial dikes. Wide sandy plains cover most of the rest of the country, falling into a few, low hills in the eastern and southern parts of the country.

Canals
The Netherlands is a land of canals, which drain the land and serve as waterways for the movement of people and freight. Amsterdam alone has more than 100 canals.

Windmills
For centuries the Dutch landscape was dotted with 10,000 windmills, which powered pumps to drain water from the land. Electric pumps now do this work in the battle to keep the sea back.

37°C (99°F) -25°C (-13°F)
16°C (62°F) 2°C (36°F)
580 mm (23 in)

Climate
The Netherlands has mild, rainy winters and cool summers. In winter northerly gales lash the coast, damaging dikes and threatening floods. Frosts sometimes freeze canals.

Land use
Almost one-third of the land has been reclaimed from the sea. These areas are known as polders and are extremely fertile. The country has large natural gas reserves in the north, and there is some offshore oil drilling in the North Sea.

Forest 3.5% Farmland 84.5%
Built-up 12%

Amsterdam
The Dutch capital is built on 70 islands, linked by about 500 bridges, which span its many canals. The best way to get around is by bicycle, and more than half a million people cycle to school or work each day. Today, Amsterdam is a centre for tourism and diamonds.

One of Amsterdam's many canals

People
The Dutch see their society as the most tolerant in Europe, with relaxed laws on sexuality, drugs, and euthanasia. The country has a long history of welcoming immigrants, often from former Dutch colonies. Most of these people are now assimilated as Dutch citizens. However, members of the small Turkish community, which makes up just one per cent, do not enjoy full citizenship.

Street scene, Amsterdam

Farming and industry
The Dutch economy is one of the most successful in Europe. Most imports and exports travel through Rotterdam, the world's biggest port. In addition to high-tech sectors such as electronics, telecommunications, and chemicals, the Netherlands has a successful agricultural industry. Productivity is high, and products such as vegetables, cheese, meat, and cut flowers are significant export earners.

Dutch tulips

418 per sq km (1,083 per sq mile) 89% Urban 11% Rural

FIND OUT MORE CANALS · DAMS · EMPIRES · EUROPE · EUROPE, HISTORY OF · EUROPEAN UNION · FARMING · NETHERLANDS, HISTORY OF · PORTS AND WATERWAYS

601

REFERENCE PAGES

Volume 5 of the Encyclopedia contains an illustrated reference section with essential facts, figures, and statistical data, divided into the five main strands described here.

International world

This strand contains a double-page map showing all the countries of the world, and data on the world's population, economy, and resources.

History

The history strand features a timeline of key historical events, stretching from 40,000 BC to the present day, together with the dates of major wars, revolutions, battles, and great leaders.

Living world

The centerpiece of this strand is a detailed guide to the classification of living things, supported by lists of species in danger, and many other facts about the natural world.

People, arts, and media

This strand is crammed full of information about television, theater, music, art, philosophy, architecture, literature, dance, and much more besides.

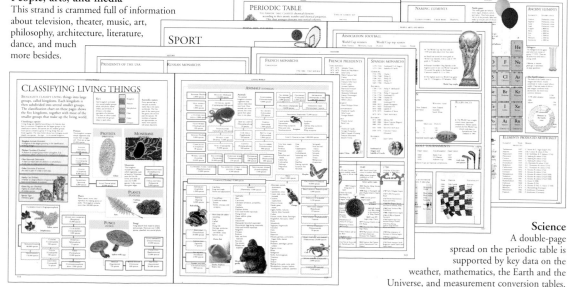

Science

A double-page spread on the periodic table is supported by key data on the weather, mathematics, the Earth and the Universe, and measurement conversion tables.

ABORIGINAL AUSTRALIANS

THE ABORIGINALS settled the Australian continent more than 40,000 years ago. They lived in total isolation from the rest of the world, existing by hunting and gathering. In the 18th century, the Europeans arrived and forced the Aboriginals off their territories. Today, many feel isolated from white society, but still try to preserve their tribal identity.

Some early peoples crossed by means of a land bridge.

Settlers stayed near the coast and rivers where more food was available.

New Guinea
Indonesian islands
Arnhem Land
Cape York
Kimberley plateau
Uluru

Aboriginal history

Aboriginals first reached Australia during the last Ice Age. Sea levels were low, and they were able to cross from Southeast Asia over land bridges and small stretches of water. When the ice melted and sea levels rose again, the continent was completely cut off. Initially, the settlers clung to the coasts and rivers, but gradually moved across the continent. By the time Europeans arrived, there were about 500 different tribal groups living in Australia.

Ways of life

Traditionally, Aboriginals lived by hunting and gathering. They were nomadic, roaming over large stretches of territory, setting up temporary camps near watering places, and moving on when food supplies were exhausted. They traded with other tribes, exchanging goods such as spears.

Hunting and gathering

Aboriginals lived by hunting animals such as kangaroos, and supplemented their diet with wild plants, nuts, and berries. The hunters used spears with stone blades and wooden boomerangs, a type of missile that flies back to the thrower. Some tribes developed an elaborate sign language so that they could send silent messages to each other when they were stalking game.

Aboriginal hunters used silent signals so they would not disturb game. The sign for kangaroo starts with a closed hand and moves to an open shape.

Corroborees

Aboriginal peoples have handed down stories, songs, and traditions from generation to generation. This culture is kept alive at corroborees, ceremonial dances where tribes gather together to retell the tales of Australia's past through songs, music, and dance.

Dreamtime

The Aboriginals believe that Dreamtime is a period when Ancestral Beings shaped the land, creating all species and human beings. These beings are thought to live on eternally in spirit form. Human beings are believed to be a part of nature, closely associated with all other living things. Images of spirits of Dreamtime, such as Lightning Man, cover sacred cliffs and caves in tribal areas.

Lightning Man was believed to have created thunder and lightning.

Barrkinj – wife of Lightning Man

Lightning Man, also known as Namarrgon

Uluru (Ayers Rock)

Aboriginals believe that the Ancestral Beings created the Australian landscape and established customs and traditions still followed today. They have left evidence of their presence in the many sacred places, such as Uluru in central Australia. This is revered as a sacred place by the local Aranda people. Once called Ayers Rock by the Australian government, the rock regained its Aboriginal name in 1988.

Aboriginals today

European colonists arrived in Australia in 1788 and displaced Aboriginal tribes from their territory. Today, there are about 250,000 Aboriginals in Australia, many of whom live in urban areas. Although there is still discrimination, Aboriginals are beginning to benefit from government aid, and to assert their civil rights.

Land rights

When the Europeans arrived in Australia, they claimed that the land was *Terra nullius*, that it belonged to no one, and that they were entitled to occupy it. More recently, the Aboriginals have campaigned to regain their lost territory and sacred sites. In 1992, the Australian government reversed its *Terra nullius* policy.

Education

During early contact with the Europeans, Aboriginal languages were lost or fell into disuse. In 1972, the government established a bilingual education program. Many children are now taught in their tribal languages before learning English. Books, radio, and television broadcasts are all available in many Aboriginal languages.

| FIND OUT MORE | ART, HISTORY OF | AUSTRALIA | AUSTRALIA, HISTORY OF | AUSTRALASIA AND OCEANIA | COOK, JAMES | MYTHS AND LEGENDS | RELIGIONS | SOCIETIES, HUMAN |

ACIDS AND ALKALIS

LEMON JUICE AND VINEGAR taste sour because they contain weak acids. An acid is a substance that dissolves in water to form positively charged particles called hydrogen ions (H⁺). The opposite of an acid is an alkali, which dissolves in water to form negatively charged ions of hydrogen and oxygen, called hydroxide ions (OH⁻). Alkalis are "anti-acids" because they cancel out acidity. Toothpaste, for example, contains an alkali that cancels out acidity in the mouth that would otherwise damage teeth.

Hydrochloric acid

The mixture bubbles fiercely as hydrogen gas is given off.

Zinc replaces the hydrogen in the acid to form zinc chloride.

Zinc nuggets

pH scale

The concentration of hydrogen ions in a solution is known as its pH. Scientists use the pH scale to measure acidity and alkalinity. On the pH scale, a solution with a pH lower than 7 is acidic, and a solution with a pH greater than 7 is alkaline. Water is neutral, and has a pH of 7. A solution's pH can be tested with universal indicator solution or paper, which changes color in acids and alkalis.

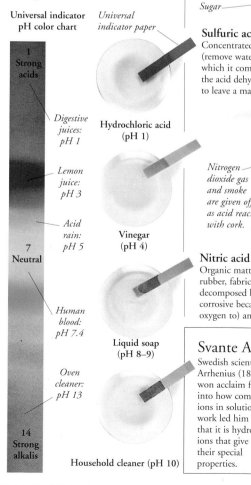

Universal indicator pH color chart

Universal indicator paper

1 Strong acids

Digestive juices: pH 1

Hydrochloric acid (pH 1)

Lemon juice: pH 3

Acid rain: pH 5

Vinegar (pH 4)

7 Neutral

Human blood: pH 7.4

Liquid soap (pH 8–9)

Oven cleaner: pH 13

14 Strong alkalis

Household cleaner (pH 10)

Strong acids

The more hydrogen ions an acid forms in water, the stronger it is, and the lower its pH. Strong acids such as sulfuric acid and nitric acid are very dangerous and must be handled carefully.

Sulfuric acid

Carbon

Sugar

Sulfuric acid
Concentrated sulfuric acid will dehydrate (remove water from) any substance with which it comes into contact. For example, the acid dehydrates sugar, a carbohydrate, to leave a mass of smoldering black carbon.

Cork

Nitrogen dioxide gas and smoke are given off as acid reacts with cork.

Nitric acid

Nitric acid
Organic matter, such as paper, cork, rubber, fabric, and skin, is rapidly decomposed by nitric acid. The acid is so corrosive because it oxidizes (supplies oxygen to) any material it touches.

Svante Arrhenius
Swedish scientist Svante Arrhenius (1859–1927) won acclaim for his research into how compounds form ions in solution. This work led him to realize that it is hydrogen ions that give acids their special properties.

Acids and metals

Even the weakest acids cannot be stored in metal containers because acids are corrosive to most metals. When an acid reacts with a metal, hydrogen gas is given off and the metal dissolves in the acid to form a compound called a salt. The reaction is very violent with metals such as potassium and sodium, and quite vigorous with metals such as magnesium and zinc.

Salts
When the hydrogen in an acid is replaced by a metal during a chemical reaction, a neutral compound called a salt is formed. For example, when copper reacts with nitric acid, the copper takes the place of the hydrogen to make the salt copper nitrate. Like other metals, copper forms a variety of salts when mixed with different acids. Most salts are crystals, and many are colored. Some salts, such as sodium chloride (table salt), occur naturally.

Copper nitrate

Nitric acid

Copper sulfate

Sulfuric acid

Hydrochloric acid

Copper turnings

Copper chloride

Acid industry

Acids are widely used in industry because they react so readily with other materials. For example, sulfuric acid is used in the production of dyes and pigments, artificial fibers, plastics, soaps, and explosives. The acid is made by mixing sulfur and oxygen together.

Sulfuric acid chemical plant

Acid rain
Burning fossil fuels to produce energy for use at home and in industry releases polluting gases into the air. The gases dissolve in water in the clouds to form nitric acid and sulfuric acid. This water falls as acid rain, which erodes stone buildings and statues, kills trees and aquatic life, and reduces the soil's fertility.

Bases and alkalis

The acidity of vinegar (ethanoic acid) can be neutralized, or canceled out, by adding chalk (calcium carbonate). Any substance that neutralizes acidity, such as chalk, is called a base. An alkali is a base that dissolves in water. An alkali's strength is measured by the number of hydroxide ions it forms in water. Strong alkalis, such as sodium hydroxide, are just as corrosive as strong acids.

Chalk and vinegar react together and release carbon dioxide gas.

The product of the reaction is a salt called calcium ethanoate.

The mixture spills out of the flask.

Testing the mixture with universal indicator solution proves that it is now neutral – the acidity has been canceled out.

Soaps and detergents

Alkalis are good at dissolving oil and grease, so they are widely used in soaps and detergents. Most dirt is bound to skin, clothes, or eating utensils by grease. The grease makes it difficult to remove the dirt with water alone, because it does not mix with water. A detergent or soap breaks the grease up into tiny drops, allowing the water to wash away any remaining dirt.

Once the liquid soap has broken down the grease, the water can wet the plate and dissolve the rest of the dirt.

Oil slicks

Accidents with oil tankers at sea can create huge oil slicks (spillages) on the water's surface. Strong detergents called dispersants may be used to break up the oil. Wildlife experts use weaker detergents, such as liquid soap, to clean the feathers of oil-coated seabirds. If the birds' feathers – which usually keep them warm and dry – become clogged with oil, the birds may lose their buoyancy and drown, or die of exposure to the cold.

Batteries

Acids, alkalis, and salts are electrolytes, meaning that they conduct electricity when in solution. Batteries consist of an electrolyte – usually in the form of a moist paste or liquid – between two rods or plates called electrodes. The most common battery is the dry cell, which uses the salt, ammonium chloride, as an electrolyte. Long-life batteries contain alkaline electrolytes, such as potassium hydroxide; car batteries have electrolytes of sulfuric acid.

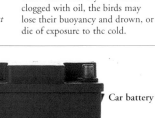

Car battery

Long-life battery

Dry cell

Alkali industry

The main raw material in the alkali industry is brine (saltwater). Sodium hydroxide, which is used to make soap and paper, is produced from brine by electrolysis (passing electricity through it). Brine will also absorb carbon dioxide to make sodium carbonate, which is used in textile treatment, photography, and glassmaking.

Electrolysis of brine to make sodium hydroxide.

Neutralizing acids

An alkali and an acid react together to give a neutral salt. In addition, hydroxide ions (OH^-) in the alkali combine with the acid's hydrogen ions (H^+) to produce water (H_2O). In daily life, problems of unwanted acidity are solved by adding an alkali of the appropriate strength.

Soil acidity

The pH of soil varies from area to area. Few crops grow well in highly acidic soil, because the acid dissolves vital minerals that the plants need for healthy growth and allows them to be washed away. Farmers treat acidic soil by spreading lime (calcium oxide) over their fields. This alkali made from limestone neutralizes the acid in the soil, making it more fertile.

Farmer liming acidic soil.

An antacid fizzes as it reacts with lemon juice (citric acid).

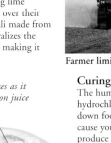

Curing indigestion

The human stomach uses hydrochloric acid to break down food. Some foods cause your stomach to produce so much acid that you feel uncomfortable. The "ache" is cured with antacid tablets, powder, or liquids. Antacids contain weak alkalis that neutralize the acidity, but do not harm your stomach, or react too vigorously with the acid.

Bee and wasp stings

A bee sting is painful because it is acidic. Treating the sting with a weak alkali, such as soap or baking soda, relieves the pain by neutralizing the acid. In contrast, a wasp sting is alkaline, so it can be neutralized by a weak acid, such as vinegar or lemon juice.

Wasp

Bee

Fritz Haber

In 1908, the German chemist Fritz Haber (1868–1934) developed a process for making the alkali ammonia, which is used to make fertilizers and explosives. The Haber process involves mixing nitrogen from the air with hydrogen at high pressure and temperature. Haber later devised a way of making nitric acid by heating ammonia in air.

Timeline

c.600 BC The Phoenicians use alkaline wood ash to make soap.

11th century AD Arab chemists make sulfuric, nitric, and hydrochloric acids.

1780s World's first sulfuric acid factory opens in France.

1865 Ernest Solvay, a Belgian chemist, develops the first commercially successful process for making the alkali, sodium carbonate, on a large scale.

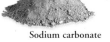

Sodium carbonate

1887 Svante Arrhenius proposes that it is hydrogen ions that give acids their special properties.

1908 Fritz Haber invents a process for making ammonia.

1909 The Danish chemist Søren Sørensen (1868–1939) devises the pH scale.

FIND OUT MORE   ATOMS AND MOLECULES   BEES AND WASPS   CHEMISTRY   DIGESTION   ELECTRICITY   MIXTURES AND COMPOUNDS   POLLUTION   ROCKETS   SOIL

ADVERTISING AND MARKETING

WHEN A COMPANY WISHES TO SELL or improve the sales of its products or services, it may decide to advertise. Newspapers and magazines carry advertisements, as do billboards, television, and radio. Marketing is the wider process of creating a product or service, advertising it, and selling it. Advertising and marketing are vast industries that affect all our lives.

Copy line gives us product information. Here, the tire company Pirelli uses humor and an eye-catching image to advertise its tires' road-holding ability.

How advertising works

Advertisements use humor and strong images to get our attention. Short, memorable catchphrases called slogans become associated with the product. An advertising campaign often combines posters and television advertisements, so repetition ensures that people remember the product.

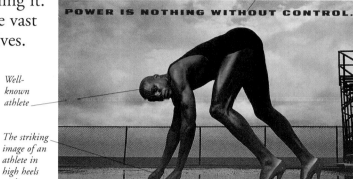

POWER IS NOTHING WITHOUT CONTROL.

Well-known athlete

The striking image of an athlete in high heels grabs our attention.

Product name

Image
Advertisers try to create a product image that will appeal to particular customers. An advertisement for perfume, for example, may project an image of beauty and sophistication. Well-known personalities may be shown endorsing a product to strengthen its image.

Marketing

A company's marketing strategy includes market research, product development, publicity, advertising, and point of sale displays. The marketing department researches the products people want and works with other departments to make sure that the products meet consumers' expectations.

Public relations
Many companies use public relations, or PR, to improve their standing with the people who buy their products. The two main branches of PR are research and communication. Research tries to find out what people think about the company and its products. Companies communicate with people through press coverage, advertising, and sponsorship.

Pepsi-Cola painted the Concorde blue to gain publicity.

Market research
The purpose of market research is to find out what sort of people are likely to buy a product, and what will make them buy one product rather than a similar product. Researchers get this information from interviews, questionnaires, and government statistics.

Point of sale
Stores use posters and display units to encourage people to buy products. Point of sale displays try to catch the customer's eye where he or she can buy the product immediately. Store window displays aim to draw customers into a store.

Advertising agencies

Companies use advertising agencies to advise them on their advertising strategy. Advertising agencies conduct market research, plan which forms of media the client's advertisements should appear in, and finally prepare the client's advertisements.

The film is combined with a sound track, and then edited.

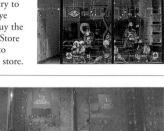

 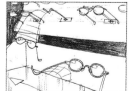

Storyboards
The first stage of producing a television advertisement is to present a storyboard of ideas to the client, showing how the final advertisement will look. A storyboard looks rather like a comic strip, with a series of pictures showing how the action will run. If the client approves the storyboard, production can go ahead.

Production
The advertising agency hires a production team to film the advertisement. The team includes a producer, who supervises the rehearsal schedule, and a director, who directs the action when the commercial is being filmed. Once the film has been shot, a sound track is added. The sound track may be a voice-over repeating the product name and a catchy tune called a jingle.

Advertisement
Once the advertisement has been completed, it is shown to the client. If the client approves the film, it is taken to the television stations to be aired. Television advertising is by far the most expensive form of advertising, but it is the most effective since it reaches people in their own homes.

FIND OUT MORE — DESIGN   FILMS AND FILM-MAKING   MONEY   SHOPS   TELEVISION   TRADE AND INDUSTRY

AFRICA

THE SECOND LARGEST CONTINENT after Asia, Africa is dominated in the north by the vast Sahara Desert and in the east by the Great Rift Valley. A rain forest lies along the equator, and open grasslands provide grazing for herds of wild animals. Africa is home to many different peoples, each with their own distinctive languages and customs. Islam and Christianity are widespread, but many Africans adhere to their own traditional beliefs.

Physical features

Most of Africa is a high plateau covered with deserts, lush rain forests, and dry grasslands. Rivers crossing it bring water to dry regions and provide a means of transportation. Although they lie on the equator, the high peaks in the east are snowcapped all year. Africa has several volcanoes.

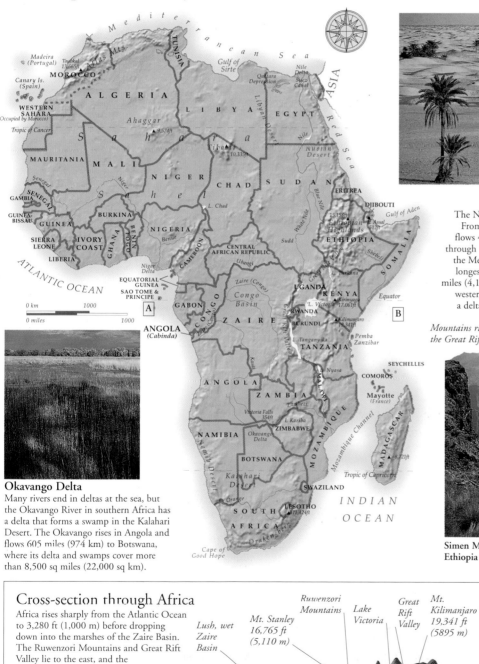

Sahara

The world's largest desert, the Sahara covers much of northwestern Africa. It has an area of 3,500,000 sq miles (9,000,000 sq km) and is rapidly expanding as land at its edges is overgrazed. With less than 4 in (100 mm) of rain a year and daytime temperatures of up to 122°F (50°C), only a few specially adapted plants and animals survive here.

Nile River

The Nile is the world's longest river. From its source in Lake Victoria it flows 4,145 miles (6,671 km) north through Uganda, Sudan, and Egypt to the Mediterranean Sea. Africa's third longest river, the Niger, flows 2,597 miles (4,180 km) in a big loop through western Africa, ending in Nigeria in a delta bigger than that of the Nile.

Mountains rise from the Great Rift Valley.

Nile River at Aswan in Egypt

Great Rift Valley

The mountains of Ethiopia are divided by the Great Rift Valley, which stretches 3,750 miles (6,000 km) north from Mozambique through east Africa and the Red Sea into Syria. The valley is formed by massive cracks in the Earth's crust. It is up to 55 miles (90 km) wide, and in millions of years will eventually divide the African continent.

Simen Mountains, Ethiopia

Okavango Delta

Many rivers end in deltas at the sea, but the Okavango River in southern Africa has a delta that forms a swamp in the Kalahari Desert. The Okavango rises in Angola and flows 605 miles (974 km) to Botswana, where its delta and swamps cover more than 8,500 sq miles (22,000 sq km).

Cross-section through Africa

Africa rises sharply from the Atlantic Ocean to 3,280 ft (1,000 m) before dropping down into the marshes of the Zaire Basin. The Ruwenzori Mountains and Great Rift Valley lie to the east, and the plateau falls gradually to the Indian Ocean.

São Tomé

Atlantic Ocean

Lush, wet Zaire Basin

Mt. Stanley 16,765 ft (5,110 m)

Ruwenzori Mountains

Lake Victoria

Great Rift Valley

Mt. Kilimanjaro 19,341 ft (5895 m)

Indian Ocean

A — Approximately 2,550 miles (4,100 km) from A to B — B

AFRICA FACTS

AREA	11,633,846 sq miles (30,131,536 sq km)
POPULATION	713,566,000
NUMBER OF COUNTRIES	53
BIGGEST COUNTRY	Sudan
SMALLEST COUNTRY	Seychelles
HIGHEST POINT	Kilimanjaro (Tanzania) 19,341 ft (5,895 m)
LONGEST RIVER	Nile (Uganda/Sudan/Egypt) 4,145 miles (6,671 km)
BIGGEST LAKE	Lake Victoria (East Africa) 26,595 sq miles (68,880 sq km)

Climatic zones

Although most of Africa is warm or hot all year round, the climate varies greatly because of the wide range of landscapes. Parts of the north coast have hot, dry summers and cooler, damp winters. Desert regions have cold nights, scorching hot days, and almost no rain at all. On the equator the climate is hot and humid, with high rainfall. Mountain regions have warm summers and cool winters.

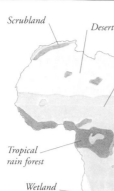

Scrubland *Desert*

Grassland

Tropical rain forest

Wetland

Mountain

Scrubland

Much of the northern coast of Africa has a warm Mediterranean climate. Coastal cliffs and hills are covered in sparse, low-growing, often fragrant plants and shrubs that are able to thrive in the poor, stony soils. Many of the plants have thorns and small, leathery leaves to prevent them from drying out in the fierce heat of the sun and frequent sea breezes.

Baie de Souhalias, Algeria

Evergreen plants are able to retain their moisture in the heat.

Fantastically shaped dunes are formed by strong desert winds.

Deserts

About 40 percent of Africa is desert. The Erg of Bilma in Niger is part of the vast Sahara. In Arabic, *erg* means a sandy expanse. The sand is blown by the wind into ripples and into huge dunes, some of which may be nearly 650 ft (200 m) high. Two other main desert areas are the Kalahari and the Namib, both in southern Africa.

Savanna

About 40 percent of Africa is covered with savanna, the name given to grassland with scattered trees and shrubs. This type of land forms a wide loop around the Zaire (Congo) basin. Vast herds of grazing animals, such as antelope and zebras, move around the savanna seeking fresh grass to eat.

Masai Mara, Kenya

Occasional stunted trees offer animals some protection from the harsh sun.

Tropical rain forest

Dense, tropical rain forest covers less than 20 percent of Africa. The most extensive areas lie close to the equator in West Africa and in central Africa's Zaire (Congo) Basin. Thousands of species of trees flourish in the hot, humid climate, which produces rain all year round. However, large-scale felling of trees for timber hardwoods, such as teak and mahogany, threatens to destroy this environment.

Many streams and rivers cross the rain forest.

Mahogany leaf

Low shrubs cover some of the mountains' lower slopes and foothills.

Mountain

Africa's highest ranges include the Drakensberg, in southeastern Africa, which runs for about 70 miles (1,130 km) through South Africa and Lesotho and forms part of the rim of the great South African Plateau. The highest point is Thabana Ntlenyana at 11,424 ft (3,482 m). Even higher mountain ranges are the Atlas range in Morocco, and the Ruwenzori on the border between Uganda and Zaire.

People

One in eight of the world's people lives in Africa, mostly along the north and west coasts and in the fertile river valleys. Although traditionally people live in small villages, a growing number are moving to towns and cities to look for work. Birth rates in many countries are high and families are large. About half the population is under 15 years old.

Ghanaian girls   Tanzanian girl   Egyptian boy

Resources

Africa has many resources, but they are unevenly distributed among the countries. Libya and Nigeria are leading oil producers, southern Africa is rich in gold and diamonds, and Zambia is a leading copper producer. Tropical forests yield valuable timber but are being felled at an alarming rate. Africa is a leading producer of cocoa beans, cassava, bananas, coffee, and tea.

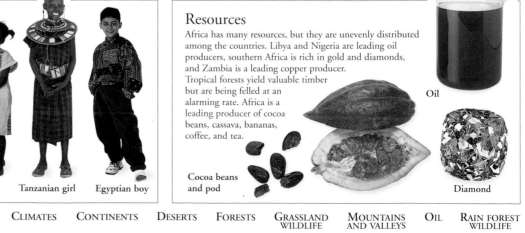

Oil

Cocoa beans and pod

Diamond

FIND OUT MORE   AFRICA, HISTORY OF   AFRICAN WILDLIFE   CLIMATES   CONTINENTS   DESERTS   FORESTS   GRASSLAND WILDLIFE   MOUNTAINS AND VALLEYS   OIL   RAIN FOREST WILDLIFE

A

AFRICA, HISTORY OF

CIVILIZATION IN AFRICA BEGAN TO appear more than 5,000 years ago with the rise of ancient Egypt. From about 2,500 years ago in sub-Saharan Africa, many other kingdoms also developed. The Sahara acted as a barrier to keep this area separate from the rest of the world until the arrival of Arab traders in the 8th century. From the 15th century, the arrival of Europeans, the subsequent slave trade, and European imperialism had a profound effect on the continent. Since the 1950s, all African nations have reclaimed independence, although modern Africa continues to struggle with its postcolonial legacy and with environmental problems.

Ancient empires

North Africa was in a good position to trade with western Asia, giving rise to rich empires to develop, including Meroë (modern Sudan, c.600 BC–AD 300) and Aksum (a trading state in northern Ethiopia, c.100 BC–AD 1000). Ghana (in West Africa, c.500–1300) developed for similar reasons.

Meroe

From the city of Meroë, the Kushites controlled trade in the Red Sea and the Nile River from 600 BC. They exported luxury goods, such as ostrich feathers and leopard skins, and built fine temples and flat-topped pyramids over the graves of their dead.

Ruined temple, Meroë

Ghana

Ghana (located on the borders of modern Mali and Mauritania), one of Africa's most important empires, controlled the trans-Saharan trade in gold. Ghana's kings wore gold jewelry, and gold-embroidered clothes and turbans. Surviving gold artifacts show the incredible wealth of this kingdom.

Heads of gold, often of royalty, played an important part in rituals.

Carving was made of wood and coated with gold.

Figures were attached to royal thrones.

Bird ornament

Rings were often decorated with flowers.

Finger rings

Aksum

From c.300, Egyptian scholars introduced Christianity to Aksum, which then became known as a holy city. During this period, Aksum took over the empire based at Meroë. Aksum's people built tall, stone stelae (monuments) to mark the tombs of dead kings.

Head weighs 3 lbs (1.5 kg).

Stela, Aksum

Early inhabitants

Humans have inhabited Africa for 4 million years. The Sahara was once a fertile land rich in plants and animals. But thousands of years ago, it dried up, and people moved south to the savanna to farm there.

Rock paintings

Rock and bone pictures often depicted everyday events, such as dancing, hunting animals, and fishing. Painters used animal fat colored with vegetable dyes.

Vegetable dye

Animals

Painted bone

Nok culture

The earliest evidence of Iron Age settlement is called the Nok culture (500 BC–AD 200), which existed in what is now central Nigeria. Nok people lived in farming communities. They produced iron weapons and tools for farming, and also made fine terra-cotta sculptures.

Terra-cotta head, Nok culture

Spread of religions

From the 8th century, trade, conquests, and colonialism spread religions such as Islam in Africa. In North Africa, Islam completely replaced traditional religions, which often included the worship of ancestors.

Festival mask

Ancestor worship

In many parts of Africa, communities had sacred shrines where they placed offerings for the spirits of their dead ancestors. Today, during certain annual festivals, members of the community wear special masks, sing, dance, and tell stories in honor of their ancestors.

Islam

By c.800, Middle Eastern Arabs had taken Islam to North Africa. From the 11th century, trade helped spread Islam across the Sahara into West Africa and up the Nile River into Sudan.

Ait Benhaddou, Morocco

Slave trade

By the 1470s, the Portuguese were trading copper, brass, gold, and slaves with Benin in West Africa. In the 1480s, the Portuguese arrived on the islands of Principe and São Tomé in the Gulf of Guinea, just off the west African coast. They established sugar plantations and forced African captives (mainly kidnapped in Senegal and Gambia) to work as slaves on the plantations. This was the beginning of European domination in Africa.

Plaque showing Portuguese soldier, 1500s

A

Colonialism

During the 1800s, Europeans colonized areas in Africa, introducing Christianity and taking economic control. They used African workers to grow or mine precious raw materials, but sent the materials to be manufactured in Europe and America – where profits stayed. During this period, slavery was at its height with Europeans kidnapping Africans to work in the Americas.

African Diaspora

The slave trade scattered more than 20 million Africans throughout the Americas and Europe, undermining African culture in the process. Over the centuries, the dispersal of these slaves and their descendents became known as the African Diaspora.

African carving of a European

Christianity

Europe sent missionaries to Africa to set up schools and churches, and to convert Africans to Christianity. They also tried to abolish African traditional religions by punishing those who still practiced them.

Traditional witch doctors

Voodoo voice disguiser

Voodoo

In 19th-century Caribbean colonies, traditional ancestor worship combined with Christianity to produce a religion called voodoo.

Scramble for Africa

In 1884, European leaders decided that their countries could claim African territories as colonies when occupied by Europeans. They started scrambling to the interior in search of new lands. By 1902, all of Africa was colonized except Liberia and Ethiopia.

Carving of Queen Victoria

Morocco
Tunisia
Algeria
Libya
Egypt
Liberia
Nigeria
British Somaliland
Sierra Leone
Ethiopia
British East Africa (Kenya)
Angola

French
British
German
Portuguese
Belgium
Spanish
Italian
Anglo-Egyptian

World Wars I and II

Although both world wars were European, thousands of Africans lost their lives as colonial rulers forced them to join the army. One cause of World War I was German resentment against other European countries during colonization. In World War II, North Africa became a battleground, as German and Italian forces invaded British- and French-ruled territories.

Troops at El Alamein, Egypt

World War I

When World War I broke out in 1914, the Ottoman Empire controlled North Africa. The Egyptians colluded with the British to overthrow Turkish rule, and they were helped from 1916 to 1918 by the eccentric soldier and author Thomas Edward Lawrence (1888–1935), who became famous as Lawrence of Arabia. After the war, Egypt became a British protectorate but signed a treaty for independence in 1922.

El Alamein

In 1941, Italian and German forces invaded North African territories held by the British. The British recruited soldiers from their colonies of Nigeria, Ghana, and Sierra Leone to join the fight on their behalf. In 1942, the British defeated the Germans at the historic battle of El Alamein. This battle was a turning point in the war.

Herero and Nama tribes fight German colonialists, Namibia, 1904

African resistance

Africans strenuously resisted colonialism. The Ethiopians fought to stay independent and won (1896); Zimbabwe and Sudan rebelled against the British (1896 and 1920); tribes in Angola tried to overthrow the Portuguese (1902); in Namibia and Tanzania, thousands were killed in uprisings against the Germans (1904–1908); and in Nigeria, tribes revolted against French rule (1920s).

Operation Torch

In 1942, American and British soldiers landed in Morocco and Algeria in an invasion called Operation Torch. Joined by the French, the Allies attacked the German and Italian armies, forcing them into Tunisia. After a bloody battle, Germany's Afrika Korps surrendered. The war on African soil was over by May 1943.

African Front

T.E. Lawrence

Haile Selassie

Emperor Haile Selassie of Ethiopia (r.1930–74) led his troops against the Italian invasion of 1935. The Italians forced the emperor into exile in 1936, but he returned in 1941. Haile Selassie instituted reforms, suppressed slavery, and worked with the Organization of African Unity. In 1974, the army overthrew the emperor, and set up military rule. He died in exile in 1975 aged 84.

A

Returning refugees, Angola

Ghanaian
Independence
Day stamps

Independence

After World War II, many Africans wanted to end colonial rule and govern their own countries. Colonial powers such as France, Portugal, and Britain fought to prevent this, and there were bloody wars of independence in Algeria, Mozambique, Angola, and Zimbabwe. By the late 1960s most African countries had gained independence, but political and economic problems remained.

Gold Coast

One of the first colonies to become independent was the former British colony of the Gold Coast. After World War II, anticolonial feeling had intensified, and, in 1957, the state of Ghana (which was named after a powerful West African medieval empire) became independent. A leading nationalist, Kwame Nkrumah (1909–72), became the new country's first prime minister. In 1960, Nkrumah declared Ghana a republic and himself president for life. He became increasingly dictatorial and distanced his country from the West. In 1966, a police-military coup overthrew Nkrumah.

OAU member states now number 50.

OAU summit, Tunisia

Organization of African Unity

In 1963, the heads of 30 independent African states met to form the OAU (Organization of African Unity). Its goal was to promote political and economic cooperation between states, and help colonies attain independence.

Angola War

In 1961, Angola's people rose in revolt against the Portuguese colonial government. The Portuguese army crushed the rebels, who fled into exile in Zaïre. While in exile, the rebels formed liberation movements and waged guerrilla warfare in Angola. In 1974, the liberation forces staged a military uprising and overthrew the Portuguese, who finally granted independence in 1975. After independence, a bitter civil war erupted between two political groups, both of whom wanted to govern Angola. One side was backed by South African troops; the other by Russian troops. The Angolan factions agreed to a ceasefire in 1994.

Electronics technician

Game park, Kenya

Apartheid

By the 1980s, only South Africa was still trying to retain white-minority power. The white government had passed the Apartheid (separateness) Policy in 1950, which classified people according to race. Under apartheid, those classified as black, colored, or Asian had few rights. Apartheid was abolished in 1994.

A taxi stand for whites, South Africa, 1967

Modern Africa

Mineral-rich Africa has a thriving mining industry. More recently, new African electronics plants specialize in assembling equipment from imported components.

Tourism

A century ago, East African governments established game reserves and parks to protect wildlife from hunters. Today, tourists pay to stay in the parks and go on safari to see the wild animals. Kenya now makes more money from tourism than from any other source.

Deforestation, Somalia

Village cooperatives

Agricultural workers (mainly women) set up village co-operatives to grow food crops, which they sell at the local market, reversing policy that existed under colonial governments. Then, small-scale farmers were forced to grow cash crops (coffee, peanuts, cocoa, and cotton) to sell to large European companies. The farmers could not grow food crops for themselves and had to buy expensive imports, such as rice.

Women's agricultural cooperative, Niger

Women are the main agricultural workers.

Food crops

Environmental devastation

In semiarid areas of Africa, such as Somalia, land is gradually turning into desert. Since the 1950s, there has been a fall in the average annual rainfall, and much of the land has become very dry. The people have often overused the land for cash crops, and cut down the trees for firewood.

Ken Saro-Wiwa

Ken Saro-Wiwa (1941–1995), a human rights campaigner, was hanged along with eight others by Nigeria's military government. His "crime" was to speak out against the pollution of tribal lands by government-backed international oil companies.

Timeline

2500 BC Climatic changes in the Sahara region force people to move southward.

c.600 BC Kushite people of Sudan expand and base their capital at Meroë.

c.AD 320–25 King Ezama of Aksum becomes Christian.

African carving

500–1300 The kingdom of Ghana controls trans-Saharan trade.

641 Arabs conquer Egypt and convert it to Islam.

600s The empire based at Aksum begins to decline.

1497 Portuguese explorers land on east coast, after sailing around Africa.

1900 Most of the Sahara region comes under French colonial rule.

1940 Italian forces invade North Africa; Germans follow one year later.

1945 League of Arab States is founded; it includes eight African nations.

1973–75 Horn of Africa suffers a severe drought.

1980 British colony of Rhodesia becomes independent. It changes its name to Zimbabwe.

FIND OUT MORE BENIN EMPIRE   GREAT ZIMBABWE   MALI EMPIRE   MANDELA, NELSON   RELIGIONS   SLAVERY   SONGHAI EMPIRE   SOUTH AFRICA, HISTORY OF

AFRICA, CENTRAL

THE EQUATOR RUNS THROUGH central Africa, affecting not only climate but also peoples' lives. There are ten countries. All were European colonies with a history of a cruel slave trade. Although they were all independent by the end of the 1960s, these countries have experienced mixed success. Cameroon is stable, while Zaire and the Central African Republic have suffered harsh dictatorships and are two of the poorest countries in the world. Most central Africans live by subsistence farming.

Physical features

The landscape varies according to its distance from the equator. Much of the region is rolling hills and valleys, with craggy mountains in the north and east. The arid Sahara Desert and Sahel cover the extreme north. Farther south is the vast equatorial basin of the Zaire River, surrounded by some unspoiled tropical rain forest.

Dry woodland
Tropical rain forests give way to woodland, where the climate is much drier. Acacia and baobab trees grow in this region. The baobabs have very thick trunks that can hold water to feed themselves. Some baobabs on Cameroon's central plateau live for 1,000 years.

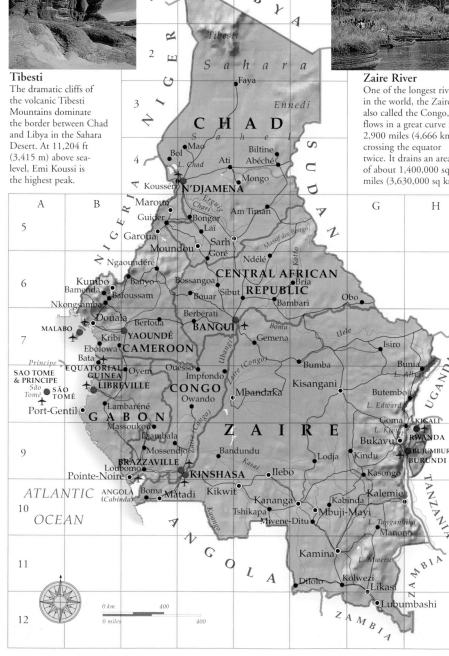

Tibesti
The dramatic cliffs of the volcanic Tibesti Mountains dominate the border between Chad and Libya in the Sahara Desert. At 11,204 ft (3,415 m) above sea-level, Emi Koussi is the highest peak.

Zaire River
One of the longest rivers in the world, the Zaire, also called the Congo, flows in a great curve for 2,900 miles (4,666 km), crossing the equator twice. It drains an area of about 1,400,000 sq miles (3,630,000 sq km).

Equatorial rain forest
The hot, humid basin of the Zaire River is Africa's largest remaining region of tropical rain forest. Competing for light, a wide variety of trees grow tall, forming a protective canopy that teems with plant and animal life.

Regional climate
The north of the region, the Sahara and Sahel area, is a broad band of dry, dusty land that is starved of rain. By contrast, in the steamy equatorial forests more than 1.5 in (38 mm) of rain falls every day in places. The south experiences the monsoon season between May and October.

84°F (29°C)   81°F (27°C)

56 in (1,434 mm)

Ethnic diversity

There are hundreds of different peoples in central Africa, each with their own customs and languages. Large groups include the Kongo and Luba, and there are several pygmy groups, including the Twa, BaKa, and Mbuti, who live in clearings deep in the rain forests. A growing number of people are moving to towns to escape war, drought, or famine, and because larger centers offer more jobs and food.

Village chief, Brazzaville, Congo

Chad

The landlocked republic of Chad is one of the world's poorest countries. Nearly half of the land is desert or lies in the Sahel, where rainfall is erratic. About 80 percent of the people work on farmland near the Chari River in the south, but lack of food is still a problem. Chad has some valuable mineral deposits, but they are unexploited.

Muslim nomads
More than 100,000 nomadic Muslims live in the desert and northern Sahel regions of Chad. They include the Kanimbo people, who are related to the Arabs and Berbers of North Africa. Every day, Kanimbo women must walk long distances in the heat to fetch water for their families.

Camels
One of the only ways to cross the vast Sahara desert is by camel. Camels are used as pack animals to transport forest products and minerals from Lake Chad, as well as for farming, pumping water, and carrying people. Herders value their milk, meat, and hides.

Dried gourds used as bowls for making butter.

Fulani
Throughout Africa a nomadic group called the Fulani herd cattle and roam wherever there is grazing land. They drink the cows' milk and use it to make butter and cheese. Bottle-shaped gourds, a type of fruit, are dried and decorated for use as water carriers and bowls.

CHAD FACTS

CAPITAL CITY N'Djamena

AREA 495,752 sq miles (1,284,000 sq km)

POPULATION 6,537,000

MAIN LANGUAGES French, Arabic, Sara

MAJOR RELIGIONS Muslim, Christian, traditional beliefs

CURRENCY CFA franc

A

Cameroon

On Africa's west coast, Cameroon was once a colony divided between the French and the British. The two parts gained independence in 1957 and became a united country. Despite initial troubles, Cameroon now has one of the most successful economies in Africa, exporting oil, bauxite, and a range of natural products including cocoa, coffee, and rubber. The country has a diverse culture with more than 200 ethnic groups.

Timber
Like many other African countries, Cameroon sells hardwood logs, including mahogany, ebony, and teak from its rain forests to earn foreign currency. Although the trade represents 11 percent of the country's total exports, it poses a serious threat to the future of the forests.

CAMEROON FACTS

CAPITAL CITY Yaoundé

AREA 183,570 sq miles (475,440 sq km)

POPULATION 13,651,000

MAIN LANGUAGES French, English, Fang, Duala, Fulani

MAJOR RELIGIONS Traditional beliefs, Christian, Muslim

CURRENCY CFA franc

Dried gourds amplify sounds made by strings.

Music
Makossa is a popular style of African folk music that originated in Cameroon. It is played on traditional instruments, including this one, known as a *mvet*. It is made using a wooden stick, horsehair strings, and hollowed-out gourds. *Mvet* players are specially trained and highly regarded in the community.

Several strings are stretched along the stick and plucked to make a range of sounds.

Soccer
One of Cameroon's leading amateur sports, soccer is widely enjoyed and people play it whenever they have time. Games draw large crowds of spectators. Cameroon's national soccer team has been acclaimed as one of the best in Africa after displaying its skills in the 1990 World Cup.

Central African Republic

Lying in the very heart of Africa, the Central African Republic, or CAR, has a complicated history. Drought and 13 years of repressive government have made the CAR one of the poorest nations in the world. Only two percent of the people live in the semiarid north, and the majority are clustered in villages in the southern rain forests.

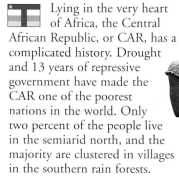

Bantu woman

Cotton
Coffee and cotton together form about 13 percent of the country's exports. Grown on large plantations, all parts of the cotton plant are used. The fiber, known as a boll, is spun into yarn to make fabric. The seed's oil forms the base of many foods; whilst the plant's stalks and leaves are plowed back into the soil to fertilize it.

After drying in the sun, cotton bolls are sorted by hand.

CENTRAL AFRICAN REPUBLIC FACTS

CAPITAL CITY Bangui

AREA 240,530 sq miles (622,980 sq km)

POPULATION 3,026,000

MAIN LANGUAGES French, Sango, Zande, Banda, Sara, Arabic

MAJOR RELIGIONS Traditional beliefs, Christian, Muslim

CURRENCY CFA franc

Millet

Cassava

People
Seven major Bantu language groups and many smaller ones make up the population of the CAR. Several thousand hunter-gatherers live in the rain forests in harmony with nature. They survive by eating forest fruits and build their homes from banana leaves.

Food
The people of the CAR grow nearly all their own food by subsistence farming. Root crops, such as cassava, yams, and vegetables, are cultivated alongside grains, including millet, corn, and sorghum. Fish from the CAR's rivers, including the Chari and Ubangi, is a vital source of protein.

Congo

The Republic of Congo was a French territory until 1960. It is a hot, humid land, and its densely forested north has few inhabitants. Nearly half the country's people are members of the Kongo group; the rest include Batéké, M'Bochi, and Sangha. The mineral and timber industries have made Congo wealthy, but many people are still subsistence farmers, growing barely enough food to survive.

Coffee beans

Each cocoa pod contains about 30 beans for use in chocolate and cosmetics.

Cocoa pods

Crops
About 50 percent of the workforce farms, growing cassava, corn, rice, peanuts, and fruit. Much food is imported. The steady export of coffee and cocoa beans has enabled Congo to remain solvent.

Animal skin is stretched across the drum.

Drum
An essential part of African life, drums are used for signaling as well as for music. Most drums are intricately carved out of a solid piece of wood and can be decorated with different woods and hides. Drums are made in all shapes and sizes – this one is almost as tall as the player.

Industry
Oil from the Atlantic Ocean accounts for 85 percent of Congo's exports, contributing largely to the country's wealth. Changing oil prices have caused some economic problems, but Congo's crop exports have remained strong. Over half of the land is forested, and more than 60 percent is scheduled to be felled for export. Huge barges on the Congo and other rivers carry timber goods as far as Brazzaville; from there the Congo Ocean Railway takes them to Pointe-Noire, Congo's only port.

CONGO FACTS

CAPITAL CITY Brazzaville

AREA 132,040 sq miles (342,000 sq km)

POPULATION 2,662,000

MAIN LANGUAGES French, Kongo

MAJOR RELIGIONS Christian, traditional beliefs,

CURRENCY CFA franc

Gabon

A palm-fringed sandy coastline 500 miles (800 km) long and lush tropical vegetation dominate Gabon's landscape. The country earns 80 percent of its foreign currency from oil and also sells timber, manganese, and uranium ore. Gabon has the potential to be wealthy, but mismanagement by the government has led to continued poverty.

Libreville
The bustling port city of Libreville was founded in 1849 by French naval officers. Meaning "free town" in French, Libreville was a new home for liberated slaves. It is now a modern, growing city and a center of culture, industry, and government. Many citizens are wealthy, but poverty still exists.

Young woman in Libreville, Gabon's capital

People
Although Gabon is one of Africa's most thinly populated countries, it contains more than 40 different ethnic groups. The indigenous Fang people form the largest group. Once fierce warriors, they now dominate the government. Most Gabonese are Christians, and 90 percent of their children attend primary schools. The Gabonese traditions of dance, song, poetry, and storytelling remain an important social and cultural part of daily life.

GABON FACTS

CAPITAL CITY Libreville

AREA 103,347 sq miles (267,670 sq km)

POPULATION 1,115,000

MAIN LANGUAGES French, Fang

MAJOR RELIGION Christian

CURRENCY CFA franc

The Trans-Gabon Railway runs from Libreville to Franceville.

Trans-Gabon Railway
Opened in 1986 to transport gold and manganese, the Trans-Gabon Railway has caused much controversy because it cut through rain forest, destroying many valuable and rare trees.

Equatorial Guinea

Two former Spanish colonies make up the country of Equatorial Guinea, located close to the equator. Río Muni, also called Mbini, is on mainland Africa, and Bioko Island, which has fertile, volcanic soil that is ideal for growing cocoa beans, is situated to the northwest, off the coast of neighboring Cameroon.

Traditional healing
Like other Africans, many people in Equatorial Guinea believe that illness is due to the influence of bad spirits. Professional healers use dancing and chants to drive out the evil spirits. They keep a range of animal bones, shells, sticks, and other plant parts in their medicine bags for use in group ceremonies.

Hippopotamus tooth

Cowrie shell

Tree root

Animal bone

Extended families
Among the people of Equatorial Guinea there is a strong tradition of large, extended families, which cling together and help one another in times of hardship.

EQUATORIAL GUINEA FACTS

CAPITAL CITY Malabo

AREA 10,830 sq miles (28,050 sq km)

POPULATION 410,000

MAIN LANGUAGES Spanish, Bubi, Fang

MAJOR RELIGION Christian

CURRENCY CFA franc

Zaire

Formerly called the Belgian Congo, this country became known as Zaire in 1971, 11 years after independence. In 1997 it adopted the name Democratic Republic of the Congo. The country consists of a plateau 3,900 ft (1,200 m) above sea level, through which the Zaire River flows. Zaire is rich in minerals and fertile land, but spendthrift governments and civil war, including conflict with Rwanda in 1996–97, have kept it poor.

Cowrie shells are sewn on to decorate the mask.

Mask

Among the many peoples of Zaire are the Kuba, a small ethnic group that has lived there for many years. Their chief wears a hunting mask like this, known as a Mashamboy mask, made of shells, beads, and raffia, to symbolize his people's power of the Great Spirit.

ZAIRE FACTS

CAPITAL CITY	Kinshasa
AREA	905,563 sq miles (2,345,410 sq km)
POPULATION	45,142,000
MAIN LANGUAGES	French, Kiswahili, Lingala
MAJOR RELIGIONS	Christian, Muslim, traditional beliefs
CURRENCY	New zaire

Creole woman selling diamonds

Farming

Zaire has much potentially cultivable land. Two-thirds of the population is engaged in subsistence farming, producing palm oil, coffee, tea, rubber, cotton, fruit, vegetables, and rice. Here, on the border of volcanic Virunga National park, the land is rich and fertile.

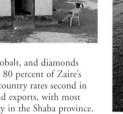

Mining

Copper ore, cobalt, and diamonds provide about 80 percent of Zaire's exports. The country rates second in world diamond exports, with most mining activity in the Shaba province.

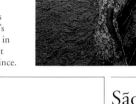

River ports

The Zaire River and its tributaries give the country 7,000 miles (11,500 km) of navigable waterways. There are many river ports with boatbuilding and repair yards, bright crafts shops, and lively markets that sell cassava, fruits, and fish, and delicacies like monkey and snake meat. Traders take their produce to sell at river markets in dugout canoes made by local craftsmen.

Ethnic strife

The present country boundaries in central Africa date back to European colonialism, and cut across logical ethnic groupings. In some places there is actual ethnic warfare, for example that between the Hutus and the Tutsis of Rwanda and Burundi. For hundreds of years, Rwanda has been dominated by the Tutsis, who ruled the Hutus. In 1959, the Hutus rebelled, and the two groups have fought ever since. The fighting has forced many people to flee their home country and live in refugee camps.

Refugee camp, Tanzania

São Tomé and Príncipe

This tiny country, formed by the main volcanic islands of São Tomé and Príncipe and four smaller islands, lies 120 miles (200 km) off the coast of Gabon. Its mountains are covered with forests, and rich soil supports farms that grow cocoa beans and sugarcane. Sea fishing has potential for development.

Pepper

The pepper plant's small, green berries redden as they ripen. Harvested quickly, the half-ripe berries are cleaned, dried in the sun, ground, and sifted to make ground black pepper.

Rwanda

One of Africa's most densely populated countries, Rwanda has been made poor by ethnic strife that has forced many thousands of people to flee to Zaire for safety. Rwanda makes its money by exporting coffee, tea, and tin and tungsten ores. Most of its people just manage to feed themselves.

Burundi

Like Rwanda, its neighbor, Burundi has been torn by conflict between the Tutsis and the Hutus, which has led to riots and thousands of deaths. Burundi has massive oil and nickel reserves beneath Lake Tanganyika, but lacks the funds to begin extraction. Most people are subsistence farmers.

Creole culture

Nobody lived on these islands until Portuguese explorers landed in 1470. The Portuguese peopled the islands with slaves from the mainland. Their mixed descendants created a culture called creole, but now only ten percent are creoles because over 4,000 left the country when it became independent.

Volcanoes Park

The *Parc des volcans* is a scenic reserve dominated by volcanic mountains, two of which are active. The park is the last refuge of the mountain gorillas, which now number less than 650.

RWANDA FACTS

CAPITAL CITY	Kigali
AREA	10,170 sq miles (26,340 sq km)
POPULATION	7,500,000
MAIN LANGUAGES	Kinyarwanda, French, Kiswahili
MAJOR RELIGIONS	Christian, Traditional beliefs
CURRENCY	Franc

Farming

Most farmers grow cassava and corn to feed their families. Some grow coffee, tea, cotton, and bananas for export. Overplanting fertile land is causing soil erosion.

BURUNDI FACTS

CAPITAL CITY	Bujumbura
AREA	10,750 sq miles (27,830 sq km)
POPULATION	5,800,000
MAIN LANGUAGES	Kirundi, French, Swahili
MAJOR RELIGIONS	Christian, Traditional beliefs
CURRENCY	Franc

SAO TOME AND PRINCIPE FACTS

CAPITAL CITY	São Tomé
AREA	372 sq miles (964 sq km)
POPULATION	136,000
MAIN LANGUAGE	Portuguese
MAJOR RELIGION	Christian
CURRENCY	Dobra

FIND OUT MORE — AFRICA, HISTORY OF · EMPIRES · FARMING · FORESTS · MONKEYS AND OTHER PRIMATES · MUSIC · OIL · PORTS AND WATERWAYS · SLAVERY · TRAINS AND RAILROADS

AFRICA, EAST

ONE OF THE WORLD'S OLDEST civilizations, Egypt, occupies the northeastern corner of East Africa, while Kenya, Tanzania, and Uganda sit farther south. Along the Horn of Africa, a piece of land that juts out into the Indian Ocean, are four of the world's poorest countries – Eritrea, Somalia, Ethiopia, and Djibouti. In recent years, Somalia, Sudan, and Ethiopia have been devastated by drought and war. Most East Africans scrape a living from farming, and some rely on food aid from abroad.

Physical features

Running through eastern Africa is the Great Rift Valley, a huge gash in the Earth that continues north through the Red Sea. Other features include the Nile, the world's longest river, and Lake Victoria, Africa's largest lake. The varied landscape includes deserts, grassland, mountains, and swamps.

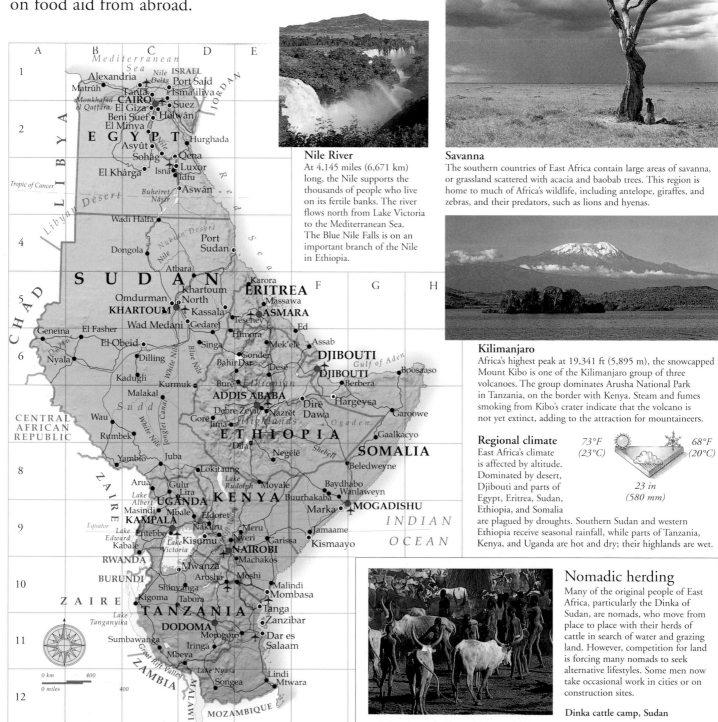

Nile River
At 4,145 miles (6,671 km) long, the Nile supports the thousands of people who live on its fertile banks. The river flows north from Lake Victoria to the Mediterranean Sea. The Blue Nile Falls is on an important branch of the Nile in Ethiopia.

Savanna
The southern countries of East Africa contain large areas of savanna, or grassland scattered with acacia and baobab trees. This region is home to much of Africa's wildlife, including antelope, giraffes, and zebras, and their predators, such as lions and hyenas.

Kilimanjaro
Africa's highest peak at 19,341 ft (5,895 m), the snowcapped Mount Kibo is one of the Kilimanjaro group of three volcanoes. The group dominates Arusha National Park in Tanzania, on the border with Kenya. Steam and fumes smoking from Kibo's crater indicate that the volcano is not yet extinct, adding to the attraction for mountaineers.

Regional climate
East Africa's climate is affected by altitude. Dominated by desert, Djibouti and parts of Egypt, Eritrea, Sudan, Ethiopia, and Somalia are plagued by droughts. Southern Sudan and western Ethiopia receive seasonal rainfall, while parts of Tanzania, Kenya, and Uganda are hot and dry; their highlands are wet.

73°F (23°C)   68°F (20°C)   23 in (580 mm)

Nomadic herding
Many of the original people of East Africa, particularly the Dinka of Sudan, are nomads, who move from place to place with their herds of cattle in search of water and grazing land. However, competition for land is forcing many nomads to seek alternative lifestyles. Some men now take occasional work in cities or on construction sites.

Dinka cattle camp, Sudan

Egypt

Today, as throughout its 5,000-year history, Egypt depends on the Nile River for much of its water, food, transportation, and energy, now generated at the massive Aswan Dam. Egypt controls the Suez Canal, a vital shipping route that links Africa, Europe, and Asia, and brings money into the country. About 99 percent of Egypt's people live along the lush, fertile banks of the river, and most are farmers, although the oil industry and tourist trade provide a growing number of jobs.

Water is drawn up to feed pipes that lead into the fields.

People

Several ethnic groups live in Egypt. Most people speak Arabic, but there are Berber and Nubian minorities. Women who live in the cities are among the most liberated in the Arab world, but, in rural families, men go to market and organize the planting and harvesting, while women cook and fetch water for the family.

EGYPT FACTS

CAPITAL CITY Cairo

AREA 386,660 sq miles (1,001,450 sq km)

POPULATION 59,713,000

DENSITY 154 per sq mile (60 people per sq km)

MAIN LANGUAGE Arabic

MAJOR RELIGION Muslim

CURRENCY Egyptian pound

LIFE EXPECTANCY 62 years

PEOPLE PER DOCTOR 1,320

GOVERNMENT Multiparty democracy

ADULT LITERACY 50%

Farming

Egypt is the world's second largest producer of dates, which are mostly grown in oases, along with melons. While some farmers use modern methods, many *fellahin*, or peasant farmers, use centuries-old techniques such as this one, where the donkey drives a wheel that scoops up water for irrigation.

Food

Reputed to be as old as the Pyramids, the traditional Egyptian dish of *ful medames* is made by boiling broad beans with garlic, onion, olive oil, and spices. The beans are served with hard-boiled eggs, lemon, and unleavened bread. Food is often accompanied by sweet tea and coffee.

Ful medames

Tourism

Thousands of people flock to Egypt every year to see the Pyramids and other remains of the country's ancient past, such as the tombs in the Valleys of the Kings and Queens, and the temples at Karnak and Luxor. The oldest pyramid is the Step Pyramid at Saqqara, which was built about 2650 BC as a tomb for King Zoser.

Soft dusters on poles are used to clean the delicate sandstone.

Ramesses II statue, Temple of Luxor

Cotton plant

Cairo

Egypt's ancient capital is the largest city in Africa, with a population of more than 6,000,000. It has at least 1,000 mosques, some built with stone looted from the Pyramids. Old Cairo's narrow streets heave with bustling bazaars, while the wealthy west bank has modern casinos and hotels.

The Sultan Hassan Mosque and surrounding area

Suez Canal

More than 20,000 cargo ships sail through the Suez Canal each year. The canal, built by French engineers in 1869, is 118 miles (190 km) long and provides a shortcut for ships between the Gulf of Suez and the Mediterranean Sea.

Cotton

Although only five percent of Egypt's land can be farmed, the country is a leading producer of cotton. Quality cloths are sold abroad or made into tunics, or *jelebas*, worn by locals.

Cotton boll

Sudan

Sudan is the largest country in Africa, measuring 1,274 miles (2,050 km) long from north to south. Desert in the north gives way to a central, grassy plain. Marshland covers much of the south. Two branches of the Nile (the White Nile and the Blue Nile) meet at the capital, Khartoum, providing fertile soil for farming. The country has good oil and mineral resources, but war and drought have weakened it.

People

There are more than 500 Sudanese ethnic groups, speaking about 100 languages and dialects. Some are nomadic herders, many of whom have now settled on farms. Most own their own plot, and live in villages of mud huts along the Nile, where farming is combined with fishing. The produce is sold at markets. Civil war and famine in the south of Sudan have created refugees.

SUDAN FACTS

CAPITAL CITY Khartoum

AREA 967,493 sq miles (2,505,815 sq km)

POPULATION 27,061,000

MAIN LANGUAGE Arabic

MAJOR RELIGIONS Muslim, traditional beliefs, Christian

CURRENCY Sudanese dinar

Religious conflict

The ruling people of the north are Arab Muslims, and the tall minarets of their beautiful mosques dominate the landscape. Farther south, the majority are divided into many ethnic groups and follow Christianity or traditional African religions. The religious, cultural, and language differences between north and south have caused bitter fighting.

A

Eritrea

A small, hot country on the Horn of Africa, Eritrea won independence from Ethiopia in 1993 after a 30-year war with Ethiopian troops that has left a legacy of destruction. Vast, but as yet unexploited, copper resources around the rugged mountains have potential for development. Eritrea's strategic Red Sea coastal position gives it access to the sea's oil fields, rich fishing grounds, and useful trade routes.

ERITREA FACTS	
CAPITAL CITY	Asmara
AREA	36,170 sq miles (93,680 sq km)
POPULATION	3,920,00
MAIN LANGUAGES	Tigrinya, Arabic
MAJOR RELIGIONS	Christian, Muslim
CURRENCY	Birr

Subsistence farming
More than 80 percent of Eritreans live by subsistence farming, many of them as nomadic herders. Farmers depend on September rains to create seasonal rivers that water the harvest, but recurring droughts have meant that Eritrea has been forced to rely on food aid from overseas.

People
The long war of independence developed a strong sense of nationalism among the people, although they belong to several ethnic groups speaking different languages. Women, 30,000 of whom fought in the war, many at leadership level, have been pressing the government for equal rights in the country's new political constitution.

Somalia

An arid, flat country bordering the Indian Ocean, Somalia has some of the longest beaches in the world. The country gained independence in 1960, but since the late 1980s there has been no effective government and the south has been in the grip of civil war waged by wealthy rival warlords. Most people are poor, and live in coastal towns in the north and in the south near rivers.

SOMALIA FACTS	
CAPITAL CITY	Mogadishu
AREA	246,200 sq miles (637,660 sq km)
POPULATION	9,077,000
MAIN LANGUAGES	Somali, Arabic
MAJOR RELIGION	Muslim
CURRENCY	Shilling

Mogadishu
Conveniently situated on Somalia's coastline, Mogadishu has long been an important port. Arabs founded the capital more than 1,000 years ago and sold it to the Italians in 1905. In 1960, it was returned to Somalia. The city's buildings are a mixture of older Arab architecture and 20th-century Italian design, but many have been damaged by war.

Civil war
Traditionally, the Somalis were organized in clans, or loyal family groups that were controlled by elder members. The government destroyed the clan system in the 1980s, provoking bitter wars. Many people are now dependent on overseas aid.

Ethiopia

The Great Rift Valley, a high plateau, and an arid desert dominate Ethiopia. The country has suffered famine, drought, and civil war, but farming reforms and good seasonal rains have enabled Ethiopians to depend less on aid from abroad. Four-fifths of the population makes a living through farming. Traditions such as storytelling, music, and dance are an important part of everyday life.

ETHIOPIA FACTS	
CAPITAL CITY	Addis-Ababa
AREA	435,605 sq miles (1,128,221 sq km)
POPULATION	51,000,000
MAIN LANGUAGE	Amharic
MAJOR RELIGIONS	Muslim, Christian, traditional beliefs
CURRENCY	Birr

Vegetable dish made from cabbage, carrots, garlic, and red lentils

Hard-boiled egg

Chicken stew with egg and red peppers

Enjera

Red onions, chilies, garlic, and ginger make wat, *a spicy sauce.*

A stew of beef, cinnamon, peppers, red chili, and tomatoes

Food
Spicy foods are standard in Ethiopia. A hot sauce known as *wat* is served with beef or chicken and mopped up with bread. Usually, a soft, flat bread called *enjera* is eaten, which is made from teff, a field crop grown mainly in Ethiopia. A wide range of fish is available to those with money. Ethiopian *kaffa*, coffee flavored with rye, is known as "health of Adam."

Orthodox church
The Ethiopian Orthodox Church is the chief Christian faith in the country. The pilgrimage center of Lalibela, in Ethiopia's central highlands, is known for its Christian churches, which date from the 10th century. *Timkat*, a yearly festival, is celebrated by Christians throughout Ethiopia.

Orthodox priests

Djibouti

A desert country on the Gulf of Aden, Djibouti serves as a port for Ethiopia. The two ethnic groups, the Afars and Issas, have a tradition of nomadic herding, but now half of them live in settled homes in the capital, Djibouti.

DJIBOUTI FACTS	
CAPITAL CITY	Djibouti
AREA	8,958 sq miles (23,200 sq km)
POPULATION	526,000
MAIN LANGUAGES	Arabic, French
MAJOR RELIGIONS	Muslim, Christian
CURRENCY	Franc

Shipping and fishing
The 19th-century city of Djibouti is one of the key Red Sea ports in the area and generates much of the country's income. The fishing industry thrives on its rich waters.

Kenya

Lying on the equator, Kenya has a varied landscape. The arid north is hot, but there is a rich farming region along the coast, and the south western highlands are warm and wet. The country has a stable, prosperous economy based on agriculture. More than 90 percent of the Kenyan people are under the age of 45 and belong to about 40 ethnic groups. Kenya is noted for its wildlife and its spectacular national parks.

KENYA FACTS

CAPITAL CITY Nairobi

AREA 224,081 sq miles (580,370 sq km)

POPULATION 28,794,000

MAIN LANGUAGES Kiswahili, English

MAJOR RELIGIONS Christian, traditional beliefs, Muslim

CURRENCY Kenya shilling

Nairobi
Founded by British colonists as a railroad town in 1899, Nairobi is Kenya's capital and a center of business and communications. Home to 1,429,000 people, the city's high-rise buildings contrast with the surrounding plains where elephants and lions roam.

Tourism
National parks are the main attraction for the thousands of tourists who visit Kenya every year. Ten percent of all Kenya is designated parkland, and there are more than 40 major national reserves. Amboseli, where many African animals (including lions, antelope, and leopards) live, enjoys a spectacular view of Kilimanjaro.

Coffee beans

Tea leaves

Crops
About 85 percent of the population works on the land. Kenya is the world's fourth largest producer of tea, which, together with coffee, is grown on plantations. Kenya leads the world in the export of pyrethrum, a pink flower that is dried to make insecticides.

Green beans

Uganda

Independence from Britain in 1962 led to ethnic conflict and poverty in Uganda, but since 1986, when peace was restored, the economy has been recovering slowly. Agriculture is still the main activity, with coffee, cotton, and cane sugar the main exports. Uganda also has good mineral deposits, including copper, gold, and cobalt. Most Ugandans live in rural villages.

UGANDA FACTS

CAPITAL CITY Kampala

AREA 91,073 sq miles (235,880 sq km)

POPULATION 19,278,000

MAIN LANGUAGES English, Kiswahili

MAJOR RELIGIONS Christian, traditional beliefs, Muslim

CURRENCY Uganda shilling

Sweet potatoes

Farming
About 80 percent of the workforce farms 43 percent of the land. Most people own small farms, producing enough cassava, corn, millet, and sweet potatoes for themselves and to trade at market.

Kampala
Uganda's capital, Kampala, stands on hills overlooking Lake Victoria. The ancient palace of the former Buganda kings stands alongside the modern Museveni University. The 773,000 people of Kampala experience violent thunderstorms on an average of 242 days a year, and rain nearly every day.

Market in Kampala

Lake Victoria
The world's second largest freshwater lake, Victoria lies between Uganda, Kenya, and Tanzania. Giant perch fish have eaten nearly all the lake's natural fish species. A hydroelectricity project at the lake's Owen Falls aims to cut Uganda's oil imports in half.

Tanzania

The islands of Zanzibar united with mainland Tanganyika in 1964, creating Tanzania. More than half the country is covered by forests, and it has a long Indian Ocean coastline. Dar es Salaam, the largest city and chief port, was until recently the capital. Farming is the main activity, but oil, diamonds, and gas have been discovered.

TANZANIA FACTS

CAPITAL CITY Dodoma

AREA 364,900 sq miles (945,090 sq km)

POPULATION 31,698,000

MAIN LANGUAGES English, Kiswahili

MAJOR RELIGIONS Traditional beliefs, Muslim, Christian

CURRENCY Tanzania shilling

Cotton
Tea, tobacco, and cotton account for two-thirds of Tanzania's exports. Most cotton is produced on government-operated farms in the north and south highlands and around Lake Victoria. Workers carry the cotton to the factory to be spun and woven into cloth.

Sisal bags

People
The 120 ethnic groups of Tanzania live together in harmony, as no single group is dominant. Nearly 77 percent of the people live in small, scattered villages, but the state *Ujamaa* policy has tried to resettle them into larger communities to provide more facilities.

Zanzibar
The island of Zanzibar and its small companion island of Pemba lie off the east coast of Tanzania. Zanzibar is one of the world's leading producers of cloves and sisal, a plant grown for making rope and bags for export.

FIND OUT MORE AFRICA, HISTORY OF   CHRISTIANITY   DAMS   EGYPT, ANCIENT   EMPIRES   FARMING   ISLAM   PORTS AND WATERWAYS   RIVERS   WARFARE

A

AFRICA, NORTHWESTERN

MOROCCO, ALGERIA, TUNISIA, and Libya, plus the disputed territory of Western Sahara, make up the northwestern corner of Africa. The region has been dominated by Arabs and their religion, Islam, for more than 1,300 years. Algeria and Libya are huge countries, but much of the land is desert. However, they and Tunisia have abundant reserves of oil and natural gas. Farming, made possible by irrigation projects, is still important in the region. Many people lead nomadic lives roaming the land with their herds of animals.

Mediterranean coast
Once occupied by the Phoenicians, Greeks, and Romans, northwestern Africa's Mediterranean coast has many ancient ruins that are particularly popular with tourists in Morocco, Algeria, and Tunisia. Most people live on the coastal plain, which has fertile land and a warm climate.

Physical features

Along the Mediterranean and Atlantic coasts is a fertile strip where most of the people live. The Atlas Mountain chain runs across Morocco and continues as rolling hills in Algeria and Tunisia. The rest of the land is desert, broken by oases and bleak mountain ranges.

Atlas Mountains
The Atlas Mountains consist of several chains of mountains that stretch 1,500 miles (2,410 km) from the Atlantic coast of Morocco to Cape Bon in eastern Tunisia. The highest peak is Djebel Toubkal at 13,665 ft (4,167 m), which lies in the High Atlas range in southern Morocco.

77°F (25°C)   -53°F (12°C)

17 in (434 mm)

Regional climate

Along most of the coast and on high ground, summers are hot and dry and winters are warm and wet. Daytime desert temperatures average about 100°F (38°C); at night they are low. Desert rainfall may be as little as 1 in (2.5 cm) a year, and irregular.

Sahara
The Sahara Desert covers about 3,320,000 sq miles (8,600,000 sq km). Only about one-fifth is sand. The rest includes vast, flat expanses of barren rock and gravel and mountains such as Algeria's Ahaggar range, peaking at 9,573 ft (2,918 m). Crops are grown in 90 large oases.

Berbers

The original people of northwestern Africa are the Berbers. Today, about 15,000,000 Berbers still live in the mountains and deserts of the region. Most are Muslim, but retain their own language and dialects. The Tuareg are a group of nomadic Berber herders who roam the North African desert.

Berber man and child

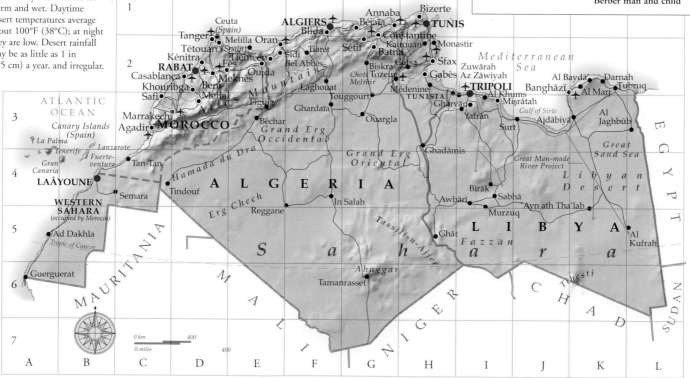

Morocco

A mix of African, Islamic, Arab, Berber, and European influences, Morocco attracts more than two million tourists each year. The country's strengths are farming and phosphate mining. Founded in Fès, in AD 859, Karueein University is the oldest in the world.

MOROCCO FACTS	
CAPITAL CITY	Rabat
AREA	177,116 sq miles (458,730 sq km)
POPULATION	28,913,000
MAIN LANGUAGES	Arabic, Berber, French
MAJOR RELIGION	Muslim
CURRENCY	Moroccan dirham

Mint tea

The traditional drink in Morocco is a refreshing mint tea, served in glasses or pots, with plenty of sugar and a sprig of mint. It is often offered free of charge in the *souks* (markets) when bargaining is about to begin.

Carpets

Hand-knotted wool carpets are one of Morocco's great craft industries. The leading carpet factories are in Fès and Rabat. The carpets have bold colors and symbolic, abstract Islamic patterns. Though sold by men, most rugs are made by women.

Polisario soldiers keep watch.

Western Sahara

Morocco has occupied the ex-Spanish colony of Western Sahara since 1975. Polisario Front guerrillas began fighting for independence in 1983, to resist mass settlement of the area by Moroccans keen to hold on to the phosphate-rich territory.

Tunisia

A former French colony, Tunisia is the smallest country in the region and one of the more liberal Arab states. Although not admitted into politics, Tunisian women make up 25 percent of the workforce. Tourism is being developed.

Couscous is steamed in a special pot that sits above the stewing meat.

TUNISIA FACTS	
CAPITAL CITY	Tunis
AREA	63,170 sq miles (163,610 sq km)
POPULATION	9,095,000
MAIN LANGUAGES	Arabic, French
MAJOR RELIGION	Muslim
CURRENCY	Tunisian dinar

Couscous

The staple food in Tunisia is granules of semolina called couscous. Originally a Berber dish, couscous is served with a meat or vegetable sauce. Tunisians like their food spicy. After the main course, dates stuffed with almond paste, or sweet pastries filled with honey and nuts are served.

Souk

A feature of Tunisian cities – and indeed all northwestern African cities – is the *souk*, or market. This is traditionally a tangle of narrow streets flanked by open stalls where people can buy anything from food to carpets or handmade jewelry.

Algeria

Under French rule from 1830, Algeria won independence in 1962. The country has a high birth rate and a young population: 86 percent is below the age of 44. Crude oil and natural gas are an important source of income. Increasingly, fundamentalist Islamic groups pose a threat to non-Muslims.

ALGERIA FACTS	
CAPITAL CITY	Algiers
AREA	919,590 sq miles (2,381,740 sq km)
POPULATION	29,350,000
MAIN LANGUAGES	Arabic, Berber, French
MAJOR RELIGION	Muslim
CURRENCY	Algerian dinar

Overpopulation

Since more than four-fifths of Algeria is desert, 90 per cent of Algerians live in the far north of the country, where it is cooler. However, as Algeria's population continues to increase at a rate of more than 2.5 percent a year, many northern towns, like Constantine, are struggling to house everybody, and slum areas are growing.

Houses are built on every available piece of land.

Black dates

Yellow dates

Dates

Algeria is the world's sixth largest producer of dates. They are grown in the fertile north as well as in the many oases of the Sahara and provide a main source of income. Date palms also yield timber; their leaves are used to thatch buildings.

Libya

Since 95 percent of Libya is desert, the Great Man-made River Project was set up to irrigate farming land. Water is piped from beneath the Sahara to populated coastal regions.

LIBYA FACTS	
CAPITAL CITY	Tripoli
AREA	679, 358 sq miles (1,759,540 sq km)
POPULATION	5,587,000
MAIN LANGUAGES	Arabic, Tuareg
MAJOR RELIGION	Muslim
CURRENCY	Libyan dinar

Oil and gas

The discovery of oil and natural gas in 1959 transformed Libya into a wealthy nation, and many people moved to the towns in search of work. In 1992, trade with the West was severely disrupted when the UN imposed sanctions because of leader Colonel Gaddafi's alleged links with international terrorist groups.

Oil workers at Calanscio

Roman ruins

Libya was abandoned by the Romans after the Arab conquest of AD 643 and was an Italian colony between 1911 and 1951. Today, some of the finest Roman ruins outside Italy can be seen at Leptis Magna, now called Labdah, to the east of the capital, Tripoli.

FIND OUT MORE | AFRICA, HISTORY OF | DESERTS | EMPIRES | FARMING | ISLAM | ISLAMIC EMPIRE | MOUNTAINS AND VALLEYS | OIL | ROMAN EMPIRE | TEXTILES AND WEAVING

AFRICA, SOUTHERN CENTRAL

SOUTHERN CENTRAL AFRICA is made up of seven countries that form part of the African mainland, and the islands of Madagascar and Comoros in the Indian Ocean. Farming is still an important source of income in these countries, but major deposits of minerals such as diamonds, copper, uranium, and iron have led many people to move to the towns and cities in search of work. Different tribal groups, each with its own language, customs, and beliefs, live in the southern central region.

Namib Desert
The Namib Desert extends for 1,100 miles (1,900 km) in a narrow strip from southwestern Angola, along the Skeleton Coast of Namibia, and down to the South African border. Although it rarely rains, the climate on the coast is humid with cold, morning fogs. Sand dunes reach down to the edge of the Atlantic and the only practical transportation is camel.

Physical features

Although lowlands fringe the coast, most of the region lies 1,200–4,500 ft (400 m–1,500 m) above sea level. The landscape includes the Namib and Kalahari deserts in the west and center, dry savanna, and humid, subtropical forests in the north.

Acacia trees, Madagascar

Savanna
Much of the region is covered by grassland, or savanna. The most common trees in these areas are thorn trees, especially acacias. They are suited to the dry conditions and grow on the edges of the Kalahari and other semidesert regions.

Regional climate

Most of the region lies in the tropics, where the climate is always hot, but there are two seasons: wet and dry. Rain is heavy in the wet season. Most of Botswana and Namibia has a semiarid climate, and much of Namibia is desert. Eastern Madagascar has a tropical wet climate.

74°F (23°C)   61°F (16°C)

38 in (964 mm)

Women's role

The traditional role of African women was to look after the home and bring up the children. Many were also expected to cultivate the crops, and some built their own houses. Today, many women in southern central Africa have additional responsibilities, because their husbands are away working in mines and cities. Despite the domestic power of women, few have official jobs or own property.

Zimbabwean woman with her baby

Angola

In 1975, after a long war, Angola became independent of Portuguese colonial rule. With fertile land and huge reserves of diamonds, oil, and natural gas, the country should have become prosperous. However, the fighting that continued after independence as a civil war between rival ethnic groups tore Angola apart and limited economic development. A truce began in 1996.

ANGOLA FACTS

CAPITAL CITY Luanda

AREA 481,351 sq miles (1,246,700 sq km)

POPULATION 11,440,000

MAIN LANGUAGE Portuguese

MAJOR RELIGIONS Christian, traditional beliefs

CURRENCY New kwanza

Oil and diamonds
Most of Angola's oil is produced in Cabinda, a tiny Angolan enclave in Zaire. Petroleum provides 90 percent of Angola's exports. Angola also ranks eighth in world output of diamonds, which are the second largest export.

Luanda
Founded by the Portuguese in 1575, Angola's capital and largest city is home for about a million people. Once used for shipping slaves to Brazil, it is still a major seaport. Modern Luanda is an industrial center with its own oil refinery.

Zambia

Bordered to the south by the Zambezi River, Zambia is a country of upland plateaus, 80 percent of which are grassland and forest. About 50 percent of the people live by subsistence farming, constantly threatened by drought. Tobacco is the only exported crop. Hydroelectric power provides much of Zambia's energy. Low copper prices in the 1980s upset finances.

ZAMBIA FACTS

CAPITAL CITY Lusaka

AREA 290,582 sq miles (752,610 sq km)

POPULATION 9,623,000

MAIN LANGUAGES English, Bemba, Tonga, Nyanja, Lozi, Lunda

MAJOR RELIGIONS Christian, traditional beliefs

CURRENCY Zambian kwacha

Cobalt is used in steel production.

Copper forms 86 percent of exports.

Copper bracelets

Copper and cobalt
Zambia is the world's fifth largest producer of copper. The seam of copper ore where the metal is mined, the Copperbelt, is 200 miles (320 km) long. The second largest producer of cobalt, Zambia also mines lead, silver, and zinc.

Urban living
About half of Zambia's people, a mix of more than 70 different ethnic groups, live in towns and cities. The most populated area is the Copperbelt, where most of them work. The capital, Lusaka, a thriving industrial and business center, is home to one in 12 Zambians.

Namibia

An ex-German colony, and ruled for 70 years by South Africa, Namibia won its independence in 1990. Rich mineral resources make mining the country's leading industry. One in seven people lives on the land, mainly rearing livestock, although drought and the expanding desert make farming difficult. Fishing is good off the Atlantic coast.

NAMIBIA FACTS

CAPITAL CITY Windhoek

AREA 318,260 sq miles (824,290 sq km)

POPULATION 1,739,000

MAIN LANGUAGES English, Afrikaans, Ovambo, Kavango

MAJOR RELIGION Christian

CURRENCY Namibian dollar

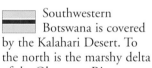

Uranium
The Rössing Uranium Mine in the Namib Desert is the world's largest, producing 2,200 tons (2,000 tonnes) of uranium every year. Namibia is the world's ninth largest producer of uranium and seventh largest producer of diamonds.

Himba woman

Hair is braided and beaded.

People
Namibia has a peaceful multiracial society. The white minority lives mostly in Windhoek, in European-style houses. Black Namibians include many groups, the largest of which are the northern Ovambo. To the west the seminomadic Himba raise cattle.

Botswana

Southwestern Botswana is covered by the Kalahari Desert. To the north is the marshy delta of the Okavango River, a haven for wildlife. Despite this wetland, however, Botswana suffers droughts. Most people live in the more fertile east. Botswana is the world's third largest producer of diamonds.

BOTSWANA FACTS

CAPITAL CITY Gaborone

AREA 224,606 sq miles (581,730 sq km)

POPULATION 1,532,000

MAIN LANGUAGES English, Tswana, Shona, Khoikhoi, Ndebele

MAJOR RELIGIONS Traditional beliefs, Christian

CURRENCY Pula

Beef stew with dried spinach

Savory porridge

San
The original inhabitants of Botswana are the nomadic San people, once known as Kalahari Bushmen, one of Africa's only remaining groups of hunter-gatherers. There are fewer than 50,000 San today, but small groups still roam the Kalahari Desert hunting small animals and eating edible plants and insects. Many San now work on cattle ranches.

Food
The Tswana people, who make up 95 percent of Botswana's population, live mostly by subsistence farming, raising cattle, and growing enough corn, sorghum, and millet for their own use. Their staple diet consists of meat stews served with a kind of porridge made from grain. Fresh vegetables are rare.

Zimbabwe

In 1980, the former British colony of Rhodesia became independent and took the name Zimbabwe, after the ancient city of Great Zimbabwe. About 75 percent of Zimbabweans live from farming: cash crops include tobacco, cotton, sugar, and corn. Coal, gold, asbestos, and nickel are mined for export. The country also has a varied manufacturing sector.

ZIMBABWE FACTS

CAPITAL CITY	Harare
AREA	150,803 sq miles (390,580 sq km)
POPULATION	11,845,000
MAIN LANGUAGES	English, Shona, Ndebele
MAJOR RELIGIONS	Traditional beliefs, Christian
CURRENCY	Zimbabwe dollar

Tourism
Zimbabwe's main tourist attractions are the spectacular Victoria Falls, the Kariba Dam, national parks, and the ruins of the city of Great Zimbabwe. Tourists enjoy active vacations, such as canoeing and rafting, on the Zambezi.

Harare
Formerly called Salisbury, the capital is Zimbabwe's commercial and industrial center and home for almost a million people. It is a clean and sophisticated city that is characterized by flowering trees, colorful parks, and modern buildings.

Madagascar

The fourth largest island in the world, Madagascar is home to some unique wildlife because of its isolated position off Africa's east coast. A high plateau runs the length of the island, dropping to a narrow, fertile strip in the east, where most people live. The country's economy is based on growing crops and raising livestock.

MADAGASCAR FACTS

CAPITAL CITY	Antananarivo
AREA	226,656 sq miles (587,040 sq km)
POPULATION	13,309,000
MAIN LANGUAGES	Malagasy, French
MAJOR RELIGIONS	Christian, traditional beliefs
CURRENCY	Malagasy franc

Vanilla
Madagascar is the world's largest exporter of vanilla. The pods of the plants are used to flavor ice cream and chocolate. Other important cash crops are cloves, sisal, cocoa, and butter beans.

Vanilla pods grow 10 in (25 cm) long.

Rural society
Most Madagascans are descended from Asians from Malaysia and Indonesia, who began to settle on the island almost 2,000 years ago. Later waves of mainland Africans intermixed to produce a uniquely multiracial society. Three-quarters of the Madagascan labor force works on the land, growing subsistence crops, such as cassava and rice.

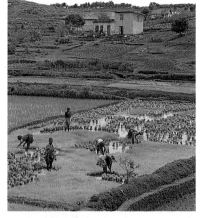

Mozambique

As a result of years of civil war, flooding, and drought, Mozambique is now one of the world's poorest countries, with a high birth rate. The land, though largely unexploited, is fertile and rich in minerals. The ports and railroads provide a trade link for landlocked Swaziland, Malawi, and Zimbabwe.

MOZAMBIQUE FACTS

CAPITAL CITY	Maputo
AREA	309,494 sq miles (801,590 sq km)
POPULATION	15,300,000
MAIN LANGUAGE	Portuguese
MAJOR RELIGIONS	Traditional beliefs, Christian, Muslim
CURRENCY	Metical

Fishing
Mozambique's main industry is fishing, and shrimp accounts for more than 40 percent of export earnings. The country's total annual fish catch totals 26,643 tons (24,170 tonnes). Cotton, tea, and sugar are also exported.

Malawi

With few natural resources, Malawi has a rural society, despite the constant threat of drought. Light industries, such as food processing, textiles, and manufacturing farm tools, are developing. Fish from Lake Malawi, which covers one-quarter of the country, is a source of food.

MALAWI FACTS

CAPITAL CITY	Lilongwe
AREA	45,745 sq miles (118,480 sq km)
POPULATION	11,552,000
MAIN LANGUAGES	Chewa, English
MAJOR RELIGIONS	Christian, Muslim
CURRENCY	Malawian kwacha

Tea grows well in the tropical climate of Malawi's hillsides.

Farming
Almost 86 percent of the Malawi labor force works in agriculture, growing cash crops, such as tea, tobacco, coffee, cotton, and sugar, as well as subsistence crops of corn, rice, cassava, and plantains. The country is self-sufficient in food.

Comoros

The three islands and few islets of the Comoros archipelago lie north of Madagascar in the Indian Ocean. They were governed by France until 1975. The economy is underdeveloped, and most of the people live by subsistence farming.

Ylang-ylang
Comoros is the world's largest grower of ylang-ylang, an aromatic tree with greenish-yellow flowers that produce a pleasantly scented oil used to make perfume.

COMOROS FACTS

CAPITAL CITY	Moroni
AREA	861 sq miles (2,230 sq km)
POPULATION	676,000
MAIN LANGUAGES	Arabic, French, local languages
MAJOR RELIGIONS	Muslim, Christian
CURRENCY	Comoros franc

FIND OUT MORE | AFRICA, HISTORY OF | AFRICAN WILDLIFE | DESERTS | EMPIRES | FARMING | FISHING INDUSTRY | GREAT ZIMBABWE | OIL | ROCKS AND MINERALS | SOCIETIES, HUMAN

AFRICA, WEST

THE ATLANTIC OCEAN borders all but three of the 15 countries that make up West Africa. Much of the area is dominated by the Sahara and the Sahel, a vast area of semidesert that the Sahara is slowly invading. Despite their potential wealth and rich resources, most of the countries are desperately poor. Long-established trade routes across the Sahara link West Africa with the Mediterranean coast to the north. For millions of West Africans, life is a perpetual struggle against a hostile climate, the threat of drought, and political instability.

Sahel
Immediately south of the Sahara Desert, stretching across West Africa, is a broad band of hot, arid, semidesert grassland called the Sahel. In Arabic, the word Sahel means "shore" of the desert. Rainfall in this region is sporadic and droughts are common.

Physical features

Most of West Africa lies 600–1,200 ft (200–400 m) above sea level. The Sahara dominates Niger, Mauritania, and Mali, and the Sahel extends south into Senegal, Burkina Faso, and Nigeria. The Senegal, Gambia, Volta, and Niger rivers irrigate the west and south.

Niger River
Africa's second longest river, the Niger flows in a great arc for 2,550 miles (4,100 km) from Guinea through Mali, Niger, Benin, and Nigeria to a vast delta on the Gulf of Guinea. A valuable source of fish and water, it is navigable for more than half its length.

Regional climate
There are four main climate regions in West Africa. From north to south, they are desert, Sahel, grassland, and tropical rain forest. Rain is rare in the northern desert and Sahel regions. The south is humid and tropical with a distinct rainy season that can last for four to six months.

78°F (25°C)   80°F (26°C)
74 in (1,879 mm)

Peanuts
Peanuts are widely grown in West Africa as a source of edible oil and as a foodstuff that is rich in protein and vitamins. Peanuts develop underground; for this reason they are also called groundnuts. The plants were introduced into West Africa from South America.

Harvesting peanuts

Mauritania

The northern two-thirds of Mauritania is desert. The only farmland lies in a narrow fertile strip along the bank of the Senegal River in the southwest. This area is scattered with small villages and oases. Nomadic Moors of Arab descent, from the north, live in Mauritania. They have often clashed with black farmers in the south.

Fishing
The waters off Mauritania have some of the richest fish stocks in the world and attract many foreign fishing fleets. All catches must be sold through the state fishing company. Fishing provides more than half of Mauritania's export earnings.

Desertification
Successive years of drought and overgrazing in the Sahel region have caused the desert to expand southward, killing livestock and forcing many nomads to move into towns.

Government schemes are attempting to reclaim the land by reducing soil erosion.

Mineral wealth
The Mauritanian desert contains the largest deposits of gypsum – used for making plaster – and some of the largest reserves of iron ore in the world. The country also exports gold. A single railroad connects mines with Nouakchott, the country's capital and main port.

Gypsum crystal

MAURITANIA FACTS

CAPITAL CITY	Nouakchott
AREA	395,953 sq miles (1,025,520 sq km)
POPULATION	2,399,000
MAIN LANGUAGES	Arabic, French, Hassaniya, Wolof, Soninké
MAJOR RELIGION	Muslim
CURRENCY	Ouguiya

Senegal

The flat, semidesert plains of Senegal are crossed by three rivers – the Senegal, Gambia, and Casamance – which provide water for agriculture, the country's main source of income. Tourism is also developing. Senegal has a mix of ethnic groups, the largest of which are the Wolofs.

Dakar
Senegal's capital and major port, Dakar is a bustling industrial center with good restaurants, shops, and markets. However, many of the one million inhabitants are poor and live in suburban slums.

Music
At festivals and ceremonies, or *griots*, a mix of historians, musicians, and poets, sing and recite traditional stories, often to the accompaniment of a *kora*.

Kora

Musicians pluck the 21 strings to give a wide range of muted sounds.

Many of Senegal's fruits and vegetables are imported and expensive.

Gourd soundbox

Farming
About 65 percent of Senegalese laborers work on the land growing cotton and sugarcane for export, and rice, sorghum, and millet for their food. Until droughts in the 1970s damaged yields, peanuts were the main cash crop. Fish is now the main export.

SENEGAL FACTS

CAPITAL CITY	Dakar
AREA	75,950 sq miles (196,720 sq km)
POPULATION	8,610,000
MAIN LANGUAGES	French, Wolof, Fulani, Sérèr, Diola, Mandinka
MAJOR RELIGIONS	Muslim, Christian, traditional beliefs
CURRENCY	CFA franc

Gambia

The fourth most densely populated country in Africa, Gambia occupies a narrow strip on either side of the Gambia River and is surrounded on three sides by Senegal. With little industry, three-quarters of the people live off the land. Peanuts make up 80 percent of exports. The main ethnic groups are the Mandinka, Fulani, and Wolof.

Tourism
Gambia is an attractive destination for winter sun-seekers from Europe. Tourism, the country's fastest-growing industry, employs one in ten Gambians. About 10,000 of those work on a seasonal basis.

GAMBIA FACTS

CAPITAL CITY	Banjul
AREA	4,363 sq miles (11,300 sq km)
POPULATION	1,106,000
MAIN LANGUAGES	English, Mandinka
MAJOR RELIGIONS	Muslim, Christian, traditional beliefs
CURRENCY	Dalasi

Guinea-Bissau

Rainfall in Guinea-Bissau is more plentiful than in the rest of Africa, enabling the country to be self-sufficient in rice. However, flooding is common along the coast because farmers have cut down mangroves to plant rice fields. Most people travel around by riverboat.

Cashew nuts

Grated coconut

Coconut

Cashew nuts
Farming employs 85 percent of the workforce. Rice, cotton, peanuts, and dried coconut are produced as cash crops, as are cashew nuts, which make up nearly 60 percent of the country's exports.

GUINEA-BISSAU FACTS

CAPITAL CITY	Bissau
AREA	13,940 sq miles (36,120 sq km)
POPULATION	1,096,000
MAIN LANGUAGES	Portuguese, Crioulo
MAJOR RELIGIONS	Traditional beliefs, Muslim, Christian
CURRENCY	Peso

Guinea

With more than 30 percent of the world's known reserves of bauxite, and deposits of diamonds, iron, copper, manganese, uranium, and gold, Guinea could be a wealthy country. However, years of poor government and lack of support from former French rulers have made Guinea's economic development difficult.

GUINEA FACTS

CAPITAL CITY	Conakry
AREA	94,926 sq miles (245,860 sq km)
POPULATION	6,897,000
MAIN LANGUAGES	French, Fulani, Malinke, Susu
MAJOR RELIGIONS	Muslim, traditional beliefs,
CURRENCY	Guinean franc

Coffee beans

Bananas

Pineapple

Fruit growing
Bananas, plantains, and pineapples grow well in the fertile Fouta Djalon hills (Guinea Highlands). Farmers cultivate coffee, palm nuts, and peanuts as cash crops and sorghum, rice, and cassava for their families.

People
Three-quarters of Guineans belong to one of three main ethnic groups – the Malinke and Fulani, who live in the north and center, and the Susu, who live closer to the coast. Two-thirds live in small rural communities, where the standard of living is one of the lowest in the world. Average life expectancy is low, at only 45 years, and only about 35 percent of people can read.

Sierra Leone

Sierra Leone was founded by the British in the early 1800s as a colony for freed slaves. Its name is Spanish for "Lion Mountains" and refers to the constant roar of thunder. Of the 12 ethnic groups, the biggest are the Mende and the Temne. Most people live in poverty.

SIERRA LEONE FACTS

CAPITAL CITY	Freetown
AREA	27,699 sq miles (71,740 sq km)
POPULATION	4,863,000
MAIN LANGUAGES	English, Krio (Creole)
MAJOR RELIGIONS	Traditional beliefs, Muslim, Christian
CURRENCY	Leone

Industry
Mining is the mainstay of Sierra Leone's economy. The chief exports are diamonds, some of which are still mined by hand, as well as gold, bauxite, and titanium ore. Farming employs more than two-thirds of the workforce, growing coffee, cocoa, palm kernels, ginger, and cassava.

Uncut diamond looks like any other stone.

Freetown
Surrounded by green hills, Sierra Leone's capital, Freetown, is a colorful and historic port and home to 500,000 people. The name is a reminder of the country's former status as a haven for freed slaves. Among Freetown's attractions are a 500-year-old cotton tree, and West Africa's oldest university, built in 1827.

Ivory Coast

With 370 miles (600 km) of Atlantic coastline and three main rivers, Ivory Coast is fertile and arable. It is among the world's top producers of coffee and cocoa. Food makes up half of all exports. Most people work in farming and forestry. Nearly all the tropical forests have been sold off as timber to pay foreign debts.

IVORY COAST FACTS

CAPITAL CITY	Yamoussoukro
AREA	124,503 sq miles (322,463 sq km)
POPULATION	14,891,000
MAIN LANGUAGES	French, Akan
MAJOR RELIGIONS	Muslim, Christian, traditional beliefs
CURRENCY	CFA franc

Farmers use pesticides on cocoa plantations, but their health is at risk because they don't wear protective clothes.

Yamoussoukro Basilica
Although only 26 percent of the population is Christian, Ivory Coast has one of the world's largest Christian churches. Able to seat 7,000 people, it dominates the city of Yamoussoukro, which replaced Abidjan as the country's capital in 1983.

Cocoa
Ivory Coast is the world's leading producer of cocoa beans. Cocoa trees need humid conditions, and many cocoa plantations lie in moist, tropical regions where rain forests were felled for timber. Factories have been set up in Ivory Coast to make cocoa butter, which is the basic ingredient of chocolate and some cosmetics.

Liberia

Founded by the US in the 1820s as a home for freed black slaves, Liberia has never been colonized. About five percent of the people descend from former slaves and American settlers. The rest are a mix of ethnic groups. About 70 percent of Liberians work on the land, growing palm trees, coffee, and cocoa, and rubber for export. Civil war has damaged trade.

LIBERIA FACTS

CAPITAL CITY	Monrovia
AREA	43,000 sq miles (111,370 sq km)
POPULATION	3,136,000
MAIN LANGUAGES	English, Kpelle, Bassa Vai, Grebo, Kru, Kissi, Gola
MAJOR RELIGIONS	Christian, traditional beliefs, Muslim
CURRENCY	Liberian dollar

Civil war
Since 1990, Liberia has been torn by a chaotic and bloody civil war, and its once prosperous economy has collapsed. The war, which began as clashes between various ethnic groups, has made thousands of people homeless and many are forced to live in large refugee camps where food shortages are a part of everyday life.

Monrovia
Reputedly the world's wettest capital city, with more than 183 in (4,560 mm) of rain per year, Monrovia is a sprawling city and major port. Liberia has the world's largest commercial fleet of ships. Almost all are foreign owned but registered in Monrovia, where taxes are low.

A

Mali

Desert and semidesert cover the northern two-thirds of Mali, and only two percent of the land can be cultivated. Most people live in the south, in farming settlements close to the Niger and Senegal rivers. Droughts, poor food, and an average life expectancy of only 49 years make Mali one of the world's poorest countries. Some gold is mined, but cotton is the biggest export.

Buildings such as this granary are made from sand bricks.

MALI FACTS

CAPITAL CITY Bamako

AREA 478,837 sq miles (1,240,190 sq km)

POPULATION 11,124,000

MAIN LANGUAGES French, Bambara, Fulani, Senufo, Soninke

MAJOR RELIGIONS Muslim, traditional beliefs

CURRENCY CFA franc

Making "mud cloth"

People

Mali's ethnic groups include the Bambara, Fulani, Tuareg, and Dogon, and smaller numbers of Songhai, and Bozo. Bozo artists, mostly women, are noted for their "mud cloth," made by painting abstract designs onto cloth using soil of various colors.

Tombouctou

Lying on the edge of the desert, Tombouctou is a city of sand still visited by camel caravans carrying salt from mines in the north for shipping up the Niger River to Mopti. This historic city is a center of Islamic learning.

Burkina

Landlocked in the arid Sahel region and threatened by the Sahara, which is expanding southward, Burkina is one of West Africa's poorest and most overpopulated countries. Faced with droughts and lack of work, many young people are forced to leave to find jobs abroad.

BURKINA FACTS

CAPITAL CITY Ouagadougou

AREA 105,870 sq miles (274,200 sq km)

POPULATION 10,628,000

MAIN LANGUAGES French, Mossi, Mande, Fulani, Lobi, Bobo

MAJOR RELIGIONS Traditional beliefs, Muslim, Christian

CURRENCY CFA franc

Fulani children

Fulani

The Fulani are nomadic cattle herders who roam West Africa with their animals. In Burkina, where they number about 75,000, they are one of more than 60 ethnic groups. Fulani herders traditionally tend cattle for local farmers in exchange for sacks of rice.

Cotton

Burkina most valuable cash crop is cotton, which brings in about 25 percent of its export earnings. However, the country's farming is threatened by the mass emigration of young workers, who send money home to their families. The country has deposits of silver and manganese, and exports gold.

Ghana

Once called the "Gold Coast" by Europeans who found gold here 500 years ago, Ghana still has reserves of gold that have recently replaced cocoa as the country's major source of income. The country is still one of the world's largest cocoa producers. Lake Volta, formed by a dam on the Volta River, is the world's largest artificial lake.

GHANA FACTS

CAPITAL CITY Accra

AREA 92,100 sq miles (238,540 sq km)

POPULATION 17,959,000

MAIN LANGUAGES English, Akan, Mossi, Ewe, Ga, Twi, Fanti, Gurma

MAJOR RELIGIONS Christian, traditional beliefs, Muslim

CURRENCY Cedi

Eseye (a kind of spinach)

Plantains

Food

A popular food in Ghana is *banku*, a mixture of cornmeal and cassava. Ghanaians mix leaves of *eseye*, a type of spinach, with palm oil to make a sauce that is eaten with boiled fish or vegetables.

People

Family ties are strong in Ghana, and the extended family is important. About half of Ghanaians are Ashanti people whose ancestors developed one of the richest and most noted civilizations in Africa. Other groups include the Mole-Dagbani, Ewe, and Ga. About 36 percent of the people live in cities and towns.

Ghanaian family

Togo

A long, narrow country, just 68 miles (110 km) at its widest point, Togo has a central forested plateau with savanna to the north and south. Nearly half the population is under 15 years of age, and few people are more than 45. Although most people are farmers, Togo's main export is phosphates, used for making fertilizers.

TOGO FACTS

CAPITAL CITY Lomé

AREA 21,927 sq miles (56,790 sq km)

POPULATION 4,264,000

MAIN LANGUAGES French, Kabye, Ewe

MAJOR RELIGIONS Traditional beliefs, Christian, Muslim

CURRENCY CFA franc

Farming

Togolese farmers produce cocoa, coffee, cotton, dried coconut, and palm kernels, mainly for export. New products include herbs, tomatoes, and sugar. For their own use, they grow millet, cassava, and corn, and fish in coastal areas.

Corn

Market women

Although politics and formal employment remain the domain of men, many Togolese women work informally in part-time jobs. The Nana Benz, wealthy women traders so-called because they all prefer to own Mercedes Benz cars, dominate Togo's markets and taxi businesses. Based in the market at Lomé, these formidable women fight hard for business and have a legendary capacity for haggling.

Nigeria

With large reserves of oil, natural gas, coal, iron ore, lead, tin, and zinc, and rich, fertile farmland, Nigeria looked set to prosper when it became independent from Britain in 1960. However, the country's economy is now in financial trouble with falling oil prices, conflicts between rival ethnic groups, and a series of military coups. Nigeria is aiming to develop new industries.

Abuja

Begun in 1980, the new, planned city of Abuja replaced Lagos as Nigeria's capital in 1991, because the government believed Lagos was too influenced by the Yoruba people. By the late 1990s, much of Abuja was unfinished as money ran low during construction.

Central mosque, Abuja

People

Nigerian society consists of an uneasy mix of more than 250 ethnic groups. Two-thirds of the population belongs to one of three groups – the Hausa in the north, the Ibo in the east, and the Yoruba in the west. About 62 percent of people live in small tight-knit villages where communal life is important.

Nigerian oil has a low sulfur content and is ideal for aircraft fuel.

Oil

Nigeria's oil production, which ranks first in Africa and twelfth in the world, accounts for 90 percent of all its exports. Almost totally dependent on this new industry, which began in the 1960s, Nigeria is vulnerable to changes in world oil prices.

Plantations

Agriculture employs more than 40 percent of all Nigerian workers. Although most farmers work on small plots with simple tools, vast plantations have been established to cultivate cash crops on a commercial scale for export, using modern machinery. Crops include cotton, coffee, cocoa beans, and palm oil.

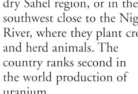

The best cloth is a mix of cotton and silk.

Cloth

Nigeria's Yoruba and Hausa peoples produce some attractive patterned textiles, hand-dyed using natural plant colors. In the Hausa town of Kano, in the north, men dye the cloth in ancient dye pits.

NIGERIA FACTS

CAPITAL CITY Abuja

AREA 356,668 sq miles (923,770 sq km)

POPULATION 88,514,501

DENSITY 248 per sq mile (96 per sq km)

MAIN LANGUAGES English, Hausa, Yoruba, Ibo

MAJOR RELIGIONS Muslim, Christian, traditional beliefs

CURRENCY Naira

LIFE EXPECTANCY 52 years

PEOPLE PER DOCTOR 5,882

GOVERNMENT Military government

ADULT LITERACY 52%

Benin

A former French colony, Benin took its name from an ancient empire, in 1975, 15 years after becoming independent. It is a long, narrow country with a short coastline on the Gulf of Guinea. Most of the land is flat and forested, with a large marsh in the south. Most people live off the land producing yams, cassava, and corn. Cotton brings in about three-quarters of the country's export income.

BENIN FACTS

CAPITAL CITY Porto-Novo

AREA 43,480 sq miles (112,620 sq km)

POPULATION 5,560,000

MAIN LANGUAGES French, Fon, Bariba, Yoruba, Adja, Fulani

MAJOR RELIGIONS Traditional beliefs, Muslim, Christian

CURRENCY CFA franc

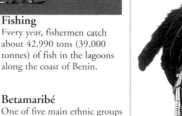

Fishing

Every year, fishermen catch about 42,990 tons (39,000 tonnes) of fish in the lagoons along the coast of Benin.

Betamaribé

One of five main ethnic groups in Benin, the Betamaribé, or Somba, live in the northwest near the Atakora Mountains. One of the first peoples to settle in Benin, they have lived free from Western influence for hundreds of years and have managed to keep many of their traditions intact.

Niger

Although it is the largest country in West Africa, Niger is two-thirds desert. The people, who are very poor, live in the dry Sahel region, or in the southwest close to the Niger River, where they plant crops and herd animals. The country ranks second in the world production of uranium.

NIGER FACTS

CAPITAL CITY Niamey

AREA 489,188 sq miles (1,267,000 sq km)

POPULATION 9,386,000

MAIN LANGUAGES French, Hausa, Djerma, Fulani, Tuareg, Teda

MAJOR RELIGION Muslim

CURRENCY CFA franc

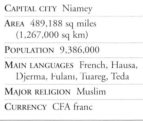

Fighting the desert

The people of Niger are waging a battle against the advance of the desert into the dry Sahel where they live. They plant trees and grass in an attempt to stop soil erosion.

Male beauty contest

Every year, in a festival known as the *gerewol*, young Wodaabé men make themselves up to try and attract a wife in an unusual beauty contest. After much dancing, the women make their choice. If a marriage proposal results, the man arranges to kidnap the woman and they set off into the desert for a nomadic life together.

FIND OUT MORE   AFRICA, HISTORY OF   BENIN EMPIRE   CONSERVATION   DESERTS   FARMING   FISHING INDUSTRY   OIL   ROCKS AND MINERALS   SLAVERY   TEXTILES AND WEAVING

A

AFRICAN WILDLIFE

NO OTHER CONTINENT matches the wealth of wildlife found in Africa. Covering the full climatic spectrum from intense heat to bitter cold, its variety of vegetation supports a wide range of animals, including mammals, birds, reptiles, fish, and insects. Among them are more than 40 species of primates, ranging from tiny galagos to huge gorillas, many different antelope, gazelles, and other hoofed animals, and 70 species of carnivores. Bird life, too, is extraordinarily rich; more than 1,500 species live south of the Sahara. In addition, Africa is inhabited by the world's fastest land animal, the cheetah; the biggest bird, the ostrich; and the largest land animal, the elephant.

Giraffe

The giraffe's great height – males reach up to 18 ft (5.5 m) – gives it the advantage of being able to spot danger from a distance and then escape quickly. It also enables the giraffe to feed on acacia leaves that are out of the reach of most other grassland animals, giving it a near monopoly of its principal food supply.

Patterned coat provides camouflage.

Long tail with coarse hair is used to deter flies.

Grassland wildlife

African grasslands (savannas) sustain over 20 species of grazing animals, from the giant sable antelope to the tiny pygmy antelope. The herds of plains game and their predators, including lions, are pursued by scavengers such as hyenas and vultures. Grassland birds include the guinea fowl and hornbills.

Long tail feathers help it balance when running.

Secretary bird

Among the most striking of Africa's grassland birds is the secretary bird, with its long legs and feathered crest. It rarely flies, preferring to walk, nodding its head with each step. It attacks snakes, spreading its wings over its body to shield itself from venomous bites, while using its feet to stamp them to death.

Long legs let it run through grass after snakes and frogs.

Zebras call to each other while grazing.

Lion

The lion is the principal predator of the African savanna. Lionesses hunt together, preying on large animals such as buffalo, zebras, and wildebeest.

Aardvark

The aardvark is a solitary, nocturnal animal. It uses its powerful claws to break into the nests of ants and termites, which it extracts with its long, sticky tongue. The aardvark can dig at an astonishing speed – faster than a person with a shovel.

Zebra

Zebras usually live in family groups of 5–20 animals, but in the dry season, they may gather in herds of a few hundred for protection against predators such as lions. Male zebras defend themselves by kicking out with their legs and hooves. Zebras eat the tough tops of the grasses.

Papyrus

The most common plant in African swamps is papyrus. It grows in clumps, often dense enough to support the weight of large animals.

Papyrus may reach 15 ft (4.5 m) in height.

Wetland wildlife

Africa's wetlands are teeming with wildlife, such as crocodiles, hippos, floodplain species such as lechwes, and fish, including the Nile perch and tiger fish. The wetlands also provide stopping places for migratory birds flying south to winter in Africa.

Lesser flamingo

Three million flamingos gather at Lake Nakuru, in Kenya, forming an amazing spectacle. They feed on the plentiful algae that flourish in the salty water, sunlight, and high temperatures in and around the lake.

Hippopotamus

Hippos spend most of the day submerged in water, with only their ears, eyes, and nostrils above the surface. They become active at dusk when they emerge from the water to graze on nearby grassland.

Long legs for wading through water.

Cichlid fish

Lakes Malawi and Tanganyika contain 265 different species of cichlids (mouth-brooding fish); all but five are unique to Africa. Great depth, isolation, and few predators have resulted in this proliferation.

Webbed feet

Addax

The addax lives in the driest and hottest parts of the Sahara – conditions few other animals could tolerate. It rarely drinks: it gets liquid from the succulent plants and tubers that it eats.

Pale coat provides camouflage in the desert.

Desert wildlife

The African deserts include the Sahara, the world's largest desert, and the deserts of the Horn of Africa, Kalahari, and Namib. Though the deserts seem barren, they are home to many animals such as bustards, sandgrouse, and the scimitar-horned oryx.

Fennec fox

The fennec lives in small colonies among sand dunes, into which it burrows to avoid the heat. It burrows so quickly, it disappears from sight in seconds.

Fox obtains all its liquid from its prey.

Sand skink

The sand skink spends most of its life underground in its burrow. It uses its flattened tail to propel itself through the sand. It preys on small mammals such as mice, as well as birds' eggs. If attacked, the sand skink can shed its tail, confusing its attacker and enabling it to get away.

Sandgrouse

Despite living in the open desert, sandgrouse must drink regularly, so they often fly many miles for water. Sandgrouse obtain water for their young by immersing themselves in water and carrying droplets back to their nests in their feathers.

Rain forest wildlife

Rain forests dominate western Central Africa. The warm, wet environment is home to many animals. Herbivores such as gorillas feed on leaves. Fruit that falls from the canopy provides food for pigs and porcupines, while animals such as tree pangolins forage in the trees.

Yellow-backed duiker

Yellow back patch

Standing 3.3 ft (1 m) at the shoulder, the yellow-backed duiker is the largest of the forest duikers. In West Africa it lives in the densest parts of the rain forest; in East Africa it lives in bamboo forests.

Red colobus monkey

The red colobus is one of five species of specialized leaf-eating primates throughout Africa. It lives in the forest canopy in family groups of about 20 animals, rarely descending to the ground.

Small spotted genet

This catlike animal spends the day asleep in the branches of a tree, becoming active at night. An agile climber, it stalks its prey – birds, small mammals, and insects – like a cat, before seizing it with a sudden pounce.

Gorillas eat many types of rain forest vegetation.

Mountain gorilla

The mountain gorilla is confined to a small area of rain forest, at a point where the boundaries of Uganda, Zaïre, and Rwanda meet. It is a massively built animal, but is not normally aggressive. The females build nests where they sleep with their young.

Gelada

The gelada is the sole survivor of a group of ground-dwelling primates now found only in Ethiopia. It lives in open country at high altitude, close to cliffs and rock faces, where it retreats if alarmed. It eats seeds, roots, grass, and fruit.

Geladas have a patch of red skin on the chest.

Mountain wildlife

The mountains of Ruwenzori, Kenya, and Kilimanjaro have distinctive plants and animals. Rodents inhabit moorland, while the scarlet-tufted malachite sunbird lives in close association with giant lobelias.

Crowned hawk eagle

One of the largest eagles, the crowned hawk eagle is widely distributed throughout the mountainous regions of East Africa and Zaïre, wherever there are suitable forests containing the monkeys that is its chief food.

Hyraxes bask in the sun for much of the day.

Giant lobelia

Africa's mountain plants include some of the most extraordinary vegetation in the world. Plants small elsewhere have grown into giants, among them the giant lobelia, tree heath, and giant groundsel, reaching 30 ft (9 m) high.

Flower spikes are more than 3.3 ft (1 m) tall.

Rock hyrax

Rock hyraxes live in colonies of 50 or more among rocky outcrops. They remain alert for signs of danger, such as eagles and leopards.

FIND OUT MORE	BIRDS	BIRDS OF PREY	DEER AND ANTELOPE	GIRAFFES	HIPPOPOTAMUSES	LIZARDS	LIONS AND OTHER WILDCATS	MONKEYS AND OTHER PRIMATES

AIR

WE LIVE, MOVE, AND BREATHE at the bottom of an immense ocean of air called the atmosphere. Air is an invisible mixture of gases, made up of a teeming mass of millions of tiny gas molecules that move randomly and at high speed. Without air, the Earth would be a lifeless planet – the gases air contains are vital to plants and animals.

Fractional distillation
The gases in air have many uses. For example, divers use tanks of oxygen to enable them to breathe underwater, and nitrogen is used in explosives. Gases are extracted from air by a process called fractional distillation. Air is cooled and compressed until it forms a blue liquid. When the liquid expands and warms up, each gas boils off at a different temperature and is collected separately.

Divers with oxygen tanks

Composition of air
Any volume of pure, dry air is 78.09% nitrogen, 20.95% oxygen, 0.93% argon, and 0.03% carbon dioxide and other gases. These colored balls represent the proportions of the different gases in air.

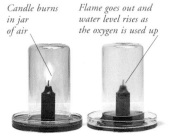

Candle burns in jar of air

Flame goes out and water level rises as the oxygen is used up

Carbon dioxide (CO$_2$)
Carbon dioxide is vital for plant life. Plants absorb carbon dioxide from the air and combine it with water gathered by their roots to help form the food they need for growth.

Tablets of nitrogen fertilizer

Red balls represent oxygen.

Green balls represent argon.

Oxygen (O$_2$)
Burning is a chemical reaction of a substance with oxygen, as this experiment shows. The candle burns in the jar of air until it has used up all the oxygen. Humans and other animals use oxygen from the air to "burn" food inside their bodies and produce energy.

Nitrogen (N$_2$)
Every living cell contains nitrogen. Plants cannot take nitrogen from the air, so they get it from the soil. Fertilizers contain nitrogen to replenish what plants remove from the soil.

Black ball represents carbon dioxide and other gases.

Blue balls represent nitrogen.

Argon (Ar)
The gas argon is called an "inert" gas because it does not react with other substances. Electric lightbulbs are often filled with argon. It prevents the bulb's filament from burning up as it would in pure air, giving the bulb a much longer life.

Air pollution
Air is not naturally "pure" and contains varying amounts of other substances, such as dust, water vapor, bacteria, pollen, and polluting gases. Air pollution from industry and traffic can cause serious health problems in towns and cities, as well as long-term damage to the environment.

Smog
Hazy air pollution that hangs over an urban area is called smog. Sulfurous smog is the result of burning fuels with a high sulfur content, such as coal. Photochemical smog occurs when sunlight causes car exhaust fumes to react together.

Water vapor
Up to 4 per cent of the volume of air may be water vapor. Warm air can hold more water vapor than cool air. A cold drink can absorb heat from the air around it. As the air cools, water vapor condenses out of the air to form droplets on the outside of the can.

Air pressure
Air exerts a force on objects because its moving molecules are constantly colliding with them. Air pressure is a measure of this force. The pressure of the open air is called atmospheric pressure. It is lower at high altitudes where the air is less dense.

Barometer
A device that measures atmospheric pressure is called a barometer. It is used to forecast changes in weather – air pressure varies slightly from day to day with changes in the air's temperature and humidity.

Sucking
When a person sucks on one end of a drinking straw, air pressure is reduced inside the straw. Atmospheric pressure on the liquid's surface pushes down on the liquid and makes it rise up the straw.

Compressed air
The pressure of air can be increased by compressing it – that is, pumping more and more of it into a limited space. Bicycle tires are filled with air that becomes compressed to give a smooth ride.

Weight of air
Air has weight, as this simple experiment proves. Identical empty balloons are attached to both ends of a stick. The balloons balance when the stick is suspended from its middle. Inflating one of the balloons tips the balance, because the balloon full of compressed air weighs more than the empty balloon.

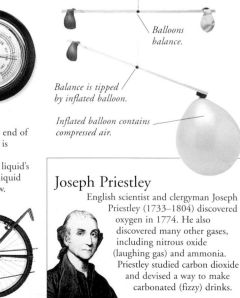

Balloons balance.

Balance is tipped by inflated balloon.

Inflated balloon contains compressed air.

Joseph Priestley
English scientist and clergyman Joseph Priestley (1733–1804) discovered oxygen in 1774. He also discovered many other gases, including nitrous oxide (laughing gas) and ammonia. Priestley studied carbon dioxide and devised a way to make carbonated (fizzy) drinks.

FIND OUT MORE   ATOMS AND MOLECULES   CELLS   FRICTION   GASES   LUNGS AND BREATHING   POLLUTION   PHOTOSYNTHESIS   PRESSURE   WEATHER

AIRCRAFT

ANY VEHICLE THAT travels through the air is called an aircraft. The ability to soar over obstacles such as oceans and mountains makes aircraft the fastest form of travel. An airliner (a large passenger plane) can fly a passenger thousands of miles in hours. The same journey would take several days by boat or car. Airliners and military aircraft are complex machines. Their frames are built with lightweight metals such as aluminium, and hi-tech materials such as plastics. Inside, their sophisticated electronic controls help pilots fly efficiently and safely. Smaller aircraft, such as gliders and hot-air balloons, are often used for sport and leisure.

Types of aircraft

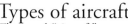

The word "aircraft" covers all flying machines – from balloons to helicopters. Most aircraft are airplanes, which have wings, and jet engines to give them speed. Other types of aircraft are gliders, which have no engine, helicopters, balloons, and airships. An aircraft's function determines its size and shape.

A

Biplanes
Many planes before World War II (1939–1945) had two pairs of wings and were called biplanes.

Transport aircraft
Armies need aircraft to transport troops and equipment. Special aircraft are designed to carry very heavy objects, such as tanks.

Balloons
Lighter-than-air craft are known as balloons. A bag is filled with gas or hot air that is lighter than the atmosphere.

Gliders
Currents of air move up and down. A glider has no engine, but flies by the effects of air currents on its wings.

Concorde
Supersonic airliners such as Concorde can travel faster than the speed of sound – about 770 mph (1,240 kmh). They can cross the Atlantic twice as fast as any other airliner, but are very noisy and need lots of fuel.

Anatomy of an airliner

Most airliners, such as this Boeing 747-400, have the same basic design. The main part is the fuselage, which is similar to a long, thin, metal tube. The wings are attached to the middle of the fuselage, and the tailplane and fin are attached at the back. A floor separates the passenger cabin from the baggage compartment.

The Boeing 747-400 can fly more than 8,451 miles (13,600 km) without stopping for fuel.

Main cabin, with economy-class seats

Fin

Tailplane

Upper deck with business-class seats

Fuselage

Fuel for engines in fuel tanks inside wings

Freighters
Airplanes that carry cargo are called freighters. The cargo is loaded through a huge door in the aeroplane's nose. The *Boeing 747* can be converted from a passenger plane to a freighter, then back again.

Forward cabin with first-class seats

Engine controls and navigation instruments

Pilot's control column

Turbofan engines hang from wings on pylons.

Cockpit
The aircraft is controlled from the cockpit. The pilot and co-pilot fly the plane using control columns, and instruments show the status of all the plane's equipment. The cockpit also contains radar and radio controls.

In-flight food
Pre-prepared meals are stored in trolleys, which lock into spaces in the aircraft's galleys until it is time for the flight attendants to serve them.

Entertainment
Some airliners feature video screens and headphones that can be tuned to music channels.

Howard Hughes

Hughes (1905–76) was an American industrialist, film-maker, and aviation enthusiast. He founded the airline TWA, and broke a number of aviation records in aircraft of his own design. Not all were successful; the *Spruce Goose* (1947) only flew once.

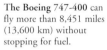

Forces of flight

An aircraft needs two forces to fly: lift to keep it up and thrust to propel it forward. Lift overcomes the plane's weight, and thrust overcomes the drag caused by the air flowing past the plane. When an aircraft is cruising, lift is equal to weight and thrust is equal to drag.

Lift

Thrust

Drag

Weight

Wings

An aircraft's wings create lift. To do this, they need air to flow over them.

The airfoil shape
If you cut an aircraft wing in two and looked at the end, you would see a special cross section called an airfoil. The top surface is longer and more curved than the bottom surface.

The airfoil at work
The air pressure beneath the wing is greater than above it, and lifts the wing up.

Lift

Angle of attack
Tilting the angle of the blades gives extra lift.

Lift

Flying controls

An aircraft is steered through the air by way of three main control surfaces – the elevators on the tailplane, the ailerons on the wings, and a rudder on the fin.

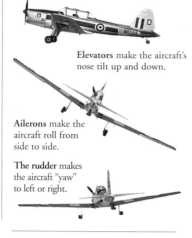

Elevators make the aircraft's nose tilt up and down.

Ailerons make the aircraft roll from side to side.

The rudder makes the aircraft "yaw" to left or right.

Airplane engines

An aircraft's engines drive it through the air by producing thrust. Different types of engines produce thrust in different ways. Piston and turboprop engines drive propellers that screw into the air, just as a ship propeller bites into water. Turbojet and turbofan engines produce a fast-moving stream of gas that pushes the aircraft forward.

Piston engines
These work in the same way as car engines. Petrol and air vapour are mixed in the engine's cylinders and they cause an explosion. The explosions push pistons, which turn a shaft. The shaft then turns a propeller.

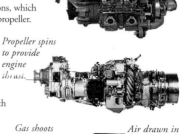

Shaft

Turboprop engines
The simplest type of jets – a turbojet engine with a propeller is called a turboprop engine. A motor turns the compressor and the propeller, which provides the main engine thrust.

Propeller spins to provide engine thrust.

Turbojet engines
Air is drawn in and compressed, then sent to a chamber where fuel burns. The gases produced are shot out of the back of the engine, which pushes the aircraft forwards, like a deflating balloon.

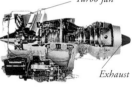

Gas shoots out

Air drawn in

Turbofan engines
A hybrid of turbojet and turboprops, the turbofan engine sucks in air, which is combined with the backdraft from a fan, and also sends air around the engine, producing the same effect as a propeller.

Turbo fan

Exhaust

Helicopters

Unlike most aircraft, which have fixed wings, a helicopter has a spinning rotor with two or more long, thin blades attached. When the blades spin, they lift the helicopter straight up into the air. A helicopter can take off from almost anywhere and does not need to use airport runways. It can hover in one place, and fly backward, forward, and sideways. It is the most versatile of all aircraft; it is very useful for transportation, surveillance, and rescue missions.

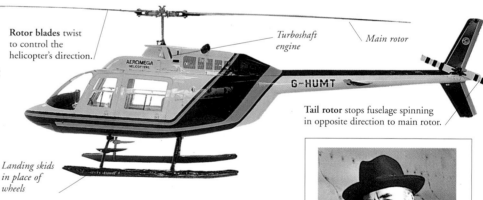

Rotor blades twist to control the helicopter's direction.

Turboshaft engine

Main rotor

Tail rotor stops fuselage spinning in opposite direction to main rotor.

Landing skids in place of wheels

Flying controls
A helicopter pilot has three flying controls. The collective pitch lever changes the amount of lift produced by the main rotor. The cyclic pitch control makes the helicopter move forward, backward, or sideways. Rudder pedals make the helicopter turn left or right.

Lifting off
Before takeoff, the main and tail rotors are speeded up. When the main rotor is turning fast enough, the pilot lifts the collective pitch lever to increase the tilt of the rotor blades. The tilt produces lift and the helicopter takes off. The higher the lever is lifted, the faster the aircraft rises.

Moving away
The cyclic pitch control makes the helicopter move in the direction the control is pushed. It tilts the main rotor so that some of the rotor's lift pulls the helicopter along. Here, the pilot has pulled the control back to make the helicopter move backward.

Igor Ivan Sikorsky
Sikorsky (1889–1972) was born in Ukraine. where he became an aeronautical engineer. In 1919 he moved to the United States where he set up an aircraft factory. He designed the first practical helicopter, the *VS-300*, which first flew in 1939. The design had to be modified many times: at one point, the helicopter flew in every direction except forward.

FIND OUT MORE

AIRSHIPS AND BALLOONS   ATMOSPHERE   ENGINES AND MOTORS   FLIGHT, HISTORY OF   TRANSPORT, HISTORY OF   WARPLANES   WORLD WAR I   WORLD WAR II

Types of aircraft
Military

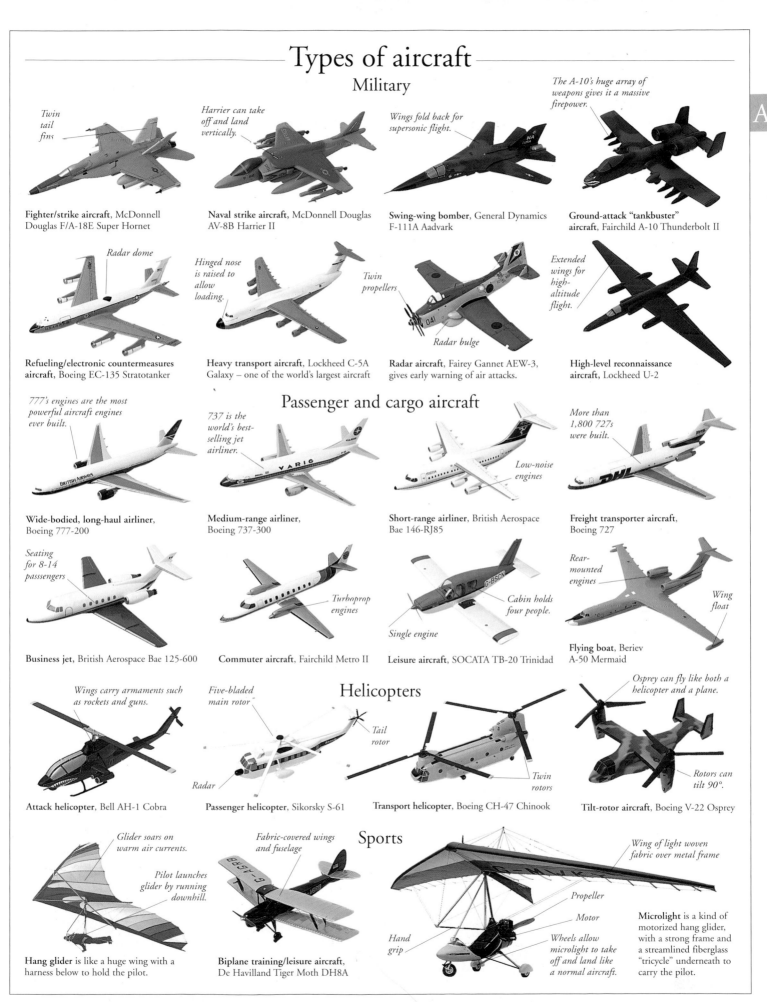

Twin tail fins

Fighter/strike aircraft, McDonnell Douglas F/A-18E Super Hornet

Harrier can take off and land vertically.

Naval strike aircraft, McDonnell Douglas AV-8B Harrier II

Wings fold back for supersonic flight.

Swing-wing bomber, General Dynamics F-111A Aadvark

The A-10's huge array of weapons gives it a massive firepower.

Ground-attack "tankbuster" aircraft, Fairchild A-10 Thunderbolt II

Radar dome

Refueling/electronic countermeasures aircraft, Boeing EC-135 Stratotanker

Hinged nose is raised to allow loading.

Heavy transport aircraft, Lockheed C-5A Galaxy – one of the world's largest aircraft

Twin propellers

Radar bulge

Radar aircraft, Fairey Gannet AEW-3, gives early warning of air attacks.

Extended wings for high-altitude flight.

High-level reconnaissance aircraft, Lockheed U-2

Passenger and cargo aircraft

777's engines are the most powerful aircraft engines ever built.

Wide-bodied, long-haul airliner, Boeing 777-200

737 is the world's best-selling jet airliner.

Medium-range airliner, Boeing 737-300

Low-noise engines

Short-range airliner, British Aerospace Bae 146-RJ85

More than 1,800 727s were built.

Freight transporter aircraft, Boeing 727

Seating for 8-14 passsengers

Business jet, British Aerospace Bae 125-600

Turboprop engines

Commuter aircraft, Fairchild Metro II

Single engine

Cabin holds four people.

Leisure aircraft, SOCATA TB-20 Trinidad

Rear-mounted engines

Wing float

Flying boat, Beriev A-50 Mermaid

Helicopters

Wings carry armaments such as rockets and guns.

Attack helicopter, Bell AH-1 Cobra

Five-bladed main rotor

Tail rotor

Radar

Passenger helicopter, Sikorsky S-61

Twin rotors

Transport helicopter, Boeing CH-47 Chinook

Osprey can fly like both a helicopter and a plane.

Rotors can tilt 90°.

Tilt-rotor aircraft, Boeing V-22 Osprey

Sports

Glider soars on warm air currents.

Pilot launches glider by running downhill.

Hang glider is like a huge wing with a harness below to hold the pilot.

Fabric-covered wings and fuselage

Biplane training/leisure aircraft, De Havilland Tiger Moth DH8A

Wing of light woven fabric over metal frame

Propeller

Motor

Hand grip

Wheels allow microlight to take off and land like a normal aircraft.

Microlight is a kind of motorized hang glider, with a strong frame and a streamlined fiberglass "tricycle" underneath to carry the pilot.

AIRPORTS

TODAY, MORE PEOPLE TRAVEL by air than ever before. Whether they are business people off to visit clients or families going on vacation, all air travelers leave from airports, which range in size from small local facilities to enormous international terminals. A large airport is like a city. It contains shops, offices, and hotels, in addition to all the buildings, runways, and taxiways needed to service the aircraft and their passengers. Airport security is always tight, because airports and aircraft have often been the targets of terrorist attacks.

Features of an airport

Airplanes take off and land on runways, which are linked to the terminal buildings by routes called taxiways. The passengers embark and disembark at the terminal buildings. For the aircraft, the airport has repair workshops, refueling facilities, and storage hangars.

Runway
To take the biggest jet aircraft, runways have to be 1.8–2.5 miles (3–4 km) long and some 165 ft (50 m) wide. They need a specially toughened surface to take the pounding they get when large jets take off or land.

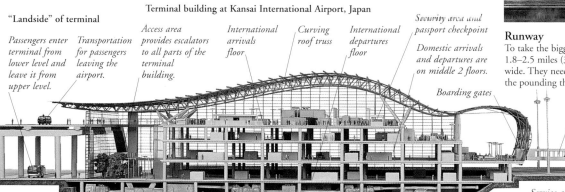

Terminal building at Kansai International Airport, Japan

"Landside" of terminal

Passengers enter terminal from lower level and leave it from upper level.

Transportation for passengers leaving the airport.

Access area provides escalators to all parts of the terminal building.

International arrivals floor

Curving roof truss

International departures floor

Security area and passport checkpoint

Domestic arrivals and departures are on middle 2 floors.

Boarding gates

"Airside" of terminal

Bridge connects boarding gate to airplane

Waiting airplane

Service area contains boilers, ventilation equipment, and other building services.

Air traffic control

At the heart of an airport is the control tower, where air traffic controllers monitor every moment of an aircraft's arrival and departure. They make sure that each pilot follows the correct flight path, that all aircraft land in the right place, and that there is a safe amount of time between each takeoff and landing.

Air traffic controllers in the control tower

Radar display screen
Airport radar tracks each aircraft as it lands, giving the controllers precise details of its position. All aircraft within 12 to 30 miles (20 to 50 km) of the airport can be tracked by radar and shown on the controllers' display screens.

Flight path
Air traffic controllers tell pilots when it is safe to land. They guide a pilot to a specific path, which the pilot must then follow as the aircraft descends to the runway. Navigation aids, such as high-frequency radio beacons, give the pilot accurate bearings.

How an aircraft lands

Fly down and right

Course is correct

Radar antenna sends out beam to guide plane onto runway.

Flight path

Antenna sends out beam to guide plane's rate of descent.

Radio waves carry information about flight path.

Runway (ground level)

Fly up and left

Dials on flightdeck tell pilot whether plane's course is correct.

Security

Airport security staff are always on their guard, trying to spot terrorists or smugglers. Metal detectors and other electronic devices alert staff when a passenger is carrying a gun or other type of weapon. There are also "sniffer" dogs that have been trained to detect the scent of explosives or illegal drugs.

Passports
A person traveling from one country to another usually carries a passport, an official document that identifies the owner and his or her place of origin. Passports are inspected at international airports.

EU passport

An X ray reveals a gun.

X ray scanner
Airport staff use X ray machines to scan the contents of passengers' luggage. A screen on the side of the X ray machine shows what is inside each bag. Different materials show up in different colors, enabling items such as guns to be found with ease.

Airports and the environment

A large airport can have a devastating impact on the local environment. Clearing the land to build an airport destroys carefully balanced ecosystems, while the air pollution can harm wildlife, and the noise may scare some animals away.

Kestrel

Airport ecosystems
Since airports cover such vast areas, birds and animals can also move into these areas and establish new ecosystems, undisturbed by people.

Animals can live in the large green spaces around a big airport.

FIND OUT MORE   AIRCRAFT   ECOLOGY AND ECOSYSTEMS   RADAR AND SONAR   TRAVEL

AIRSHIPS AND BALLOONS

AIRSHIPS AND BALLOONS are known as lighter-than-air aircraft because instead of wings, they use a large envelope, or bag, full of gas or hot air that is lighter than the air in the atmosphere around it. The air pushes the envelope upward, just as water pushes a submerged air-filled ball upward. In 1783, the Montgolfier brothers achieved the first manned flight ever by sending a hot-air balloon over Paris. Balloons fly where the wind blows them; airships have engines and can be steered. Today, airships are used for aerial photography and coastguard patrols, and ballooning is a popular sport.

Anatomy of a modern airship

The main part of an airship is its envelope, which contains bags of helium gas. The gas is slightly pressurized to keep the envelope in shape. A fin and tailplane keep the airship steady as it flies slowly along. The crew travels in a gondola attached to the underside of the envelope.

Gas-proof coated polyester envelope *Elevator flaps*

Automatic ballonet valve *Gondola* *Skyship 500 HL (semirigid airship)* *Rudder to steer the airship.*

The Hindenburg, 1937
Airship disasters
Several terrible disasters made people lose trust in airship travel. Airships were usually lost for two reasons: either they were uncontrollable in bad weather; or the highly inflammable hydrogen gas used inside the envelope exploded. Today, airship pilots use the much safer helium gas in special nylon envelopes. However, they still have to be careful in bad weather.

Types of airships

Practical airships could be built only after the lightweight internal-combustion engine had been developed. The earliest airships were "nonrigid" (they are still used today). These were followed by the "rigid" and the less usual "semirigid" types of airship.

Nonrigid airships have a flexible fabric envelope, from which the load hangs, suspended by ropes.

Rigid airship's envelope is built around a rigid framework. This skeleton contains bags of the lifting gas – helium.

Ferdinand von Zeppelin

German count Ferdinand von Zeppelin (1838–1917) began experimenting with air travel in 1891. In 1900, he devised the first airship, a 128-m (420-ft) rigid craft named the LZ1. During World War I, some 100 Zeppelins were built for military use.

Balloons

Balloons were first used for aerial reconnaissance during the French Revolution, and used again during the Civil War. During World Wars I and II, balloons were used to spot targets for artillery attacks, and barrage balloon defended cities against aircraft.

Weather and research balloons
To study what is happening in the upper reaches of the atmosphere, pilots send up helium-filled weather balloons carrying measuring instruments, but not people. The instruments measure temperature, wind speed, and so on, and send their results to the ground or to satellites by radio.

Balloon festivals
Today, ballooning is a popular sport. During the summer, ballooning enthusiasts gather at festivals to enjoy the dazzling prospect of dozens of brightly colored balloons flying together. Some of the balloons are owned by companies and are made in the shapes that advertise their products.

Flight

Hot-air ballooning requires a perfectly clear day with a gentle breeze. Too high a wind puts the balloon at risk on takeoff and landing. After take-off, a ground crew follows the balloon in a vehicle to recover both it and the crew after landing.

1 The balloon is laid on the ground. Burners heat air to fill the balloon.

2 The balloon's envelope expands as the hot air starts to inflate it.

3 The expanding balloon becomes buoyant and rises into the air.

4 Guy ropes hold the balloon down until the crew boards.

5 The crew blasts hot air into the envelope to keep the balloon afloat.

FIND OUT MORE ATMOSPHERE GALILEO GALILEI GASES FLIGHT, HISTORY OF JOHNSON, AMY RENAISSANCE WEATHER FORECASTING

A

Airships and balloons

Balloons

Lavishly decorated character from *The Thousand and One Nights*

Easter egg envelope is decorated to celebrate Easter.

Golf ball, an uncomplicated, yet realistic balloon shape

False basket

Upsidedown balloon has a false basket that is attached to the top.

Fabergé egg, the trademark jewel of a famous Russian jeweler

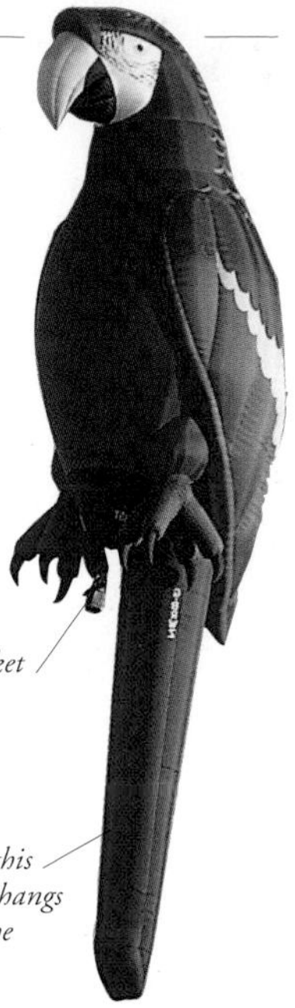

Basket

Part of this balloon hangs below the basket.

Red, blue, and yellow panels of this balloon's envelope represent the exotic plumage of a parrot.

Modern tractor has its basket hanging where the back axle would be.

Carmen Miranda, a 1940s' singing star

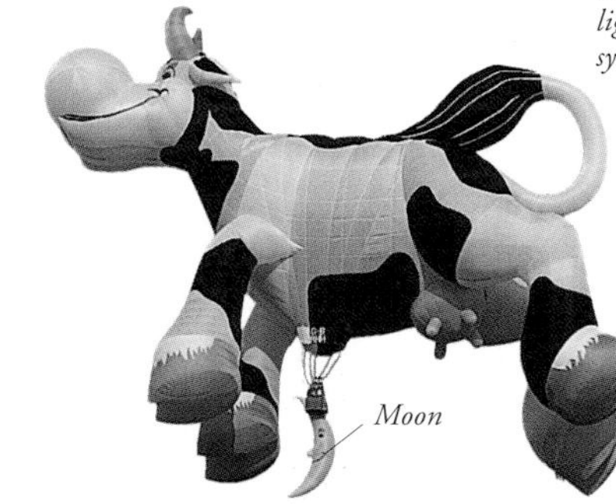

Uncle Sam, a lighthearted symbol of the US

Moon

A **"cow jumps over the moon"** is a very complicated balloon shape inspired by the famous nursery rhyme.

Face-shaped balloons are relatively simple to create.

Upturned eaves

Japanese temple whose envelope comes complete with authentic upturned eaves and balcony rails.

Soda can, the first nontraditional balloon shape

Santa Claus, an aerial Christmas decoration

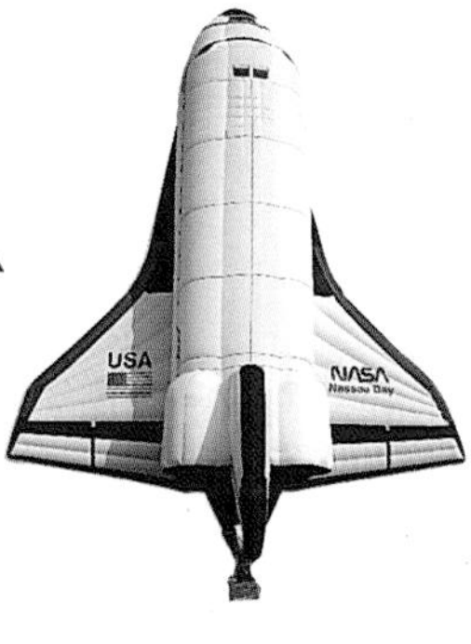

NASA rocket celebrates space exploration.

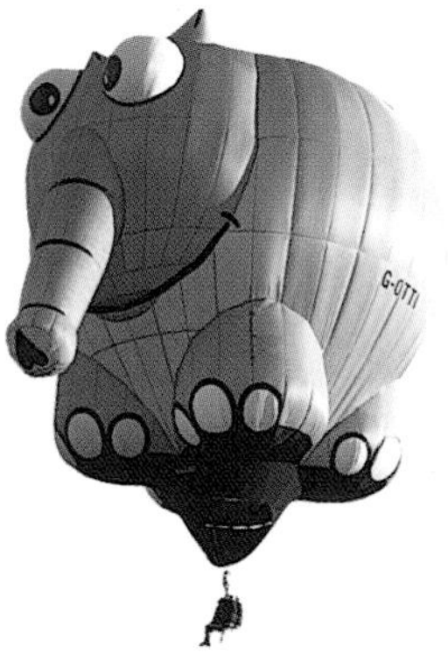

Elephant, complete with trunk and a surprised look!

Airships

Spectacular eagle has a very complicated and realistically painted envelope.

Aerial tours are often run by companies that have both airships and balloons.

Modern airships, because of their visibility and size, are often used to advertise products or services.

Rupert the Bear is a favorite fictional character for children all over the world.

ALEXANDER THE GREAT

IN LESS THAN FOUR YEARS, a brilliant young general created the largest empire the world had ever seen. The empire was the creation of Alexander the Great of Macedon, a gifted leader who inspired tremendous loyalty from his troops. It stretched from Greece in the west to India in the east. Alexander's sudden death at age 33 led to the empire's collapse, but it lived on in a series of towns that spread Greek culture eastward. These cities, all called Alexandria after their founder, opened a trade route between Asia and Europe that lasted for centuries.

Early life
Alexander was born in 356 BC, the son of King Philip of Macedon (r. 359–336 BC). As a young man he went on military campaigns with his father. Alexander won fame for taming a wild black horse called Bucephalus, which stayed with him throughout his whole life.

Aristotle
Alexander was taught by the Athenian philosopher Aristotle (384–322 BC). Aristotle's interests ranged from politics and morality to biology and literature. He shared his enthusiasm for new ideas with his young pupil.

Greece
The heartland of Alexander's empire was his home state of Macedon, in northern Greece. Before Alexander became king, Greece was divided into rival city states and was threatened by the powerful Persian Empire.

Terra-cotta figure of the Greek love goddess, Aphrodite

Alexander's empire
When Alexander became king of Macedon in 336 BC, Greece was dominated by Persia. In a series of brilliant military campaigns, Alexander defeated Persia and created his vast empire.

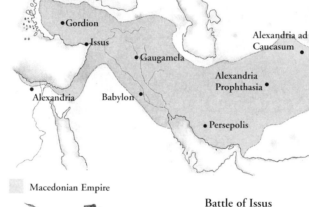

- Gordion
- Issus
- Gaugamela
- Alexandria ad Caucasum
- Alexandria
- Babylon
- Alexandria Prophthasia
- Persepolis

Macedonian Empire

Persia
The rich empire of Persia occupied much of modern Iraq, Turkey, and Iran. After Alexander had conquered the area, he tried to unite Macedonia and Persia by encouraging his generals to marry Persians. Alexander himself married Roxana, a princess from eastern Persia.

Stag from palace at Persepolis.

Persian silver stag ornament

Egypt
In 332 BC, Alexander conquered Egypt and was accepted as the new pharaoh. He founded the city of Alexandria in northern Egypt, which became the most important city of the Greek-speaking world. When Alexander died in 323 BC, he was buried in a vast tomb in the center of the city.

Alexander wears the pharaoh's crown

Battle of Issus
In 333 BC, the Macedonian army overwhelmed the more powerful Persian army led by Darius III (r. 336–330 BC) at the battle of Issus, Syria. The Persians were defeated again in 331 BC at Gaugamela near the Tigris River. After this battle, the Persian capital, Persepolis, was destroyed and the empire collapsed.

Relief of the Battle of Issus

Eastern empire
By 326 BC, Alexander had marched through Persia and had conquered Afghanistan and the Punjab. Although his troops were very loyal to him, they refused to go farther than the Indus River.

Coin from Indus area

Death of Alexander

In 323 BC, Alexander caught a fever in the city of Babylon. Although he was only 33, he died. This sudden death meant that Alexander did not have time to consolidate his rule or even name his successor. Within a few years of his death, the huge Macedonian Empire had collapsed.

Alexander's sarcophagus

Carved relief shows Alexander leading his troops.

Sarcophagus from the royal cemetery of Sidon, said to be the tomb of Alexander.

ALEXANDER THE GREAT

356 BC	Born in Macedon
336 BC	Succeeds his father to the Macedonian throne; quells rebellions in Greece
334 BC	Leads his army into Persia and defeats a Persian army at the Granicus River
333 BC	Defeats Darius III at Issus
331 BC	Defeats Darius III again at Gaugamela, completing his conquest of the Persian Empire
326 BC	Reaches the Indus, but is forced to turn back by his troops
323 BC	Dies of fever in Babylon

FIND OUT MORE

ASIA, HISTORY OF · EGYPT, ANCIENT · GREECE, ANCIENT · PERSIAN EMPIRES · PHILOSOPHY

AMERICAN CIVIL WAR

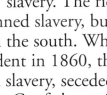

A

LESS THAN 80 YEARS after independence, the US split in two over the issue of slavery. The richer, industrial northern states had banned slavery, but slaves were used on plantations in the south. When Abraham Lincoln became president in 1860, the southern states, fearing he would ban slavery, seceded from the Union, and established the Confederate States of America. Fighting began in 1861 and lasted four years. At first the sides were evenly matched, but the strength of the Union wore down the Confederacy. Upon the Confederate surrender, slavery was abolished throughout the country.

Divided nation

Eleven southern slave states left the Union of states, declaring independence as the Confederacy. Four other slave states refused to break away; West Virginia split from the rest of the state and stayed in the Union.

Slave states in the union

Confederate states

Union states

Washington

Charleston

First modern war

The American Civil War was the first recognizably modern war. Railroads transported men and supplies to the battlefield, and iron ships were used for the first time. Commanders talked to each other by field telegraph, and the war was photographed and widely covered in newspapers.

Much of the fighting was trench warfare, but troops were also prepared for a pitched battle.

Soldiers
More than three million people fought in the two opposing armies, most of them as infantrymen (foot soldiers).

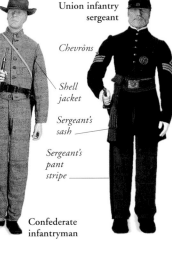

Union infantry sergeant

Chevrôns

Shell jacket

Sergeant's sash

Sergeant's pant stripe

Confederate infantryman

Union soldiers and guns

Gunner

Field gun

Officer

Percussion musket

Abraham Lincoln
Lincoln was born in Kentucky in 1809. He was elected to the state legislature in 1834, was elected president in 1860, and led the Union states to victory in the civil war. He was assassinated in 1865.

Merrimack and Monitor
The Confederate ironclad ship *Merrimack* fought the Union's vessel *Monitor* on March 9, 1862. The outcome of the battle was inconclusive, but the encounter marked the first use of iron ships in naval warfare.

Gettysburg Address
Lincoln was an inspired orator. In 1863, he dedicated a cemetery on the site of a battlefield in Gettysburg, Pennsylvania. In his speech, he hoped that "these dead shall not have died in vain; that this nation, under God, shall have a new birth of freedom, and that government of the people, by the people, for the people, shall not perish from the earth."

Appomattox
On April 9, 1865, at Appomattox, Virginia, Confederate general Robert E. Lee surrendered to Union general Ulysses S. Grant. More than 600,000 Americans died in the four years of fighting, and many more were injured.

Signing the surrender documents

Timeline

April 1861 After 11 states leave the Union, war breaks out when Confederate troops fire on the Union garrison at Fort Sumter, South Carolina.

1861 Confederates under generals Jackson and Beauregard win the first major battle against Unionists at Bull Run, near Washington.

Ulysses S. Grant

1862 Confederates win Seven Days' Battle (near Richmond, Virginia) and Battle of Fredericksburg, Virginia.

1863 Union wins its first major battle at Gettysburg; Lincoln's Emancipation Proclamation frees slaves.

1864 Ulysses S. Grant becomes Union commander-in-chief.

1864 General Sherman's Union army marches through Georgia, destroying the state capital and weakening the Confederacy.

Civil War cannon

April 1865 Lee's Confederate army surrenders at Appomattox, Virginia.

May 1865 Last Confederate army surrenders.

December 1865 Slavery is banned throughout the US by the 13th amendment.

FIND OUT MORE AMERICAN REVOLUTION ARMIES NORTH AMERICA, HISTORY OF SHIPS AND BOATS SLAVERY UNITED STATES, HISTORY OF WARFARE WASHINGTON, GEORGE

AMERICAN REVOLUTION

IN 1783, A NEW NATION WAS BORN – the United States of America. Its struggle for independence is called the American Revolution. It began in 1775, when 13 American colonies went to war against Britain. Britain governed the colonies and imposed high taxes. The colonists, who were not represented in the British Parliament, resented the taxes. Protests and demonstrations broke out, and the colonists formed a Continental Congress to negotiate with Britain. A skirmish led to war, and in 1776, the American colonists, inspired by ideals of freedom, declared independence. The British surrendered in 1781, and two years later recognized the new country.

Maine (to Massachusetts)
New Hampshire
Massachusetts
New York
Rhode Island
Pennsylvania
Connecticut
New Jersey
Virginia
Delaware
Maryland
N. Carolina
S. Carolina
Georgia

Thirteen colonies
After the Revolution, Britain's 13 original colonies formed the first 13 states of the new United States.

Stamp tax

The colonists set their own taxes. But in 1765, Britain introduced a stamp tax on legal documents. The angry colonists stated that "taxation without representation is tyranny." They refused to buy British goods.

Boston Tea Party
Britain withdrew the stamp tax, but set tax on glass and tea. Three groups of protesters, dressed as Mohawk Indians, boarded tea ships in Boston Harbor and threw their cargo into the water.

Colonists pour tea into Boston Harbor, in protest at British taxes

Lexington and Concord

In April 1775, the war began with skirmishes near Lexington and Concord. American patriots forced the British to withdraw at Lexington. They marched back to Boston under continuous fire.

Paul Revere
Paul Revere (1735–1818) rode through Massachusetts on the night of April 18, 1775, to warn that the British were coming. He was part of an anti-British group called the Sons of Liberty.

Revere on horseback

Thomas Jefferson

A planter from Virginia, Thomas Jefferson (1743–1826) attended the Continental Congress in 1775. He drafted the Declaration of Independence, reformed the laws of his native state, and went on diplomatic missions to Europe. He became the third president of the US in 1801 and served until 1809.

George Washington

The commander of the colonial army was George Washington (1732–99). He was an inspiring general, who kept the morale of his troops high in spite of several defeats at the beginning of the war. When France joined the war on the colonial side in 1778, followed by Spain in 1779, victory was assured.

Washington

Cocked hat
Cartridge box belt
Backpack strap
Brush for musket lock
Musket
Gaitered pants
Musket

American soldier

Cocked hat
Crossbelt
Red coat
Bayonet
Brush for musket lock
Breeches
Leather spatterdash
Shoe

British infantryman

Surrender at Yorktown
The fighting lasted until spring 1781, when the colonists cut the British off from their supplies at Yorktown. They finally surrendered on October 19.

Declaration of Independence
On July 4, 1776, the 13 colonies signed the Declaration of Independence. This document stated that "all men are created equal..." and its belief in "Life, Liberty, and the Pursuit of Happiness" later inspired the French Revolution.

Revolutionary war

The war lasted for six years. Washington's leadership played a vital part in the American victory. He led his troops to victories at Brandywine (1777) and Yorktown (1781).

The opposing armies
The British were well trained but poorly led. Their orders came from 2,500 miles (4,000 km) away. The Americans were less well trained, but knew the terrain and had good leaders.

Timeline

1765 Britain introduces the stamp tax. Protests break out. Britain withdraws the stamp tax, but other taxes remain.

1773 Boston Tea Party. Americans, dressed as Mohawks, dump tea in Boston Harbor as a protest against heavy taxes.

1774–75 Continental Congress. Representatives draft a petition to Britain insisting on no taxation without representation.

1775 Battle of Lexington. Congress takes over government of the colonies, and appoints Washington Commander-in-Chief.

1777 British general John Burgoyne (1722–92) forced to surrender at Saratoga.

1778 France joins the war on the American side.

1781 British surrender at Yorktown.

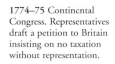

French private soldier

FIND OUT MORE FRENCH REVOLUTION UNITED KINGDOM, HISTORY OF UNITED STATES, HISTORY OF WARFARE WASHINGTON, GEORGE

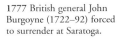

AMPHIBIANS

COLD-BLOODED animals, amphibians are vertebrates (animals with a backbone) that evolved from fish. They are adapted for life on land, but most must return to water in some form to breed. Amphibians undergo a process known as metamorphosis in their development from larvae to adult, hence the Greek origin of their name: *amphi* meaning "double"; *bios* meaning "life." There are three groups of amphibians and more than 2,500 species.

Amphibian features

Apart from the caecilians and a few species of salamander, adult amphibians have four legs, each with four or five digits. Most species take to the water to mate and produce their eggs, but some make nests on land, occasionally in burrows in the ground or in moss.

European common frog

Long legs for leaping.

Frog leaps after prey such as an insect.

Webbed toes for swimming.

Marbled newt

"Marbled" color extends along the tail.

Newts and salamanders
The tailed amphibians – newts, salamanders, and the eel-like sirens of North America – live in tropical forests, temperate woods, mountain streams, and lakes. Some have very specialized life styles: a few even live in the total darkness of caves.

Amphibian groups

There are three groups of amphibians: the wormlike caecilians; the tailed amphibians, including newts and salamanders; and the tailless frogs and toads, probably the most diverse group.

Couch's spadefoot toad

Distribution of amphibians
Amphibians live everywhere. Desert species survive the driest season by staying underground inside a membranous sac, which they secrete themselves. Some temperate species hibernate in pond mud in the winter.

Caecilians
Caecilians are legless, carnivorous amphibians most of which live in the tropics. Some species burrow in the ground; others are aquatic. They have small eyes and ears and sensory tentacles on the head.

Frogs and toads
In temperate regions, frogs are more aquatic than toads, have slimier skin and longer legs. In the tropics, some species of frogs and toads are fully aquatic and live in trees or underground.

Skin

Amphibian skin is thin and scaleless. It is usually kept moist with mucus to increase the flow of oxygen through the skin for breathing. Skin can be smooth or rough. It secretes certain chemicals: pheremones can attract potential mates; poisons deter predators. As they grow, amphibians shed the top layer of skin.

Great crested newt   Square marked toad

Mandarin salamander   Tree frog

Texture
Many frogs and toads have smooth skin covered by mucus. Other amphibians, such as the mandarin salamander and many dry-skinned toads, have raised nodules.

White's tree frogs

Color
Amphibians may have skin colors that absorb or reflect heat. Color also varies with temperature, becoming pale when warm and darker if cold and damp.

Camouflaged tree frogs

Camouflage
Many frogs and toads are camouflaged to avoid detection by predators. Most have a combination of forest colors and disruptive patterning. Some rain forest species are shaped to look like dead leaves.

Defense
The bright colors of Colombian poison-dart frogs warn predators of their highly toxic skin. The tadpoles develop their skin poisons as their colors develop. Marine toads secrete a strong toxin through large glands behind the head.

Poison-dart tadpoles

Metamorphosis

The development from an aquatic larva that breathes through gills, or spiracles, to an air-breathing adult is called metamorphosis. It involves the growth of legs and the loss of the tail in frogs and toads.

Newt egg

Frog spawn

Eggs
Amphibian eggs are laid singly, in clumps, or in strings of clear "jelly" called spawn. They have no shell and require a moist environment to survive.

Tadpoles
Larvae, or tadpoles, hatch from the eggs. Salamander tadpoles have limbs, but frogs and toads develop these during metamorphosis. Salamander larvae are carnivorous, but most frog and toad tadpoles are herbivorous.

Frog tadpole

Gills

Salamander tadpole

Axolotl
Some salamanders may stay as larvae all their life. The axolotl is a form of the Mexican tiger salamander.

FIND OUT MORE   EVOLUTION   FROGS AND TOADS   POISONOUS ANIMALS   SALAMANDERS AND NEWTS

ANGLO-SAXONS

BY THE END of the 8th century, Britain's people, known as the Anglo-Saxons, had created a rich culture that included masterpieces of jewelry, architecture, and literature. Originally these people had come from northern Germany and southern Denmark, where they were known as the Angles, Saxons, and Jutes. In the 3rd and 4th centuries, these tribes traveled to various parts of the Roman Empire, including Gaul, or present-day France, where their influence was short-lived. They traveled to Britain in the 5th century, where they settled and formed several separate kingdoms. Eventually the kingdom of Wessex became the dominant power.

Culture

Cultural life centered on the monasteries and on the royal court. Alfred the Great gathered scholars and artists around him, and himself translated many of the Latin classics into Anglo-Saxon, or Old English.

Architecture

Anglo-Saxon churches, like the one at Earls Barton, England, often have square towers decorated with stone relief. This pattern may be based on timber buildings of the period, which have all perished.

Decorated manuscripts

Monks produced quality manuscripts. One monk wrote the work, while a second illustrated it with figures, such as St. Dunstan (c.909–988) kneeling before Jesus, and a third decorated it.

Possible image of Alfred the Great

Jewelry

This jewel is inscribed "Alfred ordered me to be made" and may have belonged to Alfred the Great. The inscription and animal-head decoration are finely worked in gold; the portrait, perhaps of the king himself, is made of enamel.

Kingdoms

There was always a struggle for supremacy among the kingdoms formed by the settlers. Northumbria was the earliest one to dominate under Edwin (d. 633). Then it was Mercia's turn under Aethelbald (d. 757) and Offa (d. 796). Finally Wessex dominated under Alfred the Great. When Vikings from Denmark attacked and occupied northern England, Alfred stopped them from pushing farther south, and the Anglo-Saxons reconquered the north in the 10th century.

King Canute and King Edward

By 1016, the Danes ruled all England under the popular Canute (c.995–1035). Canute's sons inherited England, but the Anglo-Saxon Edward the Confessor (c.1003–1066) regained the country in 1042. He had no children and, when he died, an unsettled England was vulnerable to conquest by the Normans.

Edward the Confessor   Canute the Great

Written records

In the 7th century, missionaries from mainland Europe, such as St. Augustine of Canterbury, converted the Anglo-Saxons to Christianity. The creation of monasteries meant that more people learned to read and write. Monks produced historical works, such as the *Anglo-Saxon Chronicle*, which today give insights into the events of the period.

Anglo-Saxon Chronicle

In the ninth century, Alfred the Great ordered the *Chronicle*, a year-by-year account of the history of England. It covers the lives of kings and church leaders, military history, and major events, such as the Viking invasions, and was last updated in 1154.

Bede (c.673–735)

Bede, an English monk and teacher in Jarrow, wrote *A History of the English Church and People*, one of the most important sources of our knowledge of Anglo-Saxon times.

Alfred the Great

Ruler of Wessex and Mercia, Alfred (c.849–c.899) was an able soldier who defended his kingdom against the Vikings. He loved learning and education, and arts and crafts flourished in his reign. He could not drive the Vikings from northern England, but most people saw him as their protector. He was the first English king to become a national symbol.

Timeline

450 Angles, Saxons, and Jutes from northern Germany and Denmark begin to arrive in England. They settle mainly along the eastern coast – East Anglia.

802–39 Reign of Egbert of Wessex. There are many Viking attacks.

871–99 Reign of Alfred the Great, famous for law-making, translating books into Old English, and defeating the Vikings at Edington in 878.

Anglo-Saxon buckle

1016 Canute the Great, a Dane, is elected king by the British; he rules until 1035.

1042 Anglo-Saxons regain power under Edward the Confessor.

1066 Last Anglo-Saxon king, Harold II, is killed by William of Normandy at the Battle of Hastings.

 **FIND OUT MORE**   CELTS   EUROPE, HISTORY OF   MONASTERIES   NORMANS   UNITED KINGDOM, HISTORY OF   VIKINGS

ANIMAL BEHAVIOR

ALL ANIMALS RESPOND to their surroundings. A cat, for example, will arch its back when threatening a rival, but lower its body when stalking a mouse. Everything that an animal does, and the way in which it does it, makes up its behavior. An animal's behavior enables it to increase its chances of survival and find a mate so that it can pass on its genes to the next generation. Some behaviors are instinctive; others are learned during the animal's lifetime.

Egg-rolling
Greylag geese nest on the ground. If an egg rolls out of the nest, the female goose automatically reaches out with her neck and pulls the egg back in. By being in the wrong place, the egg acts as a sign stimulus that causes the female to carry out the fixed-action pattern of egg-rolling.

Instinctive behavior

"Instinct" is a term used to describe behavior that an animal performs automatically without having to learn it. Instinctive behavior is programmed by an animal's genes. It consists of unchanging components called fixed-action patterns. The fixed-action pattern often begins when an animal responds to a feature in its surroundings or on another animal, called a sign stimulus.

Web spinning
Many species of spiders, including this black widow, spin webs in order to trap their insect food. Web spinning is purely instinctive. A spider would not have time in its limited life to learn how to construct such a complex structure.

Sign stimulus
In the spring, when these freshwater fish breed, the male's throat and belly turn red. If one male intrudes into the territory of another male, its red color acts as a sign stimulus that produces a fixed-action pattern: the occupying fish drives out the intruder.

Bright spring colors

Bright colors fade after the breeding season.

Learned behavior

Learning occurs when an animal adapts to its surroundings by changing its behavior. By responding to experiences and adapting to changing conditions, an animal increases its chances of survival. Learning takes time, and animals that are dependent on learned behavior have long lives and large brains.

Trial-and-error learning
An animal will associate an action it carries out with a successful result, such as getting food or defeating a rival. This "reward" motivates the animal to alter its behavior to improve the result of future actions.

Puppies play-fight and perfect their hunting skills.

Young ducklings follow their mother.

Imprinting
Some young animals make a strong bond with their parent soon after hatching or birth. Young ducklings, for example, stay close to their mother and improve their chances of survival under her protection.

Learning tool use
Some animals learn to use simple "tools" in order to feed. Sea otters, found off the coast of California, US, swim on their backs with a stone on their chests on which they smash the shells of clams and mussels to get at the juicy contents. Young otters learn tool use from their parents.

Insight learning
This involves a form of reasoning. Some animals can solve new problems by drawing on past experiences. Chimpanzees, having learned to extract termites or ants from a nest with a stick, can exploit other nests of any shape.

Communication

Animals communicate by sending out signals that are recognized by other animals and alter their behavior in some way. The signals can be sights, sounds, or scents. Communication is used, for example, to find a mate, threaten rivals or enemies, defend a territory, warn of danger, or hold a group together.

Song thrush sings from a perch.

Visual signals
Animals may use visual signals to threaten or to attract a mate. This puss moth caterpillar adopts a warning posture if threatened. An enemy that ignores the warning is rewarded with a stinging squirt of formic acid.

Puss moth caterpillar

Bright colors add to the warning.

Sound
Many animals – including crickets, bullfrogs, peacocks, and whales – use sound to communicate. This male song thrush sings to proclaim his territory, to warn rivals to stay away, and to attract a female.

Chemicals
Some animals release chemicals called pheromones, which, when detected, affect the behavior of other members of the same species. Female gypsy moths release pheromones that attract males from several miles away.

Gypsy moth

Courtship

Mating in most mammals and birds takes place only at certain times of the year. Courtship describes the behaviors used by a male animal to attract a female and mate with her. It informs a potential mate that the intention is breeding and not aggression. During courtship, males usually compete with one another to attract females, advertise that they are ready to mate, and encourage females to be sexually responsive. Females select males by the quality of their courtship display.

Male is aware that the female may lash out at him.

Male is attentive to the female.

Female is sexually responsive and rolls.

Domestic cats
A female cat comes into heat, or is sexually responsive, about twice a year. She produces scents and calls loudly to attract males. Several males may compete for her by fighting. The successful male encourages the female by touching her and calling softly.

Bird of paradise
Most birds have fixed courtship displays that make sure they attract a mate of the same species. Male birds often have brighter plumage than females, and this is especially true of the emperor bird of paradise. Males compete for females by quivering their long feathers and calling loudly.

Territorial behavior

Many animals defend their territory to maintain access to food, water, shelter, and somewhere to reproduce. Territories can be large or small and held by one animal or by a group. Birdsong or the marking of territorial boundaries may deter rivals from entering a territory and avoid conflict and possible fatal injuries.

Cats
Most cats are solitary and maintain a territory on their own. Cheetahs patrol their territory and mark its boundaries by spraying urine on trees and other landmarks. The scent warns neighboring cheetahs not to intrude.

Kittiwakes
Like many gull species, kittiwakes nest in colonies on narrow cliff ledges. Each pair of birds defends a small territory on the ledge just large enough for the female to lay eggs and raise their young.

Aggression

Animals show aggression to other members of their species when competing for food, water, shelter, or mates. Some animals use horns, some use teeth or claws, and others kick. In many cases, animals signal their aggressive intent. This may defuse the situation and prevent injury.

Fighting bighorn sheep

Inflated porcupine fish

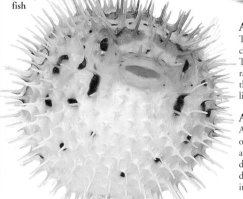

Aggression within a species
These bighorn sheep use their horns to clash head-on in competition for mates. The winner of the fight gains higher social ranking and more females. Aggression like this is highly ritualized, and neither male is likely to be injured.

Aggression between species
Animals may be aggressive toward members of other species that are threatening or attacking them. Some animals use a threat display, often making themselves bigger to deter enemies. This porcupine fish inflates its body like a balloon and erects its spines.

Social behavior

Social animals live in groups. Individuals cooperate to find food, defend themselves, and look after the young. Social groups range from shoals of fish, that form for protection, to societies of honeybees, whose social organization affects all aspects of each animal's life.

Worker bee

Male bee, called a drone

Section of a beehive

Helping others
African wild dogs are social animals and often help one another. Male dogs will look after pups that are not their own but were fathered by a brother or close relative. In this way, they help pups survive.

Living in large numbers
Many fish species swim close together in large groups called shoals. A shoal moves and turns in a coordinated manner that mimics a single large living organism. Predators find it difficult to focus on one individual within the shoal.

Konrad Lorenz

Austrian zoologist Konrad Lorenz (1903–89) pioneered the study of animal behavior. As part of his work on individual and group behaviour, Lorenz discovered imprinting. Lorenz shared a Nobel Prize in 1973 for his work.

Social insects
Within a colony of social insects, such as bees, there are groups that carry out certain tasks. In a bee colony, a single queen lays eggs while sterile female workers look after the young, collect food, and defend the colony. Male bees fertilize the queen.

FIND OUT MORE   BIRDS   FISH   GENETICS   INSECTS   MAMMALS   SONGBIRDS

ANIMALS

MORE THAN a million and a half species of animals have been identified, and there are many millions more yet to be discovered. Animals are living organisms found in nearly all of the Earth's habitats, including the depths of the oceans, the freezing Arctic, and even inside other animals and plants. The animal kingdom is divided into animals without backbones, (invertebrates), such as snails and lobsters, and animals with backbones, (vertebrates), such as frogs and monkeys. Invertebrates make up 97 percent of all animal species.

Large eyes enable the leopard to see in dim light.

The body is covered with insulating fur and supported internally by a skeleton.

Long tail is a balancing aid.

Black leopard
The leopard is a mammal. Its well-defined head is equipped with sense organs including eyes, nose, tongue, and whiskers. Sharp teeth in the mouth allow the leopard to kill prey and tear off flesh. Muscular legs enable it to walk, run, and pounce.

Air is breathed in through nostrils.

What is an animal?

Animals are made up of many cells. Most move actively, and those that are fixed in one place, or sedentary, move their body parts. Animals live by taking food into their bodies. They have sensors and nervous systems that enable them to detect what is happening around them and respond appropriately.

Animal classification

Animals are classified into groups according to their similarities and whether they have common ancestors. There are 35 major groups called phyla (singular phylum). Each phylum is divided into subgroups. The smallest of these is the species, which contains animals of just one type.

Giant land flatworm

Sponge processed for human use   **Sea anemones**

Sponges
The simplest animals are sponges (phylum Porifera). There are about 5,000 species, most of which live in the sea attached to rocks and other objects. Water is drawn in through holes, or pores, in the sponge's body wall, and bits of food are filtered out and eaten by the sponge's cells.

Cnidarians
There are more than 9,000 species of cnidarians (phylum Cnidaria), most of which are found in the sea. They include jellyfish, sea anemones, hydras, and corals. Cnidarians catch food using tentacles armed with stinging threads called nematocysts.

Flatworms
These worms (phylum Platyhelminthes) have a flattened body with one opening, the mouth, on the underside. There are about 18,500 species including those, such as tapeworms, that are parasites of humans and other animals.

Nematodes
Roundworms, or nematodes (phylum Nematoda), have a thin, cylindrical body that is pointed at both ends. Free-living nematodes are found in many habitats and occur in very large numbers in soil. Many nematodes are parasites of plants and animals.

Threadworm

Annelids
Animals in the phylum Annelida include earthworms, marine bristleworms, such as ragworms, and leeches. There are about 12,000 species, each of which has a body made up of segments with a mouth at one end and an anus at the other.

King ragworm

Stalked eye

Coiled shell protects the soft body.

Snail emerging from its shell

Mollusks
Mollusks (phylum Mollusca) form a highly diverse group of about 50,000 species. These include snails and slugs, mussels and clams, and squids and octopuses. They are soft-bodied animals that may be protected by a shell. Most live in water, but some, such as snails, are found on land.

Snail moves on a muscular foot.

Sensory tentacle

Head and foot fully extended

Echinoderms
All echinoderms (phylum Echinodermata) live in the sea. The 6,500 or so species include sea urchins and starfish. Most have five parts radiating from a central point, hard plates under the skin, and many tube feet.

Cushion star

Bloody Henry starfish

Cushion star

Arthropods have hard, jointed external skeletons.

Arthropods
With at least one million known species, Arthropods (phylum Arthropoda) are the largest group of animals. They include insects, crustaceans (such as crabs), arachnids (such as spiders), and centipedes.

Sharp teeth grasp food.

Chordates
There are about 48,000 species of chordates (phylum Chordata). Most are vertebrates, such as fish, amphibians, reptiles, birds, and mammals. Vertebrates are the most advanced animals.

Tail used for movement or balance is typical of many vertebrates.

Caiman

Tarantula

Animal skeletons

The skeleton is a supportive framework that maintains the shape of an animal and enables it to move. Most skeletons are hard structures, either inside or outside the animal's body, to which muscles are attached. The skeleton may also protect internal organs and, in the case of an insect's external skeleton, prevent the animal from drying out.

Limbs and head attached to backbone

Crab's exoskeleton

Salamander's endoskeleton

Internal skeletons
A skeleton found inside the body is called an endoskeleton. Most vertebrates have a skeleton made of cartilage and bone. Joints between the bones allow the animal to move. The endoskeleton grows with the rest of the body.

External skeletons
A hard outer skeleton that covers all or part of the body is called an exoskeleton. An insect's outer cuticle and a snail's shell are examples of an exoskeleton. An insect's exoskeleton does not grow and must be shed, or molted, periodically to allow the animal to grow.

Earthworm

Hydrostatic skeleton
The hydrostatic skeleton is an internal skeleton found in soft-bodied animals such as earthworms. It consists of a fluid-filled core surrounded by muscles, and maintains the shape of the worm.

Worm gets longer when it contracts its muscles.

Movement of an eel through water

Eel moves by throwing its body into curves that push against the water.

Animal movement

The ability to move is characteristic of animals, which move to find food, escape from predators, and find a mate. The way in which an animal moves depends on its complexity, lifestyle, and where it lives. The wide range of movement includes swimming through water, walking and creeping on land, and flying or gliding in air.

Wings sweep downward to produce forward thrust.

Movement in air
Insects, birds, and bats are capable of powered flight using wings. Birds have lightweight, streamlined bodies. They use energy to flap their wings, which pushes them forward. As air passes over the wings it creates the lift that keeps the bird in the air.

Young chaffinch in flight

Moving in water
Many aquatic animals are adapted for movement in water by having streamlined bodies. Most fish move by pushing their tail fin from side to side. This pushes the water backward and sideways, and propels the fish forward. Whales move in a similar way, except that the tail moves up and down.

Asian elephant

Feet expand under the elephant's weight as they are put down.

Movement on land
Animals move on land in a variety of ways. Many have limbs that raise the body off the ground, support it, and enable the animal to walk, run, or hop. The animals move forward by pushing the ends of their legs, or feet, backward against the ground.

Animal senses

The main senses are vision, hearing, taste, smell, and touch. Animals use their senses to find out what is going on around them. A stimulus from outside, such as a sound, is detected by a sense organ, such as the ear. Nerve impulses from sense organs are interpreted by the animal's brain which "decides" how to respond.

Dragonfly eyes

Eyes
Eyes contain sensors that are sensitive to light. When stimulated they send nerve impulses to the brain, which enable it to build up a picture. Insects have compound eyes made up of many separate units, or ommatidia.

Antennae
These are found on the head of arthropods such as insects. They are used to detect odors and may detect chemicals called pheromones released by insects to communicate with each other. Antennae also detect vibrations and movements in the air or in water.

Longhorn beetle

External ear flaps channel sounds into the ear.

Ears
Some animals can detect sounds with ears. The ear converts sounds into nerve impulses that can be interpreted by the animal's brain. Animals use sounds to communicate with each other and to detect approaching predators or prey.

Domestic Basenji dog

Feeding

All animals feed by taking in food. They use a range of feeding strategies and can be grouped accordingly. Some animals kill and eat others, some graze or browse on plants, others filter food particles from water. After feeding, or ingestion, food is digested so that it can be used by the body.

Mormon caterpillar consuming a leaf

Giant clam

Filter feeders
These are animals that feed by sieving food particles from water that flows into their body. Many are sedentary and draw in a current of water. Some whales are filter feeders that eat small animals called krill.

Herbivores
Animals that feed solely on plants are called herbivores. Many use specialized mouthparts, such as grinding teeth, to break up tough plant tissues. Plant material is not a rich food source, and most herbivores eat a lot to obtain the necessary nutrients.

Carnivores
These types of feeders are adapted to detect prey animals, to catch and kill them, and to cut them up to eat them. They include cats, eagles, and some insects. Dragonfly larvae live in water and they can catch small fish to eat.

Dragonfly larva with stickleback

FIND OUT MORE   AMPHIBIANS   ANIMAL BEHAVIOR   BIRDS   FISH   FLIGHT   INSECTS   MAMMALS   REPTILES   SNAILS AND OTHER MOLLUSKS

A

ANTARCTICA

WITH THE SOUTH POLE at its heart, Antarctica is the world's windiest, coldest, and most southerly continent. The last region on Earth to be explored, this huge landmass is not divided into countries, but seven nations claimed territories there. In 1959, however, the Antarctic Treaty suspended those claims and stated that the continent is to be used for peaceful purposes only. Antarctica's sole inhabitants are visiting scientists, working in research stations.

Physical features

Antarctica is almost entirely covered by a vast sheet of ice, in places 3 miles (4.8 km) deep. It contains 90 percent of the Earth's ice, and 70 percent of the world's freshwater. The vast Ronne and Ross ice shelves are formed where the ice sheet extends over the ocean.

ANTARCTICA FACTS

AREA 5,366,790 sq miles (900,000 sq km)

POPULATION 4,000 international researchers

NUMBER OF COUNTRIES None

HIGHEST POINT Vinson Massif, 16,863 ft (5,140 m)

AVERAGE THICKNESS OF ICE CAP 8,000 ft (2,450 m)

Icebergs
Currents beneath Antarctica's vast ice shelves cause giant slabs of ice to break away, the largest of which may be 125 miles (200 km) long. As these enormous icebergs drift north, they slowly break up and melt. Only the top third of an iceberg shows above the water.

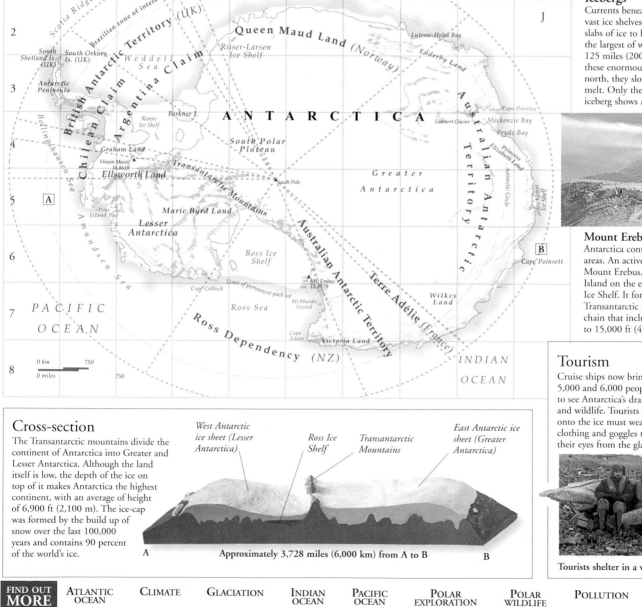

Mount Erebus
Antarctica contains volcanic areas. An active volcano, Mount Erebus, lies on Ross Island on the edge of the Ross Ice Shelf. It forms part of the Transantarctic mountain chain that includes peaks up to 15,000 ft (4,570 m) high.

Tourism
Cruise ships now bring between 5,000 and 6,000 people each year to see Antarctica's dramatic coastline and wildlife. Tourists who venture onto the ice must wear insulated clothing and goggles to protect their eyes from the glare.

Tourists shelter in a whale skull

Cross-section
The Transantarctic mountains divide the continent of Antarctica into Greater and Lesser Antarctica. Although the land itself is low, the depth of the ice on top of it makes Antarctica the highest continent, with an average of height of 6,900 ft (2,100 m). The ice-cap was formed by the build up of snow over the last 100,000 years and contains 90 percent of the world's ice.

West Antarctic ice sheet (Lesser Antarctica)

Ross Ice Shelf

Transantarctic Mountains

East Antarctic ice sheet (Greater Antarctica)

A   Approximately 3,728 miles (6,000 km) from A to B   B

FIND OUT MORE ATLANTIC OCEAN • CLIMATE • GLACIATION • INDIAN OCEAN • PACIFIC OCEAN • POLAR EXPLORATION • POLAR WILDLIFE • POLLUTION • VOLCANOES

ANTEATERS, SLOTHS AND ARMADILLOS

A BIZARRE GROUP of animals makes up the order of mammals known as the edentates. They include anteaters, armadillos, and sloths, all of which, except the nine-banded armadillo, live in the tropical regions of South and Central America. The name "edentate" means "without teeth," but it is a misleading term since only the anteaters are toothless. In fact, some armadillos have more teeth than any other land mammal.

Young
A female anteater gives birth to a single young. The young anteater travels on its mother's back for the first year of its life, by which time it is almost half the size of its mother.

Anteater
There are four species of anteaters. The giant anteater lives in grasslands; the other three species live in forests and have prehensile (grasping) tails with which they hang from trees. Anteaters have long snouts and tongues to enable them to collect the termites and ants on which they feed. They locate their prey with their acute sense of smell. Their foreclaws are so large that they need to walk on their knuckles. The claws are used to break open termite nests and for defense. If threatened, they rear up on their hind legs and try to rip their opponent with their claws.

Giant anteater breaking into a termite mound

Tongue
Anteaters have long, sticky tongues that can be pushed deep into termite nests. The tongue is covered with little spines that point backward, making it very difficult for ants and termites to escape.

Curved spines on tongue

Long, bushy tail

Giant anteater

Armadillo

Of the 21 species of armadillos, the largest is the giant armadillo, which is 3 ft (91.5 cm) long. It has up to 100 peglike teeth – twice as many as most mammals – that are shed when the animal reaches adulthood. The smallest species, the fairy armadillo, is less than 6 in (15 cm) long. Armadillos give birth to up to four young. The nine-banded armadillo, from North America, gives birth to quadruplets of the same sex.

Claws
Armadillos have large, curved claws. They use them to dig into the ground to make burrows, to escape predators, and to find food. The giant armadillo's middle claw is the largest claw in the animal kingdom, measuring 7 in (18 cm) around the curve.

Nine-banded armadillo

Bony plates

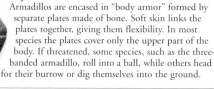

Large claws

Hairy stomach

Nine-banded armadillo

Body armor
Armadillos are encased in "body armor" formed by separate plates made of bone. Soft skin links the plates together, giving them flexibility. In most species the plates cover only the upper part of the body. If threatened, some species, such as the three-banded armadillo, roll into a ball, while others head for their burrow or dig themselves into the ground.

Sloth

Adapted to living upside down, sloths hang by their claws from the branches of trees. They can rotate their heads through a 270° angle, allowing them to keep their heads upright while their bodies remain inverted. They eat, mate, give birth, and spend their entire life-cycle upside down. Sloth's fur lies in the opposite direction from other animals' to allow rain to run off. Only when asleep do they adopt a more normal position, by squatting in the fork of a tree. There are seven species of sloths; all are herbivorous.

Female three-toed sloth with baby

Green algae cover the sloth's coat.

Movement
Sloths are very slow movers. They rarely descend to the ground and can only just stand. They cannot walk, but drag themselves along with their claws. However, they are good swimmers.

Sloth swimming

Camouflage
Because of high humidity levels in the rain forest, infestations of green algae grow within a sloth's fur and cover its coat. This acts as a camouflage and makes the sloth less conspicuous. As the seasons change, the algae change color to match the color of the trees.

Pangolin
There are seven species of pangolins, or scaly anteaters. They have much in common with edentates, but they belong to a different order – the Pholidota. They are covered with scales attached to the skin. Some species have a long, prehensile tail that is used to grasp branches and also to lash out at predators. They feed on termites, ants, and larvae, which they catch with their long tongues.

Malayan pangolin

GIANT ANTEATER	
SCIENTIFIC NAME	*Myrmecophaga tridactyla*
ORDER	Edentata
FAMILY	Myrmecophagidae
DISTRIBUTION	South America
HABITAT	Grasslands and savannas
DIET	Termites, ants, and larvae
SIZE	Length, including tail: 6 ft (1.83 m)
LIFESPAN	25 years (in captivity)

FIND OUT MORE   ASIAN WILDLIFE   CAMOUFLAGE AND COLOR   CONSERVATION   GRASSLAND WILDLIFE   MAMMALS   RAIN FOREST WILDLIFE   SOUTH AMERICAN WILDLIFE

ANTS AND TERMITES

Bull ant

Antennae are used to pick up the scent of pheromones.

Eyes

Spiked jaws used to attack prey and predators

FOR EVERY HUMAN, there are 1,000,000 ants. Ants and termites are social insects that live in large colonies and have developed complex systems of communication. Ants are found worldwide, but, like termites, most of the 9,500 species of ants live in the tropics. There are more than 2,400 types of termites; many are blind, spending their lives inside nests, never seeing the light of day.

Ants

Ants have two pairs of compound eyes, three single eyes, or ocelli, two antennae, and three pairs of legs. Only queens and males have wings. A narrow waist connects the thorax and abdomen. Ants undergo complete metamorphosis, from an egg to larval and pupal stages, before emerging as adults. They live in huge groups and each ant has a particular role. The queen runs the nest and mates with male ants. Workers are female and gather food and nurse the eggs, larvae, and pupae. Soldier ants, also female, guard the nest.

Eyes

Pheromones are released from the abdomen.

Legs are attached to the thorax.

Thorax

Wood ants

Communication
Ants lay trails of pheromones – chemicals that smell – so that other ants can follow them by using their sensitive antennae to pick up the smell. This helps foraging teams find food.

Defense
If a nest is attacked, the ants release pheromones to warn each other. Most run for cover, but soldier ants get aggressive and defend the colony. They attack enemies with their large jaws, or sting them with formic acid, which causes extreme pain. Some ants even explode to shower an attacker in venom.

Ant nest
Most ants live in nests or colonies, usually underground. However, weaver ants build nests out of leaves in trees, and army ants build "live nests" of worker ants. Normally, there is one queen in a nest, but there are sometimes several. Nests of Australian bull ants contain up to 600 ants, while some wood ants' nests can house more than 300 million.

"Live nest" made by army ants

Feeding
Many ants are omnivores and eat seeds, nectar, and invertebrates. Army and driver ants are more carnivorous, and kill and eat prey such as worms, spiders, and even some lizards. Leaf-cutting ants are one of a few species of herbivorous ants. They feed on a type of fungus, which grows on the chewed-up remains of leaves and flowers that the ants take back to their nests.

Ants carry pieces of leaves back to their nest.

Leaf-cutting ants

Termites

Although often called white ants, termites belong to a totally different order, the Isoptera. Like ants, termites live in large colonies. Unlike ants, termites do not have waists, and the male, called a king, does not die after mating, but lives with the queen. They do not go through complete metamorphosis, but grow up gradually through several nymphal stages.

Soldiers
Like ants, termites have soldiers. Termites cannot sting, but defend themselves in other ways. Some soldiers have large jaws that can cut through flesh; others squirt a poisonous sticky liquid from a special nozzle on their heads. Some nests have no soldiers – the termites defend themselves by vibrating their bodies against the side of their nest, making the sound of a hissing snake.

Pincers

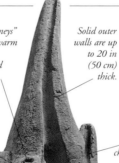

"Chimneys" allow warm air to rise and escape.

Solid outer walls are up to 20 in (50 cm) thick.

Air channel

Living quarters

Soft inner walls

Food stores

Termite mounds
Each species of termite has its own type of nest. Some build towers more than 20 ft (6 m) tall, which help maintain the correct temperature and humidity of the nest at the base. Others build mushroom-shaped mounds – the domed top deflects the rain away from the nest below and has given these insects their name of umbrella termites. Many termites do not build nests above ground, but live below the soil or inside logs. Termites that live in trees build their nests on branches.

Workers
Worker termites build the nest, collect food, and feed the soldiers, king, and queen. The nest is made from saliva, soil, and their own feces. Most workers feed on wood and have microscopic organisms in their guts to break down the wood into a more easily digested form.

Queen and king
A queen termite can reach more than 6 in (15 cm) in length. Her ovaries make her so large. She can lay up to 30,000 eggs a day. The king remains by the queen's side and mates with her several times to fertilize all the eggs.

Fungus gardens
are areas where fungi grow on termites' feces and break down the cellulose within them. The termites feed on the products released and the fungi itself.

Queen

Ground level

Nurseries

Royal chamber

Termites spread water on walls to cool the nest.

Thick pillar supports nest.

WOOD ANT

SCIENTIFIC NAME *Formica rufa*

ORDER Hymenoptera

FAMILY Formicidae

DISTRIBUTION Europe

HABITAT Woods and forests

DIET Omnivorous, feeding on seeds and invertebrates

SIZE Workers 0.24–0.31 in (6–8 mm) in length; queen 0.4–0.5 in (10–13 mm) in length

LIFESPAN Workers live for 3–4 months; the queen lives for about 15 years

| FIND OUT MORE | ANIMAL BEHAVIOR | ARTHROPODS | INSECTS | MONGOOSES AND CIVETS | MUSHROOMS AND OTHER FUNGI | NESTS AND BURROWS | WOODLAND WILDLIFE |

ARCHAEOLOGY

HUMANKIND HAS ALWAYS been fascinated by the question of who we are, where we came from, and how we used to live. Archaeology is the study of our past, from early prehistory onward, using the material remains of our ancestors and the possessions they left behind. Over thousands of years, evidence of human activity, such as artifacts, burial sites, and monuments, becomes buried. Archaeological teams discover these sites and uncover this evidence by careful excavation. The material is then preserved and studied in order to help the archaeologist piece together a picture of how people lived and died in the past.

Discovery

Iron Age fort, England

Archaeological sites are found during construction work, through reading historical documents, geophysical surveys (the study of the soil's structure), and field walking (recording above-ground objects).

Aerial photography
Horizontal and vertical lines seen from the air often show medieval strip fields, ancient roads, walls, and ditches. Aerial photography done when the sun is low shows varying surface levels, moisture levels, and vegetation most clearly.

Excavation

Archaeological sites are excavated by layers. Workers remove the top, most recent layer, and work down, uncovering older, deeper levels. The study of these layers and the items they contain is called stratigraphy.

Stratigraphy
By revealing features such as ditches, post holes, and floors, stratigraphy gives information about the history of a site and the people who lived there. In urban areas, ground levels rise as landfill is used as a foundation for rebuilding. Because it shows a chronological sequence, stratigraphy was used to date sites before radiocarbon dating was invented.

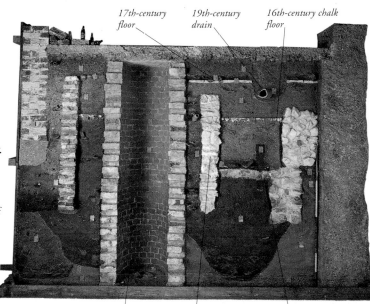

17th-century floor   *19th-century drain*   *16th-century chalk floor*

Cross-section of a dig, City of London

Brick-lined well, c.1800   *14th-century cesspit*   *Roman tiled floor*

Tools

Pick ax

Trowel   *Measuring tape*

Archaeologists use shovels and handpicks to remove the topsoil. Then smaller hand tools, such as dental picks, teaspoons, and trowels, are used to excavate delicate objects.

Finds
Archaeologists usually draw or photograph the artifacts (objects) to make a visual record. They carefully measure and record the shapes, colors, decorations, and ages of any artifacts or features. These details help archaeologists link different objects and sites.

Investigation

Buried objects are fragile and decay quickly after excavation. To stabilize them, they are cleaned and preserved. After preservation, an object can be studied. Archaeologists then record the material of the object, its use, and its date. It may then be photographed and displayed in a museum.

Salt water has caused corrosion.

Pewter jug

A cradle hoisted the ship from the seabed.

Underwater archaeology

Sites beneath the sea or in lakes are more difficult to excavate than those on land because shifting silt or sand causes poor visibility. However, marine sites often preserve materials, such as the wood of the 16th-century ship the Mary Rose, which would usually be lost on dry land. Preservation may involve treatment with water, sealing with chemicals, or careful drying.

To preserve the wood, chilled water is sprayed on the ship 20 hours a day.

Mary Rose, in dry dock

Timeline

1748 Pompeii discovered.

1799 An officer in Napoleon's army discovers the Rosetta Stone, which features 6th century BC hieroglyphs.

1812 Abu Simbel discovered.

1822 Scholars decipher Egyptian hieroglyphs.

1861 Evans and Prestwich confirm the antiquity of humans and humans' association with extinct animals.

1891 *Homo erectus* material found.

1922 Howard Carter discovers the tomb of Tutankhamun.

1931 Louis Leakey begins excavations at Olduvai Gorge.

1940 Archaeologists discover prehistoric Lascaux cave paintings.

1949 Radiocarbon dating is developed.

1974 Donald Johanson discovers "Lucy," an early hominid.

Australopithecus, an early human ancestor

Mortimer Wheeler

Wheeler (1890–1976), a field archaeologist, set up the Institute of Archaeology, London. Worldwide, modern field archaeology stems from the new excavation techniques he pioneered. In 1944, India made him director-general of archaeology. While there, he investigated the Indus Valley Civilization.

FIND OUT MORE   ASIA, HISTORY OF   BRONZE AGE   EUROPE, HISTORY OF   HUMAN EVOLUTION   PREHISTORIC PEOPLE   STONE AGE

Archaeological finds from the Mary Rose

Weapons

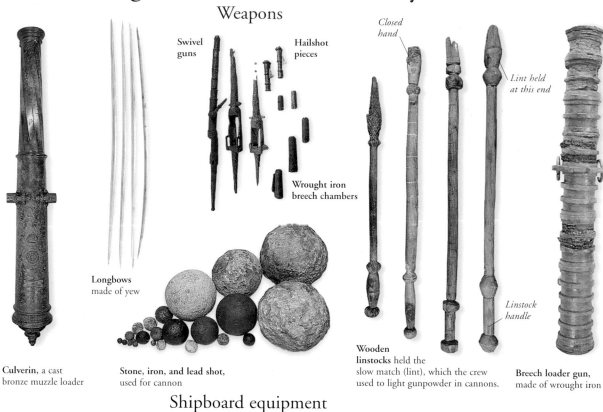

Swivel guns

Hailshot pieces

Closed hand

Lint held at this end

Wrought iron breech chambers

Longbows made of yew

Linstock handle

Wooden **linstocks** held the slow match (lint), which the crew used to light gunpowder in cannons.

Demi cannon, a cast bronze muzzle loader

Culverin, a cast bronze muzzle loader

Stone, iron, and lead shot, used for cannon

Breech loader gun, made of wrought iron

Shipboard equipment

Wooden razor handles

Apothecary's balance

Deadeye

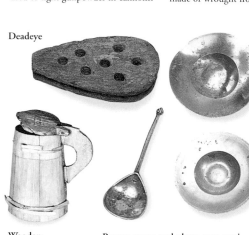

Personal sundial

Ceramic medicine jar

An angel, a 1545 gold coin worth about a dollar

Bronze cooking pot, used for communal meals

Wooden tankard

Pewter spoon and plates were used at the captain's dinner table.

Clothing and personal

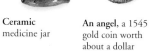

Manicure set, made of bone

Wooden comb

Inkpot, made of horn

Leather jerkin

Backgammon set

Yew and spruce inlay

Leather flask for storing wine or water

Leather book cover

ARCHITECTURE

FROM A TOWERING SKYSCRAPER to a functional factory, architecture is the art of planning a building. The word also refers to the different building styles seen throughout history. Looking at changes in architecture tells us about earlier societies: the materials that were available to their builders, the skills mastered by their engineers, and the social ideals that they wished to express in their public buildings.

Ornamentation

Early in the 20th century, many Western architects abandoned the use of all forms of building ornamentation. This is rare: most buildings from other periods and cultures use it extensively, and even a simple building would have some decoration to reflect the taste of its owner. The ancient Greeks, for instance, carved the tops, or capitals, of columns to dignify their most prestigious buildings. The distinct decorations were based on styles called orders.

Doric order

Ionic order

Corinthian order

Architectural features

The main structural and functional features of a building are the roof, arches and walls, doors, and windows. The architect combines the practical knowledge of how to construct these features with a sense of shape, space, and light to enhance the function of the building itself.

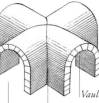

Groin

Vault

Groin vault, where two barrel vaults intersect

Main arch

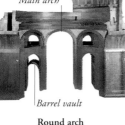

Barrel vault

Round arch

Arch and vault

An arch is a curved or pointed structure that bridges a gap; it must carry the weight of the wall, floor, or roof above. Its structure allows it to support greater weight than a flat slab can. A vault is simply an arched ceiling.

Cross and orb

Lantern (turret with windows) provides light

Dome metaling, Church of the Sorbonne, Paris, France, 17th century

Round-arched window

Dome on a circular base

Pitched roof, supporting frame

Eaves

Main rafter (inclined beam)

Horizontal beams add strength to structure.

Dome

Domes – curved, solid roofs – were first built on palaces and religious buildings as symbols of the building's importance. They are often difficult to build, and have been constructed in various shapes: the Dome of the Rock in Jerusalem is hemispherical; the "onion"-shaped dome is a popular feature of many Russian and Bavarian buildings.

Roof

All roofs are designed to provide protection from the weather. The design and covering used reflects the local climate: for instance, in a rainy area a sloping (pitched) roof will let the water run off easily. Apart from being practical, roofs can also be ingenious and beautiful, such as those of an ornate castle.

Classical Europe

Classical architecture is that of the ancient Greeks and Romans. Both built by laying stones on top of each other, or by resting beams on columns. The Romans also developed the arch, vault, dome, and the use of concrete to develop curved spaces.

Brunelleschi

Italian architect Filippo Brunelleschi (1377–1446) returned to the use of Classical features, rejecting the Gothic style. Architects all across Europe followed his example.

Eight-sided spire, built using scaffolding and wooden cranes

Turretlike pinnacle

Building innovations

The pointed arch and flying buttress were innovations that allowed Gothic churches to soar higher than buildings built earlier. Pointed arches can support heavier, taller structures than round arches. The flying buttress is a stone rib that extends down and away from the walls, transferring weight to the ground and giving extra support to a roof or walls.

Symbolism

The Pantheon is a temple built to all the Roman gods. Light comes through an opening in its vast dome and moves around the interior, lighting the curved walls. It is as if even the Universe turns around the center of the building, symbolizing the power of the Roman deities.

Gothic

This distinctive, ornate European style emerged in the 12th century and was used mainly in cathedrals and churches. Features include pointed arches and windows, and elaborate stone tracery used to divide the openings in window arches.

Use of concrete

Cheap and durable, this material allowed Roman architects to cover vast curved spaces that were impossible to construct before.

Opening

Dome, 142 ft (43 m) across

Walls 21 ft (6m) thick

Entrance porch, or portico

Outer wall faced with brick

Corinthian column

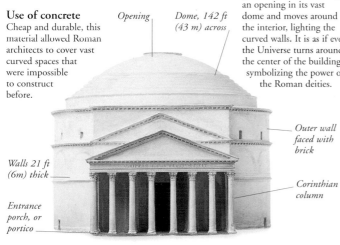

The Pantheon, Rome, Italy, completed c.AD 128

Pointed arch filled with tracery

Pitched roof

Buttress

Pointed arch

Flying buttress

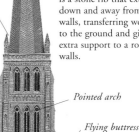

Old St. Paul's Cathedral, London, England, 1087-1666

A

Southeast Asia and the Middle East

The traditional architectural styles of Asia and the Middle East changed very little for centuries, and were heavily influenced by religious belief: Buddhism and Hinduism in southern Asia, and Islam in the Middle East. The style of buildings was determined by climate and by the materials available to local builders. As early as the 7th century, wooden temples and monasteries were being built in China and Japan.

Pagoda in Burmese style, 9th–10th century

Gilded crown

Islamic decoration uses geometric patterns and calligraphy.

South and East Asia
Many of the distinctive features of this area's architecture originated in Buddhist India. An example is the multistoried pagoda, a temple that seems to stretch toward Heaven. It was developed initially in Japan and China, but was based on the spires found on early Indian temples. An important feature of many traditional Asian buildings is their imaginative roof forms.

Minaret

Islamic architecture
The most important buildings in Islamic countries are usually mosques and tombs. The mosque is the center of a Muslim community and provides space for group worship. It contains a prayer hall, often with a domed roof, and a minaret, from which the faithful are called to prayer. It may also have a courtyard.

Early American civilizations

The Aztecs, who ruled in what is now Mexico from the 14th to 16th centuries, built stone pyramids to their gods. The remains of five separate temples have been found at Tenochtitlan, built one on top of the other as new rulers erected bigger temples on the same site.

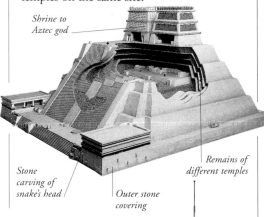

Shrine to Aztec god

Stone carving of snake's head

Outer stone covering

Remains of different temples

Baroque and Neoclassical

The Baroque style emerged in early 17th-century Europe and was noted for its ornate decoration, complex shapes, and dramatic lighting. It was followed by the Neoclassical style, which revived the more restrained Classical traditions. This was partly as a reaction to Baroque excess.

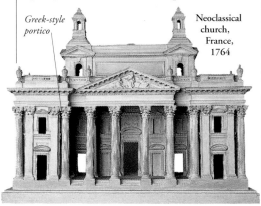

Greek-style portico

Neoclassical church, France, 1764

The 19th and 20th centuries

The development of new and stronger materials made it possible to construct buildings that were often highly original in style and owed little to the past. With advanced technology, architects turned to glass, steel, and concrete to express their vision of modern architecture.

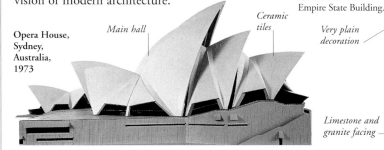

Opera House, Sydney, Australia, 1973

Main hall

Ceramic tiles

Interlocked vaults
The dramatic profile of the Opera House dominates Sydney Harbour. The building's roof of interlocked vaults, made from reinforced concrete covered with gleaming tiles, resembles the sails of a ship.

Skyscrapers
The invention of elevators during the 19th century made it practical to build skyscrapers. The first skyscrapers appeared in Chicago, Illinois, in the 1880s. Today, skyscrapers are built as offices and as apartment buildings.

Steel
Following the invention of reinforced steel, tall structures could be built for the first time. An internal steel skeleton supports the weight of a skyscraper, such as the 102 stories of the Empire State Building.

Empire State Building, New York, 1931

Very plain decoration

Limestone and granite facing

Le Corbusier
Le Corbusier was the name used by Swiss-French Charles-Édouard Jeanneret (1887–1965), the most influential 20th-century architect. Le Corbusier promoted the use of new materials and construction techniques. His most innovative designs used plain, often severe, geometric forms.

Proposed design

Architects
An architect designs a building and oversees its construction. Successful architects become very well-known. Until recently, architects drafted their building plans, called blueprints, by hand. Much of this work is now carried out on computer.

Timeline

2650 BC The Step Pyramid in Egypt is designed.

c.300 BC Buddhist temple mounds appear in India.

AD 82 Colosseum built in Rome. Dozens of stone arches support the walls of this arena.

690–850 Early Islamic buildings are designed around courtyards.

1100–1500 Europe: Gothic churches built.

c.1420 Renaissance begins in Italy; architects return to the elegant, ordered values of Classical builders.

19th century Industrial Revolution: mass-produced materials transform construction.

1920s International Modernism begins, typified by glass-and-steel towers and flat-roofed, white houses.

1970s Postmodernism develops. It refers to past styles, in a humorous way. Strong colors are popular.

1990s Eco-friendly architecture reflects environmental concerns about energy-saving and recycling.

FIND OUT MORE

BUILDING AND CONSTRUCTION

CHURCHES AND CATHEDRALS

CITIES AND TOWNS

MOSQUES

Architecture
Gothic, Renaissance, and Baroque

Magnificent Gothic cathedral

Notre Dame, Paris, France, built from 1163 to 1250

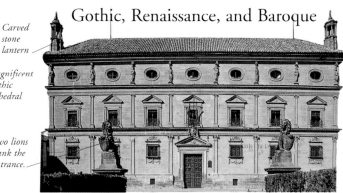

Carved stone lantern

Two lions flank the entrance.

Palacio de las Cadenas, Ubeda, Spain: built during the mid-16th century. The Classical facade shows the elegance of Renaissance buildings.

St. Paul's Cathedral, London, Britain: built in the Baroque style

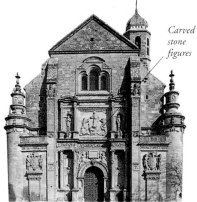

Carved stone figures

Capilla del Salvador, Ubeda, Spain: one of Spain's finest Renaissance churches, it was designed by three 16th-century architects.

Ribbed dome designed by Michelangelo

Facade by Carlo Maderno (c.1556–1629)

St. Peter's, Rome, Italy, took 108 years to build (1506–1614). It involved all the great architects of the Roman Renaissance and Baroque, including Michelangelo Buonarroti (1475–1564).

135 spires crown the roof

Milan Cathedral, Italy, is one of the largest Gothic churches in the world. Building began in the 14th century, but was not completed for 500 years.

Modern architecture

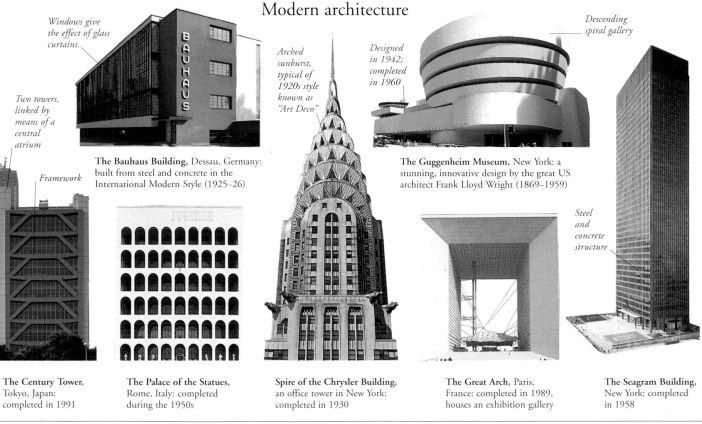

Windows give the effect of glass curtains.

The Bauhaus Building, Dessau, Germany: built from steel and concrete in the International Modern Style (1925–26)

Two towers, linked by means of a central atrium

Framework

Arched sunburst, typical of 1920s style known as "Art Deco"

Designed in 1942; completed in 1960

Descending spiral gallery

The Guggenheim Museum, New York: a stunning, innovative design by the great US architect Frank Lloyd Wright (1869–1959)

Steel and concrete structure

The Century Tower, Tokyo, Japan: completed in 1991

The Palace of the Statues, Rome, Italy: completed during the 1950s

Spire of the Chrysler Building, an office tower in New York: completed in 1930

The Great Arch, Paris, France: completed in 1989, houses an exhibition gallery

The Seagram Building, New York: completed in 1958

ARCTIC OCEAN

ONE OF THE COLDEST places on Earth, the Arctic Ocean is surrounded by the northern parts of Europe, Asia, North America, and Greenland. These icy lands are rich in minerals and wildlife, but are home to few people. In summer, when temperatures reach 32°F (0°C), warm currents from the Pacific and Atlantic melt some of the ice. With the help of icebreakers to clear their path, ships are able to sail along the coasts of Asia and North America.

Physical features

The Arctic is the smallest and shallowest of the world's oceans. Much of its surface is covered by a frozen mass of floating ice about 6 ft (2 m) thick. The north pole lies in the center of the ocean on drifting pack ice.

ARCTIC OCEAN FACTS

AREA	5,440,000 sq miles (14,089,600 sq km)
AVERAGE DEPTH	4,360 ft (1,330 m)
AVERAGE ICE THICKNESS	4.9–9.8 ft (1.5–3 m)
LOWEST TEMPERATURE	-94°F (-70°C) on northeastern tip of Greenland

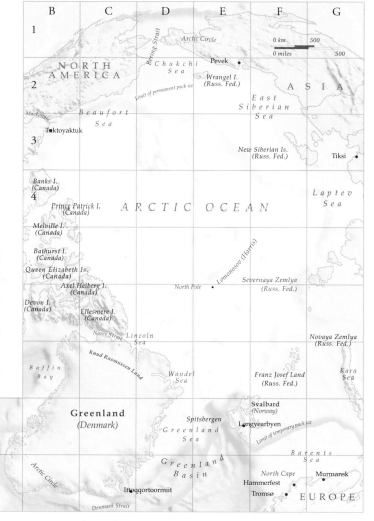

Icebergs
Giant icebergs break off glaciers in Greenland and drift south into the North Atlantic Ocean. They rise up to 400 ft (120 m) above sea level. As only a fraction of an iceberg shows above water, they are a shipping hazard.

Northern lights
On dark nights, spectacular colored lights, or Aurora, can be seen in the sky. Caused by electricity in the upper atmosphere, they are brightest in mid-winter when the sun never rises and invisible in summer when it does not set.

Arctic peoples
About 800,000 indigenous people live in the Arctic. The Yu'pik of Alaska are part of the Eskimo group that includes Inuit in Canada and Greenland, and Yuit in Siberia. Many have given up nomadic life and live in villages. The Arctic is the workplace of 2,000,000 engineers and traders from the south.

Yu'pik family from Alaska

Greenland

Although Greenland is the world's largest island, its permanent ice cover means few people live there. Most people live on the southwestern coast, where the climate is less extreme than the bleak center. The island is a self-governing territory of Denmark.

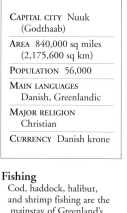

Halibut

Haddock

Cod

GREENLAND FACTS

CAPITAL CITY	Nuuk (Godthaab)
AREA	840,000 sq miles (2,175,600 sq km)
POPULATION	56,000
MAIN LANGUAGES	Danish, Greenlandic
MAJOR RELIGION	Christian
CURRENCY	Danish krone

Fishing
Cod, haddock, halibut, and shrimp fishing are the mainstay of Greenland's economy. Fish-processing factories freeze and can the fish for export to Europe and the US. Much of the cod is made into fish sticks.

FIND OUT MORE   ATMOSPHERE   CLIMATE   FISHING INDUSTRY   GLACIATION   NATIVE AMERICANS   OCEANS AND SEAS   POLAR EXPLORATION   POLAR WILDLIFE   TUNDRA

ARGENTINA, CHILE, AND URUGUAY

THE SOUTHERN PART of South America is occupied by three countries: Argentina, Chile, and Uruguay. Lying between the Pacific and Atlantic Oceans, South America's southernmost point, Cape Horn, is only about 640 miles (1,000 km) from the northern tip of Antarctica. Once part of the Spanish Empire, all three countries still show strong European influences. Their vast mineral resources have resulted in some prosperity, but all have agricultural economies and have suffered under a series of unstable governments.

Physical features

Dominating the west of the region, running north to south, the Andes Mountains form a rugged frontier between Chile and Argentina. The hot, humid land of the Gran Chaco covers the northeast, turning to rolling grassland, known as pampas, in the center. South of this and the arid plateau of Patagonia, lie the windy islands of Tierra del Fuego.

Andes

Forming a barrier between Chile and its eastern neighbors, Bolivia and Argentina, the vast Andes mountain chain stretches for about 5,000 miles (8,000 km). Nearly half of its mighty snowcapped peaks lie along Chile's long eastern border with Argentina, including Mount Aconcagua, an extinct volcano, which, at 22,835 ft (6,960 m), is the highest peak in South America.

Atacama Desert

The hot Atacama Desert is one of the world's driest places. It covers the northern 600 miles (965 km) of Chile's long coastal strip and receives less than ½ in (13 mm) of rain in a year. By contrast, the Patagonian Desert, in the far south of Argentina near Antarctica, is a vast, icy-cold expanse of windswept rocks.

Pampas

Also known as the Entre Rios, the vast natural grasslands of the pampas cover about 20 percent of Argentina and extend north into Uruguay, where three-quarters of the land is rich pasture. Much of the pampas has hot summers, warm winters, plenty of rain, and deep, fertile soil, making the area ideal for growing crops and for raising cattle and sheep.

Mestizos

More than three-quarters of the people in this region are descended from Europeans, most of whom moved from Spain or Italy in the 20th century. Many Europeans intermarried with Native Americans, giving rise to *mestizos*, people of mixed ancestry. Like their ancestors, most people are Roman Catholic and are close to their extended families. Many of them run successful businesses.

Man and child at an Easter festival

48°F (9°C)   70°F (21°C)

30 in (762 mm)

Regional climate

Chile's long, narrow shape gives it an extremely varied climate. Desert and mountains in the north give way to fertile valleys, with hot, dry summers and mild, moist winters. Argentina's southern Andean peaks and Patagonian glaciers have year-round snow; the north is hotter and wetter. Uruguay is mild and pleasant.

Argentina

After Brazil, Argentina is the second largest country in South America. It is separated from Uruguay by the Río de la Plata estuary, on which its capital, Buenos Aires, stands. Argentina is one of the wealthiest countries in South America, with fertile soil, a wealth of mineral resources, and a skilled workforce. However, years of political instability and poor leadership have left a huge overseas debt for the new democratic government to clear.

Couple dancing the tango

People

More than 88 percent of Argentina's people live in towns and cities and most enjoy a high standard of living. However, city slums, or *orillas*, illustrate the sharp contrast between the country's rich and poor. It was in the slums that the tango, the traditional dance of Buenos Aires, originated, in the late 1800s. Many tangos contain lyrics that express the frustrations of the immigrants who came from Spain, Italy, Austria, France, Germany, and Britain. The tango is now danced worldwide.

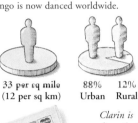

| 33 per sq mile (12 per sq km) | 88% Urban | 12% Rural |

Buenos Aires

Situated on the South Atlantic coast, Argentina's capital has been an important trade port since it was founded by the Spanish in 1536. Buenos Aires is a wealthy, sophisticated city, with expensive shops, fine avenues, and modern buildings, as well as a spectacular old cathedral. The city is the center of government, industry, and culture. Almost 40 percent of Argentinians, numbering about 11,256,000, live in the metropolitan capital, referred to as "Baires."

Government buildings

Clarin is Argentina's best-selling newspaper.

Food

High-quality beef, which is produced throughout Argentina, is used as a base for many local dishes, such as *empanadas*, or savory mince pies. Every restaurant has a barbecue grill, or *parillada*. As a cheaper alternative to meat, many people eat small potato dumplings called *noquis*, which were introduced by Italian immigrants.

Noquis

Newspapers

More than 200 daily newspapers are published every day in Argentina. Most are in Spanish, but English, French, and German papers are widely available. In the past, dictatorships have imposed censorship on the media, and today's government withdraws advertising from those that do not support its policies.

Farming

Agriculture accounts for about 60 percent of Argentina's export earnings. The country is a major producer of wheat, barley, and corn, which flourish on the pampas, and is the world's third largest producer of soybeans. Fruit, especially oranges, grows well in the warm climate, and grapes are produced for wine-making.

Harvesting barley on the fertile pampas

Gauchos

Tough, independent gauchos, or cowhands, have roamed the pampas on horseback for more than 300 years, tending cattle and horses. Modern gauchos work mainly on huge *estancias*, or ranches, owned by wealthy landlords, where they rear animals and mend fences. Gauchos are experts in handling herds and are the national heroes of Argentina.

Bolas rope used to slow down cattle

Wool poncho, or cloak, for warmth at night

Strong boots have heels to fit into stirrups.

Industry

About 30 percent of the labor force works in industry. Textiles, food production, and chemical products dominate business. The country is self-sufficient in oil and gas, and rich in minerals.

Falkland Islands

Britain and Argentina have fought over ownership of the Falkland Islands, or Islas Malvinas, since the British claimed the islands from the Spanish in 1833. In 1982, an Argentine invasion of the islands was overthrown, and the British continue to hold them.

Schooling

Literacy is high in Argentina, and free state primary and secondary education is provided. Schooling is compulsory for all children between the ages of six and 14, and more than one-third of all students go on to one of Argentina's 45 universities. Buenos Aires has the largest university in South America, with 140,000 students.

These women work in a fish-packing plant and must wear hats for hygiene.

The Falkland Islands lie 300 miles (480 km) east of Argentina.

Chile

A long and extremely narrow country, Chile measures, at most, only about 267 miles (430 km) wide. Most Chileans live in cities and towns in the Central Valley between the low coastal mountains on the west and the towering Andes on the east. The cold, stormy southern coast is flanked by thousands of islands. The waters provide rich fishing grounds. Chile has a strong economy rooted in its natural resources: minerals, fruit, sea products, and timber.

Santiago

Located in the heart of Chile, the capital, Santiago, is a bustling, modern city. The city and suburbs house about five million people. Santiago is known for severe traffic congestion, and has one of the highest taxi densities in the world, with one per 100 inhabitants. About 2,236 miles (3,600 km) of the Pan-American Highway run through Santiago, but high smog levels over the city concern environmentalists.

Some of Santiago's 14,500 buses on Avenue Campama

Mapuche Indians

Descended from the original inhabitants of South America, the Mapuche Indians are also known as the Araucanians. About 800,000 Mapuche Indians live in reservations in the south of Chile, which were established during the 1880s. They are Roman Catholics and speak their own language as well as Spanish. The Mapuche people have fought for independence since the 16th century and are still at odds with the Chilean government. Quechua and Aymara Indians also live in Chile, in the north.

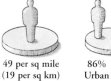

49 per sq mile (19 per sq km)

86% Urban   14% Rural

Copper

Chile leads the world in the production of copper ore, of which it owns about 20 percent of known reserves. The Central Valley, which extends for 994 miles (1,600 km), has the world's largest underground copper mine, located at El Teniente. Chuquicamata, in the bleak Atacama Desert, is one of the largest opencast copper mines in the world. The country also mines iron, gold, and silver.

The Chuquicamata copper mine, 2,200 ft (670 m) deep

Wine

Vineyards first planted by Spanish colonists in the 1500s have benefited from the hot, dry summers in the Central Valley. Today, about 350,000 tons (320,000 tonnes) of Chilean wines, red from Cabernet Sauvignon grapes and white from Chardonnay grapes, are exported all over the world.

Cabernet Sauvignon grapes and wine

ECHEVERRIA
RESERVA 1992
CABERNET SAUVIGNON
MOLINA - CHILE

Crabs are put into small baskets.

Fishing

Although less than one percent of the people work in the fishing industry, Chile is fourth in world fish production. An average 6,502 tons of sardines, anchovies, mackerel, and salmon are caught and processed each year. Punta Arenas, on the Strait of Magellan, is the industry's center.

CHILE FACTS

CAPITAL CITY Santiago

AREA 292,258 sq miles (756,950 sq km)

POPULATION 14,436,000

MAIN LANGUAGE Spanish

MAJOR RELIGION Christian

CURRENCY Chilean peso

LIFE EXPECTANCY 72 years

PEOPLE PER DOCTOR 943

GOVERNMENT Multiparty democracy

ADULT LITERACY 94%

Uruguay

One of the smallest countries in South America, Uruguay is also one of the most prosperous and harmonious. More than 40 percent of its people, about 1,348,000, live in Montevideo, the capital, chief port, and largest city. The rest are scattered over the vast lowland pastures. Uruguay has a high tourist rate, mainly because of its sandy beaches and fine weather.

People

There are 11 times as many sheep, cattle, and horses as people in Uruguay. Most Uruguayans are of Spanish or Italian descent, enjoying considerable prosperity, largely due to the wealth from earlier cattle ranching in the country.

Hydroelectricity

More than 86 percent of Uruguay's power is generated through hydroelectricity. The main hydroelectric plants are situated on the country's major rivers, the Uruguay and its tributary, the Río Negro, which both widen into the Río de la Plata estuary. Huge turbines have been built across the rivers, so that as the water rushes through, it turns the turbines and makes electricity.

URUGUAY FACTS

CAPITAL CITY Montevideo

AREA 68,498 sq miles (177,410 sq km)

POPULATION 3,240,000

MAIN LANGUAGE Spanish

MAJOR RELIGION Christian

CURRENCY Uruguayan peso

Wool

Three-quarters of Uruguay is rich pasture that provides excellent grazing land for its 25,000,000 sheep and 10,000,000 cattle. The land provides work for nearly half the population. Uruguay is one of the world's top ten wool producers and textiles made from wool account for about 20 percent of the country's exports.

Handmade scarf

FIND OUT MORE — CHRISTIANITY — DANCE — DESERTS — ENERGY — FARMING — GRASSLAND WILDLIFE — NATIVE AMERICANS — SOUTH AMERICA, HISTORY OF — TEXTILES AND WEAVING

ARMIES

FROM ANCIENT TIMES to the present day, the role of an army has always remained the same – to attack enemy territory and defend the country from attack. Armies usually work in close partnership with air and naval forces. Throughout history, foot soldiers called infantry have done most of the fighting, supported by troops on horseback called cavalry. Today, cavalry have been replaced on the battlefield by armored tank units.

Ancient Greece
Each Greek city-state had its own army. Greek soldiers were so well regarded that other countries hired them to fight on their behalf.

History of armies
The world's first armies, raised in Assyria, Egypt, China, and India, were poorly trained civilians forced to fight for their leaders. The ancient Greeks introduced compulsory military service and rigorous training for their civilian army. Later, the Romans established the first professional (paid) army to protect its empire.

The modern army
Combat troops fighting in the front line need plenty of support. Engineers, for example, repair damaged roads and bridges to help troops cross rough terrain. Other support staff includes doctors and nurses to treat wounded soldiers, cooks to feed the army, and communications experts.

British SAS personal equipment

Gas mask

Knife sheath

Balaclava

SAS survival kit

Miniature harpoons

Wire saw

Steel fire lighter

Fire-kindling tin

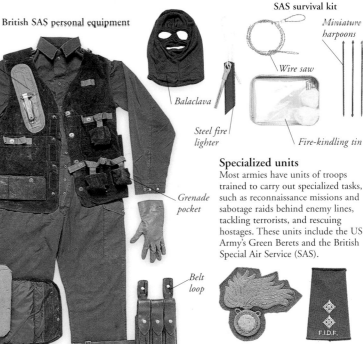

Leather glove

Body armor

Grenade pocket

Belt loop

Magazine pouch

Thigh strap

Leather boots

Reinforced toe cap

Recruitment
In some countries, the army is made up entirely of volunteer recruits who willingly join the army for a fixed period of time. In other countries, the army is made up largely of conscripts – that is, young people required by law to spend a number of years in the army.

British Army recruitment poster

Training
Modern weapons use advanced technology, so troops need to be not just physically fit but also able to make split-second decisions and operate highly complex computerized equipment. For this reason, technical instruction is just as important a part of a soldier's training as exercise and marching drills.

Specialized units
Most armies have units of troops trained to carry out specialized tasks, such as reconnaissance missions and sabotage raids behind enemy lines, tackling terrorists, and rescuing hostages. These units include the US Army's Green Berets and the British Special Air Service (SAS).

British officer's shoulder strap   **Italian officer's cap badge**

Officers
An army needs a strong chain of command, from the highest to the lowest ranks, so that orders are passed on quickly and clearly. Officers receive training in leading and inspiring their troops. Officers' ranks are shown by special symbols on their uniforms.

Terrorist armies
Sometimes armies are set up by groups of people struggling to overthrow the existing government or achieve independence for their country or region. Their supporters call them freedom fighters, but those who oppose them call them terrorists. Such groups often stage spectacular bomb attacks to gain publicity for their cause.

Terrorist bomb damage

Noncombat roles
When a nation is at peace, its army still has a vital role to play. For example, when natural disasters occur – such as earthquakes, floods, or famines – an army can bring in medical supplies and food, and restore communications links and electricity and water supplies. Armies can also help establish peace in other war-torn countries.

Peacekeeping
To separate warring sides in a civil war or to keep the peace once a ceasefire has been negotiated, the United Nations (UN) often sends multinational forces consisting of troops from many different armies.

Crisis response
Armies need to react quickly and efficiently in times of crisis. Huge cargo planes carry supplies, trucks, and even small tanks to the crisis area, while passenger planes take troops and other personnel.

FIND OUT MORE   ARMS AND ARMOR   COLD WAR   FEUDALISM   GREECE, ANCIENT   KNIGHTS AND HERALDRY   ROMAN EMPIRE   UNITED NATIONS   WARFARE   WARPLANES   WARSHIPS   WEAPONS

ARMS AND ARMOR

WARRIORS OF THE PAST attacked with slashing swords, sharp spears, flying arrows, deadly axes, and crushing clubs. All of these arms, or weapons, could kill, so fighters protected themselves with armor: tough coverings of wood, leather, or metal. The invention of firearms in the 14th century made armor useless, because metal plates thick enough to deflect bullets were too heavy to wear. By the 16th century, arms and armor were strictly for show. Modern soldiers may still wear shiny breastplates and carry swords or spears on parade, but they swap them for guns and bulletproof vests on the battlefield.

Armor

A suit of armor had to protect against weapons, yet also had to be comfortable enough to wear all day. Different cultures used various materials, such as leather or metal, to achieve these goals.

Horns
Iron mask

Samurai, 1300s

Pauldron and besagew protect shoulder and armpit.
Bevor protects lower face.

Japanese samurai
Samurai armor was made of many small metal or leather scales laced together with silk ties. Armor became more decorative when firearms removed its protective value.

European knight
Knights wore chain mail (linked metal rings) to protect them. In the 14th century, armorers introduced metal plates (plate armor) for extra protection.

A mace was effective against plate armor.

European knight, 1300s

Arms

The simplest arms – clubs – are extensions of a fighter's fist, delivering a knock-out punch from a greater distance. Most hand arms, however, aim to wound by cutting the body. Swords, daggers, and lances do this for hand-to-hand combat; arrows and boomerangs do it from a distance, killing or injuring foes that may be out of sight.

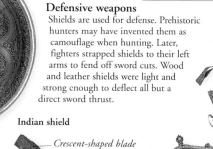

Benin warrior
Soldiers of this great 15th-century African empire wore heavily quilted garments as armor. Light bamboo shields were easy to carry and protected warriors from glancing blows from iron-tipped spears or javelins.

Benin bronze plaque

Four circular bosses covered the handle attachment.

Defensive weapons
Shields are used for defense. Prehistoric hunters may have invented them as camouflage when hunting. Later, fighters strapped shields to their left arms to fend off sword cuts. Wood and leather shields were light and strong enough to deflect all but a direct sword thrust.

Indian shield

Boomerang
Parrying shield
Crescent-shaped blade

Tiger heads studded with gems

Tabars, Indian steel axes

Mughal dagger

Sheath

Attacking weapons
Over the centuries, warriors have used various weapons for different kinds of fighting. Sabers (curved swords) delivered the deadliest cuts, but straight swords were better for thrusting strokes. Clubs and axes had to be heavy and sharp, yet short enough to swing easily. Small, easily hidden daggers were often used for secret assassinations.

Aboriginal weapons
Club
Shamshir, a classic Indian saber

Full armor for a horse weighed 75 lbs (34 kg).
Spike

Italian horse armor, 1570

Tassels on headpiece protected the horse's face from flies.
Gilt

Charm made of copper bells

Leather saddle

Animal armor
African horse armor, such as that of the Fulani people of West Africa, was quilted cotton stuffed with kapok. During battle, horses also wore chain mail across the flanks and around the head. In Europe, metal horse armor was expensive, and knights often armored only their horses' heads.

Fulani horse armor

Modern armor
Artificial fabric, such as nylon, provides soldiers and police officers with more protection than thick metal armor. Bulletproof vests are made of 16 or more layers of nylon. A bullet flattens when it hits the outer layer; lower layers slow it down so that the wearer is bruised, rather than killed or seriously injured.

Riot police

| FIND OUT MORE | ABORIGINAL AUSTRALIANS | BENIN EMPIRE | EUROPE, HISTORY OF | GUNS | INDIA, HISTORY OF | JAPAN, HISTORY OF | METALS | WARFARE | WEAPONS |

Arms and Armor
Helmets

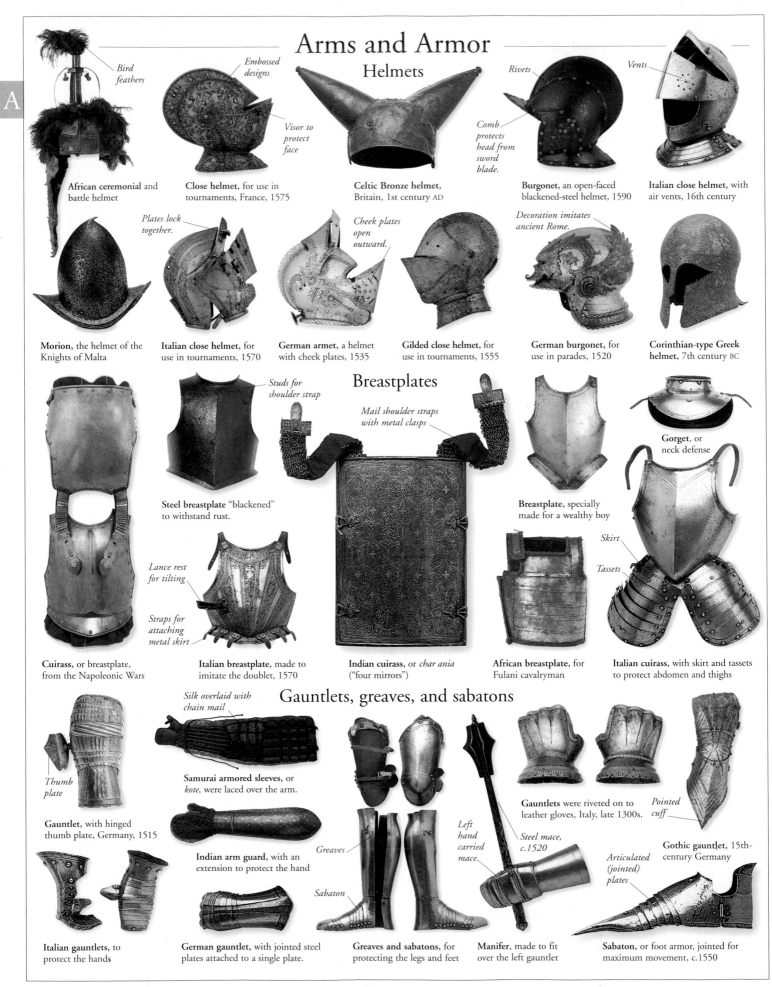

Bird feathers

African ceremonial and battle helmet

Embossed designs

Visor to protect face

Close helmet, for use in tournaments, France, 1575

Celtic Bronze helmet, Britain, 1st century AD

Rivets

Comb protects head from sword blade.

Burgonet, an open-faced blackened-steel helmet, 1590

Vents

Italian close helmet, with air vents, 16th century

Plates lock together.

Morion, the helmet of the Knights of Malta

Italian close helmet, for use in tournaments, 1570

Cheek plates open outward.

German armet, a helmet with cheek plates, 1535

Gilded close helmet, for use in tournaments, 1555

Decoration imitates ancient Rome.

German burgonet, for use in parades, 1520

Corinthian-type Greek helmet, 7th century BC

Breastplates

Studs for shoulder strap

Mail shoulder straps with metal clasps

Steel breastplate "blackened" to withstand rust.

Gorget, or neck defense

Lance rest for tilting

Straps for attaching metal skirt

Cuirass, or breastplate, from the Napoleonic Wars

Italian breastplate, made to imitate the doublet, 1570

Indian cuirass, or *char ania* ("four mirrors")

Breastplate, specially made for a wealthy boy

African breastplate, for Fulani cavalryman

Skirt

Tassets

Italian cuirass, with skirt and tassets to protect abdomen and thighs

Gauntlets, greaves, and sabatons

Silk overlaid with chain mail

Thumb plate

Gauntlet, with hinged thumb plate, Germany, 1515

Samurai armored sleeves, or *kote*, were laced over the arm.

Indian arm guard, with an extension to protect the hand

Greaves

Sabaton

Left hand carried mace.

Steel mace, c.1520

Gauntlets were riveted on to leather gloves, Italy, late 1300s.

Pointed cuff

Articulated (jointed) plates

Gothic gauntlet, 15th-century Germany

Italian gauntlets, to protect the hands

German gauntlet, with jointed steel plates attached to a single plate.

Greaves and sabatons, for protecting the legs and feet

Manifer, made to fit over the left gauntlet

Sabaton, or foot armor, jointed for maximum movement, c.1550

ART, HISTORY OF

FROM THE EARLIEST TIMES, people have tried to express their thoughts, feelings, and understanding of the world around them by creating art. Over the centuries, styles in the visual arts (sculpture, painting, and drawing) have changed. These differences reflect the changing beliefs and traditions people held as their societies developed. Materials have changed as well, allowing artists to try new ways of reflecting the world around them.

Early art

The earliest works of art seem to have had a religious or magical purpose: to represent a god, for example, or to bring a hunter luck as he hunted animals.

Sumerian sculpture
A rich artistic tradition grew up in ancient Sumer (now southern Iraq) during the 3rd millennium BC. This statue, which shows a Sumerian ruler, is carved from stone. It represents the strength and dignity of a good leader.

Caves at Lascaux
These extraordinary pictures of wild animals were painted in French caves more than 17,000 years ago. The outlines were painted by hand and the vivid colors were filled in by spraying pigment through tubes of bone.

Classical art

Western art derives from the traditions of the ancient Mediterranean world and especially the art of ancient Greece and Rome. Sculpture from these civilizations is remarkably lifelike, or naturalistic, and concentrates on the human figure.

Fresco from Pompeii

Roman wall painting
Most ancient paintings have not survived. This one was preserved by volcanic ash at Pompeii. It shows figures from Roman mythology, and was painted on a wall to decorate the interior of a Roman house.

Hermes and Dionysus, 4th century BC

Hermes and Dionysus
This Greek marble statue shows the messenger god, Hermes, holding a baby Dionysus, the god of wine. The work displays a sure knowledge of human anatomy, such as the structure of bone and muscle. It also represents the human body as an ideal form, at its peak of physical beauty. It is believed to be by Praxiteles, the most famous ancient Greek sculptor.

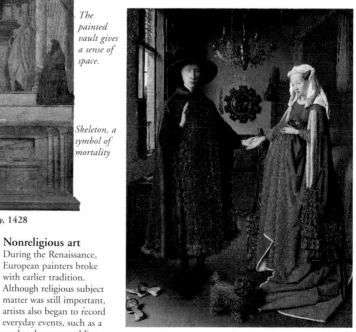

Masaccio, *The Holy Trinity*, 1428

Perspective
The Italian Tomaso Masaccio (1401–28) was the first painter to use perspective since classical times. Perspective creates the illusion that depth exists behind the flat surface of a painting.

Nonreligious art
During the Renaissance, European painters broke with earlier tradition. Although religious subject matter was still important, artists also began to record everyday events, such as a market day or a wedding.

The Renaissance

After the fall of the Roman Empire, classical art was considered too pagan for the Christian civilizations that developed in Europe. By the 15th century, painters, sculptors, and architects began to revive the classical tradition, creating highly lifelike works of art. This revival is called the Renaissance, from the French for "rebirth." It began in Italy and spread through Europe. Influential artists included the painter and sculptor Michelangelo (1475–1564).

The painted vault gives a sense of space.

Skeleton, a symbol of mortality

Jan Van Eyck, *The Arnolfini Marriage*, 1434

Early paint making

The materials used to produce a painting affect the way it looks. Before the 15th century, artists painted on wet plaster with tempera, a mixture of egg and paint pigment. Oil paints arrived in the 15th century. They were more flexible and gave a more realistic finish, so they soon became the favorite medium.

Mineral, ground into pigment

Egg tempera
Egg (either the yolk or both yolk and white) provides a strong medium for colors, but is quick-drying, making it difficult to apply.

Egg yolk

Oil paint
As a medium, oil has the advantage of being slow to dry, allowing artists to make changes while they work.

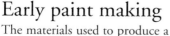

Oil for binding paint pigment

Value of color
Certain colors, such as gold, have always been more expensive than others. Until the 17th century, dark blue was the most costly because it was made from lapis lazuli, a semiprecious stone.

Lapis lazuli

Scales weigh the pigment.

A

A

Baroque art

The term "Baroque" describes a style of 17th-century European art. Rome, the centre of the Catholic church, was its birthplace. During the 16th century, the Christian church split into Roman Catholic and Protestant factions. By the 17th century, the Catholic church was using art to spread its teachings. To appeal to the viewer, it promoted a style of art that was theatrical and emotional. Painters were encouraged to use light and shade for dramatic contrasts, sculptors to show figures in dynamic poses. To achieve these effects, artists had to develop great technical skills.

Dramatic facial expression

Arrow is a symbol of God's love.

Bernini
The Italian painter, sculptor, and architect Gianlorenzo Bernini (1598–1680) was an outstanding influence on Baroque art. He had an exceptional ability to convey great emotion and drama in stone, designed to inspire those who saw his work to greater faith. This sculpture depicts the vision of St. Teresa, in which an angel pierced her with an arrow.

Bernini, *The Ecstasy of St. Teresa*, 1652

Caravaggio, *The Calling of St. Matthew*, c.1598–99

Light and shade
The Italian painter Michelangelo Caravaggio (1573–1610) shows the moment when Christ calls Matthew to become a disciple. A ray of light illuminates Matthew but Christ is hidden by shadow.

Friedrich, *Wanderer among the Mists, 1818*

The lonely universe
The German artist Caspar David Friedrich (1774–1840) was spiritually inspired by natural landscapes. There is an intense mysticism to this painting, as a solitary figure contemplates the mighty Alps.

Romanticism

The early 19th century in Europe is known as the Romantic Age. It was in part a reaction to 18th-century art, which had emphasized balance and order. Romantic artists questioned the place of human beings in the Universe. They stressed the importance of human emotion and the imagination, and celebrated the wild power of nature in dramatic landscape paintings.

A powerful landscape, shrouded in mist, conveys the strength and mystery of nature.

Change in the 19th century

From the mid-19th century, artists broke with the tradition established by earlier generations. Where they were once told what to depict by patrons who paid them, they now produced what they wanted, and then tried to sell their work.

Camille Pissarro, *Place du Théâtre Français*, 1898

Selection of colors from Renoir's palette

Lead white *Vermilion* *Emerald green* *Naples yellow* *Cobalt blue*

Impressionism
This school of painting grew up in France in the late 19th century. Artists such as Camille Pissarro (1830–1903), Claude Monet (1840–1926), and Auguste Renoir (1841–1919) painted their impressions of a brief moment in time, in particular, the changing effects of sunlight. They were criticised at first, for viewers expected paintings to look more realistic, but have been very influential.

20th-century art

During the 20th century, artists explored new theories about the world, religion, and the mind. They asked the public to confront things that they might wish to ignore, and explored many different styles. After nearly 2,500 years, the grip of Classical art seemed to have been broken.

Surrealism
During the 1920s, the fantastical art made by the Surrealists explored theories about the way the brain works. New ideas had suggested that people consciously used only a tiny part of their brains, and that they were unaware of subconscious activity over which they had no rational control. The bizarre, dreamlike paintings of Surrealists, such as the Spanish artist Salvador Dali (1904–89), were inspired by these ideas.

Salvador Dali

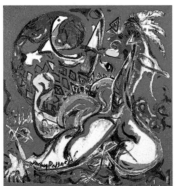

Modern art
Much modern art is specially created to be seen in a museum or gallery, and not for houses, palaces, or churches as in the past. It often prefers to baffle, tease, and provoke its audience rather than make its meaning obvious.

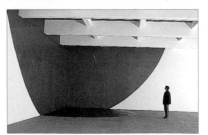
Yoki Terauchi, *Air Castle*, 1994

Abstract art
Abstract artists do not represent objects as we see them every day. Color and shape alone suggest ideas or emotions. In this way, abstract art is like music: neither describe anything that can be defined in words, but both can be expressive and moving. The artists Jackson Pollock (1912–56) and Mark Rothko (1903–70) are two of the most famous abstract painters.

Jackson Pollock, *The Moon, Woman Cuts the Circle*, 1943

Ambroise Vollard

The French art dealer Ambroise Vollard (1865–1939) made a living buying, selling, and exhibiting modern art. He gave early 20th-century artists unprecedented financial and creative freedom to paint as they wished. Artists such as Paul Cezanne and Henri Matisse achieved success in Vollard's gallery in Paris in the 1900s.

Art in Africa

African art has a long tradition, although a lack of written records make its history hard to trace. Sculpture and masks are major art forms. Most art seems to have been made for religious or ritual purposes. Wood-carving and bronze-casting techniques were highly developed.

Sculpture

The rich tradition of sculpture in West Africa begins with the pottery figures made by the Nok people from 500 BC. Around the 13th century AD, the Ife of Nigeria began to cast outstanding bronze heads and figures in a highly realistic style. These may have influenced sculptures made in Benin, Nigeria, from the 16th to 19th centuries.

Ife sculpture, 13th century

Masks

African masks may represent a spirit or ancestor, or be purely decorative. Their meaning comes from the masquerade (dance, drama, and music) of which they are a part. Wood, beads, ivory, and shells are important materials. This capped mask, carved in a bold, vital style, is from Cameroon.

Wooden mask, 20th century

Asia

Traditionally in Asian art the symbolic meaning behind the subject of a painting, sculpture, or carving is more important than the illusion of realism. In China, for instance, landscape paintings are stylized to express the ideals of religious thought: natural harmony, peace, and grace. In China and Japan, calligraphy was seen as a high form of art. The inscriptions are usually of short, poetic situations.

Brief poetic description of the scene

T'ang Yin, Dreaming of Immortality in a Thatched Cottage, Ming dynasty

Chinese landscape

In China the art of painting developed from calligraphy. Landscape artists painted on paper or silk, using brush and ink. They did not paint from real life. The flow and vigor of the brush strokes were more important.

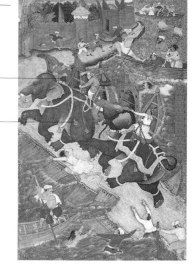

16th-century Mughal manuscript

Vividly colored

High level of detail

Miniatures

During the Mughal Empire (16th–17th centuries), figurative miniature painting flourished in India. These artworks were richly colored and exceptionally delicate. This illustration comes from a chronicle of the emperor's exploits.

Hokusai

Katsushika Hokusai (1760–1849) is perhaps the best-known Japanese printmaker. His famous wood-cuts include landscapes as well as scenes of daily life (called *ukiyo-e*). They are dramatically colored and composed.

The Great Wave of Kawagawa, 1831

Native American art

Sophisticated Native American societies, such as the Aztec and Maya in Mexico and the Inca in Peru, created distinct artistic and architectural styles. Nearly 3,000 years ago, nomadic peoples in North and South America marked awe-inspiring "sculptures" on to the land, or created vast earthworks whose shapes can only be seen from high in the air.

Tlingit totem pole

Totem poles

Complex in design, and carved with great skill, totem poles showed the status of many Native North American chiefs.

Sand paintings

In the Southwest, Native North Americans trickled colored sand and ground stones on to a smooth background to create temporary symbolic paintings with a ritual importance.

Navajo sand painting shows mythological figures.

Easter Island statues

Between AD 400 and 1680, the people of Easter Island carved huge heads, up to 40 ft (12 m) high, from volcanic rock. They commemorate the divine ancestors of tribal chiefs.

Pacific art

Contact with European Christian cultures from the 18th century onward had a destructive effect on ancient local lifestyles in the Pacific islands. Much art has been lost, although some remarkable sculptures have survived, because of their durability. Wood and stone carvings, bark cloth paintings, spirit masks, and intricate body tattoos are among the important art forms of the Pacific area.

Statues face out to sea.

Statues, Easter Island

Timeline

30,000 BC Earliest known works of art produced.

30,000–10,000 BC Cave paintings made in France.

c.500 BC Lifelike human figurines produced by the Nok in West Africa.

100 BC–AD 300s Roman Empire spreads Classical art around Europe.

Warrior, Greece, 520 BC

618–907 T'ang dynasty, China: great tradition of landscape painting develops.

15th century Beginning of the Renaissance in Europe.

16th century Mughal dynasty holds power in India.

17th century Dutch Golden Age of painting.

19th century Photography invented.

1860s–90s Impressionism develops in France. It is very influential.

Metal tubes are invented in the 1840s.

19th-century oil paints

20th century Time of incredible diversity of styles in the visual arts, including Cubism (1907–20s), abstract art (1910–50), surrealism (1920s), and Pop Art (mid-1950s).

FIND OUT MORE   AFRICA, HISTORY OF   ARCHITECTURE   MONET   NATIVE AMERICANS   PAINTING AND DRAWING   PHOTOGRAPHY   PICASSO   RENAISSANCE   SCULPTURE

A

ARTHROPODS

MORE THAN ONE MILLION species of arthropods exist, making them the largest group in the animal kingdom. They live in almost all habitats, from mountaintops to ocean depths. Arthropods are invertebrates – animals without backbones. They come in many shapes and sizes, from tiny mites to large crabs. Their bodies are divided into segments, and they have distinct heads with antennae or eyes. Rigid exoskeletons encase their bodies, but flexible leg joints allow them to move around, and give them their name.

Types of arthropods

Arthropods vary in size, from minute creatures a fraction of an inch long to oversized sea dwellers weighing several pounds. There are four main types of arthropod – insects, arachnids, crustaceans, and myriapods. Insects are the largest group, accounting for almost 90 percent of all arthropods.

Spiders have 8 legs.

Red-kneed tarantula

Arachnids
Arachnids include spiders, scorpions, and mites. They have eight legs; scorpions use the front pair as claws. Spiders and scorpions are carnivores that live mainly on land. Spiders often kill their prey with poisonous fangs; scorpions use their venom-filled sting.

Delicate wings

Large compound eyes helps it to catch prey in flight.

Broad-bodied chaser dragonfly

Insects
Insects are the most diverse group of arthropods. They live in all kinds of land and freshwater habitats. All adult insects have six legs, and most have wings – they are the only arthropods that can fly.

Asian giant millipede

Antenna

Two pairs of legs on each body segment

Myriapods
Myriapods include millipedes and centipedes. They have more legs than other arthropods – as many as 200 in some species. Their bodies are long and tubular. They live in the soil or in piles of leaves.

European lobster

Hard exoskeleton

Crustaceans
Crustaceans include crabs, shrimps, and lobsters. Most live in the ocean or in freshwater and have five pairs of legs. Lobsters and crabs have very thick exoskeletons and some grow extremely large.

Exoskeletons are made mainly of a substance called chitin.

Exoskeleton of a fiddler crab

Exoskeleton

The exoskeleton of an arthropod is a tough outer layer covering the entire body, including the eyes, antennae, and legs. It protects and supports the muscles and soft organs within the body and helps retain moisture.

Molting and metamorphosis
Exoskeletons are fixed in size. In order to grow, an arthropod must shed, or molt, this rigid layer. Its body then rapidly expands before a new exoskeleton hardens in place of the old one. Molting is part of a process called "incomplete metamorphosis". The young, called nymphs, emerge from eggs looking like tiny adults. They molt many times before reaching adult size. In "complete metamorphosis", the animal changes form as well as size.

Molting

1 An emerging adult grasshopper has cracked open its old exoskeleton and is starting to wriggle its body free, headfirst. Before this final molt, the nymph will already have been through four previous molts.

Nymph on twig

Adult is almost free of the nymph's skin.

2 The adult has pulled its legs and most of its body out of the old skin. It is already expanding in size now that it is free from its shell.

Old, empty exoskeleton

Adult waits as blood pumps into its wings before it flies away.

3 Molting is now complete. The adult rests while its new exoskeleton hardens and its wings unfurl. Its old exoskeleton, now empty and brittle, still clings to the twig.

Reproduction
Reproduction is diverse among arthropods. Fertilization may take place inside or outside the female's body. Normally eggs are laid; some are guarded, others are hidden and left alone. The young of some arthropods, such as garden spiders, are tiny versions of adults called nymphs; others start life as larvae and look different from the adults.

Cluster of young garden spiders

Feeding

Arthropods feed on plant and animal matter, both living and dead. Some arthropods, such as praying mantises, have pincers to gather food; others use their front legs. Many have cutting and chewing teethlike structures, while those that feed on fluids, such as true bugs, have mouths modified for sucking. Small aquatic arthropods eat by filtering food particles from water.

Herbivores
Some arthropods, such as chafer beetles, eat only plant matter. Adults feed on stems, leaves, and buds, while larvae eat plant roots.

Field chafer beetle

Carnivores
Many arthropods feed on other animals. Garden spiders, for example, feed mainly on insects. Some meat eaters also eat dead animals and are called scavengers. Sand crabs scavenge on dead birds and other debris found on the beach and ocean floor.

Web spun around wasp

Garden spider feeding on a wasp

Defense

Since arthropods are generally small in size, they are the target for a great many predators. Their hard exoskeleton, which acts as a tiny suit of armor, provides the first line of defense. Some arthropods, such as pill millipedes, take a passive form of defense and roll up into a ball if danger threatens. Other arthropods have special protective weapons, including stings and pincers. Many ant species have glands on their abdomens from which they secrete formic acid to drive off enemies.

Stings and pincers
Some arthropods have pincers and stings, which they use to defend themselves against attackers. Scorpions also use their large pincers to catch animals. They then use their venom-filled stings to paralyze their prey.

Sting

Eyes

Fat-tailed scorpion

FIND OUT MORE   **ANTS AND TERMITES**   **BEETLES**   **CAVE WILDLIFE**   **CRABS AND OTHER CRUSTACEANS**   **FLIES**   **GRASSHOPPERS AND CRICKETS**   **INSECTS**   **POISONOUS ANIMALS**   **SPIDERS AND SCORPIONS**

ASIA

STRETCHING from the frozen Arctic to the equator, Asia is the world's largest continent. It is also a continent of extremes, containing the world's highest point, Mount Everest, as well as its lowest, the Dead Sea. China has the world's greatest population, while Asia's largest country, the Russian Federation, extends into Europe. Asia is separated from North America by the Bering Sea, and from Europe by the Caspian Sea, Turkey, and the Ural Mountains. In the southeast, it breaks into a mass of tiny islands.

Physical features

Much of Southwest and Central Asia is covered with barren desert, such as the Gobi and Syrian deserts. The Himalayan Mountains separate the bleak north from the fierce heat of the Indian subcontinent and the tropical rain forests of Southeast Asia. Asia has many great rivers, including the Huang He, Mekong, and Indus, flanked by fertile plains and valleys.

Lake Baikal
Siberia, the northern region of Asia, has the oldest and deepest lake in the world. At its deepest point, Lake Baikal, which contains more than 20 percent of the world's unfrozen freshwater, reaches a depth of 5,371 ft (1,637 m). Covering an area of 12,150 sq miles (31,468 sq km), Baikal is the world's eighth largest lake.

Himalayas
The snowcapped Himalaya Mountains, the highest range in the world, form a massive natural barrier between the Indian subcontinent and northern Asia. They were pushed up millions of years ago when the Indian plate collided with the Asian plate.

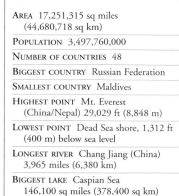

Island countries
Two Southeast Asian nations, Indonesia and the Philippines, have more than 20,000 islands between them. Most were formed by volcanic activity in the ocean, and there are several active volcanoes in the region. Southeast Asia is prone to earthquakes.

ASIA FACTS

AREA 17,251,315 sq miles (44,680,718 sq km)

POPULATION 3,497,760,000

NUMBER OF COUNTRIES 48

BIGGEST COUNTRY Russian Federation

SMALLEST COUNTRY Maldives

HIGHEST POINT Mt. Everest (China/Nepal) 29,029 ft (8,848 m)

LOWEST POINT Dead Sea shore, 1,312 ft (400 m) below sea level

LONGEST RIVER Chang Jiang (China) 3,965 miles (6,380 km)

BIGGEST LAKE Caspian Sea 146,100 sq miles (378,400 sq km)

Cross-section through Asia

From the Indian Ocean, the land rises to the Vindhya Range in northwestern India, descending to the Ganges Plain, watered by the Himalayas. In the east, the mountains drop to the Great Plain of China. Across the Yellow Sea, the Korean Peninsula juts out close to Japan in the Pacific Ocean.

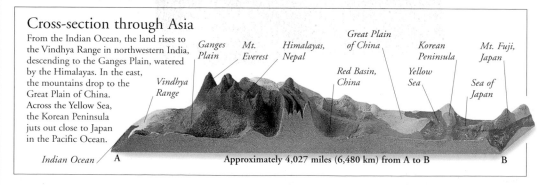

Ganges Plain — Mt. Everest — Himalayas, Nepal — Great Plain of China — Red Basin, China — Korean Peninsula — Yellow Sea — Mt. Fuji, Japan — Sea of Japan — Vindhya Range

Indian Ocean — A — Approximately 4,027 miles (6,480 km) from A to B — B

Climatic zones

Asia has every kind of climate and landscape. In the far north, Siberia is covered in tundra, where part of the ground is permanently frozen. South of the tundra are coniferous forests and open grasslands (steppes). Central and southwest Asia are mostly desert and mountains, while the east has deciduous forests. Tropical rain forests cover much of the south and southeast.

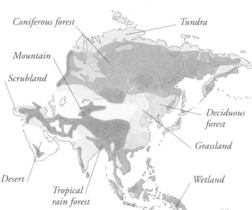

Coniferous forest
Tundra
Mountain
Scrubland
Deciduous forest
Grassland
Desert
Tropical rain forest
Wetland

Tundra

In the bitterly cold and treeless tundra region of Siberia, the subsoil remains frozen – a condition known as permafrost. With temperatures of less than 14°F (-10°C) and covered by snow for six to ten months of the year, the topsoil thaws only briefly in the summer. The tundra has rich mineral resources.

Mosses, lichens, and a few flowers appear briefly during the warmer months.

The steppes are the Asian equivalent of the pampas and prairies of the Americas.

Taiga

The Siberian taiga, which lies to the south of the tundra, is the world's largest coniferous forest. The main trees are fir, larch, pine, and spruce. In the spring, much of the taiga becomes flooded as the lower reaches of the north-flowing rivers thaw, while their mouths remain frozen. In summer, some ground remains swampy; in winter it freezes.

Steppes

The wide, open grasslands that cover Mongolia and southern Siberia are known as the steppes. Livestock is grazed on these broad, treeless plains, which, in places, merge into semidesert. The soil is mostly fertile and, with irrigation, many areas have become productive farmland.

Harsh conditions make trees stunted and sparse. Ice and snow cover the region for half the year.

Dunes form as sand drifts in the prevailing wind.

Temperatures average 70°F (21°C) with 79 in (2,000 mm) of rain per year.

Trees lose their leaves in winter as a means of protecting themselves from wind and cold.

Taklimakan Desert, China

Deserts

Asia has both hot and cold deserts, as well as many regions of semidesert where animals can be grazed. Middle Eastern deserts are hot and dry all year, with cold nights. The Gobi and Taklimakan deserts of central Asia have scorching summers, but are bitterly cold in winter.

Wetlands

Mangrove swamps are found along many coasts of southern Asia, from India to the Philippines. The mangrove trees have long, spreading roots, producing a forest that looks as if it is on stilts. Logging and pollution are destroying many mangroves.

Mangrove roots help stop coast eroding in storms.

Tropical rain forest

There are tropical rain forests in India, Southeast Asia, and the Philippines. They flourish on the southern slopes of the Himalayas, and in Burma (Myanmar), the Malay Peninsula, and the western part of the island of Irian Jaya. Home to 40 percent of all plant and animal species, the world's rain forests are threatened as people cut down trees for the timber industry and to clear space for farming.

Deciduous forest

Asia has comparatively few broadleaf forests of deciduous trees that shed their leaves in winter. They occur mainly in eastern Asia – China, Japan, and the Koreas – or in cooler upland areas such as the mountains of Nepal.

People

Asia contains two-thirds of the world's population, and the birth rate is still rising in many countries. Most people live in the southern and eastern regions and in the fertile river valleys. Many are farmers, although increasing numbers are moving into expanding cities in search of work.

Israeli boy   Vietnamese girl   Japanese boy

Resources

Asia's natural resources include farmland, which provides work for 60 percent of the people, and the fishing grounds of the Pacific Ocean. Minerals include oil and natural gas from the Gulf States, as well as bauxite, copper, coal, diamonds, gold, iron, lead, manganese, mercury, tin, and titanium.

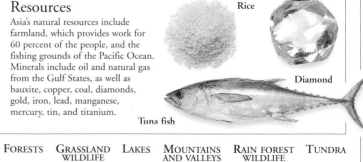

Rice
Diamond
Tuna fish

FIND OUT MORE ASIA, HISTORY OF · ASIAN WILDLIFE · CLIMATE · CONTINENTS · DESERTS · FORESTS · GRASSLAND WILDLIFE · LAKES · MOUNTAINS AND VALLEYS · RAIN FOREST WILDLIFE · TUNDRA

ASIA, HISTORY OF

ASIA IS THE WORLD'S LARGEST continent and the birthplace of the world's earliest civilizations, such as Sumer, China, and India. The emergence of these civilizations had a profound impact on history, both ancient and modern, as did the emergence of three major world religions: Hinduism, Buddhism, and Islam. Colonial interference affected Asia's development over the centuries, but after decades of independent growth, today's Asian economies are booming. There are still conflicts, however, and those in Southeast Asia and the Middle East affect world politics.

Early development

Early civilizations in Asia were largely isolated from each other and from the rest of the world by barriers of deserts, mountains, and oceans. Only the Middle East had strong connections with Europe. Therefore Asian civilizations and cultures developed independently for thusands of years. Over time, major civilizations, such as those of India and China, began to affect other Asian countries.

Central Asia

For centuries the only travelers in the inhospitable landscape of Central Asia were traders using the Silk Road. In 1398, the Mongolian warrior Timur (1336–1405) swept down from the steppes and founded a Central Asian empire.

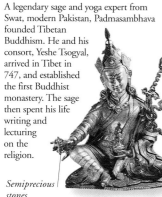

Typically tiled Samarkandian roof

Samarkand

In 1369, Timur moved his capital to the prosperous city of Samarkand, in modern Uzbekistan. The city experienced a golden age and became the architectural jewel of Central Asia, as Timur and his descendants built palaces, astronomical observatories, and Islamic colleges. In the early 1500s, nomadic Uzbeks attacked the city.

Uleg Beg Medrasa, Uzbekistan

Swat, Pakistan

Kushan Empire

In c.170 BC, a northern Chinese clan, the Yuezhi, moved west to Central Asia. By the 3rd century AD, they had founded an empire that stretched from eastern Iran to the Ganges in India. The Kushans controlled fertile river valleys and were at the center of the silk trade. They encouraged Buddhism and religious art, but declined in the 4th century.

Padmasambhava

A legendary sage and yoga expert from Swat, modern Pakistan, Padmasambhava founded Tibetan Buddhism. He and his consort, Yeshe Tsogyal, arrived in Tibet in 747, and established the first Buddhist monastery. The sage then spent his life writing and lecturing on the religion.

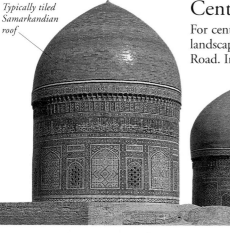

Semiprecious stones

Ancient civilizations

The Sumerians of western Asia evolved the world's first civilization, but it was the early civilizations of India and China that affected Asia the most. Their religions had special impact: Hinduism (the religion of the people of India) and Buddhism (founded by Siddhartha Gautama and one of the three great religions of China) spread over Asia.

Chola dynasty

From 850–c.1200, a powerful dynasty known as the Cholas began to dominate much of India. Cholas built many Hindu temples and spread their religion to Sri Lanka. They extended their naval power over the seas of Southeast Asia, spreading Hinduism as far as Sumatra and Bali.

Kogyuro openwork cup

Kogyuro dynasty

By the 7th century, China's influence was increasing, and Chinese monks converted Korea to Buddhism. The Kogyuro rulers (1st century BC–AD 7th century) were the last native Korean dynasty. From Korea the missionaries went to Japan, which adopted not only Buddhism but also Chinese script, architecture, and culture.

Southeast Asia

For 1,000 years, India was the major shaping force of this region and provided a mold for Southeast Asian culture, art, and religion. Its influence declined after c.1300.

Siam

Over centuries, waves of migrants from the north entered Siam (Thailand) and intermarried with the native tribes. In the 13th century, one tribe, the Thais, unified Siam into a single nation with one monarch and one religion – Buddhism.

Sea routes

From c.300, Indian traders sailed to Thailand, Malaysia, Indonesia, and the Philippines. From the 1200s, Arabian merchants spread Islam along sea trade routes. From c.1500, the region also traded with Europe.

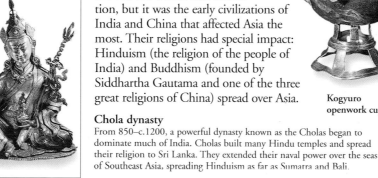

Dhow leaving Muscat, Oman

Thai tribal woman

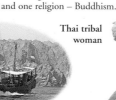

A Hindu temple in Bali, Indonesia, attests to the great influence of the Chola dynasty.

Trade and culture

During the 17th, 18th, and 19th centuries trade thrived, though some Asian countries were closed to outsiders. Russia and European countries bought silk, tea, and porcelain from China. India traded with the world and was noted for its handmade textiles, such as "paisley," which was a traditional Indian pattern. During this period, Western powers became increasingly interested in annexing Asian territories for trade purposes.

Manchu Dynasty

China's Manchu Dynasty (1644–1911) was expansionist and spread its culture by acquiring other territories, such as Mongolia (1697), Tibet (1751), and eastern Turkestan (1760). At home, however, economic conditions worsened.

Yellow lotus is a sacred flower.

A rich woman's silk robe, 19th century

Asian resistance

In the 17th and 18th centuries, China, Japan, Korea, and Siam (Thailand) resisted European expansion. China confined European trade to Macao and Canton, Japan traded only with Holland at Nagasaki, and Korea remained closed to the west. In 1688, a revolution in Siam ended French attempts to gain influence in Bangkok.

Gold-coated roof

Grand Palace, Bangkok

Great Game

During the 1800s, Russia expanded into Central Asia. The British feared the Russians were aiming to take over India, and both sides began to spy on each other. The British called this the Great Game; to the Russians it was known as the Tournament of Shadows.

Mountains of Lake Baikal, Russia

Nineteenth-century colonization

In the 19th century, European powers colonized much of Asia. The British took over Burma, Malaya, North Borneo, and Hong Kong; France dominated Indochina; the Dutch controlled Indonesia; and Russia annexed Central Asian provinces.

Britain
Russia
France
Netherlands
Japan

Conversion of the Philippines

In the late 1500s, the Spanish colonial government encouraged Filipinos to become Roman Catholics, and gave financial support to missionaries. By the 18th century, most Filipinos in towns and lowland areas had converted to Catholicism. The island of Mindanao, however, embraced Islam, which was brought to them by Muslim traders.

Paoay church, Ilocos Norte Province, Philippines

Engraving of Anglo-Burmese wars, 1824

Anglo-Burmese wars

In 1886, Burma lost its independence to Britain after a series of wars. This takeover was strategic rather than trade-based: the British wanted to prevent the French from gaining too much influence in Asia.

Golden East

As Europe gained in military and industrial strength in the 19th century, it expanded, and Asia became a rich source of food and raw materials. European planters developed tea, coffee, and rubber plantations, founded tin mines, exploited Asian timber, and prospected for gold, silver, and precious stones.

Indian tea

Vietnamese mahogany

Rama V

Chulalonkorn (1853–1910) became Rama V, King of Siam, in 1868. He traveled widely throughout Asia, and was determined to strengthen his country by a process of modernization. In the 1880s, he created a modern army, civil service, and education system. Although Thailand lost some provinces to Britain and France, it managed to preserve its prestige and independence.

The king and queen of Siam

Rebellion

From the 1850s, there were rebellions against European interference in Asian affairs. In 1857, the Sepoy Rebellion took place in India, and, in 1900, there was the Boxer Rebellion in China. Both revolts were protests against Western strength and culture. They were crushed by Western or colonial government forces.

Cover of *Le Petit Parisien*, 1900, "Death to Foreigners"

Timeline

4000–c.2500 BC The world's earliest civilization flourishes in Sumer, western Asia.

c.2500 BC Indus Valley period, India's earliest civilization.

1800 BC Shang period: China's earliest civilization starts to build its first cities.

c.330 BC Alexander the Great destroys the Persian Empire.

138 BC First recorded journey on the Silk Road.

c.50 Buddhism reaches China from India.

206 BC– AD 220 Height of the Chinese Han Empire.

 FIND OUT MORE ARCHITECTURE · ART, HISTORY OF · CHINA, HISTORY OF

A

Growth of nationalism

After World War I, Asian nationalism (a belief in independence) grew. In 1918, Arab leaders overthrew Turkish rule. The desire of Jews to create an independent state in Palestine gained support. By 1933, 238,000 Jews had settled in Palestine, and, in 1948, the state of Israel was created.

Living quarters

Jewish settlers in Palestine, 1930s

Independence movements

After 1945, many Asian countries threw off colonial rule. In 1947, India and Pakistan struggled for and won independence from Britain. In 1948, a Jewish homeland, Israel, came into being. Indonesia won independence from the Netherlands in 1949, after a four-year battle. France also tried to prevent Vietnamese independence, but was defeated in 1954; the other French colonies, Laos and Cambodia, became independent in 1954 and 1953 respectively.

With the decline of European empires, there were eventually 48 independent countries in post-war Asia.

World War II

In 1941–42, Japan occupied Burma, Indochina, and Indonesia. After the horrors of occupation, these areas rejected all foreign rule. In China, communist guerrillas resisting the Japanese, gained popular and political support.

Two war veterans on the Death Railroad, Kwai River, Thailand, 1990s

Death Railroad

During World War II, the Japanese built a railroad to link Burma and Thailand to supply Japanese troops in Burma. Many thousands of Asian workers and Western prisoners died from malnutrition, disease, and exhaustion building the 260-mile (420-km) railroad, and it became known as the Death Railroad.

Dragon economies

In the 1980s, Singapore, Taiwan, Hong Kong, and South Korea used their well-educated populations and high investment to become prosperous "dragon" economies. In the 1990s, Thailand, Malaysia, and Indonesia also developed rapidly.

Taiwanese factory

Taiwanese exported goods

Taiwan traditionally exported agricultural products, such as sugar, pineapples, and bananas; but by the 1980s it also exported advanced electronic products, such as personal computers, televisions, and portable phones.

Communist Asia

In 1949, the communists established the People's Republic of China – the world's largest communist state. In 1954, the North Vietnamese created an independent communist state. From the 1960s, communist movements in Indonesia and Malaysia threatened to overthrow existing governments.

US troops carry wounded soldiers from a helicopter.

Oil rigs, Middle East

Middle East conflicts

Since 1948, Arab-Israeli territorial conflict, such as the war of 1973 (when Egypt and Syria attacked Israel), has dominated the Middle East. There have also been conflicts between Arab countries, such as the Iran-Iraq war (1980–88). Although the oil boom has eased conflict somewhat by lessening poverty, the situation in the Middle East remains unstable.

Vietnam War

From 1954, communist North Vietnam sought to reunite with non-communist South Vietnam by force. Originally a civil war, the Vietnam War escalated into an international conflict with the gradual intervention of the United States in the 1960s. Following defeats and heavy casualties, the US agreed to withdraw in 1973. In 1975, northern forces unified both halves of Vietnam.

Chaim Weizmann

Weizmann (1874–1952) was born near Pinsk in Belarus and studied chemistry in Switzerland. In his youth he became a passionate Zionist and eventually was made head of the World Zionist Movement. After World War II, Weizmann campaigned for the creation of Israel, and in 1948, became the state of Israel's first president.

Timeline

c.618–907 The sophisticated T'ang dynasty dominates China.

1211 Mongol warrior Ghengis Khan invades China.

1300s Silk Road is shut.

1368 Ming dynasty expels Mongols from China.

1397 Mongols invade India.

1350–1460 Collapse of Khmer Empire, Cambodia.

1453 Fall of Constantinople to the Turkish Ottoman Empire.

Toy dog, Thailand, 1926

c.1488 Ming emperors rebuild the Great Wall of China.

1526–1707 Domination of Mughals in India.

1600–1614 British, French, and Dutch form East India companies.

1757 British take control of Bengal, India.

1839–42 Opium War.

1736–96 Manchu China prospers under Emperor Qianlong.

c.1750 Cultural and artistic peak in Japan.

1907 Anglo-Russian agreement ends the Great Game in Central Asia.

1949 Chinese Revolution.

1950–53 Korean War.

1954–75 Vietnam War.

Toy robot, Japan, 1956

FIND OUT MORE

CONFUCIUS   EMPIRES   EXPLORATION   GANDHI, MOHANDAS   INDIA, HISTORY OF   JAPAN, HISTORY OF   MUHAMMAD   PERSIAN EMPIRES   WARFARE

ASIA, CENTRAL

MAINLY ARID DESERT and mountainous, central Asia is made up of five countries. The Silk Road, an ancient trade route between China, the Middle East, and Europe, once passed through the region, boosting the textile industry, and making handwoven rugs from central Asia world famous. From 1922 until 1991 the whole area, apart from Afghanistan, was part of the Soviet Union. Under communist rule, the countries were partly modernized. Today, however, as independent nations they face an uncertain future. Afghanistan, which lies farthest south between Iran and Pakistan, has a turbulent history. Divided by a bitter civil war, it remains undeveloped.

Physical features

Much of central Asia is covered by two hot, dry deserts: the Karakumy and the Kyzyl Kum. The rest is largely rugged mountain chains. There is a small area of farmland that has been expanded by irrigation.

Kyzyl Kum

The name Kyzyl Kum means "red sands." This desert region lies south of the Aral Sea between the rivers Syr Daria and Amu Darya, mostly in Uzbekistan. Few people apart from nomads live here. Much of it is covered by low hills and sandy wasteland.

Tien Shan

The literal translation of Tien Shan is "Heavenly Mountains." This range of ice-capped peaks runs for 1,864 miles (3,000 km) from eastern Kyrgyzstan into China. The highest point is Pobeda Peak, 24,406 ft (7,439 m). Mountain rivers form broad, fertile valleys, which are used for farming.

Karakumskiy Ship Canal

The Karakumskiy Ship Canal is being built from the Amu Darya, one of central Asia's main rivers, across the Karakumy Desert. It will link the river with the Caspian Sea, 870 miles (1,400 km) away.

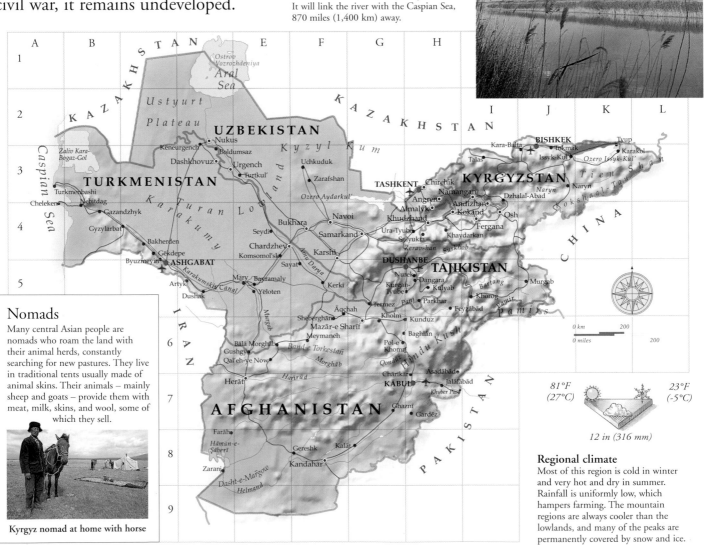

Nomads

Many central Asian people are nomads who roam the land with their animal herds, constantly searching for new pastures. They live in traditional tents usually made of animal skins. Their animals – mainly sheep and goats – provide them with meat, milk, skins, and wool, some of which they sell.

Kyrgyz nomad at home with horse

81°F (27°C)   23°F (-5°C)

12 in (316 mm)

Regional climate

Most of this region is cold in winter and very hot and dry in summer. Rainfall is uniformly low, which hampers farming. The mountain regions are always cooler than the lowlands, and many of the peaks are permanently covered by snow and ice.

Turkmenistan

Only two percent of Turkmenistan's arid land can be farmed. With irrigation, cotton, fruit, wheat, and vegetables are produced. Many people live in nomadic tribes, and there is much tension between groups. Turkmenistan is the world's eighth largest producer of natural gas.

TURKMENISTAN FACTS

CAPITAL CITY	Ashgabat
AREA	188,455 sq miles (488,100 sq km)
POPULATION	4,260,000
MAIN LANGUAGES	Turkmen, Russian
MAJOR RELIGION	Muslim
CURRENCY	Manat

Akhal-Teke
Known as the "wind of heaven," Akhal-Teke race-horses have been bred in the south of the Karakumy Desert for centuries. Fast, hardy, and well suited to the hot, harsh climate, Akhal-Tekes compete in traditional horse races at the Ashgabat hippodrome.

Akhal-Teke

Saddlecloths

Carpets
For centuries, Turkmenistan has produced beautiful, velvety carpets in deep, varying shades of red, brown, and maroon. Women hand-knot each carpet using fine wool from karakul sheep. They make several sizes, including *khali* (large) and *ensi* (welcome mats), as well as weaving curtains, sacks, bags, and pouches.

Uzbekistan

More than two-thirds of Uzbekistan is dry steppe and desert, but its areas of fertile land and resources of oil, gas, gold, copper, and coal make it one of central Asia's wealthier countries. Fruit, silk cocoons, and vegetables are exported to Moscow. Uzbekistan has the world's largest single gold mine.

UZBEKISTAN FACTS

CAPITAL CITY	Tashkent
AREA	447,400 sq miles (172,741 sq km)
POPULATION	23,308,000
MAIN LANGUAGES	Uzbek, Russian
MAJOR RELIGION	Musllm
CURRENCY	Som

The Tillya-Kari is an Islamic seminary in Registan Square.

An intricate mosaic covers building.

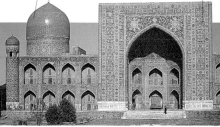

Cotton
Uzbekistan is the world's fourth largest producer of cotton. However, the irrigation system used to water crops has seriously depleted the Aral Sea.

Samarkand
Home to 370,000 people, the ancient city of Samarkand was once the center for trade in silk from China. Today, the production of silk and cotton textiles is still the city's main industry. Samarkand's Registan Square contains some magnificent 14th-century Islamic architecture.

Kyrgyzstan

Dominated by the arid Tien Shan mountains, Kyrgyzstan is a mainly rural country. Only seven percent of the land is cultivable. Half is used for growing fodder for livestock; the rest supports vegetables, wheat, fruit, cotton, and tobacco.

KYRGYZSTAN FACTS

CAPITAL CITY	Bishkek
AREA	76,640 sq miles (198,500 sq km)
POPULATION	4,754,000
MAIN LANGUAGE	Kyrgyz
MAJOR RELIGION	Muslim
CURRENCY	Som

People
The population of Kyrgyzstan is made up of 50 percent Kyrgyz people. The rest are mainly Russians and Uzbeks. Many Russians are leaving as a result of the strong nationalist feelings that have grown in the country since the end of Soviet rule. Ethnic tension also exists with the Uzbeks.

Gold

Resources
Gold and mercury are mined for export, as well as smaller amounts of other minerals including iron ore, tin, lead, copper, zinc, and bauxite. Kyrgyzstan also has reserves of oil, coal, and gas, and its many rivers and lakes give it great potential for hydroelectric power.

Tajikistan

The poorest of the former Soviet republics, Tajikistan has been torn by civil war ever since independence. The main conflict is between ethnic Tajiks, who make up about two-thirds of the population, and Uzbeks, who make up one-quarter. Tajikistan has rich mineral resources.

TAJIKISTAN FACTS

CAPITAL CITY	Dushanbe
AREA	55,251 sq miles (143,100 sq km)
POPULATION	6,155,000
MAIN LANGUAGES	Tajik, Uzbek
MAJOR RELIGION	Muslim
CURRENCY	Tajik rouble

Watermelon

Uranium
Tajikistan has 14 percent of the world's uranium, used as nuclear fuel. It is a major export, but the end of the nuclear arms race has reduced its value.

Farming
Only about six percent of Tajikistan is suitable for farming. The main farming areas are in the northwest, near Khudzhand, and the southwest, south of Dushanbe. Melons, grapes, and peaches are grown in fertile soils washed down from the mountains into the valleys.

Afghanistan

Linking central Asia and the Indian subcontinent, Afghanistan has been fought over for centuries. Since the 1980s, it has been in the grip of civil war between rival Islamic groups and is one of the world's poorest countries.

Peoples
Pashtuns – Afghanistan's largest ethnic group – make up about one-third of the population. The main minorities are Tajiks, Hazaras, and Uzbeks. Ethnic conflicts between these strongly Muslim groups have led to continuing feuding since 1992. Women have few rights in this increasingly Islamic fundamentalist society.

AFGHANISTAN FACTS

CAPITAL CITY	Kabul
AREA	251,770 sq miles (652,090 sq km)
POPULATION	19,494,000
MAIN LANGUAGES	Persian, Pashto
MAJOR RELIGION	Muslim
CURRENCY	Afghani

FIND OUT MORE

ASIA, HISTORY OF · DESERTS · FARMING · HORSES · ISLAM · MOUNTAINS AND VALLEYS · NUCLEAR POWER · ROCKS AND MINERALS · TEXTILES AND WEAVING · TRADE AND INDUSTRY

ASIAN WILDLIFE

ASIA STRETCHES FROM frozen Arctic in the north to warm tropics in the south. Although much of Asia is undulating plain, it also boasts the awesome mountain range of the Himalayas. Much of the interior receives little rain, but parts of India hold the world record for annual rainfall. This continent of contrasts provides many habitats, each with its own characteristic plants and animals. Many of the world's best known endangered species, such as giant pandas and tigers, live in Asia. But many less publicized, smaller animals and plants are also threatened by the steady spread of human population.

Temperate forest wildlife

Asian temperate woodlands are rich in broad-leaved trees. Summers are mild, but winters can be cold, and after the leaves have fallen, there is little food or shelter. Some animals migrate or hibernate; others, such as the Japanese macaque, are adapted to the cold.

Monkey eating snow

Thick, shaggy coat

Japanese macaque
Living throughout most of Japan, the Japanese macaque lives in a more northerly climate than any other monkey. In winter it grows a thick coat for protection, and some troops sit in hot springs to avoid the chill of a snowstorm. Roots, buds, and shoots form its winter diet.

Japanese emperor butterfly
Only the male Japanese emperor has an iridescent purple sheen, but both sexes have spotted wings. This pattern breaks up their outline, making it difficult to see where they land on sun-flecked foliage. Their caterpillars are leaf green, to camouflage them on the leaves of celtis trees, on which they feed.

Purple iridescence of male

White spots

Rain forest wildlife

Asia's rain forests are warm all year round, but they do have short dry seasons. They are festooned with lianas and epiphytes. The rain forest provides homes for animals at all levels, from fruit bats in the canopy to tigers on the forest floor.

Long aerial roots

Banyan tree
Some fig trees, such as the banyan tree, start life as a tiny seedling that grows in the crown of another rain forest tree. The banyan tree sends aerial roots down to the ground that enmesh and kill the host tree.

Striped coat provides camouflage in forest.

Tiger
The tiger spends much of its day roaming through its rain forest territory, stalking prey. Tigers love water, and to avoid the heat of the day, they cool down by basking in shallow pools.

Saltwater crocodile
Large reptiles, such as saltwater crocodiles, lie out on the shores of rain forest rivers in the morning sun to warm up their bodies. Later on, when the Sun gets too hot, the crocodiles return to the water to cool down.

Bill is used to kill snakes and scorpions.

Rhinoceros hornbill
With its loud call and noisy wingbeats, the rhinoceros hornbill is a very noticeable rain forest inhabitant. It uses its huge bill with great dexterity to pick fruit and kill prey.

Grassland wildlife

Asia has both tropical savannas and vast plains of temperate steppes with hot, dry summers. However, grasses and drought-resistant shrubs do grow there. Large animals have adapted to conserve moisture; smaller ones shelter in burrows.

The papery orange lanterns enclose berries.

Chinese lantern
The Chinese lantern is a drought-resistant plant. Its roots spread deep into the soil to reach any available water. New shoots appear each spring, that bear flowers and edible fruits.

Heavy snout

Saiga antelope
Herds of saiga antelope migrate south in winter to escape severe weather. They return north in summer, when the grasses are more plentiful. Saigas have a mucus-lined sac in their snout that warms inhaled air in winter and filters out dust in the hot, dry summer.

Tawny eagle
The tawny eagle nests in shrubs and trees by watercourses. It flies long distances over steppes and semi-arid deserts in search of food. The tawny eagle is a skillful hunter, but it increases its chances of getting enough food by feeding on carrion and stealing other predators' prey.

Hooked beak for tearing flesh of prey

Eagle has pushed off ground to launch itself into the air.

Mountain wildlife

The steep crags and valleys of the Himalayas provide many refuges for wildlife. Forests on the lower slopes become high altitude meadows, then snowfields. Animals of the higher slopes, such as the yak, are adapted to survive the winters; others migrate to warmer, lower slopes.

Himalayan griffon

The Himalayan griffon is a large, aggressive vulture that soars over some of the highest mountain slopes in search of food. The diet of vultures is almost entirely restricted to carrion. The Himalayan griffon's powerful hooked bill is strong enough to rip open the leathery hide of a dead yak to feast on the entrails.

Hooked beak helps pull apart prey.

A

Rhododendron

When in flower, rhododendrons set the mountainside ablaze with a riot of color. Their tiny seeds are readily spread by wind or water.

Yak

Domesticated for centuries, the yak is still found living wild in some parts of its mountain range. With its long, shaggy coat, a yak can survive temperatures as low as –40°F (–40°C). It grazes on whatever plants are available, including mosses and lichens, and can use snow as a source of water.

Sharp spines on head and neck provide protection.

Armored pricklenape agama

This lizard lives in the treetops in mountain forests. Its greeny-brown scales conceal it among twigs and leaves. Pricklenape agamas have sharp claws that give them a sure grip, as they run and leap through the branches.

Long toes and claws grip when climbing.

Boreal forest wildlife

Northern bat

In summer, this hardy bat forages for insects in the forest and even up into the Arctic Circle. To survive the winter, it hibernates in caves or buildings. Its distribution is dictated by the availability of suitable roost sites.

Just south of the Arctic tundra is a vast forest of conifer trees. In Asia, this boreal forest is called the taiga. Wildflowers, and animals such as the sable are adapted to exploit the brief summers and withstand the long, harsh winters.

Norway spruce

Narrow-crowned spruces are a characteristic feature of the taiga. Snow slides easily from their curved branches without breaking them. Norway spruce grows at the western reaches of the taiga, soon giving way to Siberian spruce. The seeds of both trees provide food for birds and rodents.

Fur for warmth

Sable

The sable hunts all year round for nestlings and rodents. It also eats shoots and berries if prey is scarce. The sable sleeps, shelters, and gives birth in hollow logs or tree holes.

Thick fur covers the whole body and even the soles of the feet.

Great gray owl

To find enough food, including voles, lemmings, and other small rodents, the great gray owl hunts by day as well as night. It may travel far to a good source of food, but returns to the dense boreal forest to breed. It chooses a secure nest site in a tree, or may use another large bird's old nest.

Desert wildlife

Not all deserts are hot all year round. Temperate deserts, such as the Gobi in Central Asia, have scorching hot summers, but icy cold winters. Nights are cold even in summer, as there is no vegetation to trap the heat. To survive here, animals must be adapted both to the dry environment and extremes of temperature.

Onager

Onagers live in small herds in the desert. There is little vegetation here for grazing animals, but the onager can cope by eating tough desert grasses and straw. Wolves, although uncommon, are their main predators. To defend themselves, onagers can run fast for long distances.

Mongolian gerbil

Like many small desert animals, these gerbils escape from temperature extremes by digging underground burrows. Living below ground also helps conserve bodily moisture. Gerbils nibble roots, shoots, seeds, and buds, and drink water if it is available. In a drought, they can get enough water from the early morning dew on their food.

Bactrian camel

Few of these desert creatures remain in the wild. A Bactrian camel has a very thick woolly coat to protect it from severe cold in winter. Fat stored in two humps on its back enables it to survive with little food or water for long periods of time.

Almost all-around vision helps them spot danger.

Pale fur for camouflage in desert

Cheek pouches stretch so gerbil can carry food in its mouth.

FIND OUT MORE ASIA BATS BIRDS OF PREY BUFFALO AND OTHER WILD CATTLE CAMELS DEER AND ANTELOPES LIONS AND OTHER WILDCATS RATS AND OTHER RODENTS TREES

ASSYRIAN EMPIRE

THE GRAND CITY OF ASHUR, beside the Tigris River in northern Mesopotamia (present-day Iraq), developed as an important trading center; by 2000 BC, it had become the capital of a great Assyrian kingdom. From 1400 BC, Assyrian armies were marching north and west to secure trade and obtain booty and taxes. Feared for their military strength, they soon came to dominate the Near East. Assyrian kings built several capital cities after Ashur, of which Nimrud and Nineveh were the most magnificent. Assyrian civilization and culture, however, were heavily influenced by Babylonia to the south. The Babylonians eventually absorbed the Assyrians into their empire.

Extent of the empire
The greatest extent of the empire was reached in the 7th century when the well-equipped soldiers of King Ashurbanipal conquered and held lands from Egypt to Iran. Assyrian governors controlled the provinces. They were expected to send taxes back to the Assyrian capital, and recruit soldiers for the army.

Bronze armor

Army

The Assyrian army was the most efficient fighting machine of its time. Its reputation alone was often enough to frighten rebellious states into surrender. At first, the army consisted of native Assyrians, but Tiglath-Pileser III (745–727 BC) recruited men from other areas of the empire. They were armed with iron helmets, armor, spears, swords, and shields. The Assyrians also used chariots and siege engines (battering rams on wheels), the most advanced weapons of the time.

Assyrian official   *King Ashurnasirpal II (r.883–859 BC)*   *Siege engine*

Stone relief of Assyrians attacking a town on the Euphrates River

Nimrud and Nineveh
By 900 BC, the city of Ashur was overcrowded. Nimrud was built in the following century; Nineveh was constructed in the 7th century BC. These cities were famous for their splendid palaces and temples.

Exotic animals from all over the empire, such as elephants and lions, filled the wildlife parks and gardens that surrounded the city of Nineveh.

Politics

At his coronation, the Assyrian king swore to expand the empire. The Assyrians believed their god, Ashur (after whom the first city was named), chose each king, so he had absolute power. He appointed all the governors of the various parts of his empire, led the army, and was responsible for all the temples. The king demonstrated his power and wealth by initiating many ambitious building projects. A network of spies reported to the king on all matters within the empire.

Gold earrings

Precious stones

Queens of Assyria
Some Assyrian queens were so powerful they became legendary. One was Sammu-rammat (Semiramis), who dominated court for 42 years in the 9th century BC. Some royal jewelry has been found in tombs at Nimrud.

Art and literature

Brightly painted stone relief carvings, the most spectacular of all Assyrian art forms, decorated palace walls from 900 BC. Artists decorated royal furniture with carvings of real or mythical animals, such as sphinxes.

Ivory-winged sphinx

Timeline

2400 BC The city of Ashur dominates trade routes; by 1900 BC, Assyrians establish trading colonies in Anatolia (modern Turkey).

1250 BC Kings of Assyria campaign as far afield as the Mediterranean and the city of Babylon.

879 BC Ashurnasirpal II builds a new capital at Kalhu (Nimrud).

744–727 BC King Tiglath-Pileser III creates an empire.

721–705 BC Sargon II builds palace at Khorsabad (Dur-Sharrukin).

Gold earring

701 BC Sennacherib leads his army to Jerusalem from his new capital at Nineveh.

689 BC Sennacherib destroys Babylon.

664 BC Ashurbanipal attacks and conquers Egypt.

612 BC Median and Babylonian armies destroy Nineveh.

609 BC Crown prince Nebuchadnezzar of Babylon finally defeats the Assyrians.

606 BC The Medes from Iran sack Nineveh.

Sennacherib

Sennacherib (704–681 BC), a strong king, spent many years building Nineveh. He established control over the coast of the Mediterranean and destroyed Babylon, but he was murdered by his jealous sons.

FIND OUT MORE ARMS AND ARMOR · ASIA, HISTORY OF · BABYLONIAN EMPIRE · HITTITES · PHOENICIANS · SUMERIANS · WARFARE

ASTROLOGY

FOR CENTURIES, people have believed that the positioning of the stars and planets has an influence on human life. The study of this influence is known as astrology. It began about 4,000 years ago in Mesopotamia (modern Iraq), and eventually spread throughout the ancient world. In most cultures, astrology was regarded as a science, and many rulers used astrology when making important political decisions. Today, many people still believe in astrology, although there is no scientific proof of its accuracy.

Casting a horoscope

To draw up your horoscope, or birth chart, astrologers need to know the exact date, time, and place of your birth. They then use careful calculations to plot the position of the Sun, Moon, and planets. Astrologers claim that they can interpret the finished chart to reveal your character.

This line represents the horizon at the time of birth.

The chart is divided into 12 houses, one for each zodiac sign.

Complicated calculations are now done with calculators.

Astrology and astronomy

The scientific study of stars and planets is known as astronomy. For thousands of years, astronomy and astrology were closely linked. Beginning in the 17th century, however, leaps in scientific knowledge resulted in astronomy becoming increasingly important, while belief in astrology began to wane.

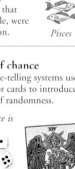

An early telescope

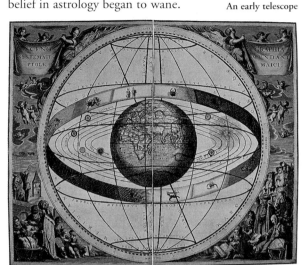

Astrological map showing the Universe in 1660

Twelve signs of the zodiac

Celestial spheres

Ancient astrologers believed that the Universe was a gigantic sphere, with the Earth at the center and the stars circling around it. They divided this sphere into 12 sections, each of which was named after a constellation of fixed stars – the signs of the zodiac.

Signs of the zodiac

Each zodiac sign takes its name from ancient mythology. Early astrologers chose names to suit the shapes formed by the constellations – the stars that make up Leo, for example, were thought to resemble a lion.

Aries
Taurus
Gemini
Cancer
Leo
Virgo
Libra
Scorpio
Sagittarius
Capricorn
Aquarius
Pisces

Chinese horoscopes

The five elements

| | Water | | Wood |
| | Earth | | Fire | | Gold |

Astrological wheel

Chinese astrology features 12 animals, each representing a different personality type. For example, people born in the year of the snake are said to be sociable, confident, and energetic.

The black and white bands represent the Universe's balancing forces of yin and yang.

Each animal sign is linked to one of the five elements.

Unlike Western astrology, which is based on the movement of the Sun and planets, Chinese horoscopes are based on the cycle of the Moon. Each Chinese year is named after a different animal – the Rat, Ox, Tiger, Rabbit, Dragon, Snake, Horse, Ram, Monkey, Rooster, Dog, and Pig.

Associations

Each astrological animal is associated with a certain food, color, and symbol. The Rat's symbol is the set of balances, its color is black, and it is linked with salty foods.

Fortune-telling

People's desire to predict the future has taken many forms that vary from culture to culture. They include crystal ball gazing, dream interpretation, palmistry, divination sticks, tarot reading, runes, numerology, and the *I Ching*, an ancient Chinese oracle.

The role of chance

Many fortune-telling systems use dice, coins, or cards to introduce an element of randomness.

Throwing dice is an ancient way of making predictions.

Consulting a fortune-teller in Hong Kong

I Ching coins

Palmistry

Each person's palm is unique, with its own distinctive pattern of lines. Palm readers believe these markings reveal the owner's character, past, and future. As well as both palms, the palmist examines the fingers and nails.

Palmistry hand

Tarot cards

Tarot cards are found worldwide. They can be dealt in many different ways and are thought to answer specific questions, as a guide to the future.

FIND OUT MORE ASTRONOMY · CHINA, HISTORY OF · SCIENCE, HISTORY OF · STARS · SUN AND SOLAR SYSTEM

ASTRONAUTS

MORE THAN 350 PEOPLE have traveled into space; 26 on missions to the Moon and the rest in orbit around Earth. For journeying into space, astronauts must be physically and mentally fit. They must also be trained to prepare them for living and working in the hostile environment of space.

Spacesuit

When astronauts work outside the spacecraft, they need to wear a suit that keeps their body at the correct temperature and protects them from fast-moving micrometeoroids. The suit must also provide oxygen for breathing and be pressurized because there is no air or atmospheric pressure in space.

Yuri Gagarin

The first person to fly into space was a Russian, Yuri Gagarin (1934-68). His flight on April 12, 1961, orbited him once around the Earth and lasted 108 minutes. No one knew how the space flight would affect a human, so Gagarin's spacecraft, *Vostok 1*, was controlled from the ground.

Pressure helmet

Visor   *Cap*

Communications headset

Communications input socket

Oxygen inlets and outlets

Water inlet and outlet

Pressure glove

Wrist clamp

Extravehicular glove

Apollo 9 spacesuit

Snap-on fastener

Urine transfer connection

Integrated thermal micrometeoroid garment

Lunar overshoe

MMU

To move away from the spacecraft, an astronaut wears a powered backpack, the Manned Maneuvering Unit (MMU). Mini nitrogen thrusters, operated from arm rests, propel the astronaut at about 65 ft/s (20 m/s).

Living in space

Daily life for an astronaut includes all the usual things, such as breathing, eating, sleeping, and going to the bathroom. The big difference, however, is living in weightless conditions. Sleeping astronauts float around the spacecraft unless strapped down, and using the toilet has to be carefully controlled.

Astronauts need daily exercise to keep fit in the weightless conditions of space.

Meal tray strapped to leg.

Vacuum-wrapped food pack

Rubber grips stop items floating away.

Space food

Meals on the space shuttle are prepared from 70 foods and 20 drinks. The meal tray is strapped down and the food eaten with the hand or utensils. Liquids are sucked from cartons or tubes.

Space toilet

The astronauts' spacesuits collect waste materials when worn outside the spacecraft. Inside the craft, the astronauts use a space toilet by firmly strapping themselves to the seat. The waste is sucked away by the toilet and collected in a secure unit.

Rubber suction cups

Suction shoes

Staying in one place in a spacecraft can be a problem. Suction-cup shoes allow astronauts to grip surfaces tightly.

Working in space

Each member of a space crew has specific tasks. These may include flying the craft, releasing a satellite into orbit, or testing new equipment. The weightless conditions of space mean that astronauts can also perform experiments not possible on Earth.

Repair work

Once a satellite is in space, it is left to work on its own. But sometimes one needs repairing. The cargo bay of the space shuttle is equipped with a robotic arm, which specially trained astronauts use to recover the satellite. They can then repair the satellite and release it back into orbit.

Experiments

Astronauts have carried out many experiments in space. These include observing how living things such as bees are affected by weightlessness.

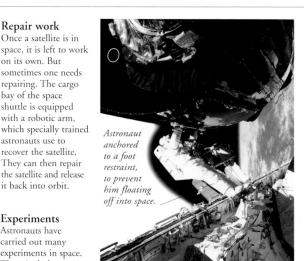

Astronaut anchored to a foot restraint, to prevent him floating off into space.

An astronaut works on the *Syncom IV-3* satellite.

Endurance record

Most astronauts spend only a few days in space, but some stay for months. Russian cosmonaut Valeri Poliakov holds the male endurance record (438 days). Shannon Lucid, an American, holds the female record (188 days).

Valeri Poliakov

Space animals

Humans are not the only space travelers; early ones included dogs, rats, and mice. Animals are no longer sent into space alone, but flies, frogs, and tadpoles occasionally accompany human astronauts.

Chimpanzee Ham returned safely from his 1961 flight.

FIND OUT MORE   EXPLORATION   GRAVITY   HEALTH AND FITNESS   MOON   ROCKETS   SPACE EXPLORATION

ASTRONOMY

ASTRONOMY IS THE STUDY OF SPACE and everything it contains. It is a subject that has been studied since ancient times when humans used their eyes to gaze out at the stars and planets. Today's astronomers use sophisticated equipment to collect information about space and how the Universe as a whole works.

Observatories

An astronomer's telescopic equipment is housed and used in an observatory. The atmosphere distorts light and electromagnetic radiation from space, so many observatories are located at high altitudes.

Kitt Peak Observatory

The largest optical telescope at Kitt Peak is the 13-ft (4-m) Mayall.

Optical observatory
The world's biggest optical observatories are on mountaintops, away from city lights and where the atmosphere is clear and dry. The Kitt Peak National Observatory, which has 15 major telescopes, is on a 6,900-ft (2,100-m) mountain in Arizona. Observatories sited in such inaccessible places need support services for the astronomers and their equipment, including housing, laboratories, and transportation.

Radio observatory
Radio waves are largely unaffected by the atmosphere, so radio telescopes can be virtually anywhere. The 1,000-ft (305-m) Arecibo radio dish (above) is in a natural hollow on the island of Puerto Rico. It is the world's largest single radio dish.

Astronomer at work

Most astronomers specialize in one area of research, such as planetary geology, interplanetary dust, stellar development, galaxy formation, or quasars. Whatever the subject, an astronomer can be found in one of two main locations: in universities and observatories.

Observation
Only a fraction of an astronomer's time is spent observing. Instead, most of the data comes from observations made and recorded by big telescopes tied to computers, or from automatic equipment on space probes. The observations are used to help build theories or to confirm an established theory, such as how stars form.

Data collection
The CCD, an electronic chip that records data from space, can collect enough data in a few hours to keep an astronomer busy for years.

Charge-coupled device (CCD)

Astronomers' tools

Astronomers collect data from space by analyzing a range of electromagnetic radiations; light and radio waves as well as wavelengths such as X ray, infrared, and ultraviolet. Astronomers use specialized telescopes with various attachments for collecting and studying the data.

Telescope
The finest and most powerful telescopes use one or more mirrors to collect light from a distant object and form an image. Electronic devices or photographic plates rather than the eye collect the data. Other attachments, such as spectroscopes and photometers, help analyze light emitted by stars.

Space observatory
Telescopes in space collect data 24 hours a day and transmit it back to Earth. The *Hubble Space Telescope*, launched in 1990, orbits Earth, collecting data from optical and ultraviolet wavelengths.

Cameras and instruments located inside.

Hubble Space Telescope

Antenna for sending data

Solar panel

Antenna for sending data

Space probe
Objects in the Solar System have been studied at close range by space probes. Instruments perform a host of investigations, including making detailed images of planets and their moons, and analyzing what they are made of. Two identical Viking probes investigated Mars in 1976.

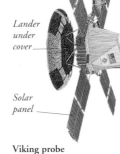

Lander under cover

Solar panel

Viking probe

Fred Hoyle
The British astronomer Fred Hoyle (b.1915) helped solve some of the most baffling questions facing 20th-century astronomers. A major break-through was explaining nucleosynthesis – how chemical elements are produced from the hydrogen inside stars.

Analysis
Data can be collected directly onto a computer and then transferred to other computers for analysis. Computers can process images and handle large amounts of information much more quickly than an astronomer.

Timeline

1609 First use of the telescope for the systematic study of space.

1781 Discovery of Uranus doubled the diameter of the known Solar System.

1863 Analysis of starlight shows stars are made of the same elements as those on Earth.

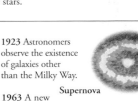

Uranus

1923 Astronomers observe the existence of galaxies other than the Milky Way.

1963 A new phenomenon, a quasar, is discovered.

Quasar

Supernova

1987 Supernova 1987A explodes, watched by observers worldwide.

FIND OUT MORE

ATMOSPHERE GALAXIES SPACE EXPLORATION STARS TELESCOPES UNIVERSE

ATHLETICS

ATHLETICS IS A GROUP of sports which take place mainly in a stadium and are divided into two main categories: track and field. Track includes running and hurdling races; field includes jumping and throwing. Some athletic events involve more than one discipline – 10 in the decathlon for men; seven in the heptathlon for women. Other events are road and cross-country running. Major competitions are the Olympics and world and continental championships.

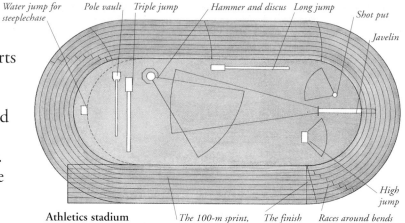

Athletics stadium
In an athletics stadium, there is a 437-yd (400-m) running track, usually marked with eight lanes. The field events take place in special areas on the grass area inside the track.

The 100-m sprint, 100-m hurdles, and 110-m hurdles are the only races run in a straight line.

The finish line is in the same place for all races.

Races around bends have a staggered start, which means athletes do not start in a straight line.

Track events

Racing takes place on the flat and over hurdles. Competitors in events up to 400 m have to stay in their lane for the whole race. The 800 m is run in lanes until the end of the first bend. A photo-finish camera is used to determine final places, and runners are timed to 0.01 second.

Athlete stays in the air as short a time as possible.

Weights in the base of the stand keep the hurdle upright.

Carl Lewis
In 1984, American Carl Lewis (b. 1961) won Olympic golds in the 100 m, 200 m, 4-by-100-m relay, and long jump. He won five more gold medals in later Olympics and retained his long-jump title three times (1988–96), becoming only the second athlete in history to win four golds in one event.

Hurdling
Athletes have to negotiate 10 hurdles in all the races – 100 m for women, 110 m for men, and 400 m for men and women. In the 3,000-m steeplechase, runners take four hurdles and the water jump on each full lap. They all use the same, fixed hurdles.

Running
Races on the track range from 100 m to the 25-lap 10,000 m. Runners use starting blocks for races from 100 m to 400 m. There are two standard relay races: 4 by 100 m and 4 by 400 m, with team members passing a baton.

Jumping events

There are four jumping events. In the high jump and pole vault, the bar is gradually raised. Competitors are eliminated if they have three consecutive failures. In the long jump and triple jump, competitors have a set number of attempts, the best one counting. The triple jump is a hop, step, and jump.

Pole vault
Poles, usually made of fiberglass, may be of any size. The vaulter plants the pole in a sunken box at the end of the runway before taking off. The pole bends and then straightens as the vaulter tries to clear the bar feet first, releasing the pole.

Long jump
Competitors must take off before reaching the end of a wooden takeoff board sunk into the runway. The jump is measured from the end of the board to the nearest part of the sand disturbed by the competitor with any part of the body, hands, or legs.

Throwing events

In the shot put, discus, and hammer, competitors throw from special circles. In the javelin, they throw from behind a curved line at the end of a runway.

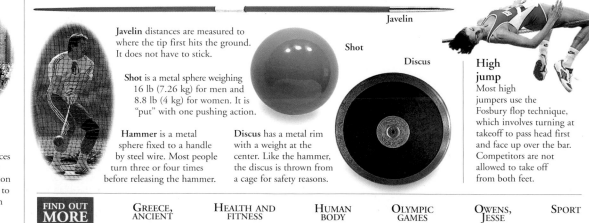

Javelin

Shot

Discus

Javelin distances are measured to where the tip first hits the ground. It does not have to stick.

Shot is a metal sphere weighing 16 lb (7.26 kg) for men and 8.8 lb (4 kg) for women. It is "put" with one pushing action.

Hammer is a metal sphere fixed to a handle by steel wire. Most people turn three or four times before releasing the hammer.

Discus has a metal rim with a weight at the center. Like the hammer, the discus is thrown from a cage for safety reasons.

The marathon
This road race is 42.195 km (26.2 miles) long. Some major races start and finish in the stadium. It derives from the Battle of Marathon in 490 BC, when a messenger ran to Athens with news of the Athenian victory over the Persians.

High jump
Most high jumpers use the Fosbury flop technique, which involves turning at takeoff to pass head first and face up over the bar. Competitors are not allowed to take off from both feet.

FIND OUT MORE

GREECE, ANCIENT — HEALTH AND FITNESS — HUMAN BODY — OLYMPIC GAMES — OWENS, JESSE — SPORT

ATLANTIC OCEAN

THE ATLANTIC IS THE WORLD'S second largest ocean, covering about one-fifth of the earth's surface. It separates the Americas in the west from Europe and Africa in the east. The Arctic Ocean lies to the north, and Antarctica to the south. There are several seas around the edges of the Atlantic, including the Baltic and the Mediterranean seas in the east, and the Caribbean in the west. The Atlantic contains some of the world's richest fishing grounds, but it is also the most polluted ocean because of the industry around its shores.

ATLANTIC OCEAN FACTS

AREA 31,660,445 sq miles (82,000,000 sq km)

AVERAGE DEPTH 12,000 ft (3,660 km)

GREATEST DEPTH 28,372 ft (8,648 m) Puerto Rico Trench

LENGTH 9,900 miles (16,000 km)

GREATEST WIDTH 4,900 miles (8,000 km)

Physical features

The waters of the Atlantic are never still. They move in huge belts of water or currents, such as the Gulf Stream. These affect the world's climate. The currents can be as warm as 86°F (30°C) or as cold as 30°F (-2°C). Many of the islands in the Atlantic are volcanic and lie on the Mid-Atlantic Ridge. Greenland and Iceland are the largest islands, bordered by the Greenland Sea in the north Atlantic.

Gulf Stream

Although the Scilly Isles lie just off the coast of Britain, in the northern Atlantic, winters there are mild due to the influence of the Gulf Stream. This warm current, which flows at about 5.6 mph (9 kmh), starts in the Caribbean, circles the Gulf of Mexico, and then heads north and east. Winds that blow over it pick up heat and raise the temperature of northern Europe, keeping ports free of ice in the winter.

Mid-Atlantic Ridge

An underwater mountain chain called the Mid-Atlantic Ridge runs down the middle of the Atlantic, where the ocean floor is splitting. Lava oozes up from the seabed and hardens, forming the mountain range. Many of the peaks surface as mid-ocean islands, such as Ascension Island. The ocean is growing wider at a rate of about 1.5 in (4 cm) a year.

Salmon

Fishing

Although Atlantic fish stocks have run low over the past 20 years because of overfishing, salmon fishing is a thriving industry, and salmon hatcheries are increasingly common.

Iceland

 The island country of Iceland lies far north in the Atlantic, midway between Europe and North America, and is increasingly important for international communications. Its position on the Mid-Atlantic Ridge means it has many volcanoes and is prone to earthquakes. Iceland has been a republic since 1944.

Climate
Owing to the Gulf Stream, Iceland's southern lowlands are mild and breezy, and snow is rare. The north is colder, but less windy.

86°F (30°C)   -33°F (-36°C)
52°F (11°C)   34°F (1°C)
34 in (860 mm)

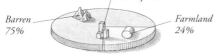

Built-up 1%
Barren 75%
Farmland 24%

Land use
The Icelandic people live in the more fertile coastal areas. Eleven percent are employed in farming, mainly raising sheep. Only about one percent of the land is used for growing crops. No one lives in the rocky center.

Reykjavik
Heated by geothermal water from boreholes, Reykjavik is a clean, modern city and home to about 100,000 people. It is a bustling hub of culture, industry, commerce, and government.

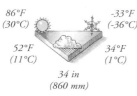

Brightly colored houses in Reykjavik's old town

Physical features
Iceland is a land of fire and ice, where steaming hot volcanic springs bubble up through glaciers. The center consists of uninhabitable plateaus and mountains. In the south are farmlands. There are many rivers, lakes, and spectacular waterfalls.

Volcanoes
The island of Little Surtsey is a volcano that rose from the sea close to Iceland in spring 1965, but disappeared again the following winter. Mainland Iceland has at least 20 active volcanoes that could erupt at any time.

Glaciers
Europe's largest ice-caps cover over one-tenth of Iceland. The biggest is Vatnajökull, which covers 3,149 sq miles (8,133 sq km) in the southeastern part of the country.

Geothermal power
Every year, thousands of people visit the Blue Lagoon, a natural pool of healing, geothermal, mineral-rich sea water. Vast resources ensure that hydroelectric and geothermal power stations generate almost all of Iceland's electricity.

Fishing
Iceland relies on exporting fish to pay for all the necessities of modern living that must be imported from abroad. Fishing and fish processing are Iceland's leading industries and employ nearly 20 percent of the workforce.

People
The first settlers in Iceland arrived from Norway in the 9th century. Today, Iceland is a prosperous society, and 80 percent of Icelanders own their own home. Most people live in towns where the standard of living is high, with extensive social security, health services, and free education.

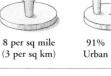

8 per sq mile (3 per sq km)   91% Urban   9% Rural

ICELAND FACTS

CAPITAL CITY	Reykjavik
AREA	39,770 sq miles (105,000 sq km)
POPULATION	300,000
MAIN LANGUAGE	Icelandic
MAJOR RELIGION	Christian
CURRENCY	Icelandic króna
LIFE EXPECTANCY	78 years
PEOPLE PER DOCTOR	376
GOVERNMENT	Multiparty republic
ADULT LITERACY	100%

Cape Verde

The volcanic Cape Verde Islands are divided into the Windward and Leeward Islands. They lie in the Atlantic, off Africa's west coast. Until 1975, they were a Portuguese colony. Poor soil and lack of fresh water forces Cape Verde to import 90 percent of its food.

CAPE VERDE FACTS

CAPITAL CITY	Cidade de Praia
AREA	1,556 sq miles (4,030 sq km)
POPULATION	400,000
MAIN LANGUAGES	Portuguese, Creole
MAJOR RELIGION	Christian
CURRENCY	Cape Verde escudo

São Nicolau
The island of São Nicolau in the Windward Islands has many Portuguese colonial-style buildings. Most of the people here are Portuguese-African Creole. Where they can, they grow bananas and sugarcane.

Atlantic Islands

The Atlantic Ocean contains hundreds of islands. Some, such as the British Isles, are part of a continent. Others, like the Azores and the Canaries, are volcanic. Ascension, Bermuda, St. Helena, and other small islands are the summits of undersea mountains and volcanic in origin.

Falkland Islands
The Falklands, with an area of 4,617 sq miles (11,960 sq km), are a British territory off the coast of Argentina. That country calls them Las Malvinas and claims ownership. Until oil was discovered, most people made a living sheep farming.

Canary Islands
The Canary Islands, off northwestern Africa, are governed as two provinces of Spain. Popular with tourists, the seven islands and six islets have a total area of 2,807 sq miles (7,270 sq km) and a population of 1,445,000.

 FIND OUT MORE   ARGENTINA, CHILE, AND URUGUAY   CLIMATE   CONTINENTS   ENERGY   FISHING INDUSTRY   GLACIATION   ISLANDS   OCEANS AND SEAS   TUNDRA   VOLCANOES

ATMOSPHERE

LIFE ON EARTH could not exist without Earth's atmosphere. The atmosphere is a colorless, tasteless, odorless blanket of gases that surrounds the Earth. It gives us air to breathe and water to drink. It not only keeps us warm by retaining the Sun's heat, it also shields us from the Sun's harmful rays. The atmosphere is approximately 440 miles (700 km) deep, but it has no distinct boundary. As it extends into space, it becomes thinner, eventually fading out. Human activity is upsetting the atmosphere's natural balance, with damaging results.

Layers of the atmosphere

The atmosphere is divided into five different layers. The composition of gases varies within these layers, as does the temperature, which drops in the troposphere, the lowest layer, and rises in the stratosphere above.

Satellite

A

Exosphere is the outer layer of the atmosphere. Here lighter gases drift into space.

In the thermosphere, gases are very thin but they absorb ultraviolet light from the Sun, raising temperatures to 3,632°F (2,000°C). The ionosphere (layer within the thermosphere) is made of gases electrically charged or ionized by the Sun's light. Radio signals can be bounced off these ionized gases.

Composition of the atmosphere

Earth's atmosphere is made mainly of two gases – nitrogen and oxygen. It also contains small amounts of argon and carbon dioxide, with tiny traces of other gases. The oxygen is made primarily by green plants, which maintain the balance of gases.

Nitrogen 78%
Oxygen 21%
Argon 0.93%
Carbon dioxide 0.03%
Other gases 0.04%

Pie chart showing the composition of the atmosphere.

Aurora – lights in the night sky, possibly caused by charged particles from the Sun striking atoms

Space shuttle

Meteorites

In the mesosphere, gases are so thin that temperatures drop rapidly to less than -166°F (-110°C). However, the air at that height is still thick enough to slow down meteorites.

Stratopause is the boundary between stratosphere and the mesosphere.

Sonar balloon

Stratosphere contains 19 percent of the atmosphere's gases, but little water vapor. It is very calm, so jets fly up here.

Ozone layer

The thin layer of ozone gas within the stratosphere protects us by absorbing harmful ultraviolet rays from the Sun. But the buildup of man-made gases called chlorofluorocarbons (CFCs) has depleted the ozone layer and holes have started to appear in it every spring over the poles.

Tropopause borders troposphere and stratosphere.

Ozone layer shields the Earth from dangerous radiation.

Greenhouse effect

Carbon dioxide and other gases in the atmosphere act like glass in a greenhouse, trapping the Sun's heat. This "greenhouse effect" keeps the Earth warm. But human activity, such as burning forests and running cars, releases too much carbon dioxide into the air and may cause global warming.

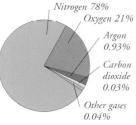

Ozone hole over Antarctica is shown as violet and pink.

Some aerosol sprays use CFC gases.

Sea level

Troposphere extends about 7.5 miles (12 km) above the ground and is the only layer in which living things can survive naturally. It contains 75 percent of the atmosphere's gases, water vapor, and clouds. Changes here create the weather.

The oxygen cycle

Gases continually circulate between the atmosphere and living things. Animals breathe in oxygen to help them release energy from food, and breathe out carbon dioxide. Green plants release oxygen back into the air and take in carbon dioxide as they absorb energy from the Sun. Oxygen is also used in burning fossil fuels.

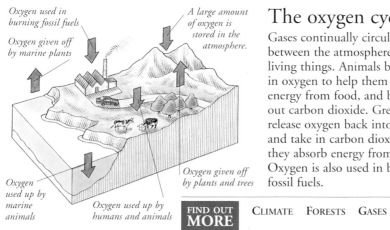

Oxygen used in burning fossil fuels
Oxygen given off by marine plants
A large amount of oxygen is stored in the atmosphere.
Oxygen used up by marine animals
Oxygen used up by humans and animals
Oxygen given off by plants and trees

James Glaisher

English meteorologist James Glaisher (1809–1903) was one of the many balloonists who, during the 19th century, took great risks when they ascended to extraordinary heights to discover more about the atmosphere. Glaisher went up almost 7.5 miles (12 km) into the troposphere without oxygen or protective clothing. Such research led to the discovery that air becomes cooler with altitude.

FIND OUT MORE CLIMATE FORESTS GASES LUNGS AND BREATHING PLANETS POLLUTION SUN AND SOLAR SYSTEM WEATHER

ATOMS AND MOLECULES

TINY PARTICLES CALLED ATOMS are the basic building blocks of all matter. Forces called bonds effectively "cement" the atoms together. A molecule is a cluster of atoms linked by bonds. There are just over a hundred different types of atoms, which are themselves made up of even smaller "subatomic" particles, such as protons, neutrons, and electrons.

Atomic structure

The center, or nucleus, of an atom contains particles called protons, which carry a positive electric charge, and neutrons, which carry none. Arranged around the nucleus in layers called shells are negatively charged particles called electrons. The atom has no charge of its own, because it contains equal numbers of electrons and protons, so the positive and negative charges are balanced.

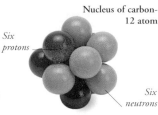

Nucleus of carbon-12 atom

Six protons

Six neutrons

Isotopes

All the atoms of an element have the same number of protons in the nucleus, but some atoms, called isotopes, have different numbers of neutrons. For example, the carbon isotope carbon-12 has six protons and six neutrons, but the isotope carbon-14 has two extra neutrons.

Quarks

Both neutrons and protons consist of three smaller particles called quarks stuck together by tiny particles called gluons. Quarks, in turn, may contain even smaller particles.

Electron shells and valency

Atoms can have up to seven shells of electrons. An atom with eight electrons in its outermost shell is very stable. Bonds form when atoms gain, lose, or share electrons in order to achieve this stable arrangement. An atom's valency is the number of bonds it can form with other atoms.

When sodium bonds, it loses an atom, leaving an outer shell of eight electrons.

A carbon atom can form up to four bonds with other atoms.

Sodium
(3 shells, valency 1)

Carbon
(2 shells, valency 4)

Nucleus   Proton (red)   Neutron (green)

Electron shells

Electrons move around the nucleus in paths called orbits.

Atom of carbon-12 cut in half

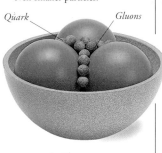

Quark   Gluons

Inside a neutron

Ionic bonds

When an electron transfers from one atom to another, the atoms become charged particles called ions. The atom losing the electron becomes a positively charged ion, and the atom gaining the electron becomes a negatively charged ion. The force of attraction between the ions' opposite charges is called an ionic bond.

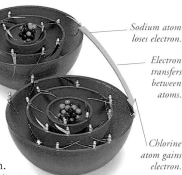

Sodium atom loses electron.

Electron transfers between atoms.

Chlorine atom gains electron.

Formation of ionic bonds in sodium chloride (NaCl)

Covalent bonds

A covalent bond forms when two atoms link up by sharing electrons. Each atom supplies an electron, and the pair of electrons orbits the nuclei of both atoms, holding the atoms together as a molecule.

Covalent bonds in ammonia molecule (NH_3)

Hydrogen atom

Two shared electrons form covalent bond.

Nitrogen atom

Nitrogen bonds with three hydrogen atoms.

Double bonds

Sometimes atoms form covalent bonds by sharing two pairs of electrons. This is called a double bond. A triple covalent bond forms when atoms share three pairs of electrons.

Atoms share four electrons.

Oxygen molecule (O_2)

Double bond links two oxygen atoms.

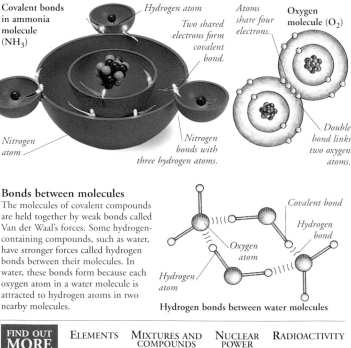

Chemical formula

Scientists use a kind of code called a chemical formula to describe a substance. The formula uses letters and numbers to show which elements are present in the substance, and in what proportions. Methane, for example, has a chemical formula of CH_4, which shows that it contains carbon (C) and hydrogen (H) combined in the ratio of one carbon atom to every four hydrogen atoms.

Hydrogen atom

Carbon atom

Methane molecule (CH_4)

Linus Pauling

The American chemist Linus Pauling (1901–94) won the 1954 Nobel Prize for chemistry for his work on chemical bonds and the structure of molecules. He calculated the energies needed to make bonds, the angles at which bonds form, and the distances between atoms. He also won the 1962 Nobel Peace Prize for his efforts to stop the testing of nuclear weapons.

Bonds between molecules

The molecules of covalent compounds are held together by weak bonds called Van der Waal's forces. Some hydrogen-containing compounds, such as water, have stronger forces called hydrogen bonds between their molecules. In water, these bonds form because each oxygen atom in a water molecule is attracted to hydrogen atoms in two nearby molecules.

Covalent bond

Hydrogen bond

Oxygen atom

Hydrogen atom

Hydrogen bonds between water molecules

FIND OUT MORE   ELEMENTS   MIXTURES AND COMPOUNDS   NUCLEAR POWER   RADIOACTIVITY

AUSTRALASIA AND OCEANIA

AUSTRALIA, New Zealand, Papua New Guinea, and the nearby islands are collectively called Australasia. The wider area known as Oceania also includes the island groups of Melanesia, Micronesia, and Polynesia and spans a huge area in the South Pacific Ocean. Australia is the largest country and a continent in its own right. Although many Pacific islands were once European colonies, the region now has closer trade links with Asia.

Coral islands

Many of the thousands of tiny islands in Oceania are the peaks of undersea volcanic mountains that are just breaking the surface of the Pacific Ocean. Reefs of coral, teeming with tropical fish, often build up close to the islands' sandy shores.

Physical features

Australasia and Oceania include a range of landscapes, from tropical rain forest in northern areas, to the arid desert of central Australia. Many islands are volcanic, with sandy beaches, high mountains, and a constant threat of earthquakes.

Geysers

These occur in New Zealand where hot rock heats water in an underground chamber. As the water boils, a fountain of scalding water and steam shoots 1,640 ft (500 m) into the air.

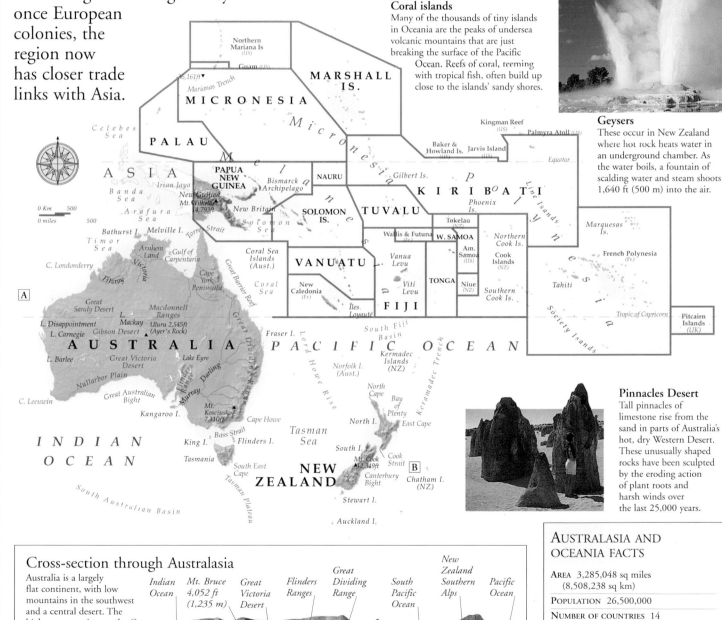

Pinnacles Desert

Tall pinnacles of limestone rise from the sand in parts of Australia's hot, dry Western Desert. These unusually shaped rocks have been sculpted by the eroding action of plant roots and harsh winds over the last 25,000 years.

Cross-section through Australasia

Australia is a largely flat continent, with low mountains in the southwest and a central desert. The highest mountains are the Great Dividing Range in the east. The Pacific Ocean between Australia and New Zealand dips to 16,405 ft (5,000 m). The Southern Alps run down New Zealand's South Island.

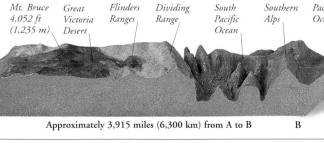

Indian Ocean · Mt. Bruce 4,052 ft (1,235 m) · Great Victoria Desert · Flinders Ranges · Great Dividing Range · South Pacific Ocean · New Zealand Southern Alps · Pacific Ocean

A   Approximately 3,915 miles (6,300 km) from A to B   B

AUSTRALASIA AND OCEANIA FACTS

AREA	3,285,048 sq miles (8,508,238 sq km)
POPULATION	26,500,000
NUMBER OF COUNTRIES	14
HIGHEST POINT	Mt. Wilhelm (Papua New Guinea) 14,794 ft (4,509 m)
LONGEST RIVER	Murray Darling (Australia) 2,330 miles (3,750 km)
BIGGEST LAKE	Lake Eyre (Australia) 3,700 miles (9,583 sq km)

Climatic zones

With a wide range of landscapes and spanning a vast area, Australasia and Oceania experience many different climates. Northern Australia and Papua New Guinea are always hot with wet and dry seasons, the east has hot summers and mild winters, and the center is dry desert. New Zealand is mild and damp. The most westerly of the Pacific islands have a wet, tropical climate.

Wetland
Desert
Tropical rain forest
Deciduous forest
Scrub
Grassland
Mountain

Many species of insects and animals live in the canopy.

Small, stunted shrubs

After rain, flowers burst into bloom.

Tropical rain forest

Steamy tropical rain forest covers most of the Solomon Islands, the mountains of Papua New Guinea, and northern Australia. Often shrouded in mist, these dense, lush forests are a haven for wildlife and contain more than 600 species of tree. As a measure to protect the environment, logging is controlled in Queensland.

Scrub

At the edges of the four major deserts that make up the interior of Australia are areas of arid brush where there is little, often unreliable, rainfall. These areas support coarse grass, scattered shrubs, and low trees.

Bushes are mostly stunted, evergreen, and spiny.

Sandstone is worn smooth and rounded by erosion.

Grassland

Australia contains vast areas of dry, open grassland, known as the "outback." The best grazing land for cattle and sheep is in Queensland and New South Wales. Scarce surface water is supplemented by underground water from artesian wells. Lush grassland covers the eastern side of New Zealand's South Island.

Eucalyptus woods

Many kinds of gum trees, also known as eucalyptus, grow in Australia. There is a species of gum tree for virtually every environment, from cold, damp mountain tops to hot, dry inland areas. Gum trees are evergreens, with leathery leaves.

Mountain gum leaves

Narrow leaves hang down to avoid drying out in the hot sun.

Coastal climate

The coastal strip between Brisbane and Melbourne in southeast Australia is backed to the west by the peaks of the Great Dividing Range, including the Australian Alps. Warm breezes blow in from the Pacific Ocean, bringing rain to this green and fertile region. The long, sandy beaches and mild, pleasant climate make this the most populated region in Australia.

Powerful waves create long, sandy beaches.

Byron Bay, New South Wales

Hot desert

The spectacular red Olgas rocks rise unexpectedly out of the arid flat expanse of Australia's scorching central desert. Situated near Uluru (Ayers Rock), this giant mass of boulders formed more than 570 million years ago and gradually eroded during the past 150 million years.

Deciduous rain forest

The west coast of New Zealand's South Island is covered with deciduous forest. Trees such as oak, beech, and hickory thrive in the mild, damp climate.

Beech forest in New Zealand's Fiordland National Park

People

The earliest inhabitants of Australasia were the Aboriginals of Australia and the Polynesians and Melanesians from the Pacific islands. White Europeans began colonizing Australia and New Zealand in the late 1700s. Since the 1970s, Australia has allowed many other peoples to settle there, including Chinese, Cambodians, and Vietnamese.

Australian children

Resources

Land is a major resource for Australia and New Zealand and is used extensively for grazing cattle and sheep, and for growing wheat. Australia is rich in minerals and leads the world in the production of bauxite (aluminum ore), diamonds, and lead ore. The main resources of the Pacific islands are fish and coconut products, such as copra, coir (rope), and matting.

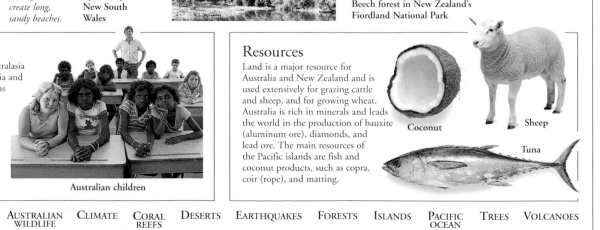

Coconut

Sheep

Tuna

FIND OUT MORE ABORIGINAL AUSTRALIANS · AUSTRALIAN WILDLIFE · CLIMATE · CORAL REEFS · DESERTS · EARTHQUAKES · FORESTS · ISLANDS · PACIFIC OCEAN · TREES · VOLCANOES

AUSTRALIA

A COUNTRY and at the same time a continent, Australia is an ancient landmass and the smallest, flattest, and, after Antarctica, driest continent. It is the world's sixth largest country, yet only 17.8 million people live there, mostly along the coast. The center of the country consists of the desert or semidesert region called the outback. Australia has six states and two territories. It has strong trade links with the US, Europe, and Asia and makes significant contributions to international affairs. The population consists of a diverse ethnic mix, making Australia a truly multicultural society.

Physical features

The center of Australia is covered by a vast, flat, arid plain called the outback – one of the hottest places on earth. Around the coast are tropical rain forests, snowcapped mountains, and magnificent beaches.

AUSTRALIA FACTS

CAPITAL CITY Canberra

AREA 7,686,850 sq miles (2,967,893 sq km)

POPULATION 17,820,000

MAIN LANGUAGE English

MAJOR RELIGION Christian

CURRENCY Australian dollar

LIFE EXPECTANCY 77 years

PEOPLE PER DOCTOR 440

GOVERNMENT Multiparty democracy

ADULT LITERACY 100%

Great Barrier Reef

Green Island forms part of the Great Barrier Reef, which stretches 1,243 miles (2,000 km) along the northeastern coast of Australia. Its coral is formed by layer upon layer of tiny anemonelike creatures, making it the largest living thing on earth. Thousands of tourists flock to see it each year, attracted by the clear, warm waters and more than 1,500 species of fish. Recent fears that divers and swimmers may be damaging the reef have led to its protection as a World Heritage Site.

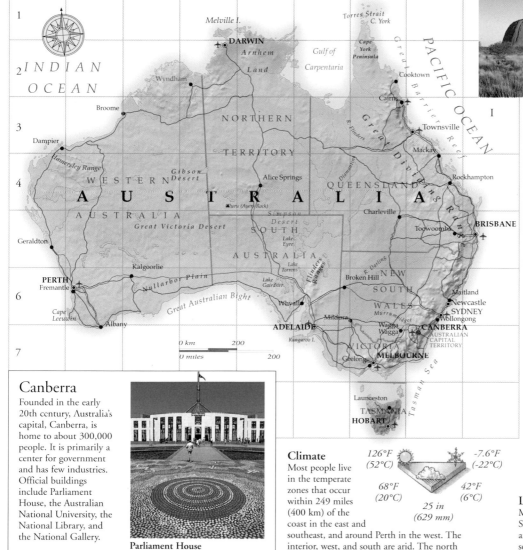

Uluru (Ayers Rock)

This giant block of red sandstone that rises from the desert is more than 1.5 miles (2.4 km) long. Once known as Ayers Rock, Uluru, meaning "great pebble," is the original name given to it by the Aboriginal people, who regard it as sacred.

Great Dividing Range

The Great Dividing Range is a series of high plateaus and low mountains that extends down the east side of Australia. It shields the arid interior of the country from the rainclouds that blow in from the Pacific Ocean. In winter, snow covers the higher peaks, and people can ski there.

Canberra

Founded in the early 20th century, Australia's capital, Canberra, is home to about 300,000 people. It is primarily a center for government and has few industries. Official buildings include Parliament House, the Australian National University, the National Library, and the National Gallery.

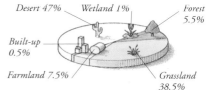

Parliament House

Climate

Most people live in the temperate zones that occur within 249 miles (400 km) of the coast in the east and southeast, and around Perth in the west. The interior, west, and south are arid. The north is hot, humid, and tropical.

126°F (52°C)
-7.6°F (-22°C)
68°F (20°C)
42°F (6°C)
25 in (629 mm)

Land use

Most of Australia's interior is inhospitable desert. Sheep and cattle are raised in the east and north, and wheat is grown in the fertile southwest and southeast. Some of the land is used to mine Australia's rich mineral deposits.

Desert 47%
Wetland 1%
Forest 5.5%
Built-up 0.5%
Farmland 7.5%
Grassland 38.5%

A

People

Aboriginal people, Australia's first inhabitants, make up between one and two percent of the population. The rest is of mainly European origin, descended either from British settlers or from Europeans who emigrated to Australia after 1945. Recent years have also seen an influx of Asians.

Multicultural society
Australian society reflects the many different nationalities that have settled in the country. Aboriginal people, English, Irish, and central and eastern Europeans have all made their mark, and, since 1972, when immigration restrictions were lifted, the arrival of Chinese, Indo-Chinese, and Indonesian peoples has added new influences. Diverse languages, customs, foods, and festivals make Australia a varied and exciting society.

5 per sq mile
(2 per sq km)

85%
Urban

15%
Rural

Farming

Less than five percent of the workforce farm, yet half the land is used for grazing cattle and sheep, and growing grapes and grains.

Livestock
Cattle roam the Australian outback, grazing on dry grass and drinking water drawn from artesian wells. They are raised on vast cattle ranches, mainly for their meat. Australia has seven times more sheep than people. They produce over one-third of the world's wool.

Grain
Although less than four percent of the land is suitable for farming cereal crops, Australia grows barley, millet, oats, and rice, and manages to rank ninth in world production of wheat. Other crops include sugarcane, fruit, and vegetables.

Grapes
The gentle climate of parts of southern Australia is ideally suited to growing grapes for winemaking. The Australian wine industry has grown by leaps and bounds in recent years, now producing about 495,000 tons (450,000 tonnes) of wine a year. Much is exported.

Industry

Australia has a strong mining industry and is a major exporter of coal, iron ore, bauxite, lead, gold, copper, and diamonds. About 16 percent of the workforce is employed in manufacturing, and two-thirds is employed in services such as banks, tourism, and government.

Diamonds

Gold

Quartz

Gold and diamonds
Australia is the world's third largest gold producer and exports more diamonds than any other country. Most of the diamonds are not gem quality and are used to make industrial cutting tools.

Leisure

Australians love the outdoors. Because most live near the coast, many people enjoy water sports such as swimming, skindiving, surfing, and sailing. Cricket is a popular spectator sport, as are rugby and the unique Australian Rules football.

Surfing
The crashing waves of Australia's east coast attract thousands to try their luck at surfing. The aptly named Surfers' Paradise, in Queensland, is a favorite spot.

Australian Rules Football
One of Australia's national winter sports is Australian Rules football. It was invented in the 1850s and is based on Gaelic football. The only other country where it is played is Papua New Guinea.

Food

Traditionally, Australians are a nation of meat eaters. They love plain foods such as fried eggs and grilled steaks, cooked on the barbecue. The influx of people from mainland Europe and Asia has brought a wide range of cuisine from China, Greece, Indonesia, and Italy.

Barbecued lamb

Grilled pumpkin

Transportation

With such a huge territory to cover, and the nearest countries so far away, Australians rely on airplanes for long-distance travel. Buses, cars, and trains are used for short distances in the cities. Trucks carry most intercity freight by road.

Road train
Heavy loads are often transported across the outback by road train. These huge trucks may pull five or six trailers over vast distances on deserted roads.

Flying Doctor
The Royal Flying Doctor Service was founded in 1928 to bring medical help to people living in the outback. Doctors are based at 12 stations where emergency callers can contact them by radio and receive treatment quickly.

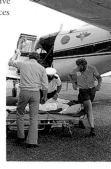

Tourism
The spectacular scenery of the Hamersley Range in western Australia is popular with tourists, mostly from Japan, New Zealand, and Southeast Asia. About one million visitors visit Australia every year, providing a welcome addition to the country's foreign earnings.

FIND OUT MORE   ABORIGINAL AUSTRALIANS   AUSTRALIA, HISTORY OF   CARS AND TRUCKS   CONTINENTS   CORAL REEFS   DESERTS   FARMING   ROCKS AND MINERALS   SPORTS

AUSTRALIA, HISTORY OF

FOR THE LAST 40,000 YEARS, Australia was inhabited by Aboriginal peoples. The Aboriginals, who came from Asia, created a rich culture based on hunting and food gathering. Their peaceful existence was destroyed by the arrival of Europeans in the late 18th century. These settlers were convicts sent from crowded British prisons; later, farmers and miners drawn by the wealth of the country, joined them. In 1901, Australia became an independent nation, sending troops to fight in both world wars. Today it is a multicultural country with a rich economy and close ties with Asia, America, and Europe.

Paddles for Aboriginal canoe

First inhabitants

The first people to inhabit Australia were the ancestors of today's Aboriginals. They reached the country about 40,000 years ago after sailing across the shallow oceans that then separated Australia from Asia. As sea-levels rose, they moved inland, using stone axes to clear trees and build shelters of wood and bark.

Outrigger canoe from Queensland

Outrigger made from solid wood

Canoe dug out of a whole tree trunk

String made of grass holds the outrigger to the main canoe.

Early sightings

In the 17th century, Spanish sailor Luis Vaez de Torres and Dutchman Willem Jansz explored the islands of Asia and the Pacific. Unplanned landings took place as ships were blown off course. In 1642–43 Dutchman Abel Tasman sailed around Australia without catching sight of it. He landed on an island he named Van Diemen's Land, now called Tasmania.

Early map of Australia

Botany Bay
In 1770, the British explorer Captain James Cook sailed into an inlet in southeastern Australia. He named the place Botany Bay and claimed the entire east coast of Australia for Britain. Joseph Banks, one of the ship's naturalists, sketched and collected hundreds of plants, that had never before been seen by Europeans.

Convict transportation
In 1787, the British decided to transport (ship out) prisoners to Australia. The first fleet, containing 759 convicts, arrived in Botany Bay in 1788. A penal settlement was established at nearby Sydney Cove, in Port Jackson. The last shipload of prisoners arrived in Australia in 1868.

Convicts were often used as servants.

The 19th century

Some 90 years after the arrival of Cook, the major settlements were all on the coast, and few people traveled inland. The first explorers mapped the Murray and Darling rivers in the southeast, while others tried to reach the heart of Australia.

Crossing the continent
The Royal Society of Victoria decided to send an expedition to cross the continent from south to north. Irishman Robert O'Hara Burke and Englishman William J Wills completed the trip in 1861, but died on the return journey. In July 1862 their rival, John Stuart, completed a similar journey, unaware that Burke and Wills had beaten him to it. He died in the attempt.

Prospectors' camp, Victoria

Gold rush
The discovery of gold in 1851 brought a rush of fortune-hunters. By 1860, the population had grown from 200,000 in 1840 to 1.1 million, and Australian gold accounted for 39 per cent of the world's total output.

Growth
The colonies prospered in the last years of the 19th century. Industry grew quickly, especially in areas such as construction and manufacturing. Social policies were forward-thinking: for example, education for all was an early goal; trade unions were organized in many areas.

Banner for trade union

Ned Kelly

Throughout the 19th century, parts of Australia were lawless. One of the most notorious outlaws, or bushrangers, was Ned Kelly (1855–80), who led a gang of robbers. The gang killed three policemen in 1878 and robbed several banks before Kelly was caught and hanged in Melbourne in 1880. His fight against the authorities made Kelly a national folk hero.

Surveyor's chain used to measure land, 1800s

Independent nation

In the early days, Australia consisted of six separate colonies. Each had its own government under the sovereignty of Britain. As the agricultural and mining industries grew in strength, the six colonies began to work closely together. In 1901, Australia gained its independence from Britain, and a federal government for the entire country was established with its capital in Melbourne. Today, the federal capital is at Canberra.

Gallipoli

On April 25, 1915, ANZAC forces landed at Gallipoli at the mouth of the Black Sea, Turkey. They hoped to take Constantinople (modern-day Istanbul) and force

Germany's World War I ally, Turkey, out of the war. The men showed extraordinary courage and spirit, but the campaign was a disaster. No important gains were made and more than 11,400 ANZAC troops lost their lives.

Gallipoli memorial

ANZAC forces

Anzac Monument, Sydney

Australian and New Zealand forces fought for Britain in the Boer War (1899–1902) in South Africa and in both world wars. They fought together as the Australia and New Zealand Army Corps (ANZAC), sending a higher percentage of soliders per capita that other warring nations. The effort forged a strong sense of national identity.

Dominion status

When Australia became independent in 1901, it remained a Dominion of the British Empire and kept close links with its former ruler. But many people had few ties to the old "Mother Country." The threat of Japanese invasion during World War II led to closer links with the US as the only power that could defend Australia.

The Federation Flag was based on the state flag of New South Wales.

Federation Flag

Immigration

In 1902, the government passed the Immigration Restriction Act to limit Chinese immigration. The act required settlers to speak a European language, and began a White Australia policy that lasted until the 1970s. Britons, Greeks, and Italians flooded into Australia in the 1950s and 1960s, with immigration from Asia later increased

Scottish emigrants leave for Australia.

Modern Australia

After World War II, Australia continued its military alliance with the US. The country sent troops to fight with the Americans in Korea during the 1950s and Vietnam in the 1960s. In recent years, those ties have weakened, and Australia has increasingly turned toward Asia, particularly Japan, for trade and investment. Today, Australia is an important trading partner with most of the powerful East Asian economies.

National symbol

Sydney Opera House, with its bold concrete roofs, has become the most widely recognized symbol of Australia.

Australian republic?

In 1992, the prime minister, Paul Keating, said he wanted the country to be a republic by the year 2000, with an Australian as the head of state, instead of the British monarch. Although Keating was defeated in 1996 elections, the debate continues.

Chinese festival, Sydney

Skyscraper, Sydney

Multicultural Australia

Modern Australia is a multi-cultural state with large Chinese and Greek populations. However, the Aboriginals have waged a long battle to be included in society and to secure their land rights and civil liberties.

Sailing in Sydney Harbour

Sports excellence

One way Australia has expressed its national identity is through a wide varieties of sports, ranging from cricket to yachting. For example, in 1983 Australia overturned a century of US dominance of the seas by winning the Americas Cup. Sydney has been chosen as the site of the Olympic Games in 2000.

Timeline

c.40,000 BC Aboriginals arrive in Australia.

1642–43 Tasman names Van Diemen's Land (Tasmania).

1770 Captain Cook lands at Botany Bay.

1788 First British prisoners arrive.

1828 Charles Sturt begins to explore Murray and Darling rivers.

1860–61 Burke and Wills cross Australia from south to north.

1868 Britain abolishes the transportation of prisoners.

Wallaby

1851 Gold discovered in Victoria and New South Wales.

1901 Australia becomes self-governing dominion in the British Empire.

1902 Immigration Restriction Act establishes the White Australia policy.

Aboriginal women's digging sticks

1914–18 60,000 Australians are killed fighting for Britain in World War I.

1927 Parliament meets for the first time in the new federal capital of Canberra.

1939–45 Australian troops fight with the Allies in World War II.

1970s White Australia policy abolished.

1992 Prime minister Paul Keating apologizes to Aboriginals for 200 years of injustice.

FIND OUT MORE ABORIGINAL AUSTRALIANS   CRIME AND PUNISHMENT   COOK, JAMES   EXPLORATION   OPERA   PREHISTORIC PEOPLE   WORLD WAR I   WORLD WAR II

AUSTRALIAN WILDLIFE

AUSTRALIA HAS BEEN ISOLATED by water for more than 30 million years, resulting in the evolution of many unique animals and plants. Half of all marsupials, such as the koala and kangaroo, live only in Australia, along with the platypus and echidna, the world's only egg-laying mammals, or monotremes. Much of Australia is desert or scrub. The animals and plants that live here are adapted to the hot, dry conditions. There are also areas of tropical and temperate forests, which contain the greatest diversity of life in Australia.

Desert wildlife

Australia's hot, dry, desert interior makes up half the continent. Drought-resistant vegetation, such as porcupine grass and acacias, grow here, providing a refuge for birds and insects. Many desert mammals rest in burrows by day to avoid the heat. Snakes and lizards are common desert animals.

Emu
Emus are large flightless birds that can run at up to 30 mph (50 kmh), although they usually walk. They cover large distances in search of grasses, fruit, and flowers. They also eat insects. Males incubate the eggs and guard the young after they hatch.

Porcupine grass
As its name suggests, porcupine grass is a spiny plant that grows in circular tussocks. It is adapted to dry desert conditions by having a thick outer covering (cuticle) to reduce water loss, and by having deep roots to reach water in the soil.

Galah
The galah, or roseate cockatoo, is one of the most common parrots in Australia. Large flocks of these birds are found not only in dry areas but also in cities. Galahs eat seeds, leaf buds, and insects.

Strong bill is used to dig up insects.

Thorny devil
This lizard's scales are drawn out into long spines. When temperatures fall at night, valuable water condenses on the spines and runs down tiny grooves towards the mouth.

Spines protect against predators.

Mulgara
This carnivorous marsupial (pouched mammal) eats insects and small vertebrates, such as mice and lizards. It bites and shakes its prey to kill it. The mulgara digs burrows in sand, in order to escape the midday sun.

Mulgara eats prey head first.

Grass forms a refuge for insects, lizards, and birds.

Long, strong legs

Lizard searches for ants.

Scrub and grassland wildlife

Covering about a third of Australia, scrub and grassland are hot and dry in summer and cooler in winter. Plants use occasional heavy rainstorms to blossom and produce seeds, and animals, such as frogs, emerge to reproduce.

Short-beaked echidna
The short-beaked echidna is an egg-laying mammal found in Australia, Tasmania, and New Guinea. It uses its sticky tongue to extract ants and termites from their nests. If threatened, the echidna rolls into a ball, or digs down into the soil.

Mallee fowl
The male mallee fowl builds a mound of vegetation and soil in which the female lays her eggs. As the vegetation rots, it releases heat that incubates the eggs.

Male checks mound temperature with his beak, and by moving vegetation.

Canopy provides shelter for animals from the midday heat.

Bottle tree
These large trees get their name from their bottle-shaped trunks. The swollen trunk stores water that helps the tree survive periods of drought. The tree also provides food for many animals, including insects, and shelter for some birds and mammals. Other vegetation common in scrubland includes dry grasses and dwarf eucalyptus.

Water is stored in bulbous trunk.

Water-holding frog
This frog survives drought by burrowing into the ground and forming a thin layer of skin around itself to conserve water. It also stores water in its bladder.

Kultarr
This small, mouselike marsupial is nocturnal. It has large eyes to help it see in the dark and to catch insects and spiders. It moves by springing off its long hind feet and tail and landing on its front feet. During the day, it takes shelter in logs, hollow stumps, and burrows.

Kultarr feeds on a spider.

A

Temperate forest wildlife

The temperate forests of southern and eastern Australia are hot and dry in summer, and cooler and wetter in winter. They are home to birds, such as parrots and kookaburras, marsupials, including the koala, and a variety of reptiles and insects. Many trees found here, such as eucalyptus, are unique to Australia.

Silver wattle
The silver wattle, also known as mimosa, is a common plant in temperate forests. These trees, with their characteristic silver-gray leaves, can withstand dry periods and also the wet season.

Bright yellow flowers provide food for insects and other animals.

Kookaburra
The kookaburra is the largest member of the kingfisher family. It is rarely found near water, however, preferring open woodland. Kookaburras swoop down from a tree branch perch to pounce on insects, lizards, snakes, and small birds and mammals. They defend their territory by making loud cackling calls that sound like human laughter.

Male lyrebird sings a loud territorial song, mimicking other birds and animals.

Lyrebird
These ground birds use their large, clawed feet to turn over stones and break open logs in search of insects. The male lyrebird has a long tail shaped like a lyre, an ancient musical instrument. He performs courtship dances to attract females by vibrating his tail over his back.

Flattened tail helps platypus swim.

Heavy beak kills reptiles and rodents.

Duck-billed platypus
This unusual-looking animal is an egg-laying mammal, or monotreme, that lives near rivers. The platypus feeds underwater on insect larvae and other food found by probing the stream bottom with its sensitive bill. It hunts mainly at night, spending most of the day in a burrow dug in the stream bank.

Long tail feathers

Koalas spend most of their time in eucalyptus trees, using their sharp claws and strong legs to climb through the branches.

Koala
Koalas are bearlike marsupials that feed on the leaves of eucalyptus trees. They eat mainly at night, spending most of the day resting or sleeping in the fork of a tree.

Tree kangaroo
The tree kangaroo is a marsupial adapted for life in the trees, by having rough paw pads and long claws for gripping. Its diet consists mainly of leaves and bark, but it sometimes descends to the ground to feed on shrubs and seedlings.

Tropical rain forest wildlife

Despite occupying only a tiny part of northeastern Australia, the rainforests contain one-third of Australia's frog and marsupial species, and two-thirds of its butterflies. The wide variety of ferns and trees, such as breadfruit trees, provide shelter and food for these animals, and many birds, bats, and insects.

Long tail helps balance in the trees.

Rainbow lorikeet
These brightly colored parrots live in screeching flocks of up to 20 birds in the upper rain forest canopy. They feed on pollen, nectar, flowers, seeds, and fruit.

Fangs are 0.5 in (1 cm) long so they can inject venom deep into their victims.

Trigger plant
When a bee lands on a trigger plant flower, the anther – the flower's male part – bends outward to dust pollen on the bee's hairy back. When the bee visits another flower the pollen sticks to the stigma – the female part of the flower, and pollinates it.

Pink flowers attract bees.

Queen Alexandra's birdwing
Found in New Guinea, this is the largest butterfly in the world. The female is larger than the male and has a wingspan of up to 11 in (28 cm). Queen Alexandra's birdwing flies in the sunlight of the upper canopy, where it feeds on flower nectar.

The male is brightly colored.

Taipan
This forest snake is active in the early morning and evening, and feeds mainly on rats and other small mammals. The taipan is one of the world's most poisonous snakes; a bite from its long fangs is often fatal to humans. Taipans normally retreat and hide when people approach, but they will become aggressive if threatened.

Brown coloration provides camouflage for taipan.

FIND OUT MORE | AUSTRALIA | BIRDS | BUTTERFLIES AND MOTHS | CAMOUFLAGE AND COLOR | FLIGHTLESS BIRDS | FROGS AND TOADS | KANGAROOS AND OTHER MARSUPIALS | REPTILES | TREES

AZTECS

A GREAT IMPERIAL power, the Aztecs came to dominate the Valley of Mexico in less than a hundred years. Egged on by bloodthirsty gods, they were a warlike people, outstanding for their military skill and well organized society. By the time the Spanish conquistador Hernán Cortés (1485–1547) arrived in 1519, the Aztecs and their allies were rulers of some 25 million people.

Rise of the Aztecs

The Aztecs were one of many tribes who invaded the Valley of Mexico soon after the collapse of the Toltecs in the late 12th century. They dominated the valley after 1438.

Human sacrifice

When they won a war, the Aztecs killed many prisoners as offerings to their gods. Aztecs believed that human sacrifices were necessary in order for the universe to continue.

Dish for human heart

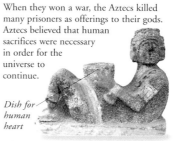

Subject peoples

The Aztecs ruled over a network of city states. Subject peoples made regular payments to their Aztec overlords, in the form of corn, cacao, or cotton. As long as this "tribute" was paid, the peoples of the Valley of Mexico were left to govern themselves and to keep their customs.

Tenochtitlán

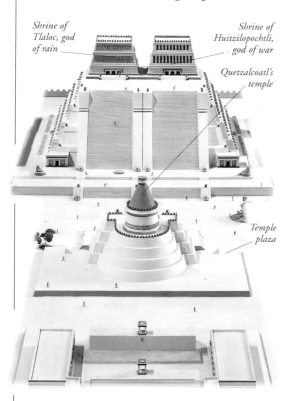

Shrine of Tlaloc, god of rain

Shrine of Huitzilopochtli, god of war

Quetzalcoatl's temple

Temple plaza

A city of canals and narrow streets, the Aztec capital was built on an island in Lake Texcoco. It was linked to the land by three narrow causeways. The city was home to 200,000 people – four or five times larger than any European city of the time. Most people lived in small houses in the narrow streets surrounding the temple precinct.

The great precinct

The center of Tenochtitlán was dominated by the Great Precinct, surrounded by a wall decorated with huge serpent heads. Inside the enclosure were the temples of the leading gods. A skull rack displayed the heads of countless victims of human sacrifice.

Aztec society

Commoners lived in small mud houses and grew crops on the marshes. They dressed and ate simply. The nobles were warriors, tribute collectors, and judges; they were rewarded for their services with land.

Mother of new baby

Chief priest

Three boys call out baby's name.

Midwife

School teacher

Customs

Aztec customs included an elaborate naming ceremony for newborn babies.

Aztecs on the eve of conquest

By the early 16th century, the Aztec Empire was showing signs of weakness. Shortly before the arrival of Cortés, priests and nobles were worried by a series of omens that seemed to forecast Aztec decline. These omens included the rumbling of the volcano Popocatépetl.

Quetzalcoatl

The Aztecs believed that the god Quetzalcoatl had been driven from his kingdom and would return to begin a golden age. When Cortés arrived, they thought he was the god. But the noise of Popocatépetl seemed to be an omen of defeat.

Quetzalcoatl, the feathered serpent

Popocatépetl

Montezuma II

The emperor Montezuma II (c. 1466–1520) was unsure if Cortés was Quetzalcoatl, and hesitated to repel the Spanish when they arrived. Cortés and his small army got as far as the capital, and Montezuma welcomed them there. But the Spanish seized the emperor and took him hostage. Montezuma died in prison, the last Aztec ruler.

Conquest of the Aztecs

In April 1519, Cortés founded Veracruz on the coast of the Gulf of Mexico, inside the Aztec Empire. With his army of 600 men and 16 horses, he advanced toward Tenochtitlán, forging alliances with Aztec enemies. By August 1521, the Spanish had occupied Tenochtitlán after laying siege with the help of many local soldiers.

Defeat by Tlaxcala

The growing thirst for human sacrifice led Aztecs to wage constant war on the neighboring Tlaxcalans. Four years before the arrival of Cortés, the Tlaxcalans inflicted a heavy defeat on the Aztec armies, greatly weakening the empire.

FIND OUT MORE   CENTRAL AMERICA, HISTORY OF   MAYA   MESOAMERICANS   OLMECS

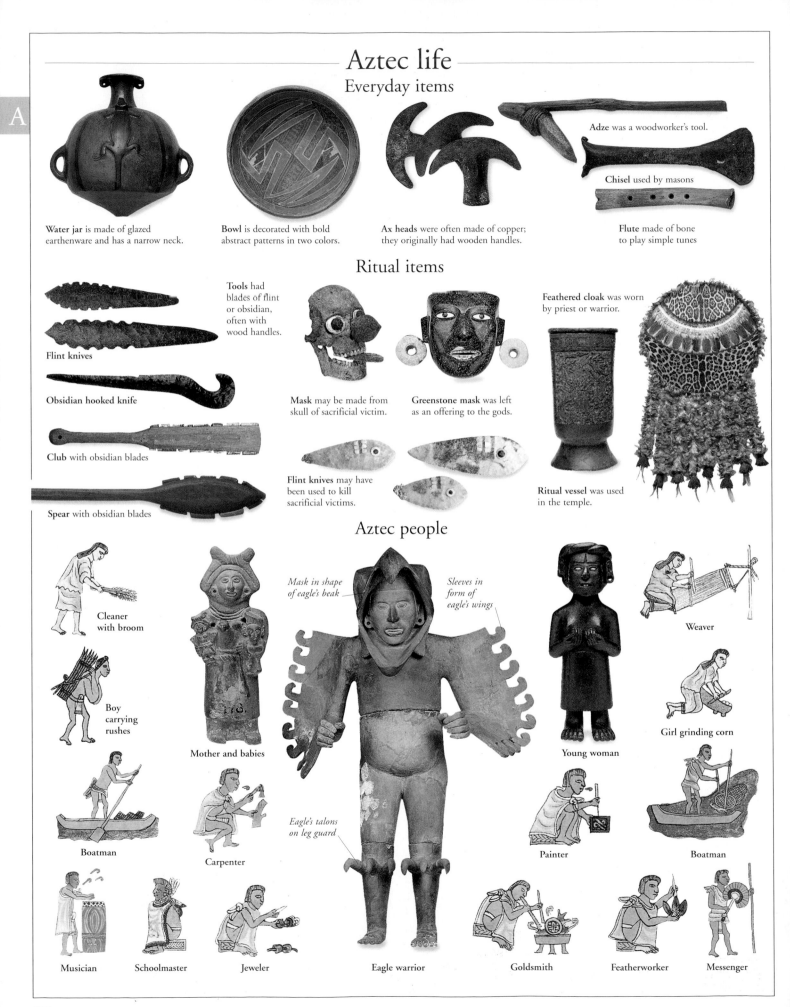

Aztec life
Everyday items

Water jar is made of glazed earthenware and has a narrow neck.

Bowl is decorated with bold abstract patterns in two colors.

Ax heads were often made of copper; they originally had wooden handles.

Adze was a woodworker's tool.

Chisel used by masons

Flute made of bone to play simple tunes

Ritual items

Tools had blades of flint or obsidian, often with wood handles.

Flint knives

Obsidian hooked knife

Club with obsidian blades

Spear with obsidian blades

Mask may be made from skull of sacrificial victim.

Greenstone mask was left as an offering to the gods.

Feathered cloak was worn by priest or warrior.

Flint knives may have been used to kill sacrificial victims.

Ritual vessel was used in the temple.

Aztec people

Cleaner with broom

Boy carrying rushes

Boatman

Mother and babies

Carpenter

Mask in shape of eagle's beak

Sleeves in form of eagle's wings

Eagle's talons on leg guard

Young woman

Weaver

Girl grinding corn

Painter

Boatman

Musician

Schoolmaster

Jeweler

Eagle warrior

Goldsmith

Featherworker

Messenger

BABYLONIAN EMPIRE

ON THE EUPHRATES RIVER, nearly 4,000 years ago, an ancient settlement became the most magnificent city in the Near East. This city was Babylon, and when Hammurabi conquered Mesopotamia, he established his capital there. Over centuries, Babylonian fortunes rose and fell, as the city was invaded by the Hittites, Kassites, and Assyrians. The Assyrians destroyed Babylon in 689 BC. In 612 BC, the Babylonians retaliated by conquering the Assyrians and again made Babylon the world's greatest city. Babylonia's splendor continued after the Persian Empire absorbed it in 539 BC.

The first Babylonian Empire
By about 1770 BC, Hammurabi had conquered most of Mesopotamia. Babylon was established as the capital of the south for the duration of the Babylonian empire.

King Hammurabi

Mesopotamia's wisest king, Hammurabi (r.1792–1750 BC), followed ancient tradition by issuing laws to protect his subjects. Using cuneiform script, he had 282 laws carved on a black stone pillar. The empire he founded collapsed in 1595 BC, when Hittites from Anatolia looted it. The Kassites from the mountains to the east of Babylon then invaded and took over.

Kassites
Between 1600 and 1190 BC, people called the Kassites ruled Babylonia. They are best known for their boundary stones (kuddurus), which marked property divisions and recorded gifts of land. These were often decorated with divine symbols. After the end of Kassite rule, Babylonia fell into a long period of chaos.

Persian Empire
In 539 BC, the Persian king, Cyrus II, took over the Babylonian kingdom and made Mesopotamia part of his empire. His son, Cambyses, was usurped by Darius I, also called "the Great," under whom the empire reached its greatest extent.

Darius I (522–486) introduced coinage.

Kudduru

Literature and art

The Babylonian Empire was renowned for its great artistic and literary achievements. Literature, such as the legendary epic of Gilgamesh, a Sumerian hero, was written on clay tablets in cuneiform script. Artistic splendors included terra-cotta plaques, superb sculpture and glassware, and, above all, the lavish and decorative entrance to the city – the Ishtar Gate and Processional Way.

Venus tablet, Kish

Science
Babylonia was famous as a home of scientists and scholars. Babylonian astrologers studied the movements of planets and stars, recorded their findings on clay tablets, and used these to predict the future. Many texts are so detailed that modern astronomers can date ancient events from them. Ancient Greeks and Romans used the Babylonian system for naming planets.

Cuneiform script

Magical spirit

The Ishtar Gate, one of Nebuchadnezzar's most spectacular structures, was made from clay bricks which were molded and brilliantly glazed with color.

Fortified tower

Stepped battlement

Dragon, symbol of the god Marduk

Bull, symbol of Adad, god of the weather

Religion
The Babylonians inherited their religion from the Sumerians. They believed that gods and spirits controlled every aspect of the world. These gods included Anu, the sky god, who gave birth to some of the most important deities, including Ishtar, goddess of love and war (represented by the planet Venus), and Ea, god of wisdom and freshwater. Ea was the father of Marduk, the god of Babylon, who created the world and made humans by mixing earth with divine blood.

Nebuchadnezzar

After the Babylonian king Nabopolasser defeated the Assyrian enemy, his son Nebuchadnezzar (r.605–562 BC) rebuilt the devastated Babylon on a grand scale. His works included the Ishtar Gate, and a temple and ziggurat tower. According to Greek tradition, he also built Hanging Gardens for his homesick wife, and these became one of the Seven Wonders of the World. In 596 BC, Nebuchadnezzar attacked the kingdom of Judah. Ten years later he returned, sacked Jerusalem, and took the Jews into exile in Babylon. They were not released until the reign of Cyrus II.

FIND OUT MORE   ARCHITECTURE   ASIA, HISTORY OF   ASSYRIAN EMPIRE   HITTITES   PERSIAN EMPIRES   SCIENCE, HISTORY OF   SEVEN WONDERS OF THE ANCIENT WORLD   SUMERIANS   WARFARE

BADGERS, OTTERS, AND SKUNKS

B

THESE THREE GROUPS OF ANIMALS are members of the weasel family – Mustelidae. Their main characteristics are a long, low-slung body, short legs, and five toes on each foot. They are carnivores, although badgers have a mixed diet. The honey badger is especially fond of honey, as its name suggests. Most mustelids discharge a thick, oily, strong-smelling fluid called musk from their anal glands. They use this mostly to send scent messages to other members of the species, usually with their droppings.

Skull
A badger eats meat and plants, and its large canines and broad molar teeth are ideal for this diet. Its jaw muscles are fixed to a rigid bone on the top of its skull, giving the animal a powerful bite.

Badgers

All badgers are thick set, with very powerful legs that they use to forage for food and to dig their often extensive burrows. They are nocturnal animals, spending the day underground with others of their social group. There are eight species of true badgers, plus the honey badger, which is classed in a subfamily of its own.

Short tail

Long, striped snout

Long, coarse hairs over a dense underfur

Badgers have a good sense of smell.

Paws
A Eurasian badger's track is unmistakable. Each foot has five toes with a kidney-shaped pad behind. The front claws usually leave marks because they are long.

Forepaw print

Hindpaw print

Eurasian badger
This is the largest badger and has the widest distribution. Females give birth to up to four cubs in February. They are weaned at 12 weeks, when they can forage for themselves.

Badger setts
During the day, badgers live underground in a complex system of tunnels and chambers called a sett. A main badger sett is easy to spot because of the entrance with piles of soil outside.

Otters

These semiaquatic mustelids live outside the polar regions on every continent except Australia. Some species are exclusively sea creatures, some use only freshwater, and others use both sea- and freshwater. Most have sleeping dens, or holts, on land.

European river otter

Asian short-clawed otter

Paws
Although all otters swim, not all have webbed feet. The European otter has a large amount of webbing, while the Asian short-clawed otter has little webbing and uses its paws to find food by touch.

Fur
An otter's coat consists of two layers. A thick underlayer of fine hairs traps air for warmth, and longer, waterproof guard hairs keep the underfur dry.

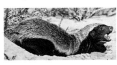

Honey badger
The African honey badger, also known as the ratel, has a thick, loose skin. Predators can find it difficult to pierce its skin, and the badger can twist around inside its skin and bite back.

Movement
With their long backs and heavy tails, otters can look clumsy on land. In the water they are graceful swimmers, propelling themselves forward by moving their hindquarters and tail up and down.

Spraints
Otters secrete a powerful scent. They mark their territory by leaving their droppings, called spraints, which smell of this scent, on high points such as rocks.

Skunks

There are 13 species of skunks, which all live in the Americas. They are best known for their ability to squirt a foul-smelling fluid from their anal glands. They aim this fluid at the eyes of an enemy, and it causes temporary blindness. Skunks search for insects and other small animals to eat, mainly at night.

Markings
Skunks have bold black and white coat markings. Like the yellow and black stripes of a wasp, these warn would-be predators of danger.

EURASIAN BADGER

SCIENTIFIC NAME *Meles meles*

ORDER Carnivora

FAMILY Mustelidae

DISTRIBUTION Europe and a wide band across Asia

HABITAT Mainly lowland farmland and woodland

DIET Worms, insects, birds, and other small animals, fruit, cereals, fungi

SIZE Length: 3.3 ft (1 m)

LIFESPAN About 7 years

FIND OUT MORE

ANIMAL BEHAVIOR

LAKE AND RIVER WILDLIFE

NORTH AMERICAN WILDLIFE

POLLUTION

WEASELS AND MARTENS

BALKAN STATES

SLOVENIA, CROATIA, Bosnia and Herzegovina, Yugoslavia, Macedonia, and Albania all lie in the western Balkans. Ruled by Turkey for nearly 500 years, all the countries, with the exception of Albania, were united as Yugoslavia in 1918. It was, however, an uneasy peace, and, in 1991, Yugoslavia split up as a result of built-up rival ethnic and religious tensions. Fighting broke out, lasting until 1995. Today, the region is struggling to overcome the damage caused by the war.

Physical features

The western Balkans are made up of limestone plateaus and steep mountain ranges separated by deep, forested valleys. In the northwest are the flat plains of the Danube River.

34°F (1°C) 73°F (23°C)

34 in (870 mm)

Regional climate

The inland plains and the coastal strip have a temperate continental climate, with hot summers and cold winters. Snow falls in the mountains in winter.

Mountains

Mixed forests of deciduous trees and conifers cover the mountain slopes that dominate the north of the region. The Dinaric Alps are barren limestone ranges, or *karst*, that rise to about 5,905 ft (1,800 m) along the Adriatic Sea coast.

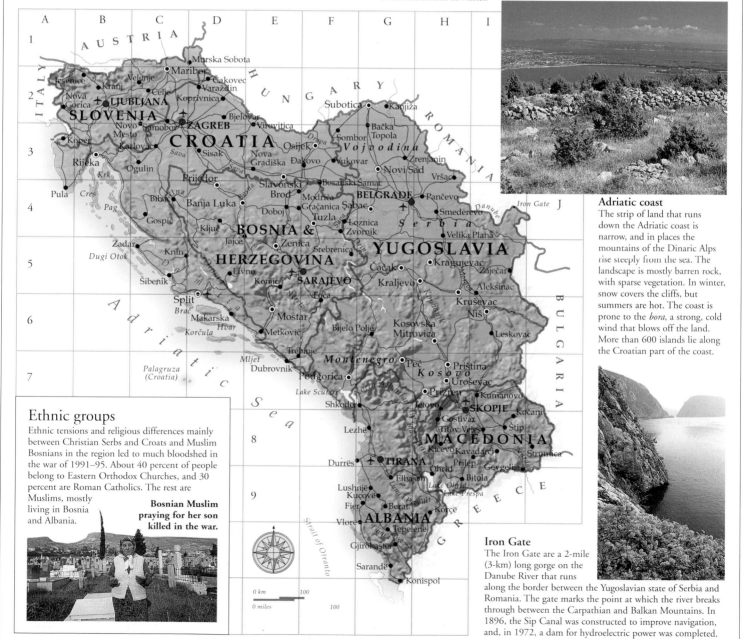

Adriatic coast

The strip of land that runs down the Adriatic coast is narrow, and in places the mountains of the Dinaric Alps rise steeply from the sea. The landscape is mostly barren rock, with sparse vegetation. In winter, snow covers the cliffs, but summers are hot. The coast is prone to the *bora*, a strong, cold wind that blows off the land. More than 600 islands lie along the Croatian part of the coast.

Ethnic groups

Ethnic tensions and religious differences mainly between Christian Serbs and Croats and Muslim Bosnians in the region led to much bloodshed in the war of 1991–95. About 40 percent of people belong to Eastern Orthodox Churches, and 30 percent are Roman Catholics. The rest are Muslims, mostly living in Bosnia and Albania.

Bosnian Muslim praying for her son killed in the war.

Iron Gate

The Iron Gate are a 2-mile (3-km) long gorge on the Danube River that runs along the border between the Yugoslavian state of Serbia and Romania. The gate marks the point at which the river breaks through between the Carpathian and Balkan Mountains. In 1896, the Sip Canal was constructed to improve navigation, and, in 1972, a dam for hydroelectric power was completed.

Slovenia

Historically and geographically, Slovenia has more in common with Austria than with the other Balkan states. The country was ruled by Austria for almost a thousand years. Slovenia has many small farms and thriving businesses. Despite economic problems caused by the conflict in areas to the south, it is the region's wealthiest country.

Resources
Slovenia mines mercury, lead, oil, and zinc for export. There are also deposits of brown coal and lignite, but they are poor quality and difficult to extract. One-third of the country's energy comes from a nuclear plant in Krsvo.

Mercury ore

People
About 90 percent of the population are Slovenes who have kept their language and traditional culture despite centuries of Austrian domination. Workers earn more than in other Balkan states, and standards of education are high. One in seven Slovenes lives in the capital, Ljubljana, which has textile, electronics, chemical, and manufacturing industries.

Tourism
Slovenia is slowly rebuilding its tourist industry, which suffered because of the war in Bosnia. Skiing, spa resorts, and lakeside scenery attract many visitors to the Alps in the north of the region.

Lake Bled is a popular tourist destination.

SLOVENIA FACTS

CAPITAL CITY	Ljubljana
AREA	7,820 sq miles (20,250 sq km)
POPULATION	2,016,000
MAIN LANGUAGE	Slovene
MAJOR RELIGION	Christian
CURRENCY	Tolar

Croatia

Ruled by Hungary for more than 800 years, Croatia became part of Yugoslavia in 1918, gaining independence in 1991. Croatia's economy was damaged by the war with neighboring Bosnia, but it is fortunate in having important ports and rich resources, including oil, coal, and bauxite. There are plans to revive tourism.

Adriatic coast
Croatia's Adriatic coast has sandy beaches and hundreds of offshore islands that once attracted up to 12 million tourists every year. However, the outbreak of war in 1991 abruptly halted all tourism. There is still an active fishing industry, with an annual catch of about 27,500 tons (25,000 tonnes).

CROATIA FACTS

CAPITAL CITY	Zagreb
AREA	21,830 sq miles (56,540 sq km)
POPULATION	4,801,000
MAIN LANGUAGE	Croatian
MAJOR RELIGIONS	Christian, Muslim
CURRENCY	Kuna

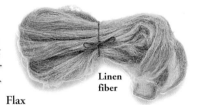

Flax stalks

Linen fiber

Flax
Fields of flax are cultivated in the fertile river valleys of northern Croatia. Flax fiber, obtained by crushing the stalks of the plant, is woven into linen and canvas, and its seeds yield linseed oil. Apricots, grapes, and plums are also grown in northern Croatia.

Zagreb
The cultural and industrial capital of Croatia is Zagreb, which has museums, art galleries, 13th-century buildings, and cathedrals, such as St. Mark's and St. Stephen's. People travel around by streetcar and bus. About 80 percent of the people are Croats and 12 percent are Serbs.

Bosnia and Herzegovina

In 1991, bitter fighting broke out in the twin states of Bosnia and Herzegovina between the Roman Catholic Croats, Muslim Bosnians, and Orthodox Serbs. In all, about 400,000 people were killed, more than 1,000,000 fled the country, and many historic cities were devastated. A precarious peace has prevailed since 1995.

BOSNIA AND HERZEGOVINA FACTS

CAPITAL CITY	Sarajevo
AREA	19,741 sq miles (51,130 sq km)
POPULATION	4,446,000
MAIN LANGUAGE	Serbo-Croatian
MAJOR RELIGIONS	Christian, Muslim
CURRENCY	Dinar

Muslims
During the war, Serbs in Bosnia forced Croats and Muslims out of areas they regarded as their own. Thousands were killed, and many Muslims fled abroad. In 1995, a peace agreement split the country into two provinces: Bosnian-Serb and Muslim-Croat.

Sarajevo
Straddling the Miljacka River, Sarajevo is the capital of Bosnia and Herzegovina. Under communist rule the city was transformed from a sleepy, Islamic town to a bustling, multi-cultural industrial center. During the civil war, however, it was shattered by 2,000,000 shells that killed tens of thousands of people. Serbs attacking the city were forced to withdraw in 1995.

Farming
Bosnia and Herzegovina's main farming region lies in the southwest; the area has fertile, spring-fed soil and hot, dry summers. Crops include citrus fruit, grapes, corn, pomegranates, figs, olives, rice, and tobacco. Sheep are raised on the hill country.

Figs

Pomegranates

Yugoslavia

Two of the former Yugoslavia's states, Serbia and Montenegro, kept the name Yugoslavia in 1992. As a result of the part Serbia played in helping Serbs fight in Bosnia and Croatia, many countries imposed sanctions and refused to trade with the new Yugoslavia. Sanctions have had a devastating effect on the economy of this nation.

People

The people of Yugoslavia speak Serbo-Croatian, which they write in the Russian-like Cyrillic alphabet. The largest minority group is Albanian (16 percent). Most people belong to the Serbian Orthodox Church.

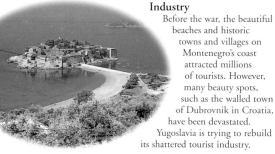

Raznjici

Cubes of grilled lamb   *Skewer*

Food

A favorite Yugoslavian dish is *raznjici*, cubes of lamb grilled on skewers and served with yogurt. *Djuvetsch*, meat with rice and vegetables, is also popular. Desserts are made from honey and nuts. The national drink is *slivovitz*, plum brandy.

Sveti Stefan was once a popular tourist destination.

Industry

Before the war, the beautiful beaches and historic towns and villages on Montenegro's coast attracted millions of tourists. However, many beauty spots, such as the walled town of Dubrovnik in Croatia, have been devastated. Yugoslavia is trying to rebuild its shattered tourist industry.

YUGOSLAVIA FACTS

CAPITAL CITY Belgrade

AREA 39,506 sq miles (102,350 sq km)

POPULATION 10,931,000

MAIN LANGUAGE Serbo-Croatian

MAJOR RELIGIONS Christian, Muslim

CURRENCY Dinar

Macedonia

The official name of the country is the Former Yugoslav Republic of Macedonia to appease the Greeks, who have a province called Macedonia. Landlocked, it is self-sufficient in energy, with efficient metal, chemical, textile, and food processing industries. Air pollution is a serious problem. Macedonia mines copper, iron ore, lead, and zinc.

Skopje

Despite having been destroyed four times by earthquakes, most recently in 1963, Macedonia's capital, Skopje, is the hub of the country's communications and industry.

Lakes

Lake Ohrid and Lake Prespa in southwestern Macedonia are two of Europe's most beautiful spots and, in peaceful times, they attract visitors for the scenery and the fishing. Ohrid is 964 ft (294 m) deep. Underground channels link the two lakes.

People

The largest group of people is made up of Eastern Orthodox (Christian) Slav Macedonians who account for two-thirds of the population. About 23 percent are Albanians, most of whom are Muslim.

MACEDONIA FACTS

CAPITAL CITY Skopje

AREA 25,713 sq km (9,925 sq miles)

POPULATION 2,093,000

MAIN LANGUAGES Macedonian, Serbo-Croatian

MAJOR RELIGIONS Christian, Muslim

CURRENCY Denar

Albania

From 1944 to 1991, Albania was a one-party state with the most rigid communist regime in the world. It is now a democracy, but, in 1997, social unrest developed. Tirana, the capital, was founded in the 17th century and has light industries as well as government buildings.

Grapes

Tomatoes

Potatoes

Watermelon

People

As a way of making the population grow rapidly, the communist government encouraged men and women to have large families. Under communism, Albania was the only official atheist state and, even today, many people are nonbelievers.

Farming

About 24 percent of Albania is cultivated. Wheat, corn, potatoes, other vegetables, fruit, and sugar beet are the main crops. Sheep, goats, and cattle are raised for meat and milk, and donkeys are bred for transportation.

Transportation

Communications are difficult. There are only 450 miles (720 km) of railroads, and 4,630 miles (7,450 km) of roads, 60 percent of which are not paved. There is only one car for every 50 people. Horses and carts are the main means of transportation.

ALBANIA FACTS

CAPITAL CITY Tirana

AREA 11,100 sq miles (28,750 sq km)

POPULATION 3,429,000

MAIN LANGUAGE Albanian

MAJOR RELIGIONS Muslim, Christian

CURRENCY Lek

FIND OUT MORE   CHRISTIANITY   EARTHQUAKES   EMPIRES   EUROPE, HISTORY OF   FARMING   FISHING INDUSTRY   ISLAM   LAKES   TEXTILES AND WEAVING   TRADE AND INDUSTRY

BALLET

ONE OF THE MOST beautiful of the arts, ballet is a combination of dance and mime performed to music. Many ballets tell a story; others are abstract and experiment with form and movement. Ballet began in Italy. It was taken to France in 1533 by Catherine de Médicis, a member of a famous Italian family, who married a French prince. In 1661, Louis XIV founded the first ballet school, L'Academie Royale de Danse. Today, children learn the basics in ballet schools around the world.

First position – heels together, feet turned out.

Second position – heels apart, feet turned out.

Arms open wide

Third position – one foot crossed halfway in front of the other.

Both arms held in front

One arm in front, the other out to the side

Fourth position (crossed) – one foot in front of the other.

One arm up, the other out to the side

Fifth position – Feet crossed and touching.

Both arms up

Ballet positions

Every step in ballet makes use of the basic positions. It was at L'Academie Royale de Danse that the five basic positions of the feet were established. To achieve them, the whole leg has to be turned out from the hips. The position of the arms is known as *port de bras*.

Benesh notation

For ballets to survive, the steps must be written down, or notated. One of the most popular notation methods was devised by Rudolf and Joan Benesh in the late 1940s. Symbols represent the position of the hands and feet.

Each line represents a part of the body: top of head; shoulder; waist; knee; floor.

Romantic ballet

In the early 1800s, the Romantic Movement, with its fascination with the supernatural, affected all the arts. One of the most important men in 19th-century ballet was the choreographer August Bournonville. His ballets were influenced by his years in Paris where Romantic ballet began.

Marie Taglione
Taglione (1804–84) was an Italian ballerina who created the role of *La Sylphide*. She perfected the art of dancing on the tips of her toes, or *en pointe*.

Giselle
The ballet *Giselle* is one of the most famous Romantic ballets. The story follows the romance between a peasant girl, Giselle, and Albrecht, a count. Giselle dies, but rises from her grave to dance with her lover.

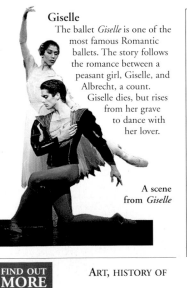

A scene from *Giselle*

Nijinsky

The Ballets Russes
Many Russian choreographers and dancers became bored with Classical ballet. Organized by Serge Diaghilev (1872–1929), they formed the Ballets Russes and toured Europe. The dancers included Vaslav Nijinsky (1890–1950), famous for his jumps.

Anna Pavlova
Russian ballerina Anna Pavlova (1881–1931) was the most famous dancer of her time. She danced with the Imperial Ballet, and also toured with the Ballets Russes. She formed her own company and toured all over the world.

Ballet in Russia

In 1847, French dancer Marius Petipa went to Russia to work with the tsar's Imperial Ballet in St. Petersburg. With his assistant Lev Ivanov, he created Classical ballets – grand lavish ballets in three or four acts, designed to show off the brilliant techniques of the dancers.

Classical ballets contain dazzling dances for the hero and heroine to perform together.

Partners have to trust each other.

Moscow City Ballet in *Sleeping Beauty*

Tchaikovsky
Russian composer Pëtr Tchaikovsky (1840–93) wrote probably the most famous ballet music of all. He worked with Marius Petipa and Lev Ivanov on the three great classical ballets, *Sleeping Beauty* (1890), *The Nutcracker* (1892), and *Swan Lake* (1895).

Ballet today

Almost every country has its own ballet company. The dancers perform Romantic and Classical ballets, ballets created by the Ballets Russes, and the works of more modern and contemporary choreographers.

New York City Ballet
The New York City Ballet (left) was founded by the Russian choreographer George Balanchine (1904–83). This is his ballet *Apollo*.

Jumps require strength.

A character from Ashton's *Tales of Beatrix Potter*

The Royal Ballet
Britain's Royal Ballet started as the Vic-Wells Ballet in 1931. It often dances works by past artistic directors Frederick Ashton and Kenneth MacMillan.

FIND OUT MORE

ART, HISTORY OF   DANCE   DRAMA   JAZZ   MUSIC   MUSICAL INSTRUMENTS   OPERA   STRAVINSKY, IGOR

BALL GAMES

BALL GAMES OF EVERY VARIETY are played around the world with all shapes and sizes of balls; on fields, courts, courses, and tables; by teams and by individuals. In addition to various football games and racket games, there are bat-and-ball games such as cricket and baseball, stick-and-ball games such as hockey, hurling, shinty, and golf; and billiard-table games such as pool, snooker, and billiards. Other ball games include basketball, played on a court, volleyball, which is usually played on a court on the beach, and bowls, in which balls are rolled along the ground.

Batting gloves

Helmet

Bat made of willow

Wicket keeping pads

Wicket-keeping gloves

Leather-cased ball

Wicket

Cricket

This game is played between two teams of 11, one team bowling and fielding against two on the batting side. The batsmen score runs by running between the wickets or hitting the ball over the boundary. The fielding side may dismiss the batsmen in several ways, including bowling at and knocking over the wicket with the ball.

Sightscreen helps the batsman see the ball.

Pitch

Cricket field
The field is usually oval but its size varies. The boundary is marked by a rope or white line. The pitch, situated at or near the middle of the field, measures 22 yd (20.12 m) between wickets and 10 ft (3.05 m) across.

Cricket equipment
Cricket is played with a hard ball, and many players wear protective clothing. The wicket keeper and batsmen wear special gloves and strapped-on leg-pads. Batsmen and close fielders may wear helmets with face guards.

Catcher's glove with hard ball

Catcher's mask

Bat

Baseball

Baseball is played between two teams of nine which take turns batting and fielding. A pitcher throws the ball and the batter attempts to hit it and run to bases without being tagged or forced out before reaching home plate. The game has nine innings. An inning is over when six batters – three from each team – are out.

Baseball equipment
The catcher, who crouches behind the batter, wears a mask and body padding. Batters wear a helmet and fielders wear a padded mitt. The ball is made of cork wrapped in yarn and encased in leather.

Outfield

Infield

Home plate

Babe Ruth

The sensational hitting of Babe Ruth (1895–1948) brought crowds to baseball in the 1920s. Originally a World Series-winning pitcher with the Boston Red Sox, he joined the New York Yankees in 1920 and slugged record after record, including his famous 60 home runs in 1927 and a lifetime total of 714.

Baseball field
The field is made up of an infield, or "diamond," and an outfield. A pitcher throws from a mound at the center of the infield, which has a base at each corner. A batter stands at home plate.

Field hockey

This is played between two teams of 11. Each player has a hooked stick, only the flat side of which can be used for playing the ball. The object of the game is to hit the ball into the opponents' goal. Goals may be scored only from inside a semicircle called the striking, or shooting, circle.

Ball, traditionally white

Goalkeeper's helmet

Hockey equipment
Players wear guards under their socks to protect their shins and ankles. The goalkeeper wears a helmet with a face mask, shoulder and elbow pads, padded gloves, substantial leg guards, and "kickers" over the boots to protect their feet when kicking the ball away.

Stick

Hurling
This is played, 15 on a side, with wooden sticks called hurleys, which are used to strike or carry a small, hard ball. Goals are like soccer goals with extended posts. Points are scored for hitting the ball under the crossbar (three points) or over it (one point).

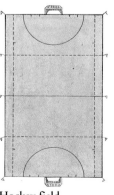

Hockey field
The pitch measures 100 yd x 60 yd (91.4 m x 54.9 m). Goals are 12 ft (3.66 m) wide and 7 ft (2.13 m) high. The shooting circles are joined quarter circles drawn from each post.

Basketball

With five a side, basketball allows free substitution from as many as seven other players. The goal is to put the ball into the opposition's basket. Baskets, or field goals, are worth three points when scored from outside the three-point line, and two points when scored from inside the line.

The player holds the ball in both hands when preparing to shoot.

Players can pivot and jump with the ball, as when shooting a "basket."

Three-point line

A moving player may take one stride with the ball.

High top sneakers are needed to support the ankles when turning and pivoting.

Basketball court
A basketball court is 91.8 ft x 49.2 ft (28 m x 15 m). The baskets stand 10 ft (3.05 m) above the ground.

Basketball

Ball is made of rubber encased in leather, rubber, or synthetic material.

Basket

Backboard

Basketball equipment
The main equipment needed for basketball is a ball and two baskets. Official time-keepers use clocks to keep track of the many time restrictions in the game, including the five-second limit on a player holding the ball.

Netball
This is played by either seven women, or girls, on a side. The goal is to throw the ball into the opponents' net. Players must stay in certain areas of the court and may not move with the ball. They wear letters to show where they should be.

Volleyball
Teams of six players aim to score points by propelling the ball over a net into the opponents' court so that they cannot return it. Players can play the ball with their hands or any part of the body above the waist. A team is allowed three hits to move the ball over the net.

Golf

The goal in golf is to take as few strokes as possible to hit a ball a certain distance into a cup set in the ground. Players have a choice of clubs with which to strike the ball. The standard course has 18 holes of different lengths and configurations.

Following through after contact

Starting a swing to hit the ball

End of follow-through

Tees

Golf balls

Bowls and bowling

Flat-green bowls is played on a flat lawn or indoors on a carpet. Players roll balls called woods, aiming to get them as close as possible to a smaller white ball called the jack. Tenpin bowling is played on indoor alleys. At each turn, bowlers have two goes to knock down as many pins as possible.

Cue-and-ball games

Games played on billiards and pool tables include snooker and pool. Players use a stick called a cue to propel a white ball into colored balls to knock them into a pocket. Billiards is played with three balls – one white cue ball for each player and a red ball.

Snooker balls

Playing a hole
Holes range from about 100 yd (90 m) to 600 yd (550 m). The first shot is played from the tee with either a wood, which is used for long shots, or an iron. Irons are used for the next shots until the putting green is reached, when the putter is used.

Wood

Iron

Putter

Flat-green wood

Indoor bowls

Jack

Golf equipment
Players are allowed up to 14 clubs, which they carry in a bag or trolley. Most players have three or four woods, nine or ten irons, and one putter. The ball is supported for the first stroke of each hole on a small stand, or tee. Players must wear studded shoes.

Bowling ball

Pool
Eight ball is the most widely played variety of pool. To win, one player must sink balls 1 to 7 in any order and then the 8, or black ball. The other player tries to sink balls 9 to 15 and then 8. Players take turns, remaining at the table until they fail to sink a ball, or commit a foul.

Snooker
Players sink a red for one point, and then any color for two to seven points, depending on the color. The colors are replaced until no reds remain and are then sunk in order of their value.

Pins

Equipment
Woods for bowls are weighted on one side so th at they curve when rolled. Bowling balls have holes for the thumb and two fingers. The ten pins are cleared and reset automatically.

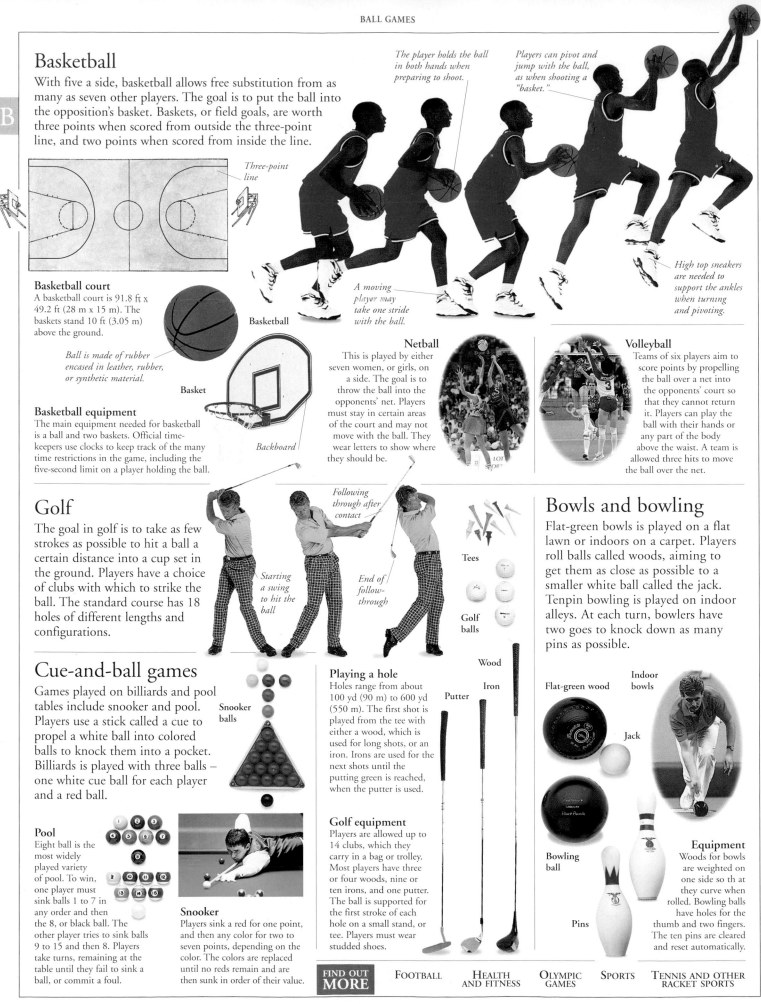

FIND OUT MORE

FOOTBALL   HEALTH AND FITNESS   OLYMPIC GAMES   SPORTS   TENNIS AND OTHER RACKET SPORTS

Ball games

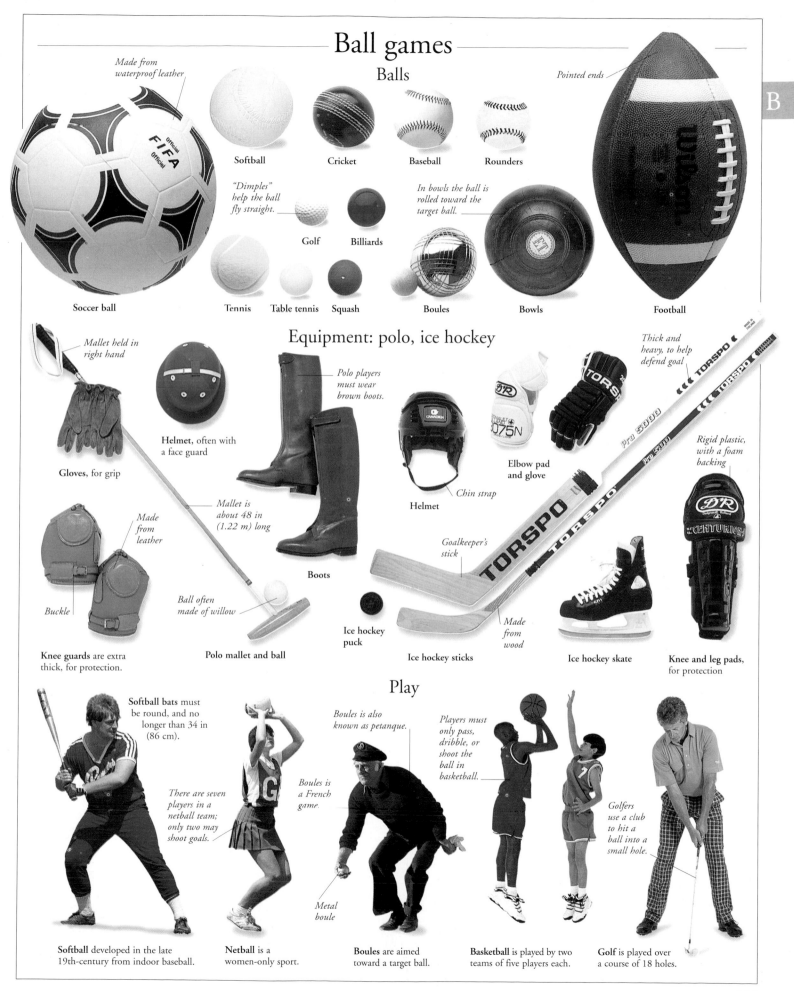

Balls

Made from waterproof leather

Softball

Cricket

Baseball

Rounders

Pointed ends

"Dimples" help the ball fly straight.

Golf

Billiards

In bowls the ball is rolled toward the target ball.

Boules

Bowls

Soccer ball

Tennis

Table tennis

Squash

Football

Equipment: polo, ice hockey

Mallet held in right hand

Gloves, for grip

Helmet, often with a face guard

Polo players must wear brown boots.

Helmet

Chin strap

Elbow pad and glove

Thick and heavy, to help defend goal

Rigid plastic, with a foam backing

Made from leather

Buckle

Knee guards are extra thick, for protection.

Mallet is about 48 in (1.22 m) long

Ball often made of willow

Polo mallet and ball

Boots

Goalkeeper's stick

Ice hockey puck

Ice hockey sticks

Made from wood

Ice hockey skate

Knee and leg pads, for protection

Play

Softball bats must be round, and no longer than 34 in (86 cm).

There are seven players in a netball team; only two may shoot goals.

Boules is also known as petanque.

Boules is a French game.

Players must only pass, dribble, or shoot the ball in basketball.

Golfers use a club to hit a ball into a small hole.

Metal boule

Softball developed in the late 19th-century from indoor baseball.

Netball is a women-only sport.

Boules are aimed toward a target ball.

Basketball is played by two teams of five players each.

Golf is played over a course of 18 holes.

BALTIC STATES AND BELARUS

THE THREE Baltic states of Estonia, Latvia, and Lithuania occupy a small area on the Baltic Sea coast to the west of the Russian Federation. Belarus, formerly known as "White Russia," sits between Russia, Poland, and Ukraine. All four countries were former Soviet republics; in 1991, after the breakup of the Soviet Union, they declared independence. Since then, they have suffered high inflation and environmental problems, but are now working to form a trade link between eastern and western Europe.

Physical features

The Baltic states have a flat landscape of plains and low hills, with forests and swampy marshes. There are thousands of rivers and lakes; the largest, Peipus, at 1,400 sq miles (3,626 sq km), is shared between Estonia and Russia.

Baltic coast and islands

Estonia, Latvia, and Lithuania all have coasts and ports on the Baltic Sea, and ice covers much of the sea in winter. Estonia has the longest coastline, and the country includes more than 1,500 islands that form a barrier protecting the Gulf of Riga.

Forests

Dense deciduous and coniferous forests cover between 30 and 40 percent of the Baltic region. Belarus is dominated by lakes and thick forests full of wildlife such as deer and mink. The east of Latvia is forested.

Forested Ganja River valley, Latvia

Pripet Marshes

Covering a vast area of southern Belarus, the Pripet Marshes are the biggest wetland area in Europe. They stretch for 15,000 sq miles (40,000 sq km), and are fed by several rivers including the Byerazino and Dnieper. The soils of the Pripet are clay or sandy, and large areas are waterlogged.

Regional climate

63°F (17°C) 23°F (-5°C)

26 in (668 mm)

Estonia, Latvia, Lithuania, and Belarus have cold winters and cool, wet summers, because of their location on the Baltic Sea. Heavy snow falls during the winter throughout the region, particularly in Belarus.

Cultural diversity

Estonia, Latvia, and Belarus have large populations of Russians, who were resettled in the Baltic states under communist rule. Their presence causes racial tension with ethnic peoples in Estonia and Latvia. In Belarus, where most people are Russian speakers, and Lithuania, where 80 per cent are ethnic Lithuanians, there is social harmony.

Folk dancer, Estonia

Estonia

 The smallest and most northerly of the Baltic states, Estonia has a long coastline and beautiful scenery that attracts many tourists from Finland and Scandinavia. Under Soviet rule, its rural economy was transformed. It is now an industrial nation, and most people live in towns. Estonians are closely related to Finns and speak a similar language.

ESTONIA FACTS

CAPITAL CITY	Tallinn
AREA	17,423 sq miles (45,125 sq km)
POPULATION	1,572,000
MAIN LANGUAGES	Estonian, Russian
MAJOR RELIGION	Christian
CURRENCY	Kroon

Flax stems are used to make linen and ropes.

Flax
Textiles made from flax and cotton are among Estonia's leading exports. Flax is harvested at different times for various purposes: young green stems make fine cloth called linen; tougher fibers are used for ropes and mats.

Tourism
More than one million tourists visit Estonia every year. The medieval buildings of Tallinn, Estonia's capital, are a major attraction, with a wealth of historical monuments. Summer regattas and boating and yachting in the sheltered waters of the Gulf of Riga are also popular.

Latvia

Sandwiched in a central position between Estonia and Lithuania, Latvia is a flat country with about 12,000 rivers. Manufacturing, encouraged under Soviet rule, is the basis of the economy. Like the other states in this region, Latvia suffered high inflation during the 1990s. Farming, fishing, and timber are valuable sources of income.

LATVIA FACTS

CAPITAL CITY	Riga
AREA	24,938 sq miles (64,589 sq km)
POPULATION	2,643,000
MAIN LANGUAGES	Latvian, Russian
MAJOR RELIGION	Christian
CURRENCY	Lats

Farming
Latvia has a larger area of fertile land than the other Baltic states. Since independence, the huge state farms introduced by the Russians have been dismantled and are now privately owned. Most are dairy farms.

People
About one-third of Latvians are of Russian origin and there are smaller numbers of Ukrainians and Belarussians. Just over half the population are ethnic Letts, or Latvians, who cling to their cultural heritage. They celebrate many traditional and religious festivals.

Women wear traditional costumes in Latvia's Rites of Spring Festival.

Lithuania

Once a powerful nation, ruling lands that extended to the Black Sea, Lithuania sits south of Latvia. Most people live in the interior of the country, working in industry or farming. The short coastline, fringed with sand dunes and pine forests, is known for its amber. Since 1991, there have been disputes with Latvia over Baltic oil.

LITHUANIA FACTS

CAPITAL CITY	Vilnius
AREA	25,174 sq miles (65,200 sq km)
POPULATION	3,782,000
MAIN LANGUAGES	Lithuanian, Russian
MAJOR RELIGION	Christian
CURRENCY	Litas

Hill of Crosses, near Siauliai, a shrine to honor the dead.

Yellow amber

Amber
The Baltic states produce two-thirds of the world's amber, the fossilized sap of pine trees. Amber is used to make jewelry in shades of yellow, orange, and deep gold.

Religion
By contrast to Estonians and Latvians, who are mainly Protestants, Lithuanians are mostly Roman Catholics. They managed to keep their faith even under Soviet rule, which discouraged religion.

Belarus

Landlocked, and with few natural resources, Belarus suffers great poverty. In 1986, an accident at the Chornobyl' nuclear reactor in the Ukraine severely contaminated farmland. Many areas remain unsafe. The shaky economy is based on the production of machines, cars, chemicals, and a large farming sector. Unlike the other Baltic states, Belarus is seeking closer ties with Russia to boost the economy.

BELARUS FACTS

CAPITAL CITY	Minsk
AREA	80,154 sq miles (207,600 sq km)
POPULATION	10,320,000
MAIN LANGUAGES	Belarussian, Russian
MAJOR RELIGION	Christian
CURRENCY	Belarussian ruble

Ceramics
Belarus produces many beautifully crafted ceramic and porcelain items, such as vases and ornaments. The country is also known for its high-quality decorated glassware, made by heating sand with salt, limestone, and old glass, then molding the molten liquid glass.

Food
The national dish of Belarus is *draniki*, made from fried, grated potatoes, and served with sour cream and pickled berries or beets. Soup made from beets is also a popular dish.

Draniki   **Sour cream**

 FIND OUT MORE   CHRISTIANITY   FARMING   FESTIVALS   FORESTS   FOSSILS   GLASS   LAKES   NUCLEAR POWER   RIVERS   SOVIET UNION   TEXTILES AND WEAVING

BANGLADESH AND NEPAL

NORTH OF THE BAY OF BENGAL, between India and Myanmar (Burma), is Bangladesh, a poor but fertile country with low-lying land that has repeatedly flooded, and largely dictated its fortunes. Nepal and Bhutan are small Himalayan states, ruled by kings, but slowly adopting democratic ideas. All three countries have a subsistence farming economy, and the majority of the people, who are a mix of Muslims, Hindus, and Buddhists, live in small, rural villages. Manufacturing industries are being developed.

Himalayas
Nepal lies in the highest part of the Himalayas, a vast mountain range that stretches 1500 miles (2,400 km) between India and China. Mount Everest, the world's highest peak at 29,029 ft (8,848 m), is part of the range and several other peaks are more than 19,685 ft (6,000 m) high, including Ama Dablam in Nepal, at 22,493 ft (6,856 m).

73°F (23°C)   52°F (11°C)

75 in (1,901 mm)

Regional climate
Bangladesh has a hot, tropical climate, and monsoon winds bring heavy floods to 67 percent of the country. Southern Nepal and Bhutan are hot and wet, but the Himalayas are cold and harsh, with much snow.

Physical features
Bangladesh is dominated by a low-lying plain created by soil caught up and carried on the great Ganges River and its tributaries. Much of the land is less than 50 ft (15 m) above sea level. By contrast, Nepal and Bhutan sit high in the mountains, with plunging forested valleys fed by many rapid streams.

Forests
About 70 percent of Bhutan is forested. Deciduous forests, which include hardwoods such as teak, grow in the south, while thick pine forests cover the steep mountains of central Bhutan. Bangladesh's flat landscape rises in the north and southeast to form wooded hills.

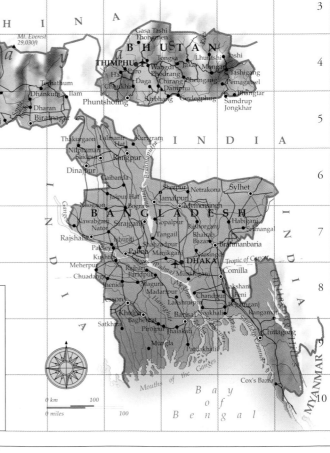

Delta
Large parts of central and southern Bangladesh are made up of the flat low-lying plains, formed by the delta of the rivers Ganges, Brahmaputra (Jamuna), and Meghna. As the rivers split continually in their journey south toward the Bay of Bengal, they become a maze of channels that often flood.

Hydroelectricity
Bangladesh, Bhutan, and Nepal share vast natural water resources in the form of hundreds of tributaries of the Ganges River system. All three countries have harnessed their waters for hydroelectricity. Bhutan's Chhukha Dam exports power to India, and there are plans to construct more dams across the fast-flowing mountain rivers in both Bhutan and Nepal.

Welding turbine wheel for hydroelectric plant, Nepal

Bangladesh

Formed in 1971 when it became independent of Pakistan, Bangladesh has a troubled political history. Democracy was restored in 1991, after a period of military rule. Bangladesh has one of the world's highest population densities and half of its people live in poverty. The country's vast water resources provide good farming conditions, but floods and cyclones wreak seasonal havoc.

B

BANGLADESH FACTS

CAPITAL CITY Dhaka

AREA 55,598 sq miles (143,998 sq km)

POPULATION 117,944,000

MAIN LANGUAGE Bengali

MAJOR RELIGIONS Muslim, Hindu

CURRENCY Taka

Stilt houses
Many people live in houses that are built on stilts to protect them from the frequent floods. The country is overcrowded, and about 80 percent of the people live in rural communities. Most grow just enough rice to live on, and fish in the Ganges.

Jute
Bangladesh is second only to India in the production of jute, a tough fiber used for sacking, rope, and carpeting. The country provides about 80 percent of the world's jute fiber. Jute products make up 13 percent of Bangladesh's exports.

Jute rope

Silkworms spin a silky thread up to 0.6 miles (1 km) long.

Dhaka
The capital of Bangladesh, Dhaka, lies on the Buriganga River, which links ports around the country. It is a center of trade and commerce. The city contains more than six million people, many of whom live in overcrowded slums.

Textiles
Many Bangladeshis work in the textile industry, with cotton and silk the country's leading fabrics. Ready-made garments are the main product, totaling 60 percent of exports. Women are the backbone of the textile industry.

Nepal

The Himalayas and their forested foothills cover most of this landlocked country. Nepal was an absolute monarchy until 1991, but now has a multiparty constitution. It is one of the world's poorest countries; the people are mostly farmers whose crops depend on the monsoon rains.

NEPAL FACTS

CAPITAL CITY Katmandu

AREA 54,363 sq miles (140,800 sq km)

POPULATION 20,813,000

MAIN LANGUAGE Nepali

MAJOR RELIGIONS Hindu, Buddhist, Muslim

CURRENCY Rupee

People
There is a wide variety of peoples in Nepal, and most are of Indian or Tibetan descent. The Sherpas of the north are skilled, tough mountaineers. About 90 percent of Nepalese people are Hindus who combine their religion with Buddhism.

Hindu holy man

Farming
Nepal is dependent on farming, which, with forestry, employs 90 percent of the workforce. Rice, corn, and sugar are grown on terraces cut into the mountainsides.

Katmandu
Lying in a valley 4,500 ft (1,370 m) above sea level, Nepal's capital, Katmandu, is a city full of ornate temples and shrines. About 400,000 people live in the city, including the Newars of the valley, famed for their wood carving.

Buddhist temple overlooking Katmandu

Trekking
Mountain climbing and trekking in the Himalayas attract 300,000 visitors to Nepal each year. Tourism attracts much-needed income, but threatens the ecology.

Bhutan

A small, isolated country, Bhutan is covered in forests and snowcapped mountains. Ruled by a monarch, known as the Dragon King, it is an isolated state, though there are plans for modernization. Three-quarters of the people are of Tibetan descent; the rest are Nepalese or Hindus. Farming, fishing, forestry, and light industry provide jobs.

Apricot

Cardamom seeds

Apple

Orange

Chili peppers

Crops
Less than three percent of Bhutan's land can be cultivated, but 90 percent of the people make a living from farming. Rice, corn, and potatoes are the staple foods, and cash crops, such as apricots, apples, chilies, cardamom, and oranges for export to other Asian countries are being developed in the fertile central valleys.

BHUTAN FACTS

CAPITAL CITY Thimphu

AREA 18,147 sq miles (47,000 sq km)

POPULATION 1,769,000

MAIN LANGUAGE Dzongkha

MAJOR RELIGIONS Buddhist, Hindu

CURRENCY Ngultrum

FIND OUT MORE

ASIA, HISTORY OF · BUDDHISM · DAMS · ENERGY · FARMING · HINDUISM · INDIA · ISLAM · MOUNTAINS AND VALLEYS · RIVERS · TEXTILES AND WEAVING

BARBARIANS

To the ancient greeks, all foreigners or outsiders were known as barbarians, but from the 3rd century on, this term was increasingly applied to nomadic mounted tribespeople from Asia, eastern Europe, and parts of Germany, such as the Huns and Goths. Organized into fearsome cavalry armies, these so-called barbarians caused havoc in their search for land, and were finally responsible for the collapse of the western Roman Empire.

Who were the barbarians?
To most Europeans, barbarian tribes included Huns and Avars (from Asia), and Saxons, Vandals, and Goths (from Germany). Huns migrating from Asia into Europe caused fear among the resident Germanic tribes, who then poured in huge numbers across the Roman Empire's frontiers. In a short time, this migration led to the fall of the empire.

Huns

The Huns were a nomadic Mongol people from the high plains, or steppes, of Central Asia who invaded southeastern Europe in c.370. Fierce in battle and famous for their skill on horseback, they conquered the Ostrogoths and drove the Vandals and other tribes westward. Under the leadership of Attila they reached the height of their influence, ravaging the Byzantine Empire and invading Gaul (modern France). In the 5th and 6th centuries, the White Huns, a related group, raided Persia (Iran) and northern India.

Huns made bows and arrows out of strips of bone.

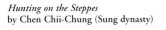

Horse saddle

**Hunting on the Steppes
by Chen Chii-Chung (Sung dynasty)**

Catalaunian Plains
The Huns were deadly in battle as mounted archers. They made short bows of bone that were light and easy to use while on horseback. They also fought with sabers at close range. Under Attila, the Huns were victorious many times, but in 451, they were finally defeated by the Romans and their allies at the Catalaunian Plains, Gaul (now Chalons-sur-Marne, France).

Attila the Hun
Attila (c.406–453) became king of the Huns in 434 jointly with his brother Bleda, whom he murdered in 445, Attila united his people into a vast tribe based in Hungary, then waged campaigns to win land and influence from the Roman and Byzantine empires. Short and crafty, the so-called "Scourge of God" was cruel to his enemies but fair to his own people. He died – possibly of poison – on his wedding night.

Ostrogoths and Visigoths

The Ostrogoths were a Germanic tribe on the Black Sea who were related to the Visigoths from the Danube area. After the Roman Empire fell in 476, the Visigoths adopted Christianity and translated the Bible from Latin into a "Gothic" script that was used for centuries in German printing.

Gothic architecture
Many medieval churches and cathedrals were built in the Gothic style. The highly decorative details, such as gargoyles, were believed by Renaissance artists to be "barbarous" when compared with the simplicity of older Roman buildings. So the artist named them after the Gothic tribes that overran Rome.

Notre-Dame gargoyles, Paris, France

Saxons

"The barbarians drive us to the sea, and the sea drives us back to the barbarians; one way or another, we die." So wrote a group of 5th-century Britons to their former masters in Rome. The seafaring barbarians threatening them were Saxons, Angles, and Jutes – Germanic tribes of skilled craftspeople and farmers who conquered and settled stretches of fertile Britain from c.500.

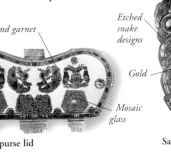

Saxon shoulder clasp

Gold and enamel

Gold and garnet

Etched snake designs

Gold

Mosaic glass

Saxon purse lid

Saxon buckle

Richborough Fort
The Romans built bases at Richborough and elsewhere on the southeastern English coast in the 3rd and 4th centuries. From these forts they could see and try to intercept Saxon raiders.

Walls were 4 ft (1.2 m) thick.

British ships destroying Chinese junks

Barbarians in the East
People in other cultures also believed that outsiders were barbarians. The 18th-century Chinese looked down on "foreign devils" and insisted that all trade between China and the west take place only in the port of Canton. The Japanese actually stopped any foreigners from entering Japan for more than 200 years, until 1854.

FIND OUT MORE  ARCHITECTURE · ANGLO-SAXONS · ROMAN EMPIRE · WARFARE

BATS

WITH ALMOST 1,000 species, bats are the second largest order of mammals after the rodents. They are the only mammals that can truly fly. The name given to their order is Chiroptera, meaning "hand wings." When bats are resting, they hang upside down. Most bats are nocturnal. They eat a variety of food, which they find either by scent and sight, as fruit bats do, or by using sound waves, a process called echolocation, as insect-eating bats do.

Types of bats

Bats are divided into two groups. They are the Megachiroptera, or megabats, which are the old world fruit bats, and the Microchiroptera, or microbats, sometimes called insect-eating bats.

Megabats

Fruit bats, or megabats, are also sometimes called flying foxes. They live in the tropical and subtropical parts of Africa, Asia, and Australasia. Most megabats eat fruit, but some also feed on flowers, nectar, and pollen.

Large eyes and nose

Epauletted fruit bat

Ears are almost as long as the bat's head and body combined.

Long-eared bat

Microbats

The term insect-eating bats is a misleading name for these bats. Many feed on fruit, meat, fish, pollen, and even blood, as well as insects. Microbats live in both temperate and tropical regions, but in cooler climates they hibernate or migrate for the winter.

Bat features

A bat's wing consists of an elastic membrane of skin that is stretched between the elongated fingers of its front limb, and back to its hind limb. Bats have lightweight bodies and strong clawed toes with which they cling to a suitable support.

Insect-eating bats have large ears, which are needed when the animal uses echolocation.

Furred body

Bats have a clawed thumb on the edge of each wing.

Wing is formed by a membrane stretched over the bones of the fingers and forelimb.

Tail is used for balance and for braking in flight.

Bat catches insect in midair.

Clawed foot

"Fingers"

Greater horseshoe bat

Roosts

Bats need a variety of places to roost, or rest. At night they rest between bouts of feeding and often settle to eat large prey. During the day, they need somewhere to sleep and groom. Females choose a safe, warm place to give birth.

Tent bats

Cave habitats

In warm climates, caves provide daytime and nursery roosts, where females give birth and look after their young. Bracken Cave in Texas has the largest colony in the world with up to 20 million bats.

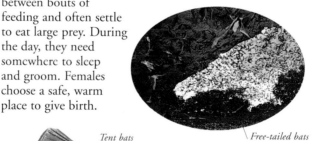

Free-tailed bats in Bracken Cave

Tree habitats

Microbats often roost in tree holes, such as old woodpecker nests, or cracks caused by storm damage. These Honduran white bats, also called tent bats, build a tent from large leaves.

Hibernation

Bats need to hibernate somewhere cold but where they will be protected from frost, which would kill them. The place where they roost, called a hibernaculum, also has to be damp so that the bats do not dry out. Suitable sites include caves, loft spaces, and tree holes.

Natterer's bat

Echolocation

To find objects in the dark, a microbat makes bursts of high-frequency sound. The sound bounces off objects, such as a moth, and the bat pinpoints the moth's position by listening to the returning echoes.

Insect prey

Returning echoes

Horseshoe bat

How a horseshoe bat catches prey

Horseshoe bats emit sounds through their noses.

1 The "horseshoe" on the bat's nose focuses the sound into a narrow beam. The bat sweeps its head from side to side as it flies along, scanning for insects.

Small eyes

Broad, rounded wings

2 The bat's large, mobile ears pick up vibrations made by the movement of an insect's wings. The bat can tell the size of an insect from the vibrations.

3 When the bat has located its prey, it scoops up the insect in its wings, often eating in midair.

The bat uses its wing membrane to put food in its mouth.

B

Feeding

Bats have a wide variety of food sources. Most bats eat insects and can consume huge amounts in one night. The smaller bats, such as pipistrelles, catch tiny gnats and mosquitoes. Larger bats, such as noctules and serotines, feed on cockchafers and dung beetles. Some bats pounce on prey that is on the ground, and pick insects off leaves. Fruit-eating bats live mostly in the tropics, where they have a year-round supply of food.

Bulldog bat

Fishing bats trail their long legs in the water to catch a fish.

False vampire bat

The bat finds its prey using echolocation.

Fishing bats
Some bats use echolocation to detect fish just below the water's surface. Fishing bats have long legs and they fly along the surface and catch the fish with long, sharp claws.

Meat-eating bats
Many larger microbats catch and eat mice, rats, frogs, and lizards. False vampire bats from Asia and America carry their catch to a suitable perch to devour it, using their thumbs and wing membranes to hold the heavy prey.

Vampire bats
True vampire bats feed on the blood of mammals or birds. Using their razor-like incisor teeth, they make a wound on an ear or ankle. As the blood flows, the vampire bat drinks it with a grooved tongue that acts as a drinking straw.

Bat drinking from a donkey.

Incisor teeth

Bats will only eat the pulp of the fruit.

Some nectar-feeding bats hover above the flower.

Spectacled flying fox

Glossophagine bat

Fruit bats
These bats squash ripe fruit against ridges on the roof of their mouth. They spit out the rind and seeds that are difficult to digest. Fruit bats sometimes eat the fruit in the tree where they pick it, but they may carry it to a safe roost to eat.

Nectar feeders
Trees that are pollinated by bats provide the animals with nectar and pollen as a reward for their services. The tongues of nectar-feeding bats have a brush-like tip which the bats use to lap up the nectar and pollen inside the flowers.

Nursery

Like all true mammals, a female bat carries her young inside her womb until she gives birth. Usually, only one bat is born at a time to minimize the extra weight a pregnant female has to carry in flight. Females gather, often in large numbers, to give birth in a nursery roost.

Young bats hang upside down while their mothers go out to feed.

A large number of bats together keep each other warm.

Females suckle their young hanging upside down. The young cling to their mother with their teeth and claws.

Most young bats cannot fly until they are three weeks old.

This nursery roost is in the roof of a building.

Young bats are born pink and hairless, so they need warm surroundings.

Each female bat can recognize the squeak of her own young.

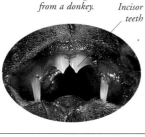

Ratsnake hunts at night.

Threats and predators
This red-tailed racer from Southeast Asia, also known as a mangrove ratsnake, catches bats in the tops of mangrove trees. Other animals that prey on bats include bat hawks, owls, and cats. Some of the greatest threats to the survival of bats around the world are habitat destruction, pesticides, and human vandalism. Many species are in danger of extinction.

Largest and smallest
The largest bat is a Malaysian flying fox which can have a wingspan of up to 5.6 ft (1.7 m). The smallest bat is the bumblebee bat, also known as Kitti's hog-nosed bat. This tiny animal is only about 1 in (30 mm) long and weighs only 0.07 oz (2 g).

GREATER HORSESHOE BAT

SCIENTIFIC NAME *Rhinolophus ferrumequinum*

ORDER Chiroptera

FAMILY Rhinolophidae

DISTRIBUTION Central and southern Europe, North Africa across to Japan

HABITAT Woodland, pasture, human settlements

DIET Insects

SIZE Length: 2.4–2.75 in (6–7 cm)

LIFESPAN Up to 30 years

FIND OUT MORE   CAVE WILDLIFE   CONSERVATION   HIBERNATION   MAMMALS   WHALES AND DOLPHINS

Bats

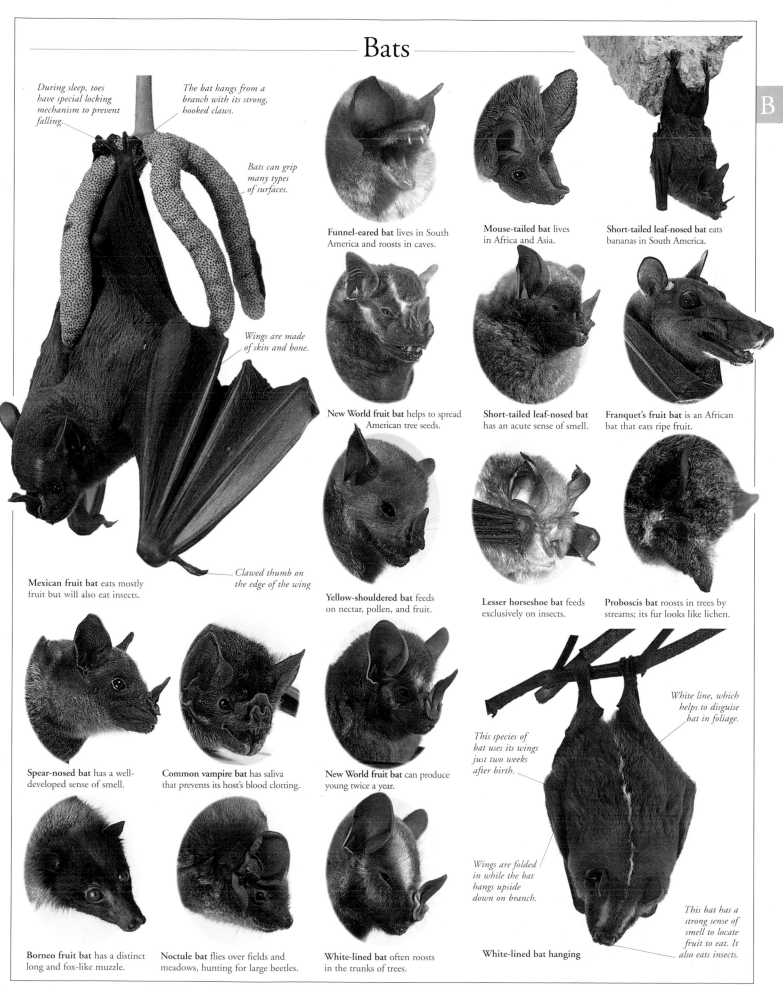

During sleep, toes have special locking mechanism to prevent falling.

The bat hangs from a branch with its strong, hooked claws.

Bats can grip many types of surfaces.

Wings are made of skin and bone.

Clawed thumb on the edge of the wing

Mexican fruit bat eats mostly fruit but will also eat insects.

Funnel-eared bat lives in South America and roosts in caves.

Mouse-tailed bat lives in Africa and Asia.

Short-tailed leaf-nosed bat eats bananas in South America.

New World fruit bat helps to spread American tree seeds.

Short-tailed leaf-nosed bat has an acute sense of smell.

Franquet's fruit bat is an African bat that eats ripe fruit.

Yellow-shouldered bat feeds on nectar, pollen, and fruit.

Lesser horseshoe bat feeds exclusively on insects.

Proboscis bat roosts in trees by streams; its fur looks like lichen.

Spear-nosed bat has a well-developed sense of smell.

Common vampire bat has saliva that prevents its host's blood clotting.

New World fruit bat can produce young twice a year.

This species of bat uses its wings just two weeks after birth.

Wings are folded in while the bat hangs upside down on branch.

White line, which helps to disguise bat in foliage.

This bat has a strong sense of smell to locate fruit to eat. It also eats insects.

Borneo fruit bat has a distinct long and fox-like muzzle.

Noctule bat flies over fields and meadows, hunting for large beetles.

White-lined bat often roosts in the trunks of trees.

White-lined bat hanging

B

119

BEARS

THERE ARE SEVEN species of bears, plus the giant panda, which has recently been classified as a primitive bear. The polar and brown bears are the largest meat-eating land animals alive today. All bears rely heavily on their acute senses of smell and hearing to find food and to locate predators. Bears that live in cool climates hibernate in dens during the winter, but those in warmer areas are active all year round.

Brown bears have a large hump of muscle and fat.

North American brown bear

Brown bears

There are nine subspecies of brown bears. The largest is the Kodiak bear, found on islands in Alaska. It may stand 12 ft (3.5 m) tall on its hind legs and is one of the most powerful animals in North America. The grizzly bear, also of North America, has white-tipped fur, giving it a "grizzled" look. The other brown bears live in Europe and temperate Asia.

Fishing
North American bears have a plentiful source of salmon when the fish swim up rivers to spawn. The bears are able to catch fish in the air as they leap up a waterfall.

Large canine teeth and powerful jaws

Asian black bear feeding

Diet

Bears belong to the order of mammals called carnivores, meaning meat-eaters. They catch and kill other animals for food and eat carrion, but they will take almost any kind of food they can find, including insects. About three-quarters of most bears' diet comes from non-animal sources, such as fruits, nuts, roots, and shoots.

Paws
There are five clawed toes on a bear's paws. The animals use their forepaws to gather food and manipulate small food items. They can kill another animal with one blow from a paw, or use their long claws to dig up roots and open bee nests.

Kermodes bear
Most American black bears are black, but some are brown, beige, or blue-black. Small isolated populations of white black bears, called Kermodes bears, live on the coast of British Columbia, Canada.

Types of bears

Brown bear This bear lives across the northern hemisphere, but in small populations only. It has disappeared from many areas.

Shaggy black fur

Sloth bear A long-coated bear from India and Sri Lanka, the sloth bear eats mainly termites, which are sucked up through its lips.

Sun bear This bear from Southeast Asia is the smallest bear. It has short, dense fur, with a yellow mark on its chest. It has a long tongue with which it licks up ants and termites.

Spectacled bear The only South American bear, this rare animal lives on the wooded slopes of the Andes. It eats mostly plant material, especially fruit, but will eat meat if it is available.

A crescent of white fur accounts for this bear's other name – moon bear.

Polar bear This white-coated bear is the most carnivorous, eating mainly seals and fish. It lives on the Arctic coast.

Asian black bear An agile climber, this bear lives in woods of Southeast Asia, from Afghanistan to China, and Japan.

American black bear Found across North America, this bear will raid garbage cans, tents, and cars for food.

Cubs' games are practise for adult conflicts.

Cubs
A female bear gives birth to her cubs in a den, where she will stay with them for up to two or three months. Each litter usually contains one to three cubs, which are born helpless and weigh only a tiny percentage of their mother's weight. They develop quickly, but will stay with their mother until nearly full-grown – two or three years in the case of the larger bears. Female bears make good mothers and will defend their cubs against any enemy ferociously.

GRIZZLY BEAR

SCIENTIFIC NAME *Ursos arctos horribilis*

ORDER Carnivora

FAMILY Ursidae

DISTRIBUTION Northwestern North America

HABITAT Mountains, forests, wilderness

DIET Almost anything, including berries, leaves, roots, small animals, fish, and carrion

SIZE Length: 6–9 ft (1.8–2.8 m) Weight: 350–500 lb (160–230 kg)

LIFESPAN 25–30 years

FIND OUT MORE | ASIAN WILDLIFE | HIBERNATION | NORTH AMERICAN WILDLIFE | PANDAS AND RACCOONS | POLAR WILDLIFE

BEATLES, THE

JOHN LENNON PLAYED rhythm guitar, Paul McCartney played bass, George Harrison played lead guitar, and Ringo Starr played the drums. Together they formed The Beatles – the most famous and influential group in the history of popular music. Their songs dominated the 1960s, when people believed that music could change the world, and the songwriting skills of Lennon and McCartney have ensured that their music lives on. Their songs still influence many musicians today.

Early life

All four Beatles were born in the English port of Liverpool and played in various rock and roll groups in the late 1950s. In 1960–61, John, Paul, George, and drummer Pete Best played at the Star Club in the German port of Hamburg, where they learned about live performance. Back in England, The Beatles played regularly at Liverpool's Cavern Club. In 1962, their manager, Brian Epstein (1934–67), replaced Best with Ringo Starr as drummer.

Live performances

The Beatles began by playing live in clubs in and around Liverpool, UK. Their lively performances were an exciting contrast to the staid and solid players who dominated popular music at the time. The Beatles' reputation was based on the songwriting abilities of John Lennon and Paul McCartney. At first they both wrote traditional rock-and-roll songs about friendship and love, but as the pair developed, their subjects became more varied.

The Beatles play a football stadium in the US

Beatlemania

In January 1964 "I Want To Hold Your Hand" reached the top of the American music charts. A new word, "Beatlemania", entered the language, as thousands of screaming fans mobbed the group wherever they went. In months, The Beatles were the biggest music group in the world.

Recording

In 1966, The Beatles stopped performing live and spent more time in the studio. There they experimented with different instruments, such as string orchestras and sitars, and with new recording techniques. Their masterpiece, *Sgt. Pepper's Lonely Hearts Club Band*, took many months to produce and made use of techniques such as tapesplicing and multitrack recording.

Plates with pictures of The Beatles

Memorabilia

The Beatles were one of the first bands to be featured on a host of souvenirs and memorabilia. The four were immortalized on everything from mugs and T-shirts to buttons, badges, posters, and other souvenirs. Many fans bought everything that featured their four favorite musicians.

Toy guitar with pictures of The Beatles

"Please Please Me"   *"Sgt. Pepper"*

Last albums

By 1969, the band was under strain as conflicts grew among the four Beatles and their musical interests took new directions. Their last albums to appear were *Abbey Road* (1969) and *Let It Be*, which was released in 1970 but recorded before *Abbey Road*. The Beatles disbanded later that year. All four continued their careers as solo musicians.

The Beatles recording tracks for *Let It Be*

George Martin

British producer George Martin (b.1926) produced almost all The Beatles' records, having accepted their first demonstration tapes at EMI in 1962. Martin was a record producer with a background in both classical and popular music. He helped The Beatles get the most out of the recording studio and the wide range of instruments used in their records, translating many of their ideas into polished musical form.

THE BEATLES

1940 John Lennon and Richard Starkey (Ringo Starr) born.

1942 Paul McCartney born.

1943 George Harrison born.

1957 John and Paul form first group, The Quarrymen.

1962 First record with EMI; Ringo Starr joins as drummer.

1964 Beatles top charts in US.

1967 *Sgt. Pepper's Lonely Hearts Club Band* released.

1970 *Let It Be* released; Beatles disband.

1980 John Lennon fatally shot in New York.

1997 Paul McCartney knighted.

FIND OUT MORE   MUSIC   ORCHESTRAS   ROCK AND POP   SOUND RECORDING

BEES AND WASPS

THEIR STINGS USUALLY bring these insects to our attention. However, by pollinating crops and killing pests, bees and wasps play vital roles in our world. There are 115,000 species of bees and wasps. Most, such as carpenter bees, are solitary, but some, including common wasps and honeybees, are social insects, living in complex colonies. People keep honeybees in hives to produce honey and wax.

Features of bees and wasps

Bees and wasps are similar in appearance, with narrow waists between the thorax and abdomen. Most species have two pairs of wings and are excellent fliers. They have two compound eyes and three small eyes, giving them good eyesight. Bees are hairier than wasps, and are normally herbivores, while wasps are generally carnivores.

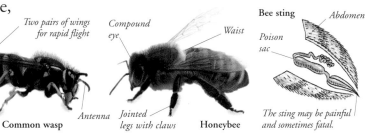

Two pairs of wings for rapid flight

Compound eye

Waist

Pointed abdomen

Claws **Common wasp**

Antenna

Jointed legs with claws **Honeybee**

Stings

The females of most species of bees and wasps have stings. The sting evolved from the egg-laying tube. Wasps have unbarbed stings that they can use repeatedly for defense or to kill prey. Bees have barbed stings that cannot be extracted, causing the bee to die. Consequently, bees only sting if provoked.

Bee sting

Abdomen

Poison sac

The sting may be painful and sometimes fatal.

Queen

Social bees and wasps have a queen in their colonies who lays eggs and runs the colony. Honeybees have one queen per hive; if two appear at the same time they fight to the death. Queens produce queen substance, a chemical that stops full sexual development of the workers.

Worker

Queen is larger than workers.

Life cycle of a honeybee

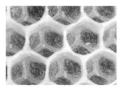

1 The queen bee spends most of her day checking cells and laying single eggs in them. She lays more than 2,000 eggs a day when there is a plentiful food supply. After 1–2 days, larvae hatch from the eggs.

2 Workers feed the larvae honey, pollen, and royal jelly. If fed extra royal jelly, larvae become queens. The larvae grow and molt, and on day 5 they spin a silk cocoon and pupate. Workers seal the cell with wax.

3 By about day 21, pupation is complete, and the adult bees chew their way out of the cells. Once the external skeleton has hardened and they can walk, the bees begin their tasks within the nest.

Nests

Common wasps' nests have the texture of paper and are made out of chewed-up wood, saliva, and water. Nests are built in hollow trees or below ground. Some other types of wasps, such as oriental stenogaster wasps, build nests out of mud. Honeybee nests are made out of wax produced from glands on the bees' abdomens. Wasps' and bees' nests usually contain combs, layers of six-sided cells in which the young grow.

Common wasp's nest

Protective layers of paper

Pupae in cocoons

Hole in nest is repaired.

Old worker wasps gather wood, chew it up, mix in saliva, and use the mixture to build nest walls.

Fertilized eggs develop into workers and queens.

Unfertilized eggs become drones.

Worker wasps spend the first week of their adult life cleaning the nest. Once able to fly, they leave the nest and hunt for insects to feed to the grubs (larvae) in the nest.

Eggs are glued into cells, since the cells face downward.

Entrance is below.

Nest walls are striped because the wood is collected from many sources.

Colonies

Social wasps and bees live in large groups called colonies. Each member of the colony has a specific duty and works for the whole nest. Wasp colonies may contain more than one million individuals; bees' nests can exceed 70,000 in number, consisting of one queen, about 69,000 workers, and 300 drones. Both queen wasps and queen bees run their nests; drones are fertile males who mate with the queen and die soon after; workers perform all other tasks. Drones appear before swarming time, when new queens leave the nest, mate, and set up nests on their own.

Food supplies

Wasps eat fruit and insects that they also feed to their young. Adult and larval bees feed on nectar and pollen that the adults collect from flowers. Bees do a dance to tell other bees the location of the flowers and navigate there by using the Sun.

Pollen carried on legs

Pollen, nectar, and honey
Bees carry pollen on hairs on their legs and store nectar in their stomachs. At the nest, they regurgitate the nectar. Water evaporates, concentrating the nectar to form honey. Honey and royal jelly, a high-protein substance made by workers, are also fed to the larvae.

Types of bees and wasps

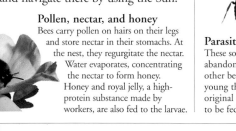

Parasitic bees
These solitary bees abandon their eggs in other bees' nests. The young then destroy the original eggs and wait to be fed by the host.

Hornets
Hornets are among the largest of the social wasps. They live in large colonies and defend their nests aggressively.

Hunting wasps
These solitary wasps paralyze other insects with a sting and lay their eggs on them. The young hatch and feed on the live host.

HONEYBEE

SCIENTIFIC NAME	*Apis mellifera*
ORDER	Hymenoptera
FAMILY	Apidae
DISTRIBUTION	Worldwide
HABITAT	Nests are built in hollow trees in the wild; also cultivated in hives
DIET	Pollen and nectar from flowers
LENGTH	Workers: 0.4–0.6 in (10–15 mm); queen: 0.6–0.8 in (15–20 mm)
LIFESPAN	Workers live for 2–3 months; queen lives for 3–5 years

FIND OUT MORE | ANIMAL BEHAVIOR | ANTS AND TERMITES | ARTHROPODS | EGGS | FLIGHT, ANIMAL | FLOWERS | INSECTS | NESTS AND BURROWS | WOODLAND WILDLIFE

BEETHOVEN, LUDWIG VAN

FROM HIS BIRTH in Bonn in 1770 to his death in Vienna in 1827, Ludwig van Beethoven lived during a time of revolution and transformation. Despite a tragically unhappy life beset with family problems and deafness, he became the major composer of his time. His symphonies, sonatas, and chamber music expanded the Classical forms, introducing exciting new musical ideas that ushered in the fiery Romantic style. Unlike previous composers, Beethoven tried to remain independent, writing for himself rather than for a single rich patron. Independence allowed him to develop his own personal expressive musical style.

Beethoven's birthplace

Early life
Beethoven was born in Bonn, Germany. His childhood was not a happy one. His father, himself a musician, forced Ludwig to practice and perform in public at an early age, hoping he would become a child prodigy. When his mother died and his father lost his job, young Ludwig had to provide for the whole family.

Vienna

Beethoven's first visit to Vienna was cut short by his mother's illness, but he returned in 1792 to study with the composer Haydn. He soon established himself as a pianist and teacher, and settled there for the rest of his life. However, as his deafness worsened, he suffered from depressions and raging tempers, and withdrew from social life. He found consolation in composing music that expressed both his despair, and his optimism and joy.

Performance
Until the onset of deafness, Beethoven earned his living as a teacher and performer. He was a superb pianist, whose emotional performances could move his audience to tears. Many of his piano compositions, especially the sonatas and concertos, explore the expressive capabilities of the instrument and are among his finest works.

Deafness
In his late twenties, Beethoven's hearing began to fail. By 1820, he was almost totally deaf. Unable to hear what he was playing, he could not earn a living from performing. Instead, he concentrated on composing.

Hearing aids

Notebooks
We can get a good idea of how Beethoven worked by looking at his manuscripts and notebooks. They show how he revised his work until he was completely satisfied with it. He wrote quickly and furiously, often crossing out and rewriting whole sections of the music.

Beethoven's Broadwood grand piano

The symphonies

Symphonies before Beethoven's time were orchestral works that followed a fairly set pattern, but in his nine symphonies Beethoven developed the form into a large and expressive work. From the third symphony, the *Eroica*, on, these works became longer and more adventurous, using new instruments and even vocalists and a choir in the ninth symphony.

Manuscript of the *Pastoral* symphony

Chamber music
Much of Beethoven's music is for small groups, such as the string quartet. This chamber music was often written for amateur players, but Beethoven found it provided an ideal way of expressing his new musical ideas.

Pastoral symphony
This symphony is unusual because it describes a scene: the countryside around Vienna where Beethoven loved to walk. It is full of the sounds of the country, including imitations of birdsong and a thunderstorm.

Eroica symphony
Beethoven originally dedicated this symphony to his hero Napoleon, but was disgusted when Napoleon proclaimed himself emperor. He scratched out the dedication, but kept the title *Eroica* (heroic).

LUDWIG VAN BEETHOVEN

1770 Born in Bonn, Germany

1792 Moves to Vienna, studies with Joseph Haydn

1796 Begins to go deaf

1802 Writes a letter, known as the "Heiligenstadt Testament," to his brothers, describing his unhappiness about his deafness

1803 *Eroica* symphony

1808 *Pastoral* symphony

1809 Piano Concerto No. 5, "The Emperor"

1824 *Choral* symphony

1827 Dies in Vienna, Austria; some 10,000 people attend his funeral

FIND OUT MORE   MOZART, WOLFGANG AMADEUS   MUSIC   MUSICAL INSTRUMENTS   NAPOLEON   ORCHESTRAS

BEETLES

THERE ARE AT LEAST 350,000 types of beetles. They make up 30 percent of all animals and 40 percent of all insects. They range in size from the 0.08 in (2 mm) long battle d'or beetle to the giant timber beetles, that grow up to 6 in (150 mm) long. Beetles live almost everywhere, from hot deserts to snowy mountaintops, but they are most numerous in the tropics. They eat a wide range of food, including crops, and are considered pests, but they perform a valuable role by breaking down dead animals and plants and returning the nutrients to the soil.

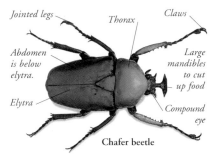

Chafer beetle

Jointed legs
Thorax
Claws
Abdomen is below elytra.
Large mandibles to cut up food
Elytra
Compound eye

Features of a beetle

Beetles have three body parts – the head, thorax, and abdomen. They have compound eyes, and antennae used for touch and smell. Their forewings have developed into hard wing cases, or elytra, that protect the hind wings. The wings, elytra, and six legs are fixed to the thorax.

How a beetle flies

1 Large beetles, such as this cockchafer beetle, take a few seconds to get airborne. First the beetle pumps air into its body by expanding its abdomen.

Beetle often opens and shuts elytra several times before taking off.

2 The beetle opens its wing cases. These act as stabilizers, similar to the tail wings of an airplane. The delicate hind wings unfold and provide the main force in flight.

Feathery antennae spread to sense the air currents.

Elytra raised

Wings unfurling, ready to beat

3 The cockchafer beetle pushes off with its legs and starts to beat its hind wings. Within a few seconds the hind wings reach the 200 beats per second needed for takeoff, and the wing cases help provide lift. During flight, the beetle uses 100 times more oxygen than it does at rest.

Cockchafer beetle

Wings beat during flight.

Outstretched hind legs help streamline the beetle.

Wood-boring beetles

Some beetles remain larvae for many years. Jewel beetle larvae may live in wood for more than 40 years. They eat the wood, making tunnels through it, leaving small holes.

Jewel beetle

Reproduction

Most beetles undergo complete metamorphosis. Larvae hatch from eggs laid by an adult female. This is the main feeding stage in a beetle's development. Once the larvae have finished growing, they turn into pupae. Inside, they change, or metamorphose, into the adult beetle that will eventually emerge from the pupa.

Mealworm beetle larva

Inside – the larva's body breaks down and changes into the adult.

Pupa develops for about 6 weeks.

Adult beetle has emerged.

Giant mealworm beetle

Fighting

Male beetles often fight with each other over a possible mate. They use their mandibles (mouthparts) as weapons. Stag beetles have huge, but not very powerful mandibles, which they use mainly to impress rivals. Despite their size, the mandibles do little harm. In this way, fighting is more symbolic, and both beetles live to fight and mate again.

The beetle clasps his rival in his huge jaws and tries to throw it on its back.

Stag beetles fighting

Feeding

Beetles' feeding habits, like beetles themselves, are diverse. Many, including spider beetles, feed on decaying leaf litter; others consume both living and dead wood. Some beetles, such as tiger beetles, actively hunt for live food. Scavengers, such as hide beetles, feed on rotting vegetation, dead animals, and dung. Some beetles, for example, rove beetles, are even parasites, living on creatures such as bats.

Ladybugs

Ladybugs are found worldwide. They prey on small insects, such as aphids and scale bugs. In this way they are helpful animals to have in the garden and can be used to control pests in place of chemicals.

Ladybug feeding on an aphid

Defense

Well-armored external skeletons and camouflage protect many beetles from predators. The bombardier beetle has an ingenious method of defense. It ejects a hot mixture of potent chemicals from its rear with an audible pop.

Bombardier beetle

Water beetles

Many beetles live in water. Diving beetles use their oarlike legs to push themselves through the water after their prey. Whirligig beetles scavenge for food that floats on the water's surface. They have special eyes that are split in two. One half looks downward for fish, while the top half scans the air for predatory birds.

Whirligig beetle

COCKCHAFER BEETLE

SCIENTIFIC NAME
Melolontha melolontha

ORDER Coleoptera

FAMILY Scarabaeidae

DISTRIBUTION Europe and western Asia

HABITAT Gardens and woods

DIET Adult feeds on sap and nectar; the larvae feed on the roots of plants, such as rose and oak

SIZE Larvae: 1.6 in (4 cm) in length; adults: 0.8–1.2 in (2–3 cm) long

LIFESPAN Larvae take about 2 years to become adults; adults live for about 2–3 months

FIND OUT MORE

ARTHROPODS   DESERT WILDLIFE   GRASSLAND WILDLIFE   INSECTS   WOODLAND WILDLIFE

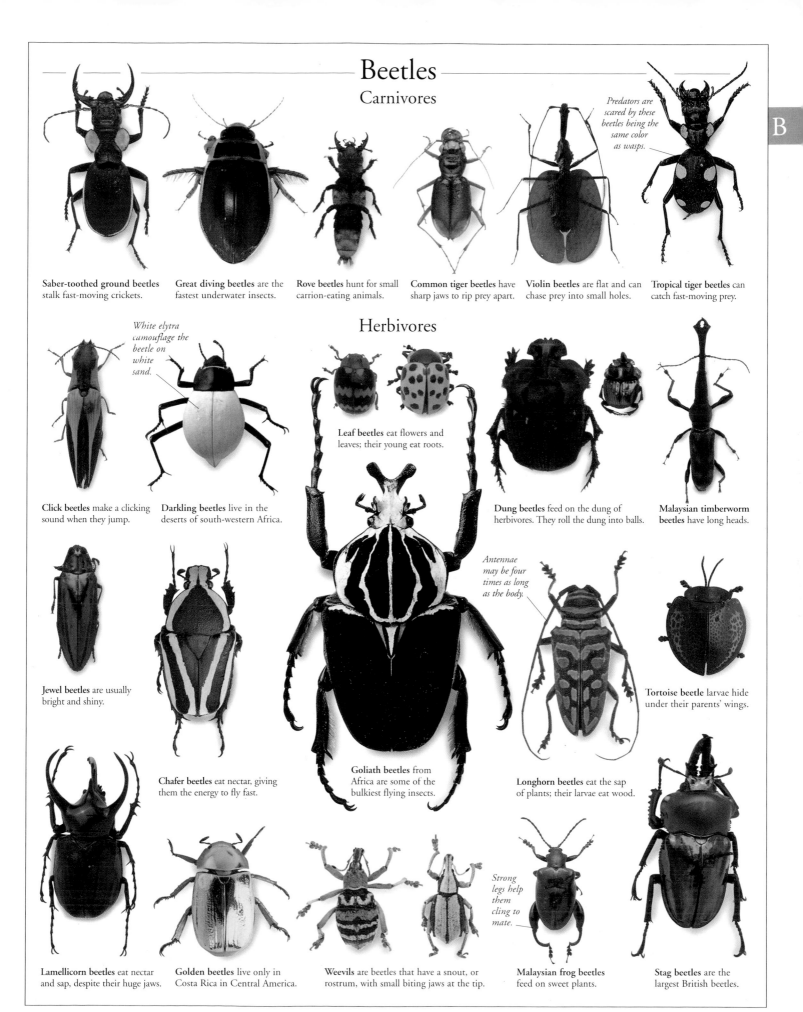

Beetles

Carnivores

Saber-toothed ground beetles stalk fast-moving crickets.

Great diving beetles are the fastest underwater insects.

Rove beetles hunt for small carrion-eating animals.

Common tiger beetles have sharp jaws to rip prey apart.

Violin beetles are flat and can chase prey into small holes.

Predators are scared by these beetles being the same color as wasps.

Tropical tiger beetles can catch fast-moving prey.

Herbivores

White elytra camouflage the beetle on white sand.

Click beetles make a clicking sound when they jump.

Darkling beetles live in the deserts of south-western Africa.

Leaf beetles eat flowers and leaves; their young eat roots.

Dung beetles feed on the dung of herbivores. They roll the dung into balls.

Malaysian timberworm beetles have long heads.

Jewel beetles are usually bright and shiny.

Antennae may be four times as long as the body.

Tortoise beetle larvae hide under their parents' wings.

Chafer beetles eat nectar, giving them the energy to fly fast.

Goliath beetles from Africa are some of the bulkiest flying insects.

Longhorn beetles eat the sap of plants; their larvae eat wood.

Lamellicorn beetles eat nectar and sap, despite their huge jaws.

Golden beetles live only in Costa Rica in Central America.

Weevils are beetles that have a snout, or rostrum, with small biting jaws at the tip.

Strong legs help them cling to mate.

Malaysian frog beetles feed on sweet plants.

Stag beetles are the largest British beetles.

BELGIUM

THIS SMALL, DENSELY POPULATED country in northwestern Europe borders France, Germany, and the Netherlands. Its current borders were settled in 1919, after World War I (1914–18). Today, Belgium is a highly developed industrial nation with a thriving economy. As a founding member of the European Union since 1957, and of the Benelux alliance (with the Netherlands and Luxembourg), Belgium plays an important role in European and international affairs.

BELGIUM FACTS

CAPITAL CITY	Brussels
AREA	11,783 sq miles (30,520 sq km)
POPULATION	10,042,000
MAIN LANGUAGES	Dutch, French, German
MAJOR RELIGION	Christian
CURRENCY	Belgian franc
LIFE EXPECTANCY	76 years
PEOPLE PER DOCTOR	309
GOVERNMENT	Multiparty democracy
ADULT LITERACY	100%

Physical features

In the north of Belgium is a flat plain stretching from Flanders to the Dutch border. The central plateau is bounded to the south by the Meuse and Sambre rivers. The Ardennes Plateau extends into Luxembourg and France.

Ardennes Plateau
The Ardennes Plateau covers 3,860 sq miles (10,000 sq km) in southern Belgium, Luxembourg, and northern France. Crossed by deep river valleys such as the Semois and Meuse, this upland area is rocky and heavily wooded and has spectacular limestone caves.

Meuse River
The Meuse flows slowly through gentle farmland and steep-sided valleys for 590 miles (950 km) from its source in France, west to east across Belgium, to the Dutch coast.

Climate
The Belgian climate is generally mild, but the skies are often cloudy. Rainfall is plentiful, especially in the mountains of the Ardennes where winter snow lingers. Summers tend to be short.

99°F (37°C) 0°F (-18°C)
64°F (18°C) 36°F (2°C)
32 in (825 mm)

Land use
Much of Belgium is built-up and densely populated. Farmers produce cereals, fruit, vegetables, and sugar beets, and raise cattle, sheep, and horses. Belgium has few natural resources and uses over 60 percent nuclear power.

Forest 35% Farmland 58% Built-up 7%

People
In southern Belgium people speak Walloon, a dialect of French. In the north people speak Dutch, formerly called Flemish. A few people in the east speak German.

852 per sq mile (329 per sq km) 97% Urban 3% Rural

Brussels
With about a million inhabitants, Belgium's capital, Brussels, is the center of government and trade. With three languages – Dutch, French, and German – it is a truly international city and the administrative headquarters of the European Union.

Gothic buildings in Brussels's Grand Place

Industry
Belgium has highly developed business and service industries, such as banking and insurance. The once-thriving coal and steel industries on the Meuse and Sambre rivers are now in crisis and are being rapidly replaced by new industries producing pharmaceuticals, chemicals, electrical equipment, and textiles. Belgium is the world's third largest exporter of chocolate, and produces fine beers.

Belgian chocolates

Luxembourg

This tiny country shares borders with Belgium, Germany, and France. Its people enjoy low unemployment and Europe's highest living standards. It is known as a banking center.

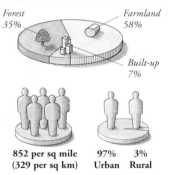

Finance center
Despite its tiny size, Luxembourg is a key member of the European Union. The headquarters of the European Parliament and the European Court of Justice are based in Luxembourg City.

LUXEMBOURG FACTS

CAPITAL CITY	Luxembourg
AREA	998 sq miles (2,386 sq km)
POPULATION	384,400
MAIN LANGUAGE	Letzeburgish
MAJOR RELIGION	Christian
CURRENCY	Luxembourg franc

FIND OUT MORE EUROPE   EUROPE, HISTORY OF   EUROPEAN UNION   FARMING   NETHERLANDS   TRADE AND INDUSTRY   WORLD WAR I

BENIN EMPIRE

ESTABLISHED IN THE 11TH CENTURY, Benin was a powerful West African kingdom that flourished in the forests west of the Niger River. The wealth of Benin was based on trading: trans-Saharan trade with African savanna kingdoms linked the Benin Empire with the Mediterranean and the Middle East, and, coastal trade linked the empire with Europe. Benin's obas, or kings, controlled the trade networks. They wielded immense power and lived in the royal palace in the capital city of Benin. In 1897, the British conquered Benin and ended the empire.

Empire boundaries

The Benin Empire was in modern Nigeria, where Benin City now stands. Both it and the modern republic west of Nigeria take their name from the old empire.

Sahara Desert

Benin City

Benin City

The empire of Benin was centered in the capital, Benin City. It was an impressive city. A wide road ran through it, and a huge dirt wall surrounded the city. The wall acted as a defense and took many years to build. Its size alone stood as a symbol of the influence held by Benin's oba. The city housed the oba's royal palace, and special areas called wards where the craftspeople lived.

Engraving of Benin City

Craft guilds

Guilds of craftspeople, such as leatherworkers, blacksmiths, drummers, weavers, carpenters, ivory carvers, and brass casters, lived in Benin City. The brass casters formed one of the most important guilds. They made the distinctive "bronze" heads and plaques for the royal palace.

Spikes to support ivory carving

Only obas wore neck rings.

Bronze head

Benin "bronze" heads are actually made of brass. They commemorated dead obas and their family members, court ceremonies – even European traders. Carved ivory adorned the heads, which were kept in shrines in the royal palace.

Memorial head of an oba

Brass plaques

Carved plaques decorated the wooden pillars that supported the oba's palace roof. They depicted court life and important events, such as the presentation of gifts from the oba to his courtiers.

Ivory carving

Ornately carved ivory tusks were among Benin's luxury goods. All trade in ivory was controlled by the oba. If elephant hunters killed an elephant, they had to give one tusk to the oba before they could sell the other.

Obas and courtiers wore ornamental weapons on ceremonial occasions.

Oba flanked by two courtiers

Carved human figures

Carvings often told of the oba's wealth and military strength.

Carved elephant's tusk

Trade

For centuries, Benin traded with African kingdoms to the north, including the Songhai Empire. The arrival of the Europeans in the 1400s disrupted these traditional relationships and established new trading outlets.

Brass manilla

Brass manillas

In Benin, merchants used bracelet-shaped objects called manillas to buy expensive purchases, but they used tiny, white cowrie shells for smaller items.

Merchants

Traveling by sea, Portuguese traders bought slaves, peppers, cloth, gold, and ivory from Benin, and paid with manillas, cowrie shells, and guns.

Portuguese flag

Ship, called a caravel

British conquest

In 1897, in revenge for an attack on a British party, the British burned and looted Benin City, exiled the oba, and brought Benin under colonial rule.

Oba Ewuare the Great

The warrior-king Ewuare (r.1440–80) rebuilt Benin City and, under his rule, the surrounding territory reached its greatest extent. Ewuare also established a tradition of secure hereditary succession.

Ewuare's leopard-shaped arm ornament

Timeline

11th century Benin Empire founded in the forests of Nigeria.

1450 Peak of Benin Empire.

1486 First European to visit Benin is Portuguese explorer Alfonso d'Aveiro; shortly afterward a Benin chief establishes a trading store for the Portuguese.

Benin ornamental sword

1500s English, Dutch, and French merchants start to trade with Benin Empire.

Early to mid-16th century King of Portugal sends Christian missionaries to Benin to convert Oba Esigie and build churches.

1688 Dutchman Olfert Dapper writes a history of Benin.

1700s Empire weakened by succession struggles.

1897 Britain takes Benin City by force.

1960 Nigeria, including the old Benin Empire, gains independence.

FIND OUT MORE

AFRICA, HISTORY OF   EMPIRES   EXPLORATION   METAL AND NONMETALS   SONGHAI EMPIRE

BICYCLES AND MOTORCYCLES

FUN AND ENVIRONMENTALLY correct, the bicycle is the simplest form of mechanical transportation. A bicycle, or bike, is a two-wheeled machine that converts human energy into propulsion; a motorcycle is a bicycle with an engine. Modern motorcycles are complex, with engine sizes ranging from 50cc (cubic centimeters) to more than 1,000cc. In many countries, such as China, most people travel or transport goods by bicycle. In other parts of the world, bicycles and motorcycles are used primarily for sport and leisure.

Parts of a bicycle

All bicycles, from a mountain bike to a racing bike or hybrid (a cross between the two), are designed to be easy to pedal and comfortable. Their weight is very important because it affects the speed at which the bike can be propelled.

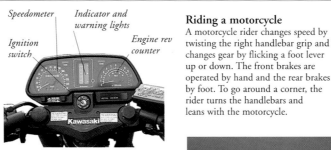

Cannondale SH600, hybrid

Saddles are adjustable, moving up and down to accommodate different riders.

Seat post slides in and out of frame to adjust seat level.

Frame, made from metal tubes, supports the rider.

Chain wheel

Gears, operated by levers, move the chain between different-sized gear wheels to change the speed at which the wheels turn.

Handlebars may be dropped for riding with less wind resistance.

Brakes are controlled by pulling levers on handlebars that force brake blocks against wheel rims to slow the bicycle down.

Brake cable

Spokes are arranged to create a strong, but lightweight, wheel.

Pedals, attached to the chain wheel, are pushed to create the force that turns the wheel.

Tires fitted on a metal wheel rim give a smooth, quiet ride over small bumps; mountain bikes have fatter tires to handle rough and rocky terrain.

Wheel hub secures the wheel to frame.

Reducing drag

Drag is the resistance of air that can slow down a bicycle or motorcycle and its rider. It is reduced by creating a streamlined shape for the air to flow around – some competitive bicycle riders even shave their legs to eliminate as much resistance as possible

Time-trial bike

Parts of a motorcycle

Like a bicycle, a motorcycle has a frame, a rear wheel that drives it along, a front wheel for steering, and controls on the handlebars. Like a car, it has an internal combustion engine and a suspension system. The suspension supports the motorcycle's body on the wheels, and stops it from being affected by bumps on the road.

Speedometer

Ignition switch

Indicator and warning lights

Engine rev counter

Motorcycle instrument panel
Motorcycles have an instrument panel in the center of the handlebars. Control switches for lights and indicators can be operated with hands on the handlebars.

Two-stroke engine with one cylinder. Larger motorcycles have more cylinders.

Lightweight frame

Fuel tank

Front suspension

1992 Yamaha FZR1000 Exup

Three-spoke alloy rear wheel, supported by suspension strut

Motorcycle tires grip the road even when the motorcycle leans into turns. These are smooth, treadless, "slick" racing tires.

Riding a motorcycle
A motorcycle rider changes speed by twisting the right handlebar grip and changes gear by flicking a foot lever up or down. The front brakes are operated by hand and the rear brakes by foot. To go around a corner, the rider turns the handlebars and leans with the motorcycle.

Small engine for speed and economy

Open "step in" frame

SFX moped

Mopeds and scooters
Small motorcycles used for short journeys in towns and cities are called mopeds or scooters. They have small engines, so they cannot go very fast, but are very economical. Mopeds, restricted to a 50cc engine, have pedals that the rider can use on steep hills.

Timeline

1839 Kirkpatrick Macmillan, a Scot, invents a lever-driven bicycle.

1863 The French Michaux brothers build the first pedal-powered bike, a velocipede.

1868 The Michaux brothers add a steam engine to a bike, creating the first motorcycle.

1885 In England, James Starley makes modern-style bicycles.

1885 German Gottlieb Daimler builds an engine-powered tricycle (below).

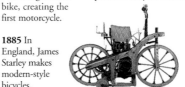

1901 The 1901 Werner is the first practical motorcycle.

1914–18 Motorcycles used extensively in World War I.

1963 Dutchman Van Wijnen designs what will become the Ecocar, covered pedal-powered transportation.

| FIND OUT MORE | AIR | CARS AND TRUCKS | ENERGY | ENGINES AND MOTORS | FORCE AND MOTION | MACHINES, SIMPLE | MOTOR SPORTS | POLLUTION | SPORTS | TRANSPORT, HISTORY OF |

Bicycles

Criterium racer allows the rider to pedal round corners easily, especially in races.

5-speed Peugeot is a traditional "ladies" bike – without a crossbar.

Mountain bikes, ideal for off-road cycling, have rugged frames and fat tires.

BMXs (Bicycle Motocross) bikes are used for rough terrain and tricks, such as wheelies."

Tricycles have three wheels for additional balance.

Triple tandems have three sets of pedals for three riders, linked by a chain to the back wheel.

Pedicabs are pedal-powered taxis. This one was made in 1980 in Bangladesh.

Kingcycle Bean, 1990, is designed to reduce drag for extra speed.

French Velocar, **1933**, is a recumbent, which allows the rider to sit back while pedaling.

Motorcycles

Harley Davidson, 1942, was adapted for military use, but was based on the civilian model.

Harley Davidson Knucklehead 61E, 1936, took the lead in American design; its engine resembled a clenched fist.

Harley Davidson Hydra Glide, 1951, has a classic chopper look with the machine stripped down to the bare essentials.

Heinkle Perle, 1956, has all the wires and cables running from the handlebars through the frame.

BMW R/60, 1956, has links to vary the angle between the "Steib" sidecar and the bike.

"Mod" scooters were popular in the 1960's: the more mirrors and lights, the more fashionable they were.

BMW R75/5, 1971, is a touring bike that combines reliability with comfort.

Honda GL1500/6 Gold Wing, 1991, has a 1500cc engine, an extra pair of cylinders, and luxuries such as a cassette player.

Husqvarna Motocross TC610, 1992, is a racing motorcyle for driving through fields or mud.

BIG BANG

AN INCREDIBLE EXPLOSION called the Big Bang is believed to have created the Universe. Observations of galaxies and heat radiation from space have helped confirm this theory. Astronomers are now working to explain exactly what happened from the point of the Big Bang explosion, which created everything in today's Universe – matter, energy, space, and time – to the present Universe, with its galaxies, stars, planets, and us.

Steady State theory

In the late 1940s and the 1950s, the Steady State theory was as popular as the Big Bang theory. It proposed that the Universe looked the same at any place and at any time. Although expanding, it would stay unchanged and in perfect balance. Material was being continuously created to keep the density of the Universe constant. As scientists found proof for the Big Bang, the Steady State theory was largely abandoned.

A Steady-State universe now (left) and later in time (right). The galaxies have moved apart, but new ones (coded orange) have been created to take their place. The density stays the same.

Georges Lemaître

In 1931, Belgian cosmologist Georges Lemaître (1894–1966) was the first to put forward the theory that the Universe started from a dense, single unit of material in a big explosion. The name Big Bang followed in 1950, introduced by Fred Hoyle, a British astronomer and supporter of the Steady State theory.

Origin of the Universe

One of the most difficult problems facing scientists in the 20th century was to explain how the Universe was created. The Universe is changing, but from what and to what? The Steady State theory suggested that the Universe had no beginning or end. The alternate, and now generally accepted, theory is the Big Bang. It proposes that the Universe was created in an explosion 15 billion years ago. From very small and simple beginnings it has grown vast and complex.

At the Big Bang, the Universe is extremely small, bright, dense, and hot.

Seething radiation

Temperature 10,000 trillion trillion degrees. Simple particles form.

Temperature 10 billion degrees. Nuclei of hydrogen and helium form.

Temperature 5,500°F (3,000°C). Clumps of gas form.

Temperature –450°F (–255°C). Quasars, ancestors of galaxies, form.

Three billion years after the Big Bang, the first galaxies start to take shape. The Milky Way forms 2 billion years later.

Temperature –454°F (–270°C)

Big Bang theory

All matter and time was created in the Big Bang. The explosion started pushing everything away and the Universe has been expanding ever since. As the Universe expanded, the temperature dropped. A fraction of a second after the explosion, the first tiny particles began to form. By the time the Universe was three minutes old, it consisted of 75 per cent hydrogen and 25 per cent helium. Everything that exists now – galaxies, stars, Earth, and humans – was created from these elements.

1 second after Big Bang

3 minutes

300,000 years

1 billion years

3 billion years

The Sun forms inside the Milky Way 10 billion years after the Big Bang. About half a billion years later, Earth is created from leftover material.

Expanding Universe

In the 1920s, analyzing starlight from galaxies showed that the galaxies are moving away from Earth. This is true of galaxies in every direction from Earth. Over time, the Universe is becoming larger and less dense. The idea that the Universe started in an explosion from a single point grew out of observations that the Universe is expanding.

Redshift: The faster a galaxy is moving away, the longer the wavelength of its starlight becomes. The starlight is said to redshift.

Background radiation

The heat produced by the Big Bang has been cooling ever since. It now has a temperature of –454°F (–270°C), detected as microwave radiation from all over the sky. The false-color map shows variations in the temperature 300,000 years after the Big Bang. The blue (cooler) patches are gas clouds, from which the galaxies formed.

The lines are shifted toward the red end of the spectrum.

More distant galaxies are speeding away faster than closer ones. Their light has a greater redshift.

Lines on the spectrum reveal a galaxy's speed.

Future of the Universe

Nobody knows for certain what is going to happen to the Universe. At present, it is getting larger and less dense. Most astronomers believe there will be a time when it stops expanding. But there is disagreement about what happens then: will the Universe live on forever, wither and die, or start to contract?

Big Crunch

The Universe may end in a Big Crunch if it starts to contract until it is hot and dense once more. But even this may not mean the end of the Universe. The Big Crunch might be followed by another Big Bang explosion, and the whole process could start over again.

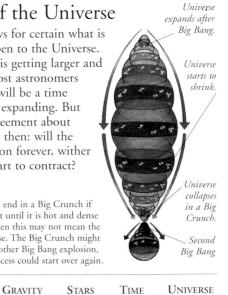

Universe expands after Big Bang.

Universe starts to shrink.

Universe collapses in a Big Crunch.

Second Big Bang

FIND OUT MORE   ASTRONOMY   BLACK HOLES   GALAXIES   GRAVITY   STARS   TIME   UNIVERSE

BIOLOGY

WHEN YOU LOOK at a running horse, you know immediately that it is alive; a beach pebble, by contrast, is nonliving. What distinguishes the two is life, or the state of being alive. Biology is the study of life and living things, and it can be divided into two main fields: zoology and botany. People who study biology are known as biologists; the living organisms they study range from animals such as horses to microorganisms such as green algae. All use energy obtained from food and released by respiration in order to fulfill their natural processes.

Classifying living things

There are more than 2 million species of living organisms, and biologists classify them into groups. The largest and most general group is called a kingdom. There are five kingdoms: Monera (bacteria), Protista (protozoa and algae), Fungi, Plantae (plants), and Animalia (animals).

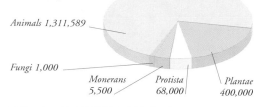

Number of life-forms in the world

Animals 1,311,589

Fungi 1,000

Monerans 5,500

Protista 68,000

Plantae 400,000

Branches of biology

Biology covers a number of different studies. Ecology examines how living things interact and where they live. Physiology looks at how organisms work. Genetics is concerned with how characteristics inherited from one generation pass to the next. Other branches include anatomy, taxonomy, microbiology, and parasitology.

Bird skeleton

Anatomists study skeletons to understand how an organism functions

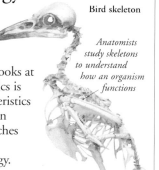

Anatomy
Anatomy is the study of the structure of living organisms. Anatomists investigate the shape and form of the parts that make up organisms. This analysis allows them to figure out things such as how bats and birds are able to fly.

Case displays butterflies and moths.

Taxonomy
The science of classifying the millions of living things into groups of related organisms is called taxonomy. Scientists called taxonomists identify and name organisms, and then group them together according to the characteristics they share and their common ancestry.

Microbiology
Microorganisms are living things that are too small to be seen without a microscope. Microbiology is the study of all aspects of the biology of these tiny organisms, which include bacteria, viruses, protists, and some types of fungi such as yeasts.

Compound microscope

Parasitology
Parasites live in or on another organism and exist at its expense; the study of parasites is called parasitology. Fleas are parasites that suck blood from their host. Tapeworms live and feed in their host's intestine.

Magnified flea image

Flea uses needlelike mouthparts to suck blood.

Zoology

Zoology is the branch of biology that is concerned with the study of animals. Animals are an amazingly diverse group of living organisms and encompass everything from sponges, spiders, and earthworms to lobsters, cats, and chimpanzees. Zoologists study the structure of animals, how their bodies function, and how they live and behave in their natural environment.

Lorenz

Ducklings imprinted on Lorenz instead of their mother.

Ethology
The study of animal behavior is called ethology. Austrian zoologist Konrad Lorenz (1903–89) helped establish the science of ethology. He discovered imprinting, a rapid learning process that occurs early in life. Imprinting to food, surroundings, or the mother happens instinctively during a short, fixed timespan early in life.

Botany

Botany is the study of plants. Plants are diverse organisms, encompassing everything from mosses and ferns to trees, cacti, and flowers. They make their own food by a process called photosynthesis, which transforms sunlight into energy. Botanists are concerned with all aspects of the structure, function, and ecology of plants.

Kew Gardens, London, England

The work of a biologist
Biologists are trained in all branches of biology, but usually focus on one specific area. Their research might involve observing animal behavior, investigating plant photosynthesis, or studying ecosystems.

Petri dishes contain control samples.

Biologist at work in a laboratory

Rachel Carson
In 1962, the American marine biologist and writer Rachel Carson (1907–64) published a book called *The Silent Spring*. In it, she warned that the indiscriminate use of pesticides and weedkillers was poisoning the natural world. Her pioneering book was fundamental in starting the environmental movement and in making ecological information accessible to the public.

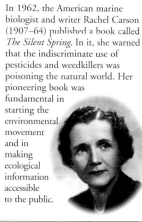

FIND OUT MORE | ANIMAL BEHAVIOR | ANIMALS | ECOLOGY AND ECOSYSTEMS | GENETICS | MICROSCOPIC LIFE | PARASITES | PHOTOSYNTHESIS | PLANTS

BIRDS

IN THE LIVING WORLD, only birds, insects, and bats are capable of powered flight. Birds are the largest and fastest of these flying animals, and are the only ones that have feathers. There are about 9,000 species of bird and they live in a huge range of different habitats – from deserts to the open oceans. They eat a variety of food, which they find mainly by sight. All birds reproduce by laying eggs. Most look after their young until they can fend for themselves.

Wings almost touch during the upstroke.

Fanned tail feathers act as a brake.

Pigeon in flight

Flight feathers are spread out as the bird prepares to land.

Feet are held against the body during flight.

Bird features

Birds have a lightweight skeleton and their feathers give them a smooth outline, that helps them move easily through the air. They do not have any teeth; they have a hard beak instead. Birds use their beaks for eating, and also for many tasks that other animals carry out with their front legs and feet, such as grasping items, or tearing up food.

Internal airspace with reinforcing struts

Legs and feet
A bird's feet and lower legs are usually covered with scales. Muscles that move them are close to the body. The feet are shaped according to their use.

Beak
A bird's beak is covered with keratin – the same substance that makes up human fingernails. The keratin keeps growing so that the edges of the beak do not wear away.

Wings
The bones in a bird's wing are similar to those in a human arm. Most birds use their wings to fly. Strong muscles pull the wings downward when the bird flies; other muscles fold them up when not in use.

Bone structure
Most of the larger bones of a bird are hollow and lightweight. They contain air spaces that connect to the special air sacs the bird uses when it breathes. Some diving birds have solid bones to make diving easier.

Skeleton
Birds have fewer bones than reptiles or mammals, and many of the bones are fused together. A large flap called the keel sticks out of the breastbone and anchors the muscles that power the wings.

Feathers

Birds use their feathers to fly, and also to keep warm and dry. Each feather is made of fine strands called barbs that carry rows of smaller barbules. In some feathers, the barbules lock together with hooks to produce a smooth surface needed for flying through the air. In others, they stay partly or fully separate. These feathers are soft and fluffy for warmth.

Microscopic hooks lock barbules together.

Macaw flight feather

A hollow quill anchors the feather in the bird's skin.

Curved tip with interlocking barbules

Continuous curved surface

Breeding colors
Male birds often have bright colors that attract mates. In some species, these colors disappear at the end of the breeding season when the birds molt and a new set of feathers grows. In other species, such as pheasants, the colors are permanent.

Central quill

Down feathers
These short, fluffy feathers do not have hooked barbs. They form an insulating layer next to a bird's skin. They trap air to stop heat from escaping from the bird's body.

Body feathers
The tips of these feathers overlap like tiles on a roof, giving the bird a smooth shape. The fluffy base of each feather is close to the body and conserves heat.

Flight feathers
These feathers are strong but flexible. They provide lift when the bird is airborne. Birds have to preen them carefully to keep them in good condition.

Tail feathers
A bird uses its tail feathers for steering and braking. Some male birds have long or brightly colored tail feathers. These play an important part in courtship.

Breeding

Birds lay their eggs either directly on the ground or in a nest. One parent – or both – keep the eggs warm by sitting on them, or incubating them. Young birds hatch from eggs at different stages of development. Some can look after themselves almost immediately; others rely on their parents for food and protection.

Eggs
Birds' eggs have a hard shell. Ground-nesting birds often lay eggs that match their background. Birds that nest in trees often lay plain eggs.

Helpless young
Tree-nesting birds usually produce poorly developed young without feathers. The young stay in the nest until they are ready to feed themselves.

Well-developed young
The young of most ground-nesting birds can feed within hours of hatching. They soon leave the nest and follow their mother.

Foster parents
Brood parasites are birds that trick others into raising their young. Here a reed warbler is feeding a cuckoo that hatched in its nest.

B

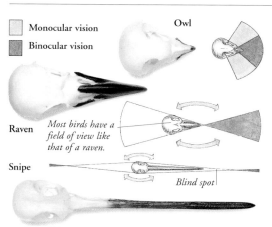

Monocular vision
Binocular vision

Owl

Raven
Most birds have a field of view like that of a raven.

Snipe
Blind spot

Vision
Birds that hunt, such as owls, have eyes at the front. This restricts their field of view, but they can judge distances accurately. Shorebirds, such as the snipe, have eyes at the side. They can spot danger in any direction, including the rear.

Senses

For most birds, vision is by far the most important sense. It guides them to their food and helps them avoid their many enemies. Hearing helps birds communicate, and is important to birds that hunt in the dark. The sense of smell is far less vital to birds than it is to many other animals, although some birds, such as the kiwi, use it to find food.

Crane
Like most birds, a crowned crane has keen eyesight. Its eyes are so big that they almost meet in the center of the skull. Its ear openings are at the base of its crown, but they are hidden by short feathers. Its nostrils are in its beak.

Crown of spiky feathers

Crowned crane

Flight

This complex way of moving requires superb coordination. Some birds stay airborne almost entirely by flapping, but others hold their wings out and glide through the air using the natural curve of their wings to provide lift. During flight, a bird adjusts the shape of its wings to alter its speed and height.

A pigeon's wings allow good maneuverability when extended, and fast flight when partially closed.

A kestrel's large wings provide lift as the bird flaps them nonstop while it hovers in the air.

A grouse's wings are shaped for load-bearing rather than speed. A grouse flies only in short bursts.

A peregrine falcon's slender wings partially fold up when it dives out of the sky on its prey.

Wing shapes
Birds have evolved a variety of wing shapes that enable them to fly in different ways. Some wings provide lots of lift but do not work well at speed. Others create as little friction as possible when they cut through the air, allowing a bird to fly faster.

Flightless birds
During the course of evolution, some birds gave up the ability to fly. Flightless birds do not need a light body, and although some are quite small, they include the biggest birds that have ever lived.

Largest and smallest
The world's heaviest bird is the ostrich. It weighs up to 275 lb (125 kg). This is about 80,000 times heavier than the rare bee hummingbird, the smallest bird. This tiny bird's eggs are the size of peas.

Feeding and diet

Birds spend much of the time looking for food. To be able to fly, birds need food that provides them with lots of energy. Many of them eat small animals, which they catch either on land, in the air, or in water. Others visit plants and eat fruits, seeds, nectar, and pollen. Some have a mixed diet. Unlike mammals, only a few birds eat grass or the leaves of other plants.

Fish eaters
The great blue heron catches fish by stabbing them with its beak. Other fish eaters snatch their prey with talons, dive-bomb them from above, or chase them through the water.

The flightless rhea comes from South America.

Seed eaters
Different birds eat different seeds. They usually crack open the seed's husk before eating the food inside. The goldfinch is a typical seed eater. It feeds on thistles.

Insect eaters
Insect-eating birds search for their food on the ground or on plants, or snap it up in midair. The goldcrest often feeds high up in trees. Like other small insect eaters, it is expert at spotting insects hidden on leaves or bark.

Meat eaters
Many birds eat small animals, but owls and birds of prey specialize in hunting larger animals, such as mammals, reptiles, and other birds. A hooked beak allows them to tear up their food before swallowing it.

FIND OUT MORE — ANIMAL BEHAVIOR · BIRDS OF PREY · EGGS · FLIGHT, ANIMAL · FLIGHTLESS BIRDS · NESTS AND BURROWS · OWLS AND NIGHTJARS · SKELETON · SONGBIRDS

Birds

Fish and meat eaters

Black-crowned night heron hunts for fish mainly after dark.

Large eyes

Inca tern flutters in the air before diving down to snatch fish from the surface of the ocean.

Spectacled owl has keen eyesight and hearing for catching small animals.

Harris's hawk uses its hooked beak to tear off meat before swallowing it.

Flamingo feeds with its head down, trailing its beak through the water.

Kookaburra is a member of the kingfisher family and feeds in woodland and forests.

Seed eaters

Scarlet eyestripe

African pygmy goose uses its broad beak to collect seeds floating on the water.

Patagonian conure lives in open grasslands of Argentina and Chile.

Mourning dove feeds on the ground in North America.

Eurasian goldfinch has a fine beak and extracts seeds from flowers.

Common waxbill is a common African finch that feeds in open grassland.

Sparrows have short, stout beaks that can crack the husks from small seeds.

Insect eaters

Kentucky warbler has a narrow beak ideally shaped for picking up small insects.

Ocher-bellied flycatcher chases after insects and catches them on the fly.

Flycatchers wait on a perch for insects to fly by that they can catch.

Didric cuckoo of Africa specializes in feeding on hairy caterpillars.

Bushy crest

Striated yuhina of Asia picks insects off leaves, and often searches under the leaves.

Racquet-tailed roller often feeds on ants and termites from the ground.

Nectar eaters

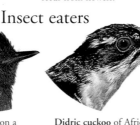
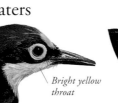

Blue-crowned hanging parrot has a brush-tipped tongue that helps it to collect nectar and pollen.

Duyvenbode's lory feeds on flowers of New Guinea forest trees, lapping up nectar with its tongue.

Yellow-fronted woodpecker feeds on fruit, probing deep into flowers to reach their nectar.

Bright yellow throat

Rufous hummingbird pumps nectar into its mouth with its tongue.

Booted racquet-tail has a rather short beak, and feeds at flowers with spreading petals.

Fruit eaters

Eurasian bullfinch feeds on buds and fruit, using its short, powerful beak.

Bearded barbet feeds mainly on figs, and uses its heavy bill to dig nest holes in wood.

Chestnut-eared aracari uses its long bill to reach for fruit on the end of long branches.

Bill has serrated edges.

Fire-tufted barbet of Malaysia eats both insects and fruit.

Splendid glossy starling gathers in isolated trees that carry ripe fruits.

Long-tailed starling searches for fruit in trees along forest edges.

Mixed food eaters

Eurasian jay feeds on acorns in fall and winter, but many foods during the rest of the year.

Alpine chough eats small animals and seeds, and also scavenges animal remains.

Blue magpie eats seeds and fruits, and small animals, including lizards and snakes.

Swainson's thrush eats insects, spiders, and fruit, particularly in winter.

Red-capped manakin hovers in front of plants to eat the fruit and also eats insects.

Red-throated ant tanager catches flying insects, and also eats fruit.

BIRDS OF PREY

At the end of a dive, the falcon opens its wings to slow down.

MOST BIRDS OF PREY, INCLUDING EAGLES, hawks, and falcons, kill and eat live animals. They soar high above the ground or dart among trees, using their excellent eyesight to search for prey. Once they spot a victim, they attack with their sharp talons, then tear up their food with their hooked beaks. Not all birds of prey feed in this way. A few species eat unusual foods, such as snails or nuts. Vultures eat carrion – animals that are already dead. They often wait for another animal to make a kill and then swoop down to the ground to feed on the remains of the carcass.

Long broad wings with finger-like tips

The falcon controls its flight by moving its long wing feathers.

Eyes
Birds of prey have superb eyesight for spotting prey on the ground from high up. Their eyes face forward, which makes the birds good at judging distances. This is essential for a bird such as the lanner falcon, because it has to know exactly when to brake as it hurtles toward its prey.

Beak
Birds do not have teeth, so they cannot cut meat into pieces before they swallow it. Instead, birds of prey tear up their food with their beaks. Despite the ferocious appearance of a bird of prey's beak, it is hardly ever used as a weapon.

Widely spread flight feathers brake the falcon's descent when it makes an attack.

Bird of prey features

With their forward-facing eyes, sharp claws, or talons, and hooked beak, birds of prey are perfectly adapted for hunting and feeding on meat. Most species have feathers covering the upper legs for warmth and protection.

Lanner falcon
This falcon lives in desert and savanna areas of southern Europe, Africa, and the Middle East. Like other falcons, it catches prey by folding its wings back and falling on it in a steep dive. Falcons also attack birds in midair by diving on them from above.

Talons
Birds of prey have large feet with long toes. Each toe ends in a talon that stays sharp by flaking into a point as it grows. The birds use their talons to kill food and carry it away. Many species can lift more than half their own weight.

Tail feathers are used to steer in flight.

Chukar partridge is prey of the falcon.

Flying styles

Splayed feathers reduce air turbulence.

Most large birds of prey, such as eagles, look for food while soaring on currents of rising air. This uses little energy, allowing the birds to fly long distances every day. Smaller species, such as hawks, usually fly in short bursts. Kestrels are unusual in being able to hover in the air.

Flight path of kestrel

Kestrel can see small animals on the ground.

Long, narrow wings

Hovering
Kestrels hover close to the ground while looking for prey. They use a lot of energy, but they can dive quickly on anything that moves below them.

Flight path of goshawk

Broad, rounded wings

Long, broad wings

Soaring
Eagles, buzzards, and vultures soar by riding on currents of rising air. They spiral around slowly as they soar upward, keeping their wings straight and steady.

Low-level flight
Hawks usually hunt by flying in short bursts. They are highly maneuverable and can swerve between trees and over hedges, using surprise to catch small birds.

Flight path of eagle

B

Roosting

These turkey buzzards from North America have gathered in a tree to roost, or settle for the night. Many vultures roost high in trees or on rocky ledges, making it easier for them to take off and become airborne when the day begins.

Vulture guards carrion while companion eats.

Long neck enables the vulture to reach into a carcass.

Vultures feeding on carrion

White-backed vulture

With a wingspan of more than 8 ft (2.5 m), this huge vulture soars high over open country in southern Europe, Asia, and Africa. Like most other vultures, it has a bare head and neck. If it had feathers there, they would become soaked with blood from the meat torn with its beak from inside a carcass.

Bare head and neck for ease of cleaning

Carrion eaters

Instead of hunting live animals, vultures feed on the remains of ones that are already dead. They live in open places such as deserts, grasslands, and mountains, and find their food by soaring and looking for animal carcasses from the air. Vultures have large beaks, but their talons are weak.

Feeding

Vultures have good eyesight. If one vulture spots a carcass and drops down to feed, others quickly follow. Soon vultures arrive from all around. The largest species usually feed first, leaving the smaller species to fight over the scraps.

Specialized eaters

Over millions of years of evolution, some birds of prey have developed very specialized diets and techniques to deal with their food. Most of these feeders eat animal food, but a few are vegetarians. Some species have learned to live alongside humans, and they eat the variety of food scraps that people throw away.

Egyptian Vulture

Egyptian vulture

The Egyptian vulture is one of only a few birds that uses tools to obtain food. It eats ostrich eggs, which it breaks open by picking up stones and hurling them against the shell until it breaks. In addition to Egypt, it lives in other parts of Africa, Europe, and Asia.

Secretary bird

Eyes face to the side instead of the front.

Slim, athletic build for hunting on the ground in open country

Feathery quills, like those once used for writing, give the secretary bird its name.

Long tail feathers provide balance.

Snail kite

The snail kite lives in marshy places from the southern US to Argentina in South America. It feeds almost entirely on freshwater snails, which it snatches from the water with one of its feet. It then scoops out the snail's body with its long, slender beak.

Palmnut vulture

The diet of this African vulture is based mainly on the fruits of oil palms, but it eats some small animals. Unlike other vultures, it does not have to fly long distances in search of food, and spends most of its time in trees.

Secretary bird raises its crest of black feathers to attract a mate

Secretary bird

This highly unusual bird of prey from Africa hunts on the ground. It has long, strong legs and kills animals by stomping them to death. The secretary bird often feeds on snakes, and when attacking them uses its wings like a shield to protect itself.

Largest and smallest

The Andean condor is the largest bird of prey, with a wingspan of more than 10 ft (3 m). It is a carrion eater. The smallest birds of prey are pygmy falcons and falconets, which feed mainly on flying insects. Some are only 6 in (15 cm) long.

LANNER FALCON

SCIENTIFIC NAME *Falco biarmicus*

ORDER Falconiformes

FAMILY Falconidae

DISTRIBUTION Southern Europe, Africa, and the Middle East

HABITAT Scrub and desert

DIET Birds, small mammals, and lizards

SIZE Length, including tail: male – 14.5 in (37 cm); female – 18.5 in (47 cm)

LIFESPAN About 10 years

FIND OUT **MORE**

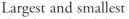

AFRICAN WILDLIFE | BIRDS | DESERT WILDLIFE | FLIGHT, ANIMAL | MOUNTAIN WILDLIFE | OWLS

Birds of prey
Eagles, hawks, and falcons

Large, broad wings

Tail is fanned out to provide lift as the kestrel hovers.

Common kestrel hovers to find its prey, instead of chasing it like other falcons.

Tawny eagle is a scavenger, feeding on carcasses, and even human garbage. It also steals from other birds of prey.

Goshawk hunts in forests and often catches birds in midair.

Black eagle is from southern Asia. It flies over forests and often snatches birds from their nests.

Feathers down to the toes as in all true eagles

American kestrel is a small falcon. It often feeds on insects.

Golden eagle lives in remote places throughout the northern hemisphere.

Harris's hawk sometimes hunts in groups, which is unusual for a bird of prey.

Imperial eagle is rare. It lives in Spain, eastern Europe, and Asia.

Caracara has long legs and toes that enable it to hunt on the ground.

Peregrine falcon is the fastest bird in the world.

Bateleur is almost tailless. This African eagle has an unusual zigzagging flight.

Vultures

Black vulture lives in the Americas. Like the turkey vulture, it has slender legs and toes.

Turkey vulture has an immense range, stretching from Canada to Tierra del Fuego at the tip of South America.

Collar of white feathers around the base of the neck

Huge flight feathers allow effortless soaring.

Worn feathers will be replaced when the vulture molts.

Andean condor is the largest bird of prey. As its name suggests, it lives in the Andes Mountains of South America.

Feet are too weak for catching food.

White-backed vulture has only a few feathers on its neck and a bare head like all vultures.

A bare neck is easy for the vulture to clean after feeding.

137

BLACK DEATH

IN THE 14TH CENTURY, a deadly epidemic swept the world. The Black Death, as it became known, was bubonic plague, a terrible disease that begins with fever, causes agonizing black swellings in the glands, and leads to death, usually within a few days of infection. Millions died. Terrified people fled infected areas and carried the plague with them. In towns the doors of plague carriers were marked with a cross to warn people to keep away. The dead were collected in carts and buried in mass graves. In Europe about one-third of the population died; a similar number probably died in Asia.

Progress of the plague

The plague reached the Black Sea from Asia in 1346. From there, it was carried by Italian traders to ports on the Mediterranean. It then spread up rivers and land routes into northern Europe. By 1350, most of Europe was affected.

Plague-free areas

Black Sea

c.1351

Prague

Paris

Milan

Constantinople

Genoa · Florence

Bordeaux

Dec. 1350

June 1350

Dec. 1349

June 1349

Dec. 1348

June 1348

Dec. 1347

Plague-free areas
Some areas, such as modern-day Poland and Milan, escaped the plague, but the reason for this is still a mystery.

Disease carriers

Plague is caused by a bacterium that lives on rodents. The disease was caught by black rats in Asia, which then traveled in ships to Europe and spread the disease among people there. An infected person could also pass the plague through the air by coughing.

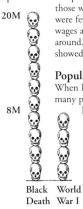

Plague bacterium
The bacterium is called *Yersinia pestis,* after the Swiss biologist Alexander Yersin, who discovered it. It is common in wild animals such as field mice, ground squirrels, and marmots.

Flea carriers
The plague bacterium lives in the digestive system of a flea and causes a blockage there. When the flea feeds, the blockage makes it vomit the newly eaten blood back onto its host, along with plague bacteria, which then infect the host.

Animal carriers
The black rat lived in towns and on ships, and scavenged in food stores and garbage dumps. Rats carry fleas, and when plague-carrying rats died of the disease, their fleas searched for other hosts. If these new hosts were people, they, too, caught the plague.

Human carriers
The plague turned into an epidemic so rapidly because human travelers helped spread it. Mongol nomads and Asian merchants carried it across Asia. The traders of the great Italian cities, such as Genoa and Venice, carried it around Europe in their ships.

Effects of the plague

The disease was so widespread that many left their families and took to the road to try to escape death. Some thought the plague was God's punishment for the sins of people, and mercilessly whipped themselves in the streets to show repentance.

Labor force
By the end of the 14th century, the smaller population of Europe meant that life was better for those who had survived. Because there were fewer peasants, they got higher wages and there was more food to go around. But recurring peasant rebellions showed that they still had grievances.

20M

8M

Population decline
When Pope Clement VI asked how many people had died from the plague, he was told at least 20 million people in Europe, and 17 million in Asia. By comparison, around eight million soldiers died in World War I.

= 2 million dead

Black Death

World War I

Dealing with the plague

Some people tried to fend off the plague by using herbal remedies, bleeding by leeches, fumigation, and even bathing in urine. A 14th-century poem, called the Dance of Death (which states that death comes for people of every rank) was often enacted and painted to remind people that death – and the plague – could strike at any time.

Lungwort

Mint

Rose

Simple lead crosses were placed on corpses in mass graves.

Tombs
During the plague, people faced death every day. Death is often realistically shown on 14th-century tombs, where images of skeletons and decaying corpses are common.

Chantries
People often left money for masses to be said for their souls. These masses were said in special chapels inside churches known as chantries. This chantry is at Winchester, England.

FIND OUT
MORE

ASIA, HISTORY OF

DISEASES

EUROPE, HISTORY OF

MEDIEVAL EUROPE

MICROSCOPIC LIFE

BLACK HOLES

ASTRONOMERS HAVE SPENT much time analyzing the life cycle of stars. One problem was to explain what happens to the most massive stars when they die. In 1967, the term "black hole" was used to describe what is left when such a star dies. Four years later, a powerful source of X rays, Cygnus X-1 was discovered; the first black hole candidate had been identified.

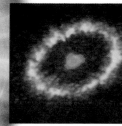

A **massive star** dies in a huge explosion, leaving a very dense core that then collapses.

Detecting a black hole

Black holes appear black because nothing, not even light, can escape from their powerful gravity. Astronomers cannot detect them directly, but can "see" them because of the effect their gravity has on everything around them, such as gas from a nearby star. The boundary of the black hole is called the event horizon. Material pulled in toward the hole is swirled around by the gravity, forming a disk, before crossing the horizon.

Gravity increases as the core of the dying star shrinks.

Event horizon

Anything trying to pull away from the gravity must travel almost at the speed of light, as the core approaches the size of the event horizon.

Once the core is smaller than the event horizon, not even light can escape.

The core continues collapsing until it takes up virtually no space. The star is a singularity, a point mass of infinitely high density inside a black hole.

Stellar collapse

Massive stars can end their lives in an explosion called a supernova that leaves behind a central core. If the core is made of the equivalent of more than three Suns, it becomes a black hole. Gravity forces the core to collapse. As the core shrinks, its gravity increases. At a certain point it reaches the critical size of the event horizon.

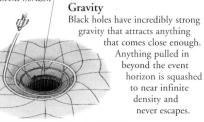

Event horizon

Gravity
Black holes have incredibly strong gravity that attracts anything that comes close enough. Anything pulled in beyond the event horizon is squashed to near infinite density and never escapes.

Gas is torn from a nearby star.

Close to the black hole, the gas glows with heat.

Black hole

Gravity pulls the gas toward the black hole.

Accretion disk

Accretion disk
The material that swirls around a black hole forms a rapidly spinning accretion disk. As the material is pulled closer to the hole, it travels faster and faster, and becomes very hot from friction. Close to the hole, the material is so hot that it emits X rays before crossing the event horizon and disappearing forever.

A black hole is black because no light or other radiation can escape and a hole because nothing that crosses the event horizon can get out.

Falling into a black hole

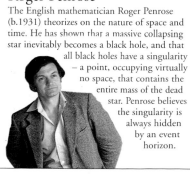

1 At the start of the fall, everything appears normal.

Astronaut becomes distorted.

2 As the astronaut approaches the hole, he starts to be stretched.

3 Light is also stretched to a longer wavelength, so the astronaut appears red.

4 Gravity stretches the astronaut until, close to the hole, he is torn apart.

Galaxy NGC 4261 in the constellation of Virgo has what appears to be a huge accretion disk – 30 million light-years across – swirling around a huge black hole.

Inside a black hole

Space and time are highly distorted inside a black hole. Anyone who fell into one would be "spaghettified" – stretched to resemble spaghetti as gravity pulled harder on the feet than the head. An observer watching a person fall would also see time running slower as the person fell toward the event horizon.

Supermassive holes

Some galaxies have very active centers that emit lots of energy. An object that has powerful gravity, such as a supermassive black hole, could be the cause of the activity. Such a hole would be a hundred million times more massive than the Sun.

Roger Penrose

The English mathematician Roger Penrose (b.1931) theorizes on the nature of space and time. He has shown that a massive collapsing star inevitably becomes a black hole, and that all black holes have a singularity – a point, occupying virtually no space, that contains the entire mass of the dead star. Penrose believes the singularity is always hidden by an event horizon.

FIND OUT MORE

FRICTION   GALAXIES   GRAVITY   STARS   SUN AND SOLAR SYSTEM   UNIVERSE

B

BOLÍVAR, SIMÓN

SIMÓN BOLÍVAR WAS the brilliant charismatic leader who led South America to independence from 400 years of foreign rule. Together with other generals, he overthrew the Spanish in just 12 years. As president of the federation of Gran Colombia, he wanted to rule the whole continent, but this dream came to nothing. To this day, he is still known as "The Liberator," and one of the South American nations, Bolivia, is named after him.

Early life

Bolívar was born into a rich family in Caracas, Venezuela, in 1783. His parents died when he was young, and he was educated by private tutors, such as Simón Rodríguez, a teacher who taught him about European ideas such as liberty.

Fighting for independence

At the start of the 19th century, all of South America except Brazil and Guiana was under the rule of the Spanish king Ferdinand VII. Many South Americans resented this and wanted to govern themselves. In response, independence movements broke out all over South America. Bolívar, eager to work in the independence movement, returned to South America and fought the Spanish in Venezuela.

Bolívar's storms to victory at the Battle of Carabobo

Bolívar in Europe

In 1799, Bolívar was sent to Madrid to live with relatives and improve his education. While in Europe, Bolívar learned of an attempt in 1806 by Francisco de Miranda to liberate Venezuela from Spanish rule. The rebellion failed, but inspired Bolívar to fight for independence.

Ferdinand VII of Spain

The first republic

In 1810, Francisco de Miranda returned from exile in Europe and was made president of the new republic of Venezuela. In 1811, it became the first South American country to declare independence from foreign rule. Bolívar joined the rebel army, but the republic collapsed. He carried on the struggle, going to Colombia to fight the Spanish there.

Francisco de Miranda in prison

The Liberator

From 1811 onward, Bolívar was the focus of independence movements across South America. In 1813, he defeated the Spanish and entered Caracas, where he was given the title of "The Liberator." In 1819, he put together an army of 2,500 men and marched them across the continent to Boyacá, Colombia. He won the resulting battle, and Colombia gained its independence.

The Angostura Congress

At a congress held in Angostura, now Ciudad Bolívar, Bolívar was elected president of Venezuela. The congress also proposed the formation of Gran Colombia, a federation that included present-day Venezuela, Colombia, Ecuador, and Panama. Between 1819 and 1822, Bolívar won a series of victories against Spain, confirming the independence of Colombia and Venezuela, and liberating Peru.

Bolívar and Sucre

Ecuador and Peru

In 1822, one of Bolívar's most talented generals, Antonio José de Sucre, defeated the Spanish at Pichincha to win Ecuador's independence. Two years later, Bolívar made a deal with the Argentinian liberator José de San Martín, whose forces were active in Peru. As a result, Sucre defeated the Spanish at Ayacucho, bringing independence to Peru. As a result of Bolívar's influence, another large area of South America was liberated.

Bolivia

In 1825, Bolívar dispatched Sucre to conquer Alto Perú, in west central South America, which was still under Spanish control. Once the Spanish were defeated, the newly independent country was named Bolivia in honor of the Liberator. By now, every South American state except Uruguay had won its independence.

Bolívar's statue at government buildings, La Paz, Bolivia

SIMÓN BOLÍVAR

1783	Born in Caracas, Venezuela.
1799	Sent to Europe.
1811	Venezuela declares its independence; Bolívar becomes a military leader.
1812	First republic is defeated.
1813	Bolívar enters Caracas as "The Liberator," but is soon defeated.
1819	Angostura Congress.
1819	Bolívar wins Battle of Boyacá to win Colombian independence.
1821	Bolívar wins Battle of Carabobo to win Venezuelan independence.
1822	Ecuador wins independence.
1825	Bolivia named in his honor.
1830	Dies of tuberculosis.

FIND OUT MORE   CENTRAL AMERICA, HISTORY OF   NAPOLEON BONAPARTE   SOUTH AMERICA, HISTORY OF   SPAIN, HISTORY OF

BOLIVIA AND PARAGUAY

BOLIVIA AND PARAGUAY are the only landlocked countries in South America. They are also two of the poorest in the continent, reliant on their neighbors for access to the sea. In a bitter war between them over ownership of the Gran Chaco, (1932–35) Bolivia lost, but both countries suffered political turmoil. Under Spanish rule between the 1530s and 1820s, Bolivia and Paraguay still bear its legacy: Spanish is an official language, and more than 90 percent of the region's population is Roman Catholic. Many people farm and, in Bolivia, some grow and sell coca, for cocaine, a drug that the government has taken steps to banish.

Physical features

The Altiplano dominates the west of Bolivia, while the east is covered by a lowland plain called the Oriente. Paraguay is divided north to south by the Paraguay River. In the west is the Gran Chaco, a region of grass and scrub; the east is covered in grassy plains and forests, and drained by the mighty Paraná River.

Altiplano
At about 12,467 ft (3,800 m) above sea level, the Altiplano, a vast, windswept, almost treeless plateau, lies between two ranges of the Bolivian Andes. Despite its cold, arid climate, about 70 percent of Bolivia's population lives here, growing a few crops and raising animals such as llamas and alpacas.

Lake Titicaca
The clear blue waters of Lake Titicaca cover 3,200 sq miles (8,288 sq km) at a height of 12,500 ft (3,810 m) above sea level, making it the highest navigable lake in the world. It is the last surviving stretch of an ancient inland sea known as Lago Ballivián.

Aymara
The Aymara are a group of Native South Americans who have farmed on the Bolivian Altiplano for hundreds of years, strongly resisting cultural change. With the Quechua, another Indian group, they make up more than half Bolivia's population, but suffer discrimination and do not contribute to politics or the economy. The state has successfully persuaded many Aymara to move into towns.

Aymaras farmers, Altiplano, Bolivia

Gran Chaco
The flat, dry plain that covers southeastern Bolivia and northwestern Paraguay is called the Gran Chaco. Since so few people live in this area of coarse grass, cactus, and thorny shrubs, a range of plants and animals thrive.

Regional climate
Bolivia's Altiplano has a cool, crisp, dry climate. The eastern part of the country is warm and humid, as is most of Paraguay. The Chaco is hot, with 20–40 in (50–100 cm) of rain a year, although it often has droughts in winter.

67°F (19°C)   55°F (12°C)

74 in (1,890 mm)

Bolivia

The highest and most isolated nation in South America, Bolivia is named after Simón Bolívar, who, in the 1800s, led wars of independence against the Spaniards. Despite rich natural resources, exporting is difficult because of Bolivia's position. About half are Native Americans; the rest are Spanish or mixed blood *mestizos*.

La Paz
Although Sucre is Bolivia's official capital, the country is governed from La Paz, which also has capital status. At 11,913 ft (3,631 m) above sea level, La Paz is the world's highest capital and Bolivia's largest city, with a population of about 1,126,000, of whom over half are Native Americans. La Paz has chemical and textile industries, but unemployment is generally high.

Chuqui

Pipes are made from a local reed. The longer the reed, the deeper the sound.

Tin

Music
Bolivian music has Incan, Amazonian, Spanish, and African influences. Rural Aymara orchestras are often composed entirely of panpipes, called *chuqui*. Other instruments include drums, flutes, and the *phututu*, made from a cow's horn.

Deforestation
Tropical rain forests in Bolivia are being cut down at the rate of 772 sq miles (2,000 sq km) a year, mostly for cattle ranching or growing coca for cocaine. Chemicals used in the manufacture of cocaine are discharged directly into the rivers of Amazonia, many of which have high pollution levels that damage plant and tree life.

Metal mining
Bolivia's tin mines lie high in the Andes mountains. Output has fallen, but the country is still the sixth largest producer in the world. It is also the third largest producer of antimony, and ranks ninth in silver.

BOLIVIA FACTS

CAPITAL CITIES La Paz, Sucre

AREA 414,162 sq miles (1,098,580 sq km)

POPULATION 8,256,000

MAIN LANGUAGES Spanish, Quechua, Aymara

MAJOR RELIGION Christian

CURRENCY Boliviano

Potatoes

Corn

Barley

Crops
Bolivian farmers living on the Altiplano grow potatoes, soybeans, barley, and wheat for themselves and their families. Rice, corn, bananas, and plantains are grown in the lowlands. Cash crops include sugarcane, cocoa beans, and coffee, although the profits from illegal coca crops greatly exceed all legal farming produce combined.

Paraguay

The Paraguay River, from which the country takes its name, divides the land in two. To the east lie the fertile hills and plains that are home to 95 percent of the people. Most are *mestizos*; the rest are Guaraní or Europeans. To the northwest is the Gran Chaco, large areas of which Paraguay won from Bolivia in the 1930s. Only five percent of the people live in the Chaco, including 10,000 Mennonites, farmers of German descent who retain their culture.

Macá bag

Macá Indians
The Macá are a small group of Indians who follow a traditional lifestyle in the Gran Chaco. They make a living from farming. Macá women also weave bags and cloth for the tourist trade.

Beef
The main industry in Paraguay's Gran Chaco is cattle ranching. Herds of animals roam the flat grasslands, tended by skilled Paraguayan cowboys called *gauchos* who round the cattle up on horseback. The farms are called *estancias* and are some of the only buildings in this open landscape.

Itaipu Dam
With a reservoir 1,255 sq miles (3,250 sq km) and 722 ft (220 m) deep, the Itaipu Dam, on the Paraná River, was undertaken as a joint project with Brazil. It provides water for the world's largest hydroelectric plant and generates enough electricity to make Paraguay self-sufficient in energy.

Dam generates 13,320 megawatts of electricity – enough to supply New York City.

PARAGUAY FACTS

CAPITAL CITY Asunción

AREA 157,046 sq miles (406,750 sq km)

POPULATION 4,576,000

MAIN LANGUAGES Spanish, Guaraní

MAJOR RELIGION Christian

CURRENCY Guaraní

Jesuits
In 1588, Spanish missionaries from the Jesuit order of the Roman Catholic Church arrived in Asunción. They converted the local Guaraní people to Christianity, and taught them trades such as weaving. The Jesuits built large stone churches.

Exports
Soybean flour and cotton make up nearly 50 percent of Paraguay's exports. The country also sells timber from its forests, vegetable oils, and processed meat. Leading trading partners include Brazil, the Netherlands, and Argentina.

FIND OUT MORE BOLIVAR, SIMON · CHRISTIANITY · DAMS · DRUGS · ENERGY · FARMING · MUSIC · NATIVE AMERICANS · ROCKS AND MINERALS · SOUTH AMERICA, HISTORY OF · TEXTILES AND WEAVING

BOOKS

FROM ENCYCLOPEDIAS TO NOVELS, books are a vital record of human life and achievement. They store the thoughts, beliefs, and experiences of individuals and societies, preserving them long after the author's death. There are many kinds of books, from religious works, such as the Qur'an, and nonfiction, such as dictionaries and educational books, to fiction such as plays and stories. The Chinese invented printing in the 9th century; it arrived in Europe during the 15th century. Printing made it possible to mass-produce books, and knowledge was spread more widely. Today, publishing is a global industry.

B

Early Chinese book made of fragile bamboo strips

Early books

The first books were not made of paper. Long before 3000 BC, the Sumerians wrote on clay tablets. Around 1300 BC, the Chinese began making books from bamboo strips bound together with cord.

Making books

Much preparation goes into making books and some take several years to produce. For example, making an encyclopedia will involve a team of people that includes authors, editors, designers, picture researchers, illustrators, photographers, and computer technicians, as well as printers.

Designer's plan, showing exact page layout

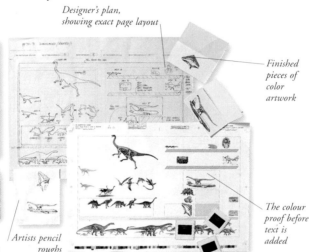

Finished pieces of color artwork

The colour proof before text is added

Editor's notes and designer's rough layout

Artists pencil roughs

Design and illustration

The designer draws a detailed plan, showing the position of each illustration. The artist makes rough sketches, which are checked, then paints each picture separately. The artwork is photographed, and carefully positioned on the page using a computer until the design is perfect.

Papyrus plants grow by the Nile.

Paper

The ancient Egyptians wrote on scrolls made from papyrus, which grew by the Nile River. Later civilizations in the Middle East wrote on parchment made from animal skin. Modern paper was probably invented in China around AD 200. It was made by pulping flax fibers, then flattening and drying them in the sun. The Chinese kept this process a secret for 600 years before they passed it on to the rest of the world.

CD-ROMS

There is a limit to how big any book can grow before it becomes too heavy and cumbersome to be practical. Now modern technology is developing compact alternatives to traditional books. One CD-ROM can contain as much text as a shelf of encyclopedias. Text and pictures from CD-ROMs can be read and transmitted by computer.

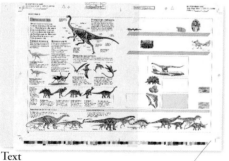

Text

After the text is written, it is edited in position on a computer screen, then photographed onto film. The text film is laid over the artwork and checked to make sure that words and images fit exactly before being sent to the printer.

Marks show the printer how to position text and color film for a perfect fit.

Pictures and text are perfectly integrated.

The color matches the original artwork as closely as possible.

Finished book

At last the book is finished and fitted with a hard cover and a protective jacket. It is now ready to be sold. The production of an illustrated book may take several years.

CD-ROMs

Paperbacks

A paperback book contains the same text as a hardback, but has a soft cover. The first modern paperback books were published in London by Penguin, in 1935, priced at six pence (about 25 cents). They are far cheaper than hardbacks, and many more people can buy them.

Timeline

c. 285 BC Egyptian pharaoh Ptolemy I establishes a library at Alexandria, Egypt.

AD 300s Books with pages first invented.

Gutenberg Bible

c.1440 Johannes Gutenberg invents the metal type.

1789 French Revolutionaries proclaim the fundamental public right to print without fear of censorship.

1796 Lithography (a technique for printing illustrations) invented.

1811 First totally mechanized printing press invented, US.

1935 First paperback books published for mass market by Penguin in UK.

1980s Electronic books for the computer published in CD-ROM format.

1990s Books first published on the Internet.

FIND OUT MORE   CHILDREN'S LITERATURE   COMPUTERS   DRAMA   EGYPT, ANCIENT   LITERATURE   POETRY   PRINTING   WRITING

BRAIN AND NERVOUS SYSTEM

EVERY THOUGHT YOU HAVE, every emotion you feel, and every action you take is a reflection of the nervous system at work. At the core of the nervous system are the brain and spinal cord, known as the central nervous system (CNS). The most complex part of the CNS is the brain; it constantly receives information from the body, processes it, and sends out instructions telling the body what to do. The CNS communicates with every part of the body through an extensive network of nerves. The nerves and the CNS are both constructed from billions of nerve cells called neurons.

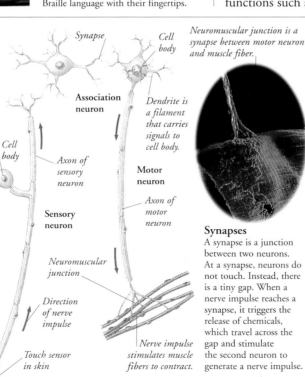

Brain is the body's control and co-ordination center.

Cranial nerves

Cervical nerves

Brachial plexus

Spinal cord relays information to and from the brain and the rest of the body.

Thoracic nerves

Lumbar nerves

Sacral nerves

Radial nerve controls the muscles in the arm and hand.

Lumbar plexus

Sacral plexus

Sciatic nerve controls the muscles in the leg and foot.

Tibial nerve controls the muscles of the calf and foot.

Nerves

Nerves form the "wiring" of the nervous system. Each nerve consists of a bundle of neurons (nerve cells) held together by a tough outer sheath. Nerves spread out from the brain and spinal cord and branch repeatedly to reach all parts of the body. Most nerves contain sensory neurons that carry nerve impulses toward the CNS, and motor neurons that carry nerve impulses away from the CNS.

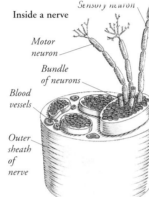

Inside a nerve

Sensory neuron

Motor neuron

Bundle of neurons

Blood vessels

Outer sheath of nerve

Nerve endings

At the ends of sensory neurons there are nerve endings called sensory receptors. If you touch an object, a sensory receptor in the skin is stimulated, nerve impulses travel to the brain along the sensory neuron, and you feel the object. In this way, visually impaired people can "read" Braille language with their fingertips.

Nervous system

The nervous system is made up of the CNS and the peripheral nervous system, which consists of the nerves. The peripheral nervous system has two sections: the somatic system, which controls voluntary actions, and the autonomic nervous system, which controls automatic functions such as heart rate.

Neurons

Neurons are long, thin cells adapted to carry electrical signals called nerve impulses. There are three types of neurons: sensory neurons, motor neurons, and association neurons. The most numerous are association neurons, which transmit signals from one neuron to another and are found only inside the CNS.

Synapse

Cell body

Association neuron

Dendrite is a filament that carries signals to cell body.

Cell body

Axon of sensory neuron

Sensory neuron

Motor neuron

Axon of motor neuron

Neuromuscular junction

Direction of nerve impulse

Touch sensor in skin

Nerve impulse stimulates muscle fibers to contract.

Nerve impulses

Nerve impulses are the "messages" that travel at high speed along neurons. Impulses are weak electrical signals that are generated and transmitted by neurons when they are stimulated. The stimulus may come from a sensory nerve ending, or from an adjacent neuron. Nerve impulses travel in one direction along the neuron.

Neuromuscular junction is a synapse between motor neuron and muscle fiber.

Synapses

A synapse is a junction between two neurons. At a synapse, neurons do not touch. Instead, there is a tiny gap. When a nerve impulse reaches a synapse, it triggers the release of chemicals, which travel across the gap and stimulate the second neuron to generate a nerve impulse.

Reflex actions

If you touch something sharp, you automatically pull your hand away without thinking about it. This is a reflex action. A sensory neuron carries impulses to the spinal cord, where an association neuron transmits impulses to a motor neuron, and the arm muscle contracts.

Receptors in hand detect the prick of a pin and send signal to spinal cord.

Brain

Sensory receptors

Motor neuron

Muscle

Sensory neuron

Santiago Ramón y Cajal

Spanish anatomist Santiago Ramón y Cajal (1852–1934) pioneered the study of the cells that make up the brain and nerves. He developed methods for staining nerve cells so they could be seen clearly under the microscope. His work revolutionized the examination of brain tissue.

The brain

The brain is the body's control center. Your brain enables you to think and to have a personality, and also regulates all your body processes. It has three main regions: the forebrain, the cerebellum, and the brain stem. The forebrain consists of the cerebrum (which is made up of two halves or hemispheres), the thalamus, hypothalamus, and the limbic system, which controls emotions and instinctive behavior.

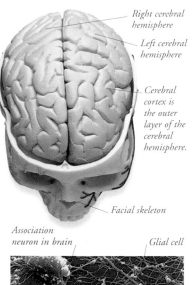

White matter

Gray matter

Section through brain tissue

Gray and white matter

Each cerebral hemisphere has two layers. The outer layer, the cerebral cortex, consists of gray matter containing cell bodies of neurons that form a communication network. The inner layer, or white matter, consists of nerve fibers that link the cerebral cortex to the other parts of the brain.

B

Thalamus relays information about the senses to the cerebrum.

Cerebrum is the site of conscious thought.

The two cerebral hemispheres are joined by a band called the corpus callosum.

Hypothalamus regulates body temperature, thirst, and appetite.

Left and right brains

The left cerebral hemisphere controls the right side of the body, and the right cerebral hemisphere controls the left side of the body. Although both hemispheres are used for almost every activity, each hemisphere has its own special skills. In most people, the left hemisphere is involved in spoken and written language, mathematical ability, and reasoning, while the right hemisphere controls the appreciation of art and music, insight and imagination, and shape recognition.

Right cerebral hemisphere

Left cerebral hemisphere

Cerebral cortex is the outer layer of the cerebral hemisphere.

Facial skeleton

Frontal lobe

Pituitary gland

Cerebellum coordinates movement and balance.

Spinal cord

Brain stem controls essential automatic functions, such as breathing and heart rate.

Brain cells

The brain consists of hundreds of billions of nerve cells. Many of these are association neurons that are constantly receiving and transmitting nerve impulses. Any one of these neurons can have links to over 1,000 other neurons, producing a complex network. The brain also contains other nerve cells, called glial cells, which hold the neurons in place.

Association neuron in brain

Glial cell

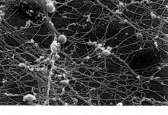

Brain areas

Certain areas of the cerebrum are involved with particular body functions. These areas can be highlighted on a brain map. Motor areas of the brain, such as the speech and basic movement areas, send out instructions to control voluntary movement. Sensory areas, such as the hearing, taste, smell, touch, and vision areas, receive information from sensory receptors around the body. Association areas, such as the frontal lobe, deal with thoughts, personality, and emotions, analyse experiences, and give you consciousness and awareness.

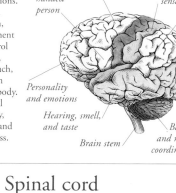

Speech area in right-handed person

Basic movements

Touch and other skin sensations

Vision

Personality and emotions

Hearing, smell, and taste

Brain stem

Balance and muscle coordination

Brain waves

The brain's neurons are constantly sending out and receiving nerve impulses. This process produces electrical signals that can be detected using a machine called an electroencephalograph (EEG). Electrodes linked to the EEG can be attached to a person's scalp in order to record the brain's electrical activities as a series of patterns called brain waves.

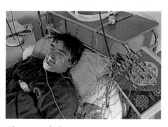

Sleep and dreams

As you sleep, you move repeatedly between phases of light REM (rapid eye movement) sleep and phases of deeper NREM sleep. These shifts can be detected using an EEG.

Metal rod

Skull of Phineas Gage

Personality

The frontal lobe of the brain plays a major role in deciding personality. The case of an American worker, Phineas Gage, proved it. In 1848, an accident sent a metal rod through Gage's cheek and frontal lobe. He survived, but his personality changed from being friendly to being aggressive.

Spinal cord

The spinal cord relays information between the brain and the rest of the body and is involved in many reflex actions. It is a flattened cylinder of nervous tissue, about 17 in (43 cm) long and as thick as a finger. It runs from the base of the brain to the lower back, surrounded by the backbone.

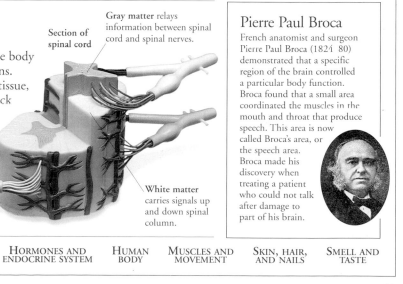

Gray matter relays information between spinal cord and spinal nerves.

Section of spinal cord

Spinal nerve relays nerve impulses to and from all parts of body.

Spinal ganglion

White matter carries signals up and down spinal column.

Pierre Paul Broca

French anatomist and surgeon Pierre Paul Broca (1824–80) demonstrated that a specific region of the brain controlled a particular body function. Broca found that a small area coordinated the muscles in the mouth and throat that produce speech. This area is now called Broca's area, or the speech area. Broca made his discovery when treating a patient who could not talk after damage to part of his brain.

FIND OUT MORE CELLS EYES AND VISION HORMONES AND ENDOCRINE SYSTEM HUMAN BODY MUSCLES AND MOVEMENT SKIN, HAIR, AND NAILS SMELL AND TASTE

BRAZIL

THE LARGEST COUNTRY in South America, Brazil is a land of opposites. Watered by the second longest river in the world, the Amazon, it has the world's largest rain forest, arid desert in the northeast, and rolling grassland in the south. Crowded cities contrast with remote areas that have never been explored. The country has many well-developed industries and a huge, successful agricultural base, but many people live in poverty. Brazilian society is a vibrant, diverse mix of cultures.

Physical features

The Amazon Basin and its forests, some mountainous, occupy northern Brazil. The southeast is a region of plateaux that vary from sunburned arid scrublands to rich fields and pastures.

BRAZIL FACTS

CAPITAL CITY	Brasília
AREA	3,286,472 sq miles (8,511,970 sq km)
POPULATION	163,577,000
MAIN LANGUAGE	Portuguese
MAJOR RELIGION	Christian
CURRENCY	Réal
LIFE EXPECTANCY	66 years
PEOPLE PER DOCTOR	670
GOVERNMENT	Multiparty democracy
ADULT LITERACY	82%

Highlands

The Brazilian Highlands extend from the Amazon Basin to the coast, rising to 10,000 ft (3,000 m). About 60 percent of the country is dominated by the plateau, where landscape ranges from tropical forest to dry, rocky desert.

Amazon rain forest

Three-fifths of Brazil is cloaked in dense rain forest. The Amazon River, 4,007 miles (6,448 km) long, runs through the north of Brazil, giving life to more than 40,000 different species of plants and animals in the forests.

106°F (41°C)   25°F (-4°C)
64°F (18°C)   72°F (22°C)
63 in (1,600 mm)

Climate

All except the extreme south of Brazil lies in the tropics, so temperatures are always high. The Amazon rain forest receives about 157 in (4,000 mm) of rain every year. By contrast, droughts are common in the northeastern corner. Farther south, summers are hot and winters can be cold with frosts.

Brasília

Brazil's modern capital city, Brasília, lies on the extreme northern edge of the plateau region. Planned in the 1950s on the site of a felled rain forest, the city replaced Rio de Janeiro as the capital. Its inland location has helped develop new areas away from the coast. There are many imaginative, futuristic buildings, including the spectacular cathedral.

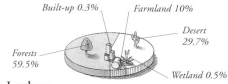

Brasília Cathedral

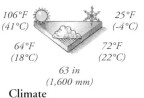

Built-up 0.3%   Farmland 10%
Desert 29.7%
Forests 59.5%
Wetland 0.5%

Land use

Thick forests cover the majority of the land, but are being cleared at an alarming rate to make way for farmland and roads. The fertile southeast, especially around São Paulo, is permanently farmed. Much of the land is desert.

People

The Brazilian people have a diverse ethnic background. There are large groups of Africans, Europeans, and Asians and the original inhabitants of Brazil form only a tiny percentage of the population. Many families are tight knit, fiercely loyal, and strictly Roman Catholic. The majority live in towns clustered along the southeastern coast.

Indian groups
Some native Brazilians still live in the rain forests, following traditional ways of life. However, about 14 groups now shelter in Xingu National Park, set up when their forest home was destroyed.

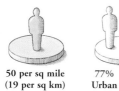

**50 per sq mile
(19 per sq km)**

**77%
Urban**   **23%
Rural**

Leisure

The mainly Roman Catholic people of Brazil celebrate many religious festivals, such as the Rio and Bahía carnivals. Sports, including soccer, basketball, and water sports along the coast, are the chief leisure activities for millions of Brazilians. The samba, one of the world's most popular dances, originated in Brazil.

Rio Carnival
Known as one of the world's largest and most spectacular festivals, the Rio Carnival, in Rio de Janeiro, is held just before Lent every year. During the carnival, processions of brightly decorated floats and a myriad of colorful singers, musicians, and dancers with imaginative costumes, fill the streets.

Soccer
Many Brazilians have a passion for soccer, either as players or spectators. The national team has won the World Cup more times than any other team. Its star player, Edson Arantes do Nascimento, known as Pelé, was the world's leading player in the 1960s and is regarded by fans as a living legend.

Farming

Brazil has immense natural resources. About 22 percent of the labor force works on the land, growing all Brazil's own food, with a vast surplus for export. The best farmland is around Rio de Janeiro and São Paulo, where water is plentiful and the climate is frost free. About 150 million cattle are raised on large ranches in this region.

**Cattle ranch,
São Paulo**

Orange

**Coffee
leaves and
berries**

Soybeans
Each berry contains two beans, which are washed, dried, and roasted.

Meat production
Brazil is the world's third largest producer of beef and veal. Cows graze on the rich green pastures of central Brazil. Large areas of tropical rain forest are cleared to create new cattle ranches, but the soil is soon exhausted and more forest has to be felled.

Bananas

Crops
Brazil is the leading producer of cocoa beans, coffee, oranges, and sugarcane, and the second largest grower of soybeans and bananas. About 22 percent of the world's coffee comes from Brazil, and millions of oranges are picked every year. These crops grow successfully in the warm, fertile soil of central and southern Brazil.

Forest products

The plants and trees of the Amazon rain forest have long been used for food, housing, and medicine by the people who live there. Some of the products, such as rubber and Brazil nuts, are now known worldwide. Other lesser-known plants are quinine, taken from the bark of chinchona and used to treat malaria; ipecac, an ingredient of cough medicine; and curare, once an arrow poison, now a life-saving muscle relaxant used in operations.

**Brazil
nuts**

Transportation

A vast network links Brazil's main centers, but only nine percent of the 1,031,693 miles (1,660,352 km) of roads are paved. Brazil has one of the world's largest national air networks. Cities with rapid growth, such as São Paulo, are expanding their subways.

Industry

The manufacturing industry employs about 15 percent of the Brazilian workforce. Machinery, textiles, cars, food products, industrial chemicals, and footwear are the main export products. Brazil has large mining, oil, and steel industries, but has suffered high inflation.

Mining
Brazil is a leading producer of gold, manganese, and tin ore. The country is noted for its precious stones, such as amethysts, diamonds, and topaz, but the quest for mineral wealth has led to much forest destruction.

Steel
South America's top steel maker, Brazil ranks ninth in world production. This, and cheap labor, has attracted many carmakers to invest in the country.

"Green" cars
About one-third of all Brazil's cars are run on so-called "green gas," or ethanol, which is made from fermented sugarcane. Because it produces less carbon monoxide than gas when it is burned, it is less harmful to the environment and is reducing pollution.

**FIND OUT
MORE**   CHRISTIANITY   CRYSTALS
AND GEMS   FARMING   FESTIVALS   FORESTS   NATIVE
AMERICANS   RIVERS   ROCKS AND
MINERALS   SOCCER   SOUTH AMERICA,
HISTORY OF

BRIDGES

CURVING MAJESTICALLY across rivers and valleys, bridges are some of the most spectacular structures engineers have ever created. They are also some of the most useful, because bridges can speed up journeys by cutting out ferry crossings, long detours, steep hills, and busy junctions. The first bridges were probably tree trunks laid across streams. Wooden beam bridges and stone or brick arches were the main types of bridge from Roman times until the 18th century, when iron became available to engineers. Most modern bridges are made of steel and concrete, making them both strong and flexible.

1 The foundations are laid, and the two pylons are erected. The concrete side spans, which will link the bridge to the shore, are assembled.

Pylon

Side span

2 The deck sections are hung from cables attached to the pylons, and the bridge begins to stretch across the river from each shore.

Cables

3 The central deck spans are lifted by crane off river barges, welded into place, and attached to cables.

Crane

4 When the last deck section is in place, the bridge is complete. The cables transfer the weight of the deck to the pylons.

Building a bridge

A cable-stay bridge is a type of suspension bridge with a deck hung from slanting cables that are fixed to pylons instead of the ground. Once the pylons are in place, the bridge is built outward in both directions from each pylon. This ensures that the forces on the pylons balance, so that there is no danger of the pylons collapsing.

Types of bridges

On a trip, you may see many different shapes and sizes of bridge, but there are really only a few main types: arch bridges, beam bridges, cantilever bridges, suspension bridges, and cable-stay bridges. The type of bridge used depends on the size of the gap it must span, the landscape, and traffic that will cross it.

Arch bridge
The arch is used to build bridges because it is a strong shape that can bear a lot of weight. To bridge a wide gap, several arches of stone or brick are linked together.

Beam bridge
In a beam bridge, the central span (or beam) is supported at both ends. Very long beams are impractical, because they would be liable to collapse under their own weight.

Cantilever bridge
A beam fixed at one end and stretching out over a gap is a cantilever. Balanced cantilever bridges have several supports, each with two beams that reach out from either side.

Suspension bridge
The deck of a suspension bridge hangs from cables slung over towers and anchored to the ground at each end of the bridge. Such bridges have spans of up to 0.62 mile (1 km).

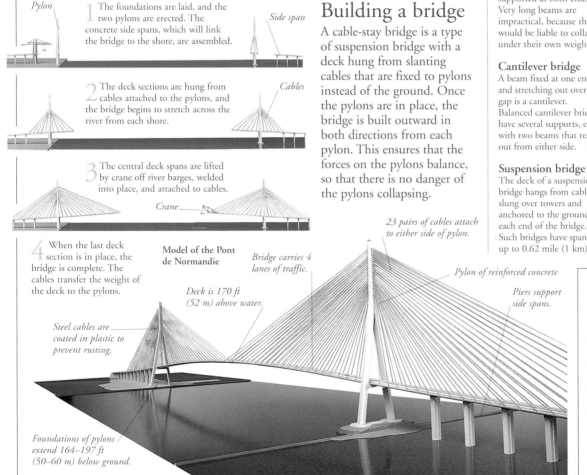

23 pairs of cables attach to either side of pylon.

Bridge carries 4 lanes of traffic.

Model of the Pont de Normandie

Pylon of reinforced concrete

Piers support side spans.

Deck is 170 ft (52 m) above water.

Steel cables are coated in plastic to prevent rusting.

Foundations of pylons extend 164–197 ft (50–60 m) below ground.

Isambard Kingdom Brunel
English engineer Isambard Kingdom Brunel (1806–59) was a genius of bridge design. Brunel designed and built two of the earliest suspension bridges. He also planned and built railroads and several huge steamships.

Aqueducts
Not all bridges carry roads or railroad tracks. An aqueduct is a bridge that carries water. The Romans built aqueducts to supply water to the baths and drinking fountains in their cities. More recent aqueducts carry canals over steep-sided valleys in order to keep the canal level. This avoids having to build long flights of locks.

Aqueduct on the River Dee, Wales

Timeline
200 BC Roman engineers build arch bridges of stone or wood, and aqueducts.

1779 The first bridge made of cast iron is built at Ironbridge, England.

1883 In the US, New York's Brooklyn Bridge is the first bridge to be supported by steel suspension cables.

1930 Switzerland's Salginatobel Bridge is constructed of reinforced concrete (concrete strengthened with steel).

Sydney Harbour Bridge, Australia

1932 Australia's Sydney Harbour Bridge opens, carrying a road and rail tracks suspended from a huge steel arch.

1998 The Akashi Kaikyo suspension bridge over Japan's Akashi Strait has the longest main span in the world.

FIND OUT MORE BUILDING AND CONSTRUCTION · IRON AND STEEL · RIVERS · ROADS · ROMAN EMPIRE · SHIPS AND BOATS · TRAINS AND RAILROADS · TRANSPORT, HISTORY OF · TUNNELS

B

BRONTË SISTERS

THREE OF THE FINEST writers of the 19th century, Charlotte, Anne, and Emily Brontë, were brought up in solitude in a small town in northern England. In spite of many difficulties, including being far away from the world of publishing in London, they produced some of the most popular novels of the period. The books portrayed characters with a new frankness and showed how difficult life could be for women of that time. Their stories still enthrall readers of today.

Haworth parsonage

The Brontë sisters were brought up in the small town of Haworth in Yorkshire, northern England. Their father was the curate (priest) at the local church, so they lived at the parsonage (clergyman's house). It was a grim stone building with a view over the graveyard.

The Brontë family
Charlotte, Emily, and Anne lived with their father, Patrick Brontë and their brother, Branwell. Their mother, Maria, died when the children were young and two other children died in infancy, so the sisters were brought up by their aunt. They had a lonely life. They mixed little with other children and had to make their own entertainment.

Education

Charlotte and Emily were sent away to Cowan Bridge school. The conditions were poor and made Charlotte ill. Lowood school, in *Jane Eyre*, is based on her time there. All three sisters later worked as teachers, or governesses – one of the few jobs then open to educated young women.

Cowan Bridge school

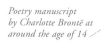

Manuscripts are still preserved at Haworth parsonage

Poetry manuscript by Charlotte Brontë at around the age of 14

Manuscripts and illustrations completed by the Brontë sisters in their teenage years

The novelists

In 1846, the Brontës started to get their works published. They began with a volume of poems, but only two copies were sold. In the following two years Emily's *Wuthering Heights*, Charlotte's *Jane Eyre*, and Anne's *Agnes Grey* were published. At the time it was not thought proper for the daughters of clergymen to write fiction, so the sisters used false names, or pseudonyms, to keep their identities secret. Lots of people bought the books and wanted to find out about the authors.

The Bell brothers

The Brontë sisters published their books under three male names – Acton, Currer, and Ellis Bell, the initials of which matched those of the sisters' own names. To begin with, even their publishers did not know who the "Bell brothers" really were.

WUTHERING HEIGHTS

A NOVEL.

BY

ELLIS BELL.

IN THREE VOLUMES.

VOL. II.

LONDON:
THOMAS CAUTLEY NEWBY, PUBLISHER,
72, MORTIMER St., CAVENDISH Sq.
1847.

Jane Eyre
Charlotte Brontë's first novel tells the story of Jane Eyre and her struggle to be an independent woman in a hostile society. Working as a governess, she falls in love with her employer, Mr Rochester, only to discover terrible secrets in his past. The novel was considered radical in its time.

Wuthering Heights
Emily Brontë's novel follows a series of tragic relationships across the generations and is especially famous for its depiction of Catherine and Heathcliff. Set against the background of the Yorkshire countryside, the novel deals with issues of social change and industrialization.

Angria and Gondal

To amuse themselves in the bleak moorland rectory, the Brontë children invented two imaginary lands, called Angria and Gondal. They wrote many stories and poems about these lands, which were peopled with heroes and heroines who lived exciting and tragic lives.

CHARLOTTE BRONTË

1816 Born Yorkshire, England.

1822–32 Educated at Cowan Bridge School and Miss Wooler's School, Roe Head, Yorkshire.

1846 Publishes her poems.

1847 Publishes *Jane Eyre*.

1849 Publishes *Shirley*.

1853 Publishes *Villette*.

1854 Marries Arthur Nicholls.

1855 Dies.

FIND OUT MORE

BOOKS • CHRISTIANITY • DICKENS, CHARLES • FILM AND FILMMAKING • LITERATURE • UNITED KINGDOM, HISTORY OF • WRITING

BRONZE AGE

IN ABOUT 3000 BC, prehistoric people began to use bronze – an alloy of copper and tin – instead of stone, to make tools, weapons, and ornaments. The dates for this development, which is known as the Bronze Age, vary from culture to culture, but the earliest bronze workers probably lived in Mesopotamia (modern Iraq). These people initially used pure gold and copper, which was easy to hammer into shape, before discovering how to make bronze. They were also responsible for developing the world's first civilizations. The Bronze Age was followed by a time when people learned to smelt and shape iron ore to produce stronger tools and weapons. This period is known as the Iron Age.

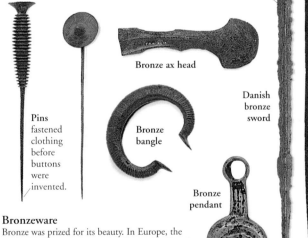

Stone wristguard with gold screws

Copper dagger blade

Pottery beaker for use in the afterlife

The Barnack grave, c.1800 BC

The first metalworkers

In the early days of the Bronze Age, metalworkers used gold, copper, and bronze for luxury items or for high-status weapons, such as the dagger in the Barnack grave, England. People still made tools from stone, because stone was harder than bronze.

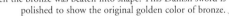

Prongs for lifting meat from a cauldron

Flesh hook

Copper
The royal family of the city of Ur in Mesopotamia used copper for jewelry, as well as for everyday items, such as this flesh hook. They used gold to make beautiful vessels for special occasions.

Ornate French sword

Bronze swords were sometimes cast, although they were stronger when the bronze was beaten into shape. This Danish sword is polished to show the original golden color of bronze.

Bronze ax head

Pins fastened clothing before buttons were invented.

Bronze bangle

Danish bronze sword

Bronze pendant

Bronzeware
Bronze was prized for its beauty. In Europe, the nobles liked to wear bronze jewelry, such as bangles and pendants, and bronze pins in their clothing. Bronze swords were high-status weapons.

Making bronze

People learned how to extract metal from ores by heating the rock. The metal could then be used to make useful or decorative objects.

Ore
This common type of copper ore was fairly easy for people to spot on the ground.

Yellow chalcopyrite

Blue bornite

Smelting
To extract the metal, Bronze Age people heated the ore to a high temperature. When the metal in the ore reached the melting point, they collected it in a round, stone crucible.

Ingots
Early metalworkers discovered how to add molten tin to copper to make bronze. Liquid bronze was poured into round molds and left to set. The blocks of bronze were called ingots.

Trace of an ingot

Casting

Bronze Age people cast objects by pouring hot, molten bronze into a mold. When the metal had cooled and set, the mold was opened, revealing the finished item. Casting was used to produce decorative items.

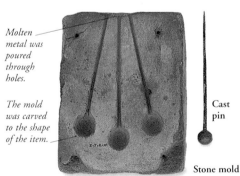

Molten metal was poured through holes.

The mold was carved to the shape of the item.

Cast pin

Stone mold

Mold
This is one half of a stone mold for casting pins. It was made in Switzerland in c.1000 BC. To use the mold, the two halves were fastened together and metal poured in through the holes at the top.

Cast pin
Bronze pins like this were cast in the stone mold. The mold used to make this pin was carved to create the delicate pattern on the pinhead.

Timeline
3800 BC The earliest known metal objects are produced by smelting. Copper is the main metal smelted in Tepe Yahya, Iran.

3000 BC Bronze objects are used throughout western Asia, where copper is being combined with tin.

2500 BC Bronze is used in the cities of Mohenjo-Daro and Harappa, Indus Valley.

2000 BC Bronze-working comes to the civilizations of the Minoans on Crete and the Myceneans in mainland Greece. These Aegean cultures trade in Europe for copper and tin.

1900 BC Iron Age starts in western Asian areas, such as Turkey, Iran, and Iraq.

1800 BC Bronze Age reaches European areas, such as modern Slovakia.

800 BC Early Iron Age starts in central Europe.

Shaft-tube ax, Hungary

FIND OUT MORE   GREECE, ANCIENT   INDUS VALLEY CIVILIZATION   METALS   MINOANS   POTTERY AND CERAMICS   STONE AGE   SUMERIANS

BUDDHA

BUDDHISM IS A WORLD faith that has changed the lives of millions of people. It began in Sakya, a small kingdom in northeast India. The founder of Buddhism was a prince, named Siddhartha Gautama, but today he is known simply as the Buddha, a title meaning "the enlightened one." When he was a young man, Siddhartha began a search for an understanding of suffering. By the end of his life, he had become the Buddha, founded the Buddhist faith and already had many followers.

Early life
According to tradition, Siddhartha was born while his mother, Maya, was on her way to visit her parents. She died soon afterward. His father was told that the boy would become either a great ruler or a Buddha. The king was afraid that Siddhartha would leave the court to become a holy beggar, so confined him to the palace grounds. But eventually he left to search for the true meaning of suffering.

Siddhartha, later called the Buddha

Maya, mother of the Buddha

The Buddha meditating

Buddha sat under a holy fig or bo tree

Enlightenment
When Siddhartha left the palace, the suffering he saw around him made him decide to become a holy man. He spent six years depriving himself of food and sleep, and learning about spiritual matters. Eventually he realized that this ascetic lifestyle made him too weak for deep reflection, so he meditated under a tree. Here he made the breakthrough understanding of the truth known as enlightenment.

Mara, the demon

Buddha

Temptations
While Siddhartha was meditating, a demon named Mara sent his beautiful daughters to tempt him from his chosen path. Mara also whipped up a storm and hurled thunderbolts at Siddhartha. But the young man continued to meditate, unmoved. He meditated for a whole night before understanding the truth, which he called *dharmma*, and reaching peace, or *nirvana*, in his heart.

Teaching
After experiencing enlightenment, the Buddha set out to teach others what he had learned. Many were converted, and the Buddha sent them off as wandering missionaries. Later, the Buddha returned to his father's court to teach his own people what he had learned. His father was among the first to be converted.

Sarnath
At Sarnath, near Varanasi, the Buddha preached his first sermon to five men who had previously sought enlightenment with him. He taught them that suffering is caused by desire, and to end suffering they must give up desire. Sarnath became the site of one of the greatest Buddhist shrines.

Buddha

Bimbisara
Even during his own lifetime, the Buddha commanded so much respect that many people left their homes to follow him and form orders of monks and nuns. When King Bimbisara gave the Buddha a generous gift of land – "the gift of the bamboo grove" – Buddha's followers built the first Buddhist monastery there.

King Bimbisara

Death of Buddha

Pilgrim

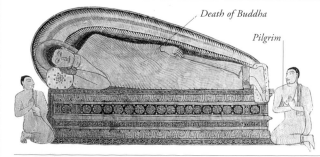

Later life
When the Buddha was 80 years old, he ate some food that had been accidentally poisoned, and died at Kusinagara in India among his disciples. Many people came to pay homage to him. His body was cremated, and the remaining bones were placed under stone mounds that have since became holy places of pilgrimage for Buddhists.

THE BUDDHA

Earliest records of Buddha's life were written more than 200 years after he died, so details are hard to verify. The following dates are accepted by most authorities.

563 BC Siddhartha Gautama, son of King Suddhodana of the Sakya, born in northeastern India.

533 BC Siddhartha leaves his father's court to become a holy man.

527 BC Siddhartha attains enlightenment, and becomes the Buddha.

483 BC Buddha dies at Kusinagara, in Oudh, India.

FIND OUT MORE | BUDDHISM | CHINA AND TAIWAN | INDIA, HISTORY OF | MAURYAN EMPIRE | MONASTERIES | SHRINES

BUDDHISM

THE BUDDHIST FAITH was founded by an Indian nobleman named Gautama Siddhartha in the 6th century BC. Gautama, who became known as the Buddha, or the "Enlightened One," told people how to achieve fulfillment. He taught that fulfillment is reached by meditation, wisdom, and correct behavior in all aspects of life. Buddhists also believe in reincarnation, in other words that a person can be reborn after death. The Buddha is revered by his followers, but not worshiped as a god. For this reason, Buddhism exists side-by-side with other religions in many countries. There are about 320 million Buddhists worldwide, although the majority live in Asia.

Rites and ceremonies

Ceremonies at Buddhist temples are usually simple. They involve reciting extracts from Buddhist scriptures and making offerings to the Buddha. A monk may give a sermon. Some Buddhist rituals also involve candlelit processions and music-making. The Buddhist year is enlivened with festivals, most of which take place at full Moon. The most famous festival is Wesak, at New Year, which celebrates the birth, enlightenment, and death of the Buddha.

Hand gestures on a statue of the Buddha

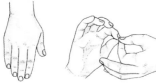

The Buddha touches earth as witness to his worthiness for Buddhahood.

This gesture shows the Buddha actively turning the wheel of law.

The Buddha reassures an approaching person.

The Buddha

Statues of the Buddha are kept in temples and homes to inspire Buddhists to live as he did. Buddhists bow before the statues to show their respect. They also carry out the ceremony called "Going for refuge," in which they recite texts that show their dedication to the Buddha, to his teaching (the Dharma), and to the community of Buddhists (the Sangha).

Teachings

The Buddha taught the Four Noble Truths, which explain the Buddhist attitude toward suffering and how fulfillment can be achieved. The Truths say that suffering is always present in the world; that the human search for pleasure is the source of suffering; that it is possible to be free from these desires by achieving a state called nirvana; and that the way to nirvana is through the Eightfold Path.

Wheel of law

Pictures in the inner circle reveal the six realms of existence.

In each realm, a Buddha-figure helps the beings there.

Three animals in the center are symbols of ignorance.

Wheel of Life

The Eightfold Path

The Path teaches that the way Buddhists lead their lives should be correct in eight important aspects: understanding, thought, speech, action, means of livelihood (work), effort, recollection, and meditation. The eight-spoked wheel of law shown above represents each of the eight stages of the Path.

Karma

Buddhists believe in the law of karma. According to this law, good and bad actions result in fitting rewards and punishments, both in this life and in later rebirths. The Wheel of Life is a symbol of rebirth. When people die, they are reborn into one of its six realms of existence.

Offerings

Buddhists regularly make offerings to the Buddha, such as flowers and food. Burning incense or candles and scattering petals around the Buddha's statue are ways of making an offering that also beautifies the temple. The light of the candles is the light of the Buddha's great wisdom, and the smoke from incense wafts the truth of the doctrine toward the devotees.

The Buddha's topknot is a sign of his princely wisdom.

His face has the serene expression of meditation.

Long earlobes symbolize his nobility.

Eyes cast down show that he is meditating.

Colored sash is changed for each season.

Candles

Incense

Lotus flowers

Meditation

Buddhists meditate in order to purify their minds and free themselves from thoughts about material things. In this way they hope to achieve "perfect mindfulness," one of the stages in the Eightfold Path. One way in which they meditate is to concentrate on feeling their breath going in and out. Concentration empties the mind of selfish thoughts – the person becomes calmer and the mind clearer.

Buddha's cross-legged position is called the lotus position.

Branches of Buddhism

From its beginnings in India, Buddhism spread around eastern and Southeast Asia, where the majority of the world's Buddhists still live. There are also Buddhist communities in other parts of Asia, and in the West. Buddhism has two main strands – Mahayana and Theravada – but other forms of Buddhism with distinctive features have also developed.

Theravada

This branch of Buddhism is closest to the teachings of the Buddha himself. It is dominant in Southeast Asia (Burma, Cambodia, Laos, Sri Lanka, and Thailand). Theravada Buddhists revere the Buddha and do not worship other figures. They aim to become "perfected saints" by following the Eightfold Path and tend to believe that people can reach the state of nirvana only through their own efforts.

Mahayana

This form of Buddhism prevails in China, Korea, Japan, Mongolia, Nepal, and Tibet. A follower's first goal is to become a bodhisattva, an enlightened being who does not pass into nirvana but remains in this world in order to help others to enlightenment. Mahayana Buddhists therefore place a high value on charity.

Chinese bodhisattva head

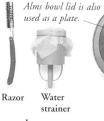

Monks are given offerings of food by locals.

Almsgiving emphasizes the close relationship between monks and laypeople.

Tibetan Buddhism

A form of Mahayana Buddhism is found in Tibet. Here, special value is placed on the Buddhist virtues of meditation and wisdom. Tibetan Buddhists have their own rituals, such as repeating sacred sayings, or mantras. Since the Chinese invasion of Tibet in the 1950s, few Buddhist monasteries remain in Tibet.

Mantra

Inside a prayer wheel is a mantra that the monk repeats while spinning the wheel.

Zen

This form of Buddhism originated in China and spread to Japan in about the 13th century. Zen Buddhists aim to lead a simple life, close to nature, using everyday actions as a means of meditation. Zen Buddhists meditate in a way that tries to see beyond logical patterns of thought and preconceived ideas.

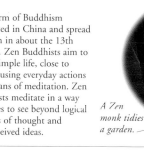

A Zen monk tidies a garden.

Monasticism

Buddhist monasteries began when the Buddha's followers built permanent settlements to live in together during the rainy season. Today there are many monks (and some nuns) who devote themselves to explaining the Buddha's teachings and setting an example by the way they lead their lives.

The monk's meditative pose suggests peace and stability.

Shaven head shows the monk has renounced worldly vanities.

Sharpening stone

Alms bowl lid is also used as a plate.

Needle and thread **Razor** **Water strainer**

Alms bowl lid

Living as a monk

Monks live apart from their families and have few personal possessions. They rely on gifts for survival, carrying alms bowls into which people place food. They obey strict rules. They must avoid entertainment in which there is singing or dancing, give up decorative clothes, and eat only at set times.

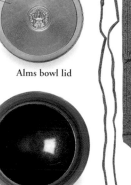

Alms bowl **Belt or girdle**

Sacred texts

Buddhism has sacred texts made up of sayings and sermons, many of them attributed to the Buddha. One of the most important books of writings is the Dharmapada, which forms part of the Pali Canon, the oldest collection of Buddhist scriptures.

In Tibetan-style libraries, manuscripts are wrapped in cloth and placed between boards.

Library in Shey Monastery, Ladakh, India

Temples

The religious buildings of Buddhism vary widely in their shape and decoration, from Japanese pagodas to Thai wats. But all contain statues of the Buddha. The statues act as a focus for devotion and for offerings. People go to the temples to carry out acts of private worship and for special ceremonies.

Wat Benchamabophit, in Thailand's capital, Bangkok, is known as the marble temple.

Stepped roofs symbolize stages of spiritual development.

Devotees gather with their offerings on the grounds of the temple.

The Dalai Lama

The Dalai Lama is the spiritual and political leader of Buddhists in Tibet, who believe that each Dalai Lama is a reincarnation of the previous one. The present Dalai Lama, Tenzin Gya-so, was born in 1935. In exile since 1959 following the Chinese takeover, he is still Tibet's most important leader.

FIND OUT MORE

ASIA, HISTORY OF   BUDDHA   CHINA, HISTORY OF   FESTIVALS   MAURYAN EMPIRE   RELIGIONS   SHRINES   SIGNS AND SYMBOLS   THAILAND AND MYANMAR

BUFFALO AND OTHER WILD CATTLE

THE FIVE SPECIES OF BUFFALO, and all other cattle, are members of the family Bovidae. They have split, or cloven, hooves, and both sexes have horns. Wild cattle use their horns for defense against predators, and also live in herds for protection. Only the anoas are solitary animals. Cattle were among the earliest animals to be domesticated. The Asiatic buffalo, yak, banteng, and gaur are examples of cattle that have been domesticated. The loss of habitat, hunting, and disease has drastically reduced the world's wild cattle. Nine of the eleven species are in danger of extinction.

Broad hooves support the weight of the buffalo.

Bison

Plains bison

Often incorrectly called buffalo, there are two species of bison. The American bison is a grassland animal which appears in two forms – the plains bison and the woods bison. The European bison, or wisent, is a forest dweller. Bison are massive animals standing more than 5 ft (1.5 m) tall and weighing more than a ton (910 kg).

American bison
The head, neck, and forequarters of the American bison are covered with long hair, which, with the large hump, makes the forequarters appear much bigger than the hindquarters. The horns are short and curved, and are grown by both sexes.

European bison
The wisent lives in Poland's Bialowieza Forest. It is taller than the American bison, has a longer, less barrellike body, and longer legs. Its hindquarters are also more powerfully built.

African buffalo

The buffalo is the only species of wild cattle found in Africa. Cape buffalo bulls are up to 5 ft (1.5 m) at the shoulder and weigh more than 1,800 lb (816 kg). Their horns have a span of up to 5 ft (1.5 m) and form a massive helmet, or boss, across the head. A smaller subspecies, the forest buffalo, lives in equatorial forests.

Asiatic buffalo
There are four species of Asiatic buffalo – the water buffalo (shown here), the lowland and mountain anoa, and the tamarau. The water buffalo lives in both domestic and wild herds, although only a few wild herds survive. Its horns are semicircular and sweep outward and backward.

Endangered tamarau

Confined to the highlands on the island of Mindoro in the Philippines, this dwarf buffalo has been relentlessly hunted. Only about 100 survive today.

Oxen

The group of wild cattle commonly called oxen contains four species – the yak, the banteng, the gaur, and the kouprey. Domestic cattle also belong to this group. Most breeds of domestic cattle are descended from the now-extinct aurochs, which at one time inhabited the plains and woodlands of Europe and Asia in great numbers.

Yak
Largest of the wild cattle, the wild yak lives in herds high up on the Tibetan Plateau in Central Asia. Yaks have long, shaggy black hair reaching almost to the ground, with a thick undercoat that protects them against the bitterly cold climate.

Banteng
Found in Southeast Asia, Java, and Borneo, the banteng is a shy animal. Females and young are a brick-red color; adult males are black.

Largest and smallest
Wild cattle range in size from the wild yak, which is more than 6.5 ft (2 m) high at the shoulder, to the mountain anoa, which is no more than 30 in (76 cm) high.

Mountain anoa

Wild yak

CAPE BUFFALO

SCIENTIFIC NAME *Syncerus caffer*

ORDER Artiodactyla

FAMILY Bovidae

DISTRIBUTION Africa, south of the Sahara

HABITAT Grassland and woodland savannas, but seldom far from water

DIET Mainly grass, occasionally supplemented with foliage

SIZE 5 ft (1.5 m) at the shoulder

LIFESPAN About 20 years

 FIND OUT MORE   DEER AND ANTELOPE   FARMING   NORTH AMERICAN WILDLIFE   SHEEP AND GOATS

BUGS

THE WORD BUG is often used to describe any crawling insect or a disease-causing germ. The true bugs are a group of insects that have long feeding tubes specially adapted for sucking fluids out of plants and animals. Bugs, such as shield bugs, are often brightly colored, and, as a group, they are remarkably varied in shape. There are about 55,000 species of bugs, including large, solitary insects such as giant water bugs and cicadas, and tiny creatures, such as scale insects, bedbugs, and aphids. It is the smaller bugs, such as aphids and leaf hoppers, that create problems for farmers because of the severe damage they do to crops.

Features of a bug

All bugs have specialized mouths with cutting implements for piercing and needlelike tubes held within a protective sheath for sucking. Some bugs, such as lantern bugs, have their membranous wings exposed when at rest; others have forewings that are partially thickened and used not for flight, but as a protective cover for the delicate hind wings.

Lantern bug with wings open

False eyes

Extension to head

True eyes

Abdomen

Two sets of wings

Forewings overlap at rest.

Jointed legs

Spines on hind legs are used for defense.

Lantern bug

Reproduction

Bugs attract a mate in many ways, such as emitting scent or vibrating the surface of water. Male cicadas attract females with their loud song, produced by drumlike organs on the abdomen. During mating, male and female bugs are often attached for hours. Females usually lay hundreds of eggs. These hatch into nymphs – tiny versions of their parents – and molt many times before reaching adult size.

Shield bugs

Shield bugs are found virtually worldwide. They are also called stink bugs since they can give off a bad smell. Females protect their eggs and young from attack.

Young shield bug nymphs being guarded by their mother.

Parthenogenesis

Aphids multiply rapidly, because they can reproduce without mating. Females produce a succession of identical female offspring from unfertilized eggs, each of which later produces more of the same, a process called parthenogenesis.

Feeding

Bugs use their mouths to cut a hole in their food and pierce the soft parts inside. They inject enzymes and digestive juices through a pair of tiny tubes to break down solids and suck up the resulting fluids. In this way, predatory bugs, such as assassin bugs, can suck their victims dry. Bedbugs are parasites that suck the blood of birds and mammals, including humans. Some bugs feed only on plant juices.

Assassin bugs

Assassin bugs are carnivores. Most prey on other invertebrates, such as millipedes. Some steal prey already caught in spiders' webs. Assassin bugs can squirt toxic saliva at would-be predators.

Feeding tube

Assassin bug feeding on a cockroach

Leaf hoppers

Leaf hoppers are herbivores. They are often considered pests because they cut holes in the leaves of plants to suck out the sap, thereby weakening the plants.

Defense

Small bugs face many enemies. To deter would-be attackers, bugs have evolved a range of defenses. Some bugs, such as tree hoppers, have developed elaborate camouflage; others, such as stink bugs, emit bad smells. The larvae of spittle bugs, also known as frog hoppers, hide within a frothy substance called cuckoo spit. Aphids employ ants to protect them by providing the ants with a nutritious sugary secretion.

Tree hoppers

Tree hoppers camouflage themselves with cuticles that resemble thorns.

Water bugs

Some bugs live in water. Water-striders skim over water on their dainty legs, while back swimmers dart below the water using paddle-shaped limbs. Underwater bugs either come to the surface to breathe, or carry around an air bubble.

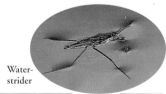

Water-strider

RED-BANDED LEAF HOPPER

SCIENTIFIC NAME
Graphocephala coccinea

ORDER Homoptera

FAMILY Cicadellidae

DISTRIBUTION Eastern US and eastern Canada

HABITAT Meadows and gardens

DIET Plant juices

SIZE Length 0.4–0.5 in (8–11 mm); wingspan 0.5–0.6 in (12–16 mm)

LIFESPAN Adults: up to 4 months

| FIND OUT MORE | ARTHROPODS | CAMOUFLAGE AND COLOR | FARMING | FLIGHT, ANIMAL | INSECTS | LAKE AND RIVER WILDLIFE | PARASITES | PLANTS, DEFENSE |

BUILDING AND CONSTRUCTION

THE SIMPLEST BUILDING is a permanent structure with a roof and four walls. Buildings come in a huge variety of shapes, sizes, and appearances – from skyscrapers and factories to schools, hospitals, houses, and garden sheds. Despite these differences, all buildings have the same basic purpose – to provide a sheltered area in which people can live, work, or store belongings. The engineers, surveyors, and construction workers who plan and build these structures also work on other projects, such as roads, bridges, dams, and tunnels.

Ancient tower house, Sana, Yemen

Early building
Since the beginning of history, people have built shelters to protect themselves from the weather, wild animals, and their enemies. The first buildings were simple, single-story structures made of materials such as wood, stone, and dried grass and mud. The first large-scale stone constructions were temples for the worship of gods and goddesses, and palaces in which powerful leaders lived. About 6,000 years ago, people discovered how to bake clay bricks. In time, engineers developed new building methods that enabled them to build higher and lighter structures.

Walls are made from mud and bricks dried in the sun's heat.

Anatomy of a building

Most buildings have certain features in common, such as walls, a roof, and floors. A large modern building, such as this airport terminal, also has a strong internal frame. Underneath this are the solid foundations on which the whole structure rests. The building is equipped with services, such as electricity and water supplies, as well as escalators, stairs, or elevators to give access to different stories, and fire escapes that enable people to leave the building rapidly in the event of an emergency.

Roof
A roof is a protective covering over a building. Roofing materials include thatch, clay tiles, slate, glass, and steel. Roofs in wet climates are shaped to make rainwater run off; in cold countries, they slope steeply to stop snow from building up; and in dry climates, they are often flat. Sloping roofs are held up by supports called roof trusses.

Roof trusses sit on frame.   *Roof truss*

Steel beams | **Overhead cutaway of roof**

Kansai Airport, Japan

Glass wall lets in a lot of light.

Roof is clad with shiny steel panels.

Floor rests on columns, which are part of frame.

Foundations
A building's foundations spread its huge load evenly into the ground, stopping the building from sinking under its own weight. Pile foundations are columns that rest on hard rock; raft foundations are concrete platforms that rest on soft rock. The foundations form the base on which the building's frame is constructed.

Internal frame
The "skeleton" of a large building is its internal frame, which supports the roof, the walls, and the floors. Frames can be made of wood, steel, or reinforced-concrete columns and beams joined together.

Foundations extend underground.

Basement houses service machinery.

Walls and floors
In a house, the walls – which may be made of wood, stone, or brick – are strong enough to hold up the floors, ceilings, and roof trusses. In a larger structure, however, the frame supports the building's weight, and the walls simply hang from the frame. The floors in a large modern building are reinforced-concrete slabs.

Structural engineers

Long before the construction of a building is under way, structural engineers begin working on the design of the building with an architect. They calculate how strong the building's structure needs to be and draw up detailed plans, usually on a computer. When the building work commences, they make sure that everything happens safely, on time, and within the financial budget.

Structural engineer on a building site

Surveyors
Accuracy is extremely important in construction work if the completed building is to have vertical sides and level walls, and be structurally safe. Even small errors in the design or assembly can result in parts not fitting together properly. People called surveyors check the building at every stage of its construction, using special instruments, such as theodolites and spirit levels, to take accurate measurements.

Hard hat

Theodolite is an instrument that measures angles to find distances, lengths, and heights.

Surveyor using theodolite

Building sites

The different stages in the construction of a large building must always take place in a certain order, starting with the preparation of the site. Materials and machinery must arrive just when they are needed: if they are too early, the site may get too crowded; if they are too late, the building work may be delayed.

Site clearance and excavation

The building site must first be cleared, which may involve demolishing other buildings, removing vegetation, and leveling the site. Holes are excavated (dug) for the foundations and basement.

Foundation laying

The next stage is to build the foundations. This involves driving steel beams, called piles, into the ground, or pouring liquid concrete into a deep pit to form a solid base that will support the building.

Frame building

The building's frame soon rises from the foundations. The frame is built either by bolting together steel beams, or by pouring concrete into molds crossed by steel rods. A shell of metal poles and wooden planks, called scaffolding, is temporarily erected around the building so that workers can reach all parts.

Completed building is ready for use.

Completion

With the frame in place, work starts on the floors, walls, and roof. Services such as water and waste pipes, heating and air-conditioning ducts, and electricity and telephone cables are installed on each story. Finally, the windows are inserted, and the interior is decorated.

Equipment

Some of the tasks on a building site, such as plastering a wall or laying bricks, are done by tradespeople using hand tools. Other tasks, such as erecting the building's frame or lifting heavy objects, may require large, specialized machines. Together, these machines are known as construction plant.

Plumb line

Set square

Spirit level

Trowel

Bricklayer's tools

Hand tools

Each tradesperson involved in building and construction uses special tools. A bricklayer, for example, uses a trowel to spread mortar onto bricks, a plumb line to ensure that a wall is vertical, and a spirit level and a set square to check that it is horizontal.

Construction plant

Powerful machines, such as cranes and cement mixers, can do jobs in a few minutes that would take manual workers hours or even days. Other machines include pile-drivers to hammer steel piles into the ground, bulldozers to level building sites, and excavating diggers.

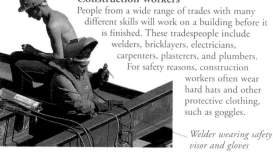

Backhoe digger

Trench-digging bucket

Hydraulic jacks steady digger.

Wide shovel tool scoops up soil.

Building materials

Some building materials, such as steel, concrete, and bricks, are structural – that is, they make up the basic structure of the building. Other materials, such as ceramics and glass, are mainly decorative. Traditional materials, such as stone and wood, have been used for many centuries and are often found locally.

Building site materials

Wooden planks for scaffolding

Steel rods for reinforced concrete

Steel girders for frame

Concrete and steel

Most modern buildings contain concrete, steel, or a combination of both. Concrete is a mixture of cement, water, and small stones (called aggregate) that hardens like rock when it sets. Steel is iron that contains a tiny amount of carbon. Concrete strengthened by steel rods is called reinforced concrete.

Types of concrete

Wood

Some houses have floors made of wooden planks and wooden beams for roof trusses. Scaffolding may have walkways of wooden planks.

Bricks

Blocks of hardened clay, called bricks, are laid in rows and joined together with mortar – a mixture of cement and sand.

Local materials

Many buildings throughout the world are built from materials that occur naturally in the surrounding area. These local materials may include straw, mud, stone, wood, and even animal dung. They can do just as good a job as modern manufactured materials, which are usually more expensive and have to be imported from elsewhere.

Decorative wooden battens

Reeds

Thatch is made of interlaced bundles of straw (dried grass or reeds).

Metal rods secure bundles.

Cutaway of a thatched roof

Straw

Construction workers

People from a wide range of trades with many different skills will work on a building before it is finished. These tradespeople include welders, bricklayers, electricians, carpenters, plasterers, and plumbers. For safety reasons, construction workers often wear hard hats and other protective clothing, such as goggles.

Welder wearing safety visor and gloves

FIND OUT MORE   ARCHITECTURE   BRIDGES   CHURCHES AND CATHEDRALS   DAMS   HOUSES AND HOMES   IRON AND STEEL   ROADS   TUNNELS

BUTTERFLIES AND MOTHS

SCALY WINGS AND A COILED feeding tube set butterflies and moths apart from other insects. Together, they form a single group of about 170,000 species, of which 90 percent are moths. Both have four stages to their life cycle in which they change from a caterpillar to an adult with wings. They feed on plants and rely on camouflage, irritating hairs or spines, or poisons in their body for protection against predators.

Scales overlap like the tiles on a roof.

Wing scales
Scales on the wings contain colored pigments. Some scales produce colors by reflecting the light.

The front and back wings of a moth are hooked together.

Moth's bright colouring indicates it is poisonous

Zygaenid moth

Moths
Most moths fly at night. They tend to have drab colors, and have a fatter body and longer, narrower wings than butterflies. When resting, moths usually hold their wings open or fold them flat over their back.

Swallowtail butterfly

Butterflies
In most cases, butterflies are more brightly colored than moths and have a thinner body. Unlike moths, they hold their wings upright when resting. The front and back wings are loosely joined together by a lobe on the back wing that grips the front wing. Butterflies are usually active by day rather than at night.

Wings are made of a tough membrane supported by a network of rigid veins.

Proboscis is rolled up when not in use.

Moth antennae have a large surface area for picking up scents.

Feeding tube
Adult butterflies and moths suck up liquid food, such as flower nectar, through a tube called a proboscis. A few moths have no proboscis because they do not feed as adults.

Antennae
Insects use their antennae for smelling, touching, and tasting. Butterfly antennae are clubbed; moth antennae range from single strands to feathery branches.

Life cycle
Butterflies and moths start life as an egg that hatches into a caterpillar. This feeds and grows until it turns into a pupa. The adult develops inside the pupa. This process of change is called metamorphosis.

Pupa protects developing adult.

Adult butterfly emerges.

Butterfly pumps blood into its wings to expand and stiffen them.

Adult Blue Morpho

Henry Bates
Henry Walter Bates (1825–92) was a British naturalist and explorer who studied camouflage in animals. He found that some harmless insects look the same as a poisonous insect so that predators leave them alone. This is now called Batesian mimicry after Henry Bates.

Defense
To escape from predators, butterflies and moths often fly away or hide. Some have irritating hairs or spines, or are poisonous. Bright colors may warn predators that a butterfly or moth is poisonous. Poisons often build up in a caterpillar from the plant it eats. These then remain in the adult.

Camouflage
Many butterflies and moths blend in with their surroundings at some stage of their life cycle. Camouflaged like this, they may escape predators.

Eye spots
False eyes on the wings can startle predators or stop them from pecking the real eyes. A damaged wing is not as serious as an injury to the head.

Mimicry
Some butterflies and moths gain protection by looking like another species of butterfly or moth. The top butterfly shown here is poisonous; the bottom one is not.

Wing color
When a butterfly is resting, only the underside of its wings shows. This is often colored for camouflage. The colors of the upper side help attract a mate.

FIND OUT MORE

CAMOUFLAGE AND COLOR   INSECTS   FLIGHT, ANIMAL

SWALLOWTAIL BUTTERFLY

SCIENTIFIC NAME	*Papilio palinurus*
ORDER	Lepidoptera
FAMILY	Papilionidae
DISTRIBUTION	From Burma to the islands of Borneo and the Philippines in Southeast Asia
HABITAT	Tropical rain forest
DIET	Flower nectar
SIZE	Wing span: 3.75 in (9.5 cm)
LIFESPAN	Varies (The adults of most butterflies live for only a few weeks or months)

Butterflies

Owl butterfly

Japanese emperor

Brown-veined white

Orange-barred giant sulphur

Great spangled fritillary

Viceroy

Common opal

Great orange tip

Common blue

Peacock

African giant swallowtail

Common blue

Blue morpho

Chequered skipper

Swallowtail

Cairns birdwing

Small copper

Hewitson's blue hairstreak

Moths

African moon moth

Goat moth

Buff-tip

Provence burnet moth

Magpie moth

Owl moth

Hornet moth

Hoop pine moth

Garden tiger

Giant agrippa

Verdant sphinx

Oak eggar

Madagascan sunset moth

Pale tussock

Hieroglyphic moth

BYZANTINE EMPIRE

IN 395, THE GREAT ROMAN EMPIRE split into eastern and western sections. The western half – still called the Roman Empire – was centered in Rome. The eastern half became the Byzantine Empire with a center at Constantinople. The Greek character – in language, customs, and dress – of Constantinople contrasted with Latin Rome. Despite efforts on the part of emperors to reunite the two halves of the old empire, the Byzantine Empire gradually grew away from Rome. The Roman Empire collapsed in 410, but the Byzantine Empire existed until 1453, when the Ottoman Turks captured it.

Extent of Byzantine Empire, c.565
Because of its fabulous wealth, superb shipbuilding facilities, and strategic position between Asia and Europe, the Byzantine Empire was under almost constant siege by its powerful neighbors – Persia, Arabia, Turkey, and some states of the Christian west.

Byzantium to Constantinople

Mosque

The ancient Greek port of Byzantium stood on the Golden Horn, a strip of land surrounded by sea on three sides. Constantine the Great (AD c.274–337) redesigned the city and re-named it Constantinople in AD 330. Soon it was one of the world's most beautiful cities.

Bridge over the Bosporus Strait, linking Asia and Europe

Art and religion

Byzantine churches were famous for their interiors. They were lavishly decorated on a huge scale, with painted icons and intricate mosaic images of Christ, the Virgin, and saints.

Icons

In the 8th century, the empire was racked by arguments over whether it was idolatrous to worship beautiful religious statues and paintings, known as icons. Finally in 843, worship of icons was declared to be legitimate, and their production increased. Later, icons were collected by Renaissance artists.

East versus west

By the 9th century, the Byzantine form of Christianity was changing from the western, or Roman, form. Greek had replaced Latin as the official language, and the Roman pope and Byzantine patriarch argued over church ritual, united only by their fear and hatred of the non-Christian Turks and Arabs.

Great Schism

In 1054, representatives of the Roman and Byzantine churches excommunicated each other. This religious split, or schism, destabilized political links between east and west, and caused mutual suspicion and hostility.

Orthodox priest

St. Gregory of Nazianzus · Virgin and Child · St. John Chrysostom

Triptych icon, 12th century · Gilt covering

Hagia Sophia

The biggest church in the eastern empire, Hagia Sophia was built in only five years (532–37). The Ottomans converted it into a mosque in the 16th century, and today it is a museum.

Fall of Constantinople

Constantinople was conquered twice: once by the west and once by the east. In 1204, it was ransacked by Christians on their way to the Holy Land. In 1453, Ottoman Turks overran it, and it became a Muslim stronghold.

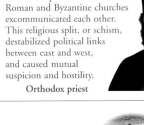
Fall of Constantinople, 1453

Mosaics

Byzantine artists pressed cubes of tinted glass, marble, or precious stones into beeswax or lime plaster to make a mosaic. The artists often decorated the images with gold and silver leaf.

Christ Pantokrator, 11th century

Emperor Justinian I

Justinian I (r.527–565) expanded the empire in the west by conquering North Africa, southern Spain, and Italy, while holding off the Persian threat in the east. In addition Justinian built Hagia Sophia, and his Codex Justinianus, or Roman Law Code, still forms the basis of the legal system in many European countries.

Timeline

395 Roman Empire divided into west (Roman) and east (Byzantine).

867–1056 Empire reaches its peak.

The Good Shepherd mosaic, 5th century

529–34 Justinian I introduces his Roman Law Code.

976–1025 Basil II, known as "the Bulgar-slayer," gains more land than any emperor since Justinian I.

1054 Great Schism: Byzantine church breaks with the Roman church and forms the Eastern Orthodox church.

1096 First Crusade: European army joins Byzantine army at Constantinople.

1204 Fourth Crusaders sack Constantinople.

1453 Ottoman Turks capture Constantinople, ending the empire.

FIND OUT MORE · ART, HISTORY OF · CHRISTIANITY · OTTOMAN EMPIRE · PERSIAN EMPIRE · ROMAN EMPIRE

CAESAR, JULIUS

JULIUS CAESAR WAS A BRILLIANT general and ruler of the Roman world. He is one of the most famous controversial figures in history. He transformed the Roman world, expanding Rome's territory into Gaul and suppressing many revolts. He was a fine administrator, reforming the Roman calendar and Roman law and bringing strong government to the republic. Caesar was also a great writer and orator. But he could be unscrupulous in pursuit of his own interests and made many enemies during his career.

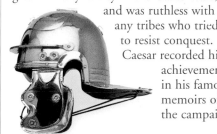

Early life
Caesar was born in Rome in about 100 BC. A member of a rich family, he had a successful military and political career, rising through various offices to become Pontifex Maximus, or high priest, in 64 BC. In 61 BC, he became Governor of Further Spain, one of the most important jobs in the Roman republic.

Triumvirate

In the years leading up to 60 BC, rival politicians competed to gain power. Order was restored when Caesar, the financier Marcus Crassus, and the army commander Pompey set up a three-man committee, or triumvirate, to rule Rome. In 59 BC, the triumvirate allowed Caesar to be elected consul, one of the two magistrates who held supreme power. As consul, Caesar strengthened and reformed the government.

Pompey
Gnaeus Pompeius Magnus (106–48 BC), known in English as Pompey, was a Roman general who conquered Palestine and Syria, and did much to get rid of opposition to Roman rule in Spain and Sicily. Although he was a member of the triumvirate and he married Caesar's daughter, he was always Caesar's rival.

Pompey the Great

Gallic wars

From 58–50 BC, Caesar waged a series of wars that led to the incorporation of Gaul (modern France and Belgium) into the Roman republic. Caesar displayed great military ability in the Gallic Wars, and was ruthless with any tribes who tried to resist conquest. Caesar recorded his achievements in his famous memoirs of the campaign.

Roman legionary's helmet

The civil war

After the death of Crassus in 53 BC, rivalry between Caesar and Pompey reached new heights. Pompey became sole consul in 52 BC and, with the support of the Roman senate (parliament), declared Caesar an enemy of the people. In 49 BC, Caesar crossed the Rubicon, the river dividing Italy from Gaul, and marched on Rome in triumph. In 48 BC, he defeated Pompey. By 45 BC, Caesar had removed all opposition, becoming master of the Roman world.

Roman catapult bolts

Roman cavalry spur

Cleopatra
Caesar followed Pompey to Egypt and remained in the country after Pompey's death. He befriended and lived with Cleopatra, queen of Egypt, and helped establish her firmly on the throne. When Caesar returned to Rome in 47 BC, Cleopatra came with him. After Caesar's death, the Egyptian queen had twin sons with the Roman soldier and politician Mark Antony (c.82–30 BC).

Caesar as soldier

Caesar crosses the Rubicon.

Pharsalus
Caesar showed his military skills when, in 48 BC, he defeated the much larger army of Pompey near the Greek town of Pharsalus. Caesar's strategic sense and better location enabled his small force to overwhelm Pompey's army, which was routed. Pompey himself fled to Egypt, where he died.

Battle of Pharsalus

Antony and Cleopatra

Dictator

In 45 BC, Caesar was appointed dictator for life. He reformed the living conditions of the Roman people by passing new agricultural laws and improving housing. He also made the republic more secure from its enemies.

Assassination
Despite his reforms, Caesar's dictatorial rule created enemies for him in Rome. On March 15, 44 BC, the Ides of March, Caesar was stabbed to death in the senate house by rival senators, including Cassius and Brutus. Caesar's work lived on in his adopted son, Octavian, who later became emperor.

Assassination of Caesar

JULIUS CAESAR

c.100 BC Born in Rome

80 BC First military service in Turkey

60 BC Forms triumvirate with Crassus and Pompey

59 BC Elected consul

58–50 BC Conquers Gaul

50 BC Roman senate declares him an enemy of the people

49 BC Starts civil war against Pompey

48 BC Defeats Pompey and follows him to Egypt

44 BC Assassinated in the senate in Rome by rival senators

| FIND OUT MORE | ARMIES | FRANCE, HISTORY OF | ITALY, HISTORY OF | ROMAN EMPIRE | UNITED KINGDOM, HISTORY OF |

CAMELS

WELL-SUITED TO DESERT LIFE, camels can withstand extreme conditions. There are two main types: the one-humped dromedary, which lives in Africa and Arabia and is usually domesticated; and the two-humped Asian Bactrian, some of which still roam wild in the Gobi Desert. Closely related to camels are four animals without humps – llamas, alpacas, guanacos, and vicunas. All six species, called camelids, belong to the artiodactyls, a group of herbivorous, even-toed mammals that also includes cattle.

Features of a camel

Camels are the largest of the even-toed mammals, standing up to 8 ft (2.4 m) at the shoulder. They have long legs and walk at an ambling pace. Camels have a split upper lip, which allows them to eat dry, spiky plants. Their lips and upright heads have given camels a reputation for arrogance. In reality this is nonsense. However, camels may spit at or bite humans if annoyed or frightened. During the mating season, male camels often fight, biting their rivals when competing for females.

Feet

Camels' feet have two toes joined by a web of skin; underneath is a soft, flexible pad that splays out when the camel walks. The camel's feet are very wide, and this, together with the pad, prevents the camel from sinking into soft sand and enables it to walk over rough terrain.

Web of skin

Foot of dromedary

Large, wide feet with soft pads allow camel to walk on sand.

Thick fur keeps camel warm during cold desert nights and helps prevent overheating in the day.

Hump

Contrary to popular belief, the camel's hump is not filled with water, but is a fat store that provides the camel with energy when food is scarce. Because fat is stored in the hump, there is less fat under the rest of the skin, enabling the camel to lose heat more easily in hot conditions.

Shaggy fur

Bactrian camel

Long legs help camel walk long distances.

Dromedary camel

Long, curved neck allows camel to reach desert vegetation.

Long eyelashes

Slitlike nostrils

Split upper lip

Head of dromedary camel

Eyes and nostrils

Camels have long eyelashes that protect their eyes from fierce sandstorms and enable them to see under difficult conditions. They can close their slitlike nostrils to reduce the amount of sand and dust blowing up the nose and minimize moisture loss from the nasal cavity.

Ships of the desert

Camels are the only animals that can carry heavy loads long distances in extreme heat and with little water. Nomadic peoples survive in deserts by using camels as pack animals as well as for meat, milk, and skins.

Salt-laden caravan, Taoudenni, Mali

Water loss

Camels can exist for long periods without water, but make up the loss quickly when water is available. Camels are also adapted to reduce water loss by producing dry feces and small amounts of syrupy urine. In addition, their body temperature can rise to 104.9°F (40.5°C) during the day, reducing the need to keep cool by sweating, a process that also causes water loss.

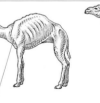

During long periods without drinking, a camel can lose 40 percent of its body mass as water.

Within 10 minutes, camels can drink sufficient water to make up huge losses.

Types of camelids

Related to camels are two species of domesticated camelids, the llama and alpaca, and two wild species, the vicuna and guanaco; all live in or near the Andes mountains in South America. Small herds of guanaco feed on grass and shrubs in shrub land and savanna up to heights of 13,900 ft (4,250 m) from southern Peru to southern Argentina.

Vicunas are a protected species.

Alpacas' wool may be black, brown, or white.

The wool, milk, and meat of llamas are all used.

Vicuna
Vicunas, the smallest of the camelids, live in family groups at high altitudes.

Alpaca
The highland people of Peru and Bolivia breed alpacas for their long, soft wool.

Llama
Llamas are used as pack animals to carry loads of up to 220 lb (100 kg), at altitudes of 16,400 ft (5,000 m) over long distances.

DROMEDARY CAMEL

SCIENTIFIC NAME	*Camelus dromedarius*
ORDER	Artiodactyla
FAMILY	Camelidae
DISTRIBUTION	Domesticated in North Africa, Middle East, southwestern Asia; feral populations in Australia
HABITAT	Desert
DIET	Any type of desert vegetation, including thorny twigs and salty plants that other animals avoid
SIZE	Head and body length 10 ft (3 m); shoulder height 6.5 ft (2 m); weight up to 1,320 lb (600 kg)
LIFESPAN	Up to 50 years

FIND OUT MORE

ANIMALS • ASIAN WILDLIFE • DESERTS • DESERT WILDLIFE • MAMMALS • PIGS AND PECCARIES • SOUTH AMERICAN WILDLIFE

CAMERAS

A LIGHTPROOF BOX with a hole or lens at one end and a strip of light-sensitive film at the other is the basic component of a camera. To take a photograph, the photographer points the camera at an object and presses a button. This button very briefly opens a shutter behind the lens. Light reflected from the object passes through the lens and reacts with chemicals in the film to produce an image.

Lenses

Different lenses achieve different effects. A wide-angle lens allows more of the scene to appear in a photograph than a normal lens. A telephoto zoom lens takes a close-up shot of a distant object. The fish-eye lens distorts images for dramatic effect.

Normal lens

Wide-angle lens

Telephoto zoom lens

Fish-eye lens

Parts of a camera

The quality of a photograph is controlled by adjusting the film and shutter speed dials, flash, and aperture scales. The final image will depend on the type of film in the camera, the amount of light that enters the lens, and the length of time that the film is exposed to light.

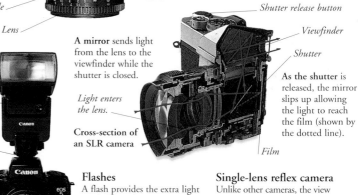

Shutter release button

Shutter and film speed dial

FM2

Self-timer lever

Lens

Lens release button

Shutter and film speed dial

Connection for flash

Film rewind knob

Shutter release button

Aperture scale

Lens

Distance scale

35mm cameras
The most popular cameras are the 35mm, named after the width of the film they use. These cameras are small and easy to manage, and often have automatic features that produce clear photographs of an object everytime by adjusting the camera's settings to variations in light and distance.

Shutter release button

Viewfinder

Shutter

A mirror sends light from the lens to the viewfinder while the shutter is closed.

Light enters the lens.

As the shutter is released, the mirror slips up allowing the light to reach the film (shown by the dotted line).

Movable flash head

Flash light sensor

Cross-section of an SLR camera

Film

Flashes
A flash provides the extra light needed for taking pictures after dark, or in dim conditions. The flash is electronically controlled to go off at the moment the shutter opens.

Single-lens reflex camera
Unlike other cameras, the view through a single-lens reflex (SLR) camera is that of the actual image that is recorded on the film. Mirrors in the viewfinder correct the upside-down image sent from the lens.

Film types

Today's plastic film comes in various sizes and speeds and is packaged as rolls or plates, in either a color or a black and white format. The speed, given in ASA/ISO or DIN numbers, indicates how quickly the film reacts to light.

Plate film

35mm film

110mm film

George Eastman

An American inventor, George Eastman (1854–1932), formed the Kodak company. In 1884, he produced the first roll film and in 1888, the first box camera, making photography an accessible hobby. In 1889, he used clear celluloid film on which the first movie pictures were taken.

Aperture and exposure time

The aperture (an opening in the lens) controls the amount of light entering the camera and the length of time the film is exposed to light. Aperture size is measured in 'f' numbers: the higher the number, the smaller the aperture.

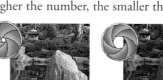

Picture taken at f16 for 1 sec

Picture taken at f5.6 for 1/8 sec

Picture taken at f2 for 1/60 sec

Digital cameras

Pictures taken by a digital camera can be seen almost instantaneously on a computer or television screen. Instead of using film, images are converted into computer data which can be stored on disks or chips.

Digital camera

Timeline

4th century BC The "camera obscura" is developed; it consists of a darkened room into which an image is projected.

1822 Frenchman Joseph Niepce takes the first photograph on a sheet of pewter, coated with bitumen.

1839 Niepce's colleague, Louis Daguerre, announces process for recording images on copper.

1839 William Fox Talbot, an Englishman, invents a process that allows photographs to be copied.

1895 The Lumière brothers of France patent their original camera/projector using celluloid film with sprocket holes at the edge.

1948 American inventor Edwin Land, develops the first instant camera, which is marketed by the Polaroid Corporation.

1956 A camera that records onto reel-to-reel magnetic videotape, rather than plastic film, is invented.

FIND OUT MORE COLOR FILMS AND FILMMAKING GLASS INVENTIONS LIGHT PHOTOGRAPHY PLASTICS TELEVISION

Still cameras

Early cameras

Image projected upside down

Shutter operated by a cord

Box made camera sturdy

Upper lens is for viewing

Fox Talbot's camera of 1835 required exposure times of over an hour.

Daguerreotype camera of mid-1800s was the first model sold to the public.

Kodak Autographic Special of 1918 was an early roll-film camera.

Ensign of the 1930s, with a side viewfinder: was popular in sports photography.

Brownie Hawkeye of the 1940s reflected the new use of plastic in design.

1950s Duaflex was modeled on the superior twin-lens cameras of the time.

35mm cameras

Shutter and film speed dial

Shutter release button

Zoom controlled by motor

Image is seen here

Manual SLR camera needs to be focused and wound manually.

Automatic SLR camera has an automatic film loading and winding mechanism.

Basic compact camera has a fixed length lens and built-in flash.

Advanced compacts are often fitted with a zoom lens, giving extra flexibility.

Leica cameras were the first to use the small-format 35mm film.

Waist-level viewfinder allows photos to be taken from waist height.

Medium- and large-format cameras

6 x 4.5 cm camera is a small, light, medium-format camera.

6 x 6 cm camera produces a square image and is used by many professionals.

Direct vision camera has range finder–focusing lenses, reducing size and weight.

6 x 7 cm camera produces a rectangular image ideal for landscape photography.

6 x 9 cm camera produces large images that make very clear enlargements.

Large-format camera uses individual sheets of film for each image.

Special cameras

Large viewfinder

Built-in flash

Bellows camera allows for a very wide range of image magnifications.

Film exit slot

Moving bellows along track alters magnification

Underwater camera has large easy-to-read dials for use in deep water.

Panoramic camera rotates to take a view of up to 360° in one exposure.

Polaroid camera produces a finished photo seconds after taking the picture.

Disposable camera is simple and light, and is used only once.

Movie cameras

Debro pavro was an early movie camera. The handle was turned to start filming.

Technicolor three-strip camera produces good, but expensive films.

Cine 8 takes still photographs in rapid succession.

Marey's rifle is a camera shaped like a rifle, with the lens in the barrel.

Magazines hold three strips of film separately

Images are recorded directly on video tape

Camcorders are handheld video cameras used by many individuals.

Trigger works like a shutter release

Matt-box keeps stray light out of the lens

CAMOUFLAGE AND COLOR

ANIMALS HAVE EVOLVED different colors, shapes, and patterns that help them survive. Some, such as birds of paradise, are brightly colored to attract a mate; others, such as the fire salamander, use colour to advertise that they are poisonous to eat. Animals, such as lapwings and polar bears, are camouflaged – colored or patterned – in such a way that they blend with their surroundings. Camouflage helps animals hide from predators, but it can also help predators creep up on their prey.

Bright colors of male make him stand out and attract females.

Newly hatched lapwings match color of straw.

Cryptic coloration

Cryptic coloration is common among birds. The plumage of many desert species blends perfectly with the ground color of their habitat. Birds of the forest canopy, such as parrots, are frequently green to match the dense foliage in which they live. Not all members of the same species are always of cryptic colors. Sometimes the female or nestlings, which are generally in greater need of concealment, have cryptic color, while the male is conspicuously colored to attract a mate.

Young lapwings in nest

Types of coloration

Coloration falls into two main categories: cryptic and phaneric. Cryptic colors and patterns help conceal an animal, thus helping protect it from enemies, or assisting in the capture of its prey. The factors that cryptic species suppress – color, movement, and shape – are exaggerated in phaneric species. Phaneric coloration makes an animal stand out. It can include the conspicuous display of brilliant colors, shapes, and actions, as demonstrated by birds of paradise.

Redheaded gouldian finch

Phaneric coloration

Phaneric coloration used by animals such as macaws and mandrills makes them stand out and be noticed. It is used between male and female in courtship displays, between parent and young and members of a group for purposes of recognition, between rival males in threat displays, and between predators and prey to warn, bluff, or deflect attack. Long ear and head plumes, fans, elongated tail feathers, wattles, and inflatable air sacs are all used to attract attention.

Camouflage

For concealment to be effective, the color and pattern of an animal's coat or skin must relate closely to those of its background. A bird's color often harmonizes with its nest; some ground-nesting birds choose a nest site with surroundings of a color similar to that of their eggs to conceal them. Color and posture can be a highly effective form of camouflage. The many types of concealment include disruptive coloration, disguise, and immobility.

Disruptive coloration

Irregular patches of contrasting colors and tones of an animal's coat divert attention away from the shape of the animal, making it harder to recognize. Tigers and giraffes show disruptive coloration.

Tiger camouflaged in long grass

Disguise

Cryptic coloration aims to disguise rather than conceal. The combination of color, form, and posture can produce an almost exact replica of a commonplace object associated with the habitat. Stick insects, for example, resemble small twigs, while nightjars, when lying down, look like stones or wood fragments.

Giant spiny stick insect

Mimicry

Mimicry is an extreme form of concealment. It occurs when a relatively defenseless or edible species looks like an aggressive or dangerous species. The mimic not only takes on the appearance of the object it is mimicking, but also adopts its behavior, assuming characteristics that are completely alien to it. For example, harmless milk snakes resemble poisonous coral snakes so that other animals will not attack them. The monarch, a poisonous butterfly, is mimicked by a non-poisonous species, the viceroy, which is indistinguishable from it.

Coral snake

Milk snake

Milk snakes have stripes of the same color as coral snakes, but in a different order.

Immobility

Effective camouflage is possible only if an animal remains still. Many animals react to danger by freezing. For example, if confronted with danger, reedbuck crouch down with their necks outstretched, and, by remaining motionless, become hard to distinguish from their surroundings. Some birds, particularly ground-nesting birds such as nightjars, squat down to reduce the shadow they make.

Reedbuck

Assassin bug

Many species of assassin bugs resemble the insects on which they feed. This enables them to get close to their prey without being detected, before seizing it and injecting a toxic fluid. One species of assassin bug, *Salyavata variegata*, lives in termite nests. It camouflages itself by covering its body in debris, including the bodies of termites, and then enters the nest unnoticed, and feed on the inhabitants.

Assassin bug covered in debris by termites' nest

Termite

Social displays

Social displays take many different forms, from threat display to courtship and bonding. Both cuttlefish and octopuses can change color; darkening and flashing different colors to intimidate rivals or enemies. The male Uganda kob, a type of antelope, establishes territorial breeding grounds by displaying along the boundary of his territory. Lowering his head, he makes a mock attack with his horns, warning rival males to keep out of his territory, while at the same time, inducing other females to join his harem.

Ring-tailed lemurs signaling with raised tails

Signaling

Signs and signals help animals maintain contact, preserve the social hierarchy, and intimidate rivals and enemies. The signals have to be conspicuous and unmistakable. The ring-tailed lemurs of Madagascar raise their long black and white tails to waft scent at their rivals and to enable all members of a group to maintain contact. The black rings encircling the cheetah's white-tipped tail enable the cubs to follow their parent, which would otherwise be invisible in the long grass. The young of ringed plovers have a white neckband that helps the parents keep the brood together.

Courtship

Many animals use courtship displays to attract a mate. The fiddler crab, for example, waves his outsize claw, the elephant seal inflates his nose, and the grouse spreads his tail and inflates his air sacs. Among the most impressive courtship displays are that of the male peacock, which spreads his brilliantly colored tail plumage, and the elaborate rituals of birds of paradise and bowerbirds. These involve vibrating the body, fanning feathers, puffing out plumage, decorating nesting areas, and calling loudly.

Tail feathers overlap and rest on the ground when relaxed.

Peacock

Peacock starts to erect tail plumage.

Male calls as he starts to display.

Strong feathers at the rear, attached to muscles, are used to raise the long feathers.

Peacock with tail feathers raised

Warning signals

Animals use many methods to frighten off other animals. Warning colors make prey appear unpalatable to discourage predators. Many poisonous and venomous animals do not need to be camouflaged; they advertise themselves with bright colored patterns of red, yellow, and black which, are recognized warning colors. Skunks' black and white coats warn they can squirt foul-smelling spray.

Red and black froghopper

Henry Walter Bates

The English naturalist and explorer, Henry Bates (1825–92) spent 11 years exploring the Amazon, returning with 8,000 species of previously unknown insects. In 1861, he published a paper on mimicry that made an important contribution to the theory of natural selection. He suggested that some harmless insects looked like harmful ones to discourage predators from attacking them.

False warning

Many animals employ bluff as a means of defense. In birds, this may take the form of fluffing up feathers, spreading wings, and clacking beaks. Many frogs and toads puff themselves up to make them appear larger; the hawkmoth caterpillar looks like a snake to intimidate enemies; and the Australian frilled lizard erects its frill and hisses loudly to intimidate intruders.

The toad raises itself on its legs to make itself appear bigger.

European common toad

The caterpillar looks like a small pit viper snake to scare predators.

Hawkmoth caterpillar

Seasonal change

Some Arctic animals, such as the polar bear and snowy owl, remain white throughout the year; others undergo a seasonal change. In far-northern latitudes, the stoat becomes completely white in winter, except for the tip of its tail, which remains black. In the warmer parts of its habitat, it can retain its russet coloration, become particolored, or change to white as needed. This ability to change color provides the stoat with effective camouflage throughout the year.

Stoat with dark summer coat

Stoat with pale winter coat

FIND OUT **MORE**   BIRDS   BUGS   DEER AND ANTELOPE   FROGS AND TOADS   LIONS AND OTHER WILDCATS   MONKEYS AND OTHER PRIMATES   OWLS AND NIGHTJARS   POISONOUS ANIMALS   SNAKES

CAMPING AND HIKING

ONE OF THE MOST popular types of vacation, camping offers people the chance to enjoy the great outdoors at close quarters. For many people, their first experience of camping is as children, setting up a tent in their own backyard. But it is also a popular activity with adults, who enjoy getting away from cities to explore the countryside, and perhaps even learning survival skills in the wild. Camping offers the freedom to choose to stay at one campsite through a holiday, or to set up camp at a different site each night. Whatever the type of vacation, it is important to take the appropriate clothing, food, and equipment.

An ideal campsite

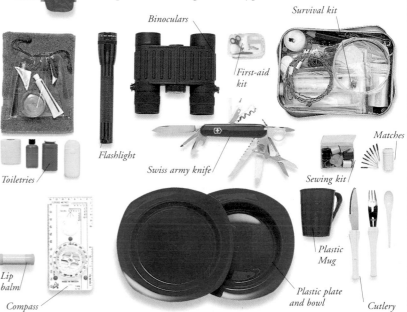

Prevailing winds

Trees provide shelter from the wind.

River is a source of water for drinking and washing.

Ground is level and there is no danger of flooding.

Choosing a campsite

Many campers stay on organized campsites with shared cooking and washing facilities. Those who prefer to camp "in the wild" look for high, level, dry ground on which to pitch a tent. The best campsites are sheltered from the wind, and not too close to any rivers or dams.

Fire ingredients

Tinder

Kindling

Small fuel

Main fuel

Large fuel

Making a tepee fire

Fires provide warmth and a means of cooking, but they can also be dangerous. Campers must make certain that a fire is permitted, safe, and will not harm their tent or the surroundings. They are especially careful if a strong wind is blowing.

1 The camper gathers the fuel he or she needs (ranging in size from twigs to branches), cuts out a square of earth, and puts a layers of sticks in the hole.

Make sure the fuel is dry.

2 The camper then balances four sticks to meet at the top in a tepee shape, making sure the tepee has enough space for tinder inside the sticks.

3 Gradually, the camper adds more sticks, making the tepee as sturdy as possible, and puts some tinder, such as leaves and dry grass, inside.

Hole for putting in tinder

4 Having set light to the tinder, the camper gradually adds more tinder, then twigs and larger pieces of fuel. He or she takes care not to knock the tepee over. When the teepee burns, it will collapse and create embers that can be used for cooking.

Keep a flashlight at the head of the sleeping bag.

Unpack things only as needed.

The head of a sleeping bag should face the door.

Living in your tent

There is very little room inside a tent, so campers need to be well organized, or they may lose things and be uncomfortable. To stop damp seeping in from the soil under a sleeping bag, campers put a waterproof sheet on the ground beneath the tent.

Things to take camping

It is better to take only the basic items of equipment camping. These include all the tools needed to set up a camp, in addition to cooking and eating utensils. In addition, campers should take durable clothes to protect them against all types of weather.

Binoculars

Survival kit

First-aid kit

Flashlight

Matches

Swiss army knife

Sewing kit

Toiletries

Lip balm

Compass

Plastic Mug

Plastic plate and bowl

Cutlery

Food and water

For healthy eating, campers aim to maintain a balanced diet, including fruit and vegetables, bread, and food containing protein, such as fish and meat. If it is difficult or impossible for campers to buy food while they are away, they take tinned or freeze-dried foods, which will not perish. Campers should only drink water from approved sources. If necessary, they take water purifiers or a portable water filter.

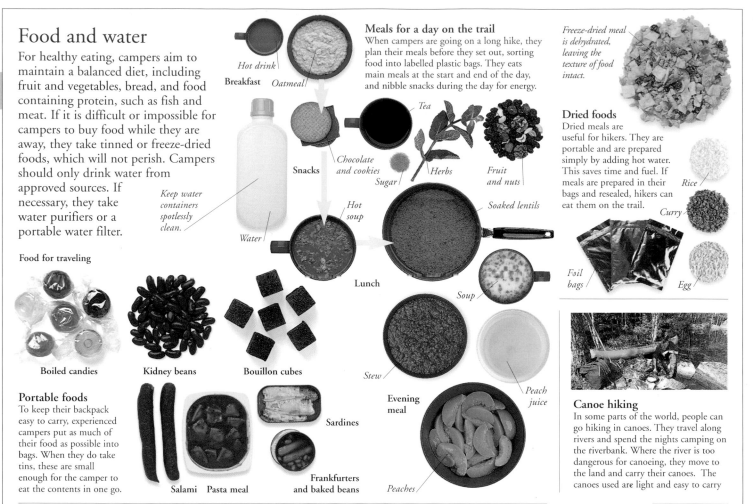

Hot drink
Breakfast *Oatmeal*

Meals for a day on the trail
When campers are going on a long hike, they plan their meals before they set out, sorting food into labelled plastic bags. They eats main meals at the start and end of the day, and nibble snacks during the day for energy.

Freeze-dried meal is dehydrated, leaving the texture of food intact.

Dried foods
Dried meals are useful for hikers. They are portable and are prepared simply by adding hot water. This saves time and fuel. If meals are prepared in their bags and resealed, hikers can eat them on the trail.

Keep water containers spotlessly clean.

Tea
Snacks
Chocolate and cookies *Sugar* *Herbs* *Fruit and nuts*

Rice
Curry

Water

Hot soup

Lunch *Soaked lentils*

Soup

Foil bags *Egg*

Food for traveling

Boiled candies   **Kidney beans**   **Bouillon cubes**

Stew

Peach juice

Canoe hiking
In some parts of the world, people can go hiking in canoes. They travel along rivers and spend the nights camping on the riverbank. Where the river is too dangerous for canoeing, they move to the land and carry their canoes. The canoes used are light and easy to carry

Portable foods
To keep their backpack easy to carry, experienced campers put as much of their food as possible into bags. When they do take tins, these are small enough for the camper to eat the contents in one go.

Salami Pasta meal

Sardines

Frankfurters and baked beans

Evening meal

Peaches

Camping with trailers

Trailers are like compact homes on wheels, and can be towed by a car, or any vehicle, to a campsite. Trailers usually have several rooms and are more comfortable to live in than tents; most trailers have stoves, beds, and toilets, and some may even have refrigerators and showers. Some campsites have permanent, fixed trailers that you can rent for your vacation if you do not have your own.

Hiking

Walking through the countryside, for a few hours or for up to several weeks, is a form of exercise enjoyed by people of all ages. Hikers walk in groups, so that if an accident occurs, at least two can go for help together, and one can stay with the injured member of the party. Hikers should be fully equipped for the sort of trip they are making and should tell someone where they are going.

Tent poles and stakes in the same bag

Keep the pack full so that heavy items stay at the top.

Sleeping bag at the bottom

Ice pick
Windproof jacket with a hood.

Ice hammer

Shoulder straps can be adjusted to fit.

Mountain walking
The most difficult and dangerous form of hiking is mountain climbing. Mountain climbers enjoy testing their strength and skill on steep rock faces. They need to be particularly fit, and use special climbing equipment.

Crampon

How to pack your sack
To keep the contents of a backpack dry, line it with a plastic bag and put everything in separate plastic bags. Pack the lighter, bulkier things at the bottom and the heavier things at the top. Spare clothes can be packed down the back to protect the spine.

Using a compass
Hikers take a map and a compass when they go on a long walk, so that they can follow the route and not get lost. A protractor compass, shown here, is popular because it is light, reliable, and accurate.

Backpacking
A comfortable way to carry belongings, backpacks range from light day packs to large packs that have space for everything needed for several days' hiking. They sit as high as possible on the shoulders, to distribute weight.

FIND OUT MORE   **EXPLORATION**   **ENERGY**   **FIRST AID**   **FIRE**   **FOOD**   **HEALTH AND FITNESS**

CANADA

THE WORLD'S SECOND LARGEST country, Canada covers the northern part of the North American continent and is made up of ten provinces and two territories. Canada borders Alaska and the Pacific Ocean to the west, and the Atlantic Ocean to the east. Winters in the northern third of the country, much of which lies within the Arctic Circle, are so severe that very few people can live there. About 80 percent of Canadians live within 200 miles (320 km) of the US border. Canada has huge forests, rich mineral resources, and open, fertile farmland.

C

113°F
(45°C)
-81°F
(-63°C)
70°F
(21°C)
12°F
(-11°C)
34 in (871 mm)

Built-up
0.5%
Wetland
2%
Grassland
1%
Forest
59%
Tundra
27%
Barren
5.5%
Farmland
5%

Ottawa

Canada's capital sits on the south bank of the Ottawa River and has a population of 921,000. The city has clean, wide streets, many lined with parks. The Rideau Canal, part of a complex of lakes and canals linking Ottawa with Lake Ontario, freezes in winter, becoming the world's longest skating rink.

Skating on the Rideau Canal

Physical features

Covered with lakes, rivers, and forests, Canada has one-third of the world's freshwater. Frozen islands lie in the Arctic, high mountains in the west, and vast prairies in the south.

Climate

Most of Canada has a continental climate with long, bitterly cold winters and hot, humid summers. Coastal areas are generally mild, especially the Pacific west coast. The glaciers and ice-caps of the north are permanently frozen.

Rocky Mountains

The snowcapped Rocky Mountains dominate western Canada, extending south into the US. Canada's highest mountain is Logan, at 19,551 ft (5,959 m).

Land use

Canada's vast prairies are used for growing wheat. The forests support a thriving timber industry. Only five percent of Canada's land area is cultivated.

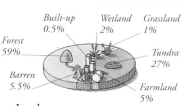

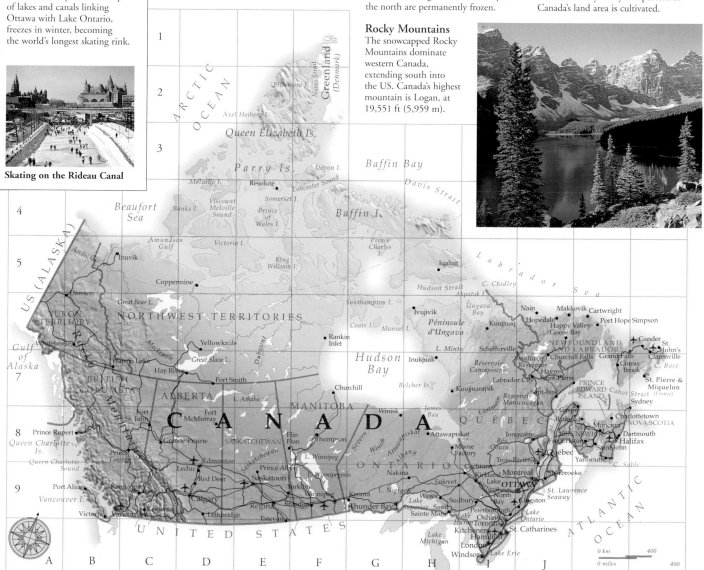

People

Most Canadians have European ancestors who emigrated to Canada from the UK, France, Germany, Scandinavia, and Italy. There are large numbers of Ukrainians, Indians, and Chinese. The native people of Canada form only four percent.

8 per sq mile
(3 per sq km)

77% **23%**
Urban **Rural**

Inuit
The Inuit are one of the country's indigenous groups, and almost 27,000 Inuits live in northern Canada. One-quarter are settled on Baffin Island, in the eastern Arctic, and speak their own language, *Inuktitut*. They live in close communities and are skilled craftworkers.

Leisure

Many Canadians enjoy outdoor activities. In the summer, people sail, raft, canoe, or simply enjoy one of Canada's many well-kept parks. The major spectator sports are hockey, baseball, and soccer.

Winter sports
Plentiful snow makes skiing and ice-skating popular with many Canadians. Ice hockey is played everywhere, from frozen backyards to national stadiums. Calgary hosted the 1988 Winter Olympics.

Hardwood stick

Tough rubber puck is hit into the goal.

Calgary Stampede
One of the world's largest rodeos, the Calgary Stampede attracts one million visitors every year. Held in July, the 10-day rodeo is an exciting re-creation of the Wild West, where people dress up in cowboy outfits and try their luck at calf roping, chuck wagon racing, and bronco riding.

Farming

Five percent of Canada's land is arable, and the country is a top exporter of wheat, oats, corn, and barley. Forest products and fish are also key exports. Cattle and pigs are raised on the pastures of the southeast. Farming employs three percent of the workforce.

Apple

Cranberries

Niagara Fruit Belt
The land between lakes Ontario and Erie is called the "Niagara Fruit Belt" because the soil and climate are ideal for growing soft fruit such as cherries and peaches. Apples and cranberries flourish in British Columbia. In the east, the maple tree (its leaf is Canada's national emblem) yields rich syrup, a favorite served with sweet pancakes.

Maple leaves

Wheat
Canada's main grain crop is wheat, and on the eastern prairies, around Saskatchewan, wheat farming is a way of life. About half of the 32,930,000 tons (29,870,000 tonnes) grown every year are exported.

Transportation

The 5,000-mile (8,000-km) Trans-Canada Highway links the east and west coasts. The St. Lawrence Seaway provides trade links for the eastern provinces. Airways, railroads, rivers, and the lakes are also used for transportation.

St. Lawrence Seaway
Opened in 1959, the St. Lawrence Seaway links the Great Lakes with the St. Lawrence River and the Atlantic. Over 450 miles (725 km), a series of locks enables oceangoing ships, from all over the world, to sail inland.

Snowplow
Canada's long, cold winters bring heavy snow and ice to the country, making traveling by road difficult and dangerous. Snowplows work through the day and night to keep roads clear. Most Canadian roads are wide to allow room for snow to be piled up on either side.

Industry

The center of Canada's industry is at the western end of Lake Ontario, a region known as "the Golden Horseshoe." Canadian factories process foods, assemble cars, and make steel, chemical products, and paper. The service industries are thriving, and tourism now employs one in ten Canadians.

Nickel

Zinc

Mining
Minerals have been one of the major factors in the growth of Canada's economy. The country is the world's largest producer of zinc ore and uranium, and second of nickel and asbestos.

Forestry
Canada's abundant forests have made it the world's second largest exporter of softwood (fir and pine) and wood pulp. Ten percent of Canada's labor force work in the lumber industry, using timber as a raw material. British Columbia, Québec, and Ontario are the major timber-producing provinces.

Québec
At the heart of French Canada, Québec City has many stone houses and 17th-century buildings, and its old town was declared a World Heritage Site in 1985. The province of Québec is home to nearly 6,900,000 people. More than three-quarters of the people are of French descent; they keep the French language and culture alive. There have been many attempts by the province to claim independence from Canada.

Château Frontenac, Québec old town

FIND OUT MORE CANADA, HISTORY OF · FARMING · FISHING INDUSTRY · FORESTS · LAKES · NATIVE AMERICANS · PORTS AND WATERWAYS · ROCKS AND MINERALS · TUNDRA · WINTER SPORTS

CANADA, HISTORY OF

FOR MOST OF ITS history, Canada has been home to Native Americans and Inuits. They were descendants of the first people to settle there during the Ice Age, and built advanced cultures based on hunting and trapping fish and animals. In 1497, the first Europeans visited the country, establishing settlements in the early 1600s. In the 18th century, French and British armies fought for control of the entire country. The British won, but a sizable French community has remained in Quebec to this day.

The first Canadians

The first inhabitants of Canada were peoples from northern Asia who crossed a land bridge from Siberia and moved south through America more than 20,000 years ago. The Inuits lived in the Arctic regions; other Native American peoples occupied the plains and coastal areas. They all developed their own distinctive cultures. For example, the tribes of the northwest coast recorded their family history on totem poles, carving out representations of the family spirits on the trunks of cedar trees.

Fur trading

European settlers were attracted to Canada by the wealth to be made from furs and skins of animals trapped in the forests. The English-owned Hudson's Bay Company, established in 1670, and other trading companies set up fortified trading posts to trade furs and other goods with local Indian tribes. Quebec (established 1608) and Montreal (1642) became important centers of the fur trade.

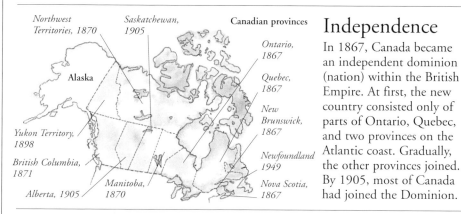

Traders traveled by canoe in order to reach the trading post.

Missionaries built churches to convert Native Americans.

Wigwams made of birch wood covered with skins or bark.

Houses and walls were built with wood from the forests.

Trading post

Jacques Cartier

The French sea captain Jacques Cartier (1491–1557) was hired by Francois I of France to look for a northwest passage to China above North America. In 1534, he sailed into the Gulf of St. Lawrence and, in 1535, discovered the St. Lawrence River. As he sailed up the river, he stopped at two Indian villages – Stadacona (modern Quebec) and Hochelaga (Montreal). As a result, French immigrants began to settle by the St. Lawrence River.

Capture of Quebec

In 1759, British forces led by General James Wolfe attacked Quebec, capital of the French colony of New France. Wolfe captured the city, arriving from the Gulf of St. Lawrence

Wolfe's flotilla arrives in Quebec

with a flotilla of 168 ships that carried over 30,000 men. However, both he and the French commander, Louis, Marquis de Montcalm, were killed. All of French North America came under British control.

Northwest Territories, 1870

Saskatchewan, 1905

Canadian provinces

Ontario, 1867

Alaska

Quebec, 1867

New Brunswick, 1867

Yukon Territory, 1898

British Columbia, 1871

Newfoundland 1949

Manitoba, 1870

Nova Scotia, 1867

Alberta, 1905

Independence

In 1867, Canada became an independent dominion (nation) within the British Empire. At first, the new country consisted only of parts of Ontario, Quebec, and two provinces on the Atlantic coast. Gradually, the other provinces joined. By 1905, most of Canada had joined the Dominion.

Immigration

At the end of the 19th century, Canada's economy expanded and several transcontinental railroads improved communications. Canada became an attractive place for European emigrants, and between 1891 and 1914, over three million people came to Canada in search of work and a new life. Canada's government encouraged Europeans to emigrate, promising future citizens health and wealth in their new home.

Canadian government poster

Timeline

1497 John Cabot, an Italian sailor, claims Newfoundland for Britain.

1534 Jacques Cartier explores the St. Lawrence River for France.

1605 French establish the first European colony at Port Royal, Nova Scotia.

1754 French and Indian War between Britain and France. France forced to relinquish Quebec to Britain.

1846 Oregon Treaty confirms present borders with USA

1949 Founder member of NATO

1968 Quebec Party formed to demand independence for Quebec

1976 French made official language in Quebec

1989 UK transfers all power relating to Canada in British Law.

Canadian flag

Quebec

Canada recognized both its English- and French-speakers as equal, but in the 1960s, many people in French-speaking Quebec began to press for their province to become independent. In 1982, Quebec was given the status of a "distinct society," but referendums seeking independence were defeated in 1980 and 1995.

FIND OUT MORE   EXPLORATION   FRANCE, HISTORY OF   NATIVE AMERICANS   NORTH AMERICA, HISTORY OF   UNITED KINGDOM, HISTORY OF   UNITED STATES, HISTORY OF

CARIBBEAN

HUNDREDS OF ISLANDS lie in the Caribbean Sea, east of the US and Central America and stretching west into the Atlantic Ocean. These Caribbean islands, also known as the West Indies, take their name from the Caribs, the original inhabitants of the region, until the Spanish arrived in 1492. Most islanders today are descendents of African slaves brought to work on plantations between the 16th and 19th centuries. The islands have a tropical climate, turquoise waters, and fine beaches, and have developed a booming tourist industry. However, many people are poor, and live by farming.

Volcanic islands
Many Caribbean islands are made of volcanic rocks that emerged from the ocean millions of years ago. Some, such as the St. Lucian Gros Piton, 2,619 ft (798 m), and the Petit Piton, 2,461 ft (750 m), are the remains of ancient volcanoes that rise up from the sea on the west coast, near the town of Soufrière. Several are still active, such as La Soufrière, at 4,000 ft (1,219 m), on St. Vincent.

Physical features

Long, sandy beaches, tropical seas, and fine natural harbors have earned the Caribbean islands a reputation for beauty. Most of the islands are forested and mountainous. Some are volcanic in origin, others are founded on coral reefs. Hurricanes, earthquakes, and active volcanoes shake parts of the region from time to time.

Coral islands
The warm, tropical seas of the Caribbean provide ideal conditions for coral. Some of the Caribbean's volcanic islands, such as Barbados and the Cayman Islands, are fringed with coral reefs, which protect them against the lashing waves. The 700 islands and 2,300 islets of the Bahamas are entirely built up of coral, which can be viewed from the bridge that links Nassau with Paradise Island.

Hurricanes
Powerful tropical storms called hurricanes sweep the Caribbean between May and October every year, often causing great damage and economic hardship. They begin as thunderstorms that are whipped up by high winds and warm waters to form destructive storm clouds. These clouds swirl around a single center at up to 220 mph (360 kmh). A hurricane can last for up to 18 hours.

Regional climate
The countries of the Caribbean all enjoy a warm, tropical climate. Mountainous islands, such as the Windwards, receive three times as much rainfall as lower areas. Most islands have a wet, hurricane-prone season between June and November. From January to March, it is generally dry and pleasant.

73°F (23°C)   82°F (28°C)

46 in (1,167 mm)

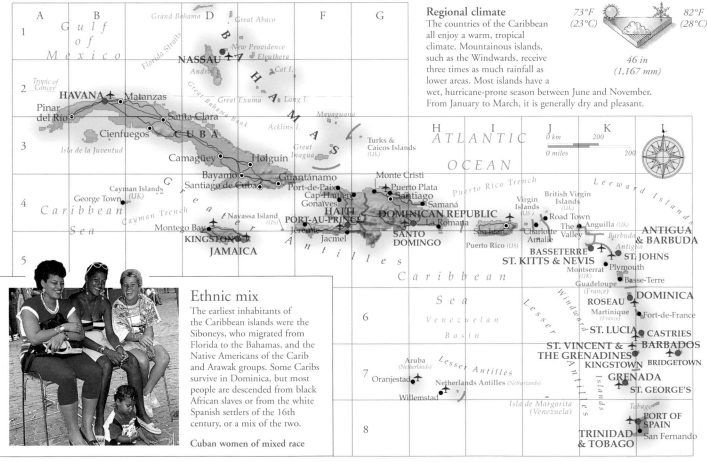

Ethnic mix
The earliest inhabitants of the Caribbean islands were the Siboneys, who migrated from Florida to the Bahamas, and the Native Americans of the Carib and Arawak groups. Some Caribs survive in Dominica, but most people are descended from black African slaves or from the white Spanish settlers of the 16th century, or a mix of the two.

Cuban women of mixed race

Cuba

The largest island in the Caribbean, Cuba has fertile lowlands set between three large mountainous regions. Sugar, rice, tobacco, and coffee are grown on the lowlands, and chromium and nickel are mined. Formerly a Spanish colony, Cuba has been a communist state since 1959. Hostile politics caused the US to impose a trade embargo, which has disabled Cuba's economy and kept it agricultural.

Sugar is extracted from the cane.

Sugar

With an annual production of 55,000,000 tons (50,000,000 tonnes), sugarcane is Cuba's largest crop. It is grown around Havana and processed in the city's factories. The country is the world's fourth largest producer; it exports much of it to Russia and Iran in exchange for oil, since Cuba's reserves are small.

Communism

The only communist state in the Caribbean, Cuba is led by Fidel Castro (b. 1926), who led the revolution in 1959. Under Castro, and with Soviet help, Cuba made considerable social and economic progress, although living standards suffered with the breakup of Soviet communism in 1991. US policies remain hostile.

Havana

Situated in a natural harbor, Cuba's chief port and capital, Havana, was founded by the Spanish in 1515. Its old town has many ancient buildings and cobbled streets. There are no shantytowns here, unlike many capitals in Central America, but of its 2,119,000 people, half live in substandard houses.

Cigars

Cuba's fertile soil and warm climate are ideal for growing high-quality tobacco. Havana cigars are popular all over the world and are made from a blend of at least five different types of tobacco. Cigars are still rolled by hand at long wooden tables.

CUBA FACTS

CAPITAL CITY Havana

AREA 42,803 sq miles (110,860 sq km)

POPULATION 11,172,000

MAIN LANGUAGE Spanish

MAJOR RELIGION Christian

CURRENCY Peso

C

Bahamas

Located to the northeast of Cuba, the Bahamas extend south for about 600 miles (965 km). Of the 3,000 coral islands and islets, only 30 are inhabited. Most of the people are black, but on Spanish Wells Island, there are about 1,290 white descendants of Puritan settlers. Tourism, fishing, and financial services flourish on the islands.

Festival

Music and dancing are everywhere in the Caribbean, but especially so at the Junkanoo Festival in the Bahamas. Held at the end of every year, Junkanoo is a lively celebration with street dancing, music, and colorful parades where people wear wild costumes and blow whistles. The festival has roots in the celebrations of a slave leader called John Canoe, and slaves' days off at Christmas.

BAHAMAS FACTS

CAPITAL CITY Nassau

AREA 5,359 sq miles (13,880 sq km)

POPULATION 281,000

MAIN LANGUAGE English

MAJOR RELIGION Christian

CURRENCY Bahamian dollar

Jamaica

The third largest island of the Caribbean, Jamaica is a land of springs, rivers, waterfalls, and sandy beaches. A few wealthy families dominate the island, but the slum areas around Kingston are controlled by violent gangs. Many of the people of those areas are Rastafarians, worshipers of the former emperor of Ethiopia. Jamaica is a prosperous country, with booming tourist, mining, and farming industries. Cricket is a popular game.

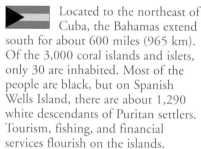

Reggae

Jamaica's distinctive form of popular music, reggae, began in the 1960s as an offshoot of rhythm and blues, with songs calling for social and political change. Bob Marley (1945–81), whose band became very popular in the 1970s, is a reggae icon, and his birthday is celebrated by all Jamaicans.

JAMAICA FACTS

CAPITAL CITY Kingston

AREA 4,243 sq miles (10,990 sq km)

POPULATION 2,572,000

MAIN LANGUAGE English

MAJOR RELIGIONS Christian, Rastafarian

CURRENCY Jamaican dollar

Women

The Caribbean women's rights movement began in Jamaica, and many Jamaican women hold senior posts in economic and political life. An increasing number of women prefer to be single mothers, especially those who have careers. Women also dominate the growing data-processing industry, largely because they work for lower wages than men.

Okra

Breadfruit

Dasheen or taro

Vegetables

Jamaicans grow a wide range of vegetables. *Dasheen*, or *taro*, is a staple vegetable. The roots and leaves are eaten. There are more than 1,000 varieties of *dasheen* and it is also used for medicinal purposes. Okra are green pods that are used in "pepperpot stews." Breadfruit, with a creamy, pulpy texture, grow to 5 in (13 cm) wide, and are eaten baked or roasted.

Bauxite

Jamaica is the world's third largest producer of bauxite, the ore from which aluminum is made. Refineries produce alumina, the next stage in producing the metal, worth ten times as much as the ore. Aluminum provides half of Jamaica's export income, and accounts for 10 percent of global output.

Haiti

Occupying the western third of the island of Hispaniola, Haiti is one of the most mountainous countries in the Caribbean. It is also the poorest. About 95 percent of its people are descendents of black slaves. The country is overcrowded and has suffered deforestation, soil erosion, and desertification, as well as a turbulent political history.

Port-au-Prince

Modern hotels have lured many visitors to Haiti's capital, Port-au-Prince. The city has two cathedrals, a university, and many government buildings. However, it also has the worst slums in the Caribbean, most of which are found north of the city. They have no sewage system and are overcrowded.

Voodoo

A Haitian blend of West African religions and Christianity, voodoo uses drumming, singing, and dance. Its followers believe that through worship of spirits, they can live in harmony with nature and their dead. Many celebrations coincide with Christmas and the Mexican Day of the Dead.

Voodooists on Gede, or All Saint's Day

HAITI FACTS

CAPITAL CITY	Port-au-Prince
AREA	10,714 sq miles (27,750 sq km)
POPULATION	7,328,000
MAIN LANGUAGES	French, French Creole
MAJOR RELIGIONS	Christian, Voodoo
CURRENCY	Gourde

Puerto Rico

About 994 miles (1,600 km) southeast of Miami, the crowded island of Puerto Rico is a self-governing territory of the US. It is home to more than 3.5 million people, of African and Spanish descent, of whom half live in the capital, San Juan. An old walled city, it has colonial buildings.

Balconies, old San Juan

Dominican Republic

Lying 600 miles (966 km) southeast of Florida, the Dominican Republic spreads across the eastern two-thirds of Hispaniola. It has the Caribbean's highest peak, Pico Duarte, 10,417 ft (3,175 m), and also its lowest point, crocodile-infested Lake Enriquillo, 144 ft (44 m) below sea level. Nickel, amber, and gold mining are important industries, and vacationers flock to the island for its long pearly beaches, modern hotels, and wildlife.

People

With a higher standard of living than neighboring Haiti, the Dominican Republic provides good health care for its people. The mixed race middle classes form about 73 percent of the population. The minority of blacks work as farmers, selling their produce at market.

Farming

About 22 percent of the labor force works on farms located in the north and east of the country, and in the San Juan valley. Sugar, tobacco, and cocoa are main crops, and although the market has slowed, most are exported to the US.

Tobacco leaves are hung upside down to dry and then made into cigars and cigarettes.

DOMINICAN REPUBLIC FACTS

CAPITAL CITY	Santo Domingo
AREA	18,815 sq miles (48,730 sq km)
POPULATION	8,050,000
MAIN LANGUAGES	Spanish, French Creole
MAJOR RELIGION	Christian
CURRENCY	Peso

Tourism

The Dominican Republic is the largest tourist destination in the Caribbean, attracting two million each year. The industry brings in half of the country's earnings and provides much-needed jobs.

St. Kitts and Nevis

The two islands of St. Kitts (or St. Christopher) and Nevis sit in the northern part of the Leeward Islands. Both are mountainous and their idyllic palm-fringed beaches attract many tourists. Most people are descendents of black Africans, and nearly all work in farming or tourism.

ST. KITTS AND NEVIS FACTS

CAPITAL CITY	Basseterre
AREA	139 sq miles (360 sq km)
POPULATION	44,000
MAIN LANGUAGE	English
MAJOR RELIGION	Christian
CURRENCY	East Caribbean dollar

Sugarcane

The main crop on St. Kitts is sugarcane, which accounts for 25 percent of exports and provides 12 percent of jobs. Low world prices and hurricane damage have created problems.

Antigua and Barbuda

The largest of the Leeward Islands, Antigua has two dependencies: Barbuda, a small coral island bursting with wildlife, and Redonda, an uninhabited rock with its own king. The blue lagoons and corals that surround Antigua teem with tropical fish.

ANTIGUA AND BARBUDA FACTS

CAPITAL CITY	St. John's
AREA	170 sq miles (440 sq km)
POPULATION	69,000
MAIN LANGUAGE	English
MAJOR RELIGION	Christian
CURRENCY	East Caribbean dollar

Yachting

The harbor at St. John's has an annual Sailing Week that attracts many visitors. Throughout the year, cruise ships and luxury boats call at the 18th-century Nelson's Dockyard.

C

Dominica

The largest and most mountainous of the Windward Islands, Dominica has some of the finest scenery in the Caribbean, with rain forests containing 200 wildlife species. Bananas and coconuts are principal exports; shrimp farming is proving successful.

DOMINICA FACTS

CAPITAL CITY Roseau

AREA 290 sq miles (750 sq km)

POPULATION 71,000

MAIN LANGUAGES English, French

MAJOR RELIGION Christian

CURRENCY East Caribbean dollar

Carib reservation

In the 1900s, the British forced the Caribs to move to a reservation. Today, the Carib reservation, on the east coast of the island, is home to more than 2,000 Caribs, descendants of the original inhabitants. Within the reservation – a popular tourist attraction – Caribs follow traditional lifestyles, although their language has died out. Many Carib craftspeople make a living selling bags made from banana leaves and grasses.

St. Lucia

The beautiful island of St. Lucia has clear seas, sandy beaches, and striking volcanic mountains. Most people work in farming, tourism, or industry. Each year, 165,000 tons (150,000 tonnes) of bananas are exported.

ST. LUCIA FACTS

CAPITAL CITY Castries

AREA 239 sq miles (620 sq km)

POPULATION 144,000

MAIN LANGUAGE English

MAJOR RELIGION Christian

CURRENCY East Caribbean dollar

Ecotourism

St. Lucia's lush rain forests, hot springs, and twin Piton peaks are attractions that lure visitors to the island. Aromatic tropical plants, trees, and flowers grow everywhere.

Barbados

Known as the "singular island," Barbados lies 100 miles (160 km) east of the Caribbean chain. Barbados retains a strong English influence, and many Britons retire to the island. The people of Barbados, called Bajans, enjoy some of the Caribbean's highest living standards.

BARBADOS FACTS

CAPITAL CITY Bridgetown

AREA 166 sq miles (430 sq km)

POPULATION 262,000

MAIN LANGUAGE English

MAJOR RELIGION Christian

CURRENCY Barbados dollar

Tourism

Barbados has one of the Caribbean's most well-developed and lucrative tourist industries. About 400,000 people visit the island every year.

St. Vincent and the Grenadines

The quiet island of St. Vincent is fertile and volcanic, while its 100 tiny sister islands of the Grenadines are flat coral reefs. Both are exclusive vacation resorts and their clear waters are popular with yachts-people. Bananas are the main export.

Arrowroot

St. Vincent is the world's largest producer of arrowroot, a starchy liquid that is removed from the arrowroot plant. It is used as a thickening agent in foods and, more recently, as a fine finish for computer paper. Arrowroot is St. Vincent's second largest export.

Arrowroot

Arrowroot powder

ST. VINCENT AND THE GRENADINES FACTS

CAPITAL CITY Kingstown

AREA 131 sq miles (340 sq km)

POPULATION 113,000

MAIN LANGUAGE English

MAJOR RELIGION Christian

CURRENCY East Caribbean dollar

Grenada

The most southerly of the Windwards, Grenada rises from a rugged coast to a high forested interior. Formerly a British colony, Grenada has built its economy on agriculture and tourism. Its people are of African or mixed origin.

Nutmeg

Ginger

Cinnamon

GRENADA FACTS

CAPITAL CITY St. George's

AREA 131 sq miles (340 sq km)

POPULATION 92,000

MAIN LANGUAGE English

MAJOR RELIGION Christian

CURRENCY East Caribbean dollar

Spices

Grenada is described as the "spice island." It grows about two-thirds of the world's nutmeg and, with Indonesia, dominates the market. Large quantities of cloves, mace, cinnamon, ginger, bay leaves, saffron, and pepper are also cultivated on the island.

Trinidad and Tobago

The low-lying island of Trinidad and its smaller partner, Tobago, lie just off the coast of Venezuela. The islands have a vivid, cosmopolitan culture, home to people from every continent. Both have fertile farmland, fine beaches, and abundant wildlife.

TRINIDAD AND TOBAGO FACTS

CAPITAL CITY Port-of-Spain

AREA 1,981 sq miles (5,130 sq km)

POPULATION 1,317,000

MAIN LANGUAGE English

MAJOR RELIGIONS Christian, Hindu, Muslim

CURRENCY Trinidad and Tobago dollar

Steel bands

Trinidad and Tobago are the home of steel bands, calypso, and limbo dancing. The first drums, or *pans*, began as empty oil containers. Today, drums are hand-decorated and tuned so that melodies can be played on them. They provide the beat for lively calypso songs.

FIND OUT MORE CARIBBEAN, HISTORY OF CHRISTIANITY FARMING FESTIVALS ISLANDS MUSIC RELIGIONS ROCKS AND MINERALS SLAVERY VOLCANOES

C

CARIBBEAN, HISTORY OF

FOR CENTURIES, the Caribbean islands were home to the Carib and Arawak peoples. Their way of life was abruptly disturbed when Europeans arrived in the 1490s. Within 100 years, most had been wiped out by new European rulers who brought thousands of Africans into the Caribbean to work on sugar plantations. The sugar-based economy continued until its decline in the late 19th century. From the mid-1960s, the islands gradually gained independence from European control.

Original inhabitants
The Caribs were expert navigators, traveling great distances in wooden canoes. The Arawaks were skilled craftsworkers, who produced baskets and furniture.

Arawak-style wooden seat from the Bahamas

Spanish conquest
The arrival of the Spanish-sponsored navigator Christopher Columbus in the Caribbean in 1492 transformed the region. Convoys of galleons laden with gold and other treasures from the Spanish empire in South America soon crossed the sea on their way back to Spain. Within a few years, Spanish armies had conquered and settled almost every island. Most of the Caribs were killed by the invaders.

Columbus's ship, the *Santa Maria*

European settlement

In the 16th century, with unofficial government backing, English, French, and Dutch pirates raided Spanish treasure ships. They also captured many of the smaller islands. Settlers from Europe arrived, and by 1750 most of the islands were under British, French, or Dutch rule.

Route of trading ships

NORTH AMERICA

Crops taken to England

Manufactured goods taken to Africa

CARIBBEAN

EUROPE

AFRICA

Slaves taken to Caribbean

Toussaint L'Ouverture

Ex-slave Toussaint L'Ouverture (1743–1803) led a revolt of slaves in French-ruled Haiti in the 1790s. He declared the country a republic, but the French regained control and took him to France, where he died.

Plantations
Europeans set up plantations to satisfy demand for sugar and tobacco in Europe. African slaves worked on the plantations. By 1750, the Caribbean produced most of the world's sugar.

Sugar-cane

Tobacco

Slave trade
Most of the Caribbean slave trade was controlled from English ports. Ships left England for West Africa with goods to barter for slaves. The slaves were shipped across the Atlantic. Sugar, tobacco, and other crops were then taken back to England for sale.

Rastafarians

Many Jamaicans are Rastafarians. They believe that the former emperor of Ethiopia, Ras Tafari, or Haile Selassie, was the new messiah who would one day lead his people back to Africa.

Cuban War
In 1895, following an earlier, unsuccessful uprising, the Cubans rose in revolt against their Spanish rulers. In 1898, the US declared war on Spain, and freed Cuba.

Emigration
After World War II, many people left the Caribbean in search of work and a better standard of living in Europe. In 1948, the *Empire Windrush* took 492 emigrants from Kingston, Jamaica, to London. Over the next 20 years, thousands of Caribbean islanders emigrated to Britain.

Fidel Castro

In 1959, Fidel Castro (b.1927) became the President of Cuba and introduced many social reforms. The US government tried to depose him in 1961, and he turned to the USSR for help. When Soviet nuclear missiles were installed in Cuba in 1962, the world came close to nuclear war.

Timeline

1300s Caribs drive out Arawak people from the eastern Caribbean islands.

1492 Christopher Columbus lands in the Bahamas.

1500s The Spanish take control of the Caribbean.

1700s French, British, Dutch, and Danes capture many islands.

1804 Haiti becomes first Caribbean island to achieve independence from European rule.

1898–1902 Cuba under rule of US.

1933 Fulgencio Batista becomes ruler of Cuba.

1948 *Empire Windrush* takes first emigrants to Britain.

Capturing a slave

1959 Cuban Revolution; Fidel Castro takes power.

1962 Cuban missile crisis brings the US and the USSR to the brink of nuclear war.

1962 Jamaica is first British Caribbean colony to win independence.

1962–83 Most British islands win independence; Dutch and French islands remain tied to Europeans.

1983 US overthrows left-wing regime in Grenada.

Flag of Jamaica

1994 US intervenes to secure democracy in Haiti, after years of dictatorship on the island.

FIND OUT MORE

AFRICA, EAST   COLUMBUS, CHRISTOPHER   EMPIRES   EXPLORATION   FRANCE, HISTORY OF   GOVERNMENTS AND POLITICS   SLAVERY   SPAIN, HISTORY OF

CARNIVOROUS PLANTS

PLANTS THAT catch and "eat" insects are called carnivorous plants. These plants fall into two groups. Some species, such as the Venus flytrap, have active traps with moving parts. Other species have passive traps, catching their victims on a sticky surface or drowning them in a pool of fluid. Carnivorous plants live in areas where the soil is poor in nitrates and other nutrients, such as bogs, peatlands, and swamps. They obtain extra nutrients by catching insects, which are digested by special juices.

Monkey-cup pitcher plant

The lid and the smooth rim are often brightly colored to attract insects.

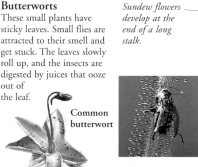

Tendril

Pitcher plants from Southeast Asia form traps that hang from their leaves.

Hanging pitcher

Passive traps

Most carnivorous plants have passive traps. Usually the leaves of these plants have evolved to catch insects in a variety of ways. Some are sticky, others form pit-fall traps with fluid at the bottom and are called pitcher plants.

Rim of the pitcher contains nectar.

Lid stays closed while the pitcher develops.

Mouth of pitcher

Insects fall into the liquid and are digested.

Development of a pitcher plant

1 A young leaf tip extends into a tendril.

2 An upturned swelling appears at the end.

3 The swelling develops into a pitcher.

4 The lid opens when the pitcher is mature.

American pitcher plants
Although they catch their prey in the same way as other pitcher plants, American pitcher plants grow up from the ground rather than hanging from leaves. The inside of the pitcher is slippery and lined with downward pointing hairs which prevent the insects from escaping. The liquid below drowns and slowly digests them.

Pitcher plant

Pitcher is made of leaves joined at the edges.

Venus flytrap
The most spectacular of the carnivorous plants is the Venus flytrap. It is related to the sundews but has evolved a more elaborate trap. The Venus flytrap grows wild only in one small patch of marshy ground on the border of North and South Carolina, US. Its trap springs closed when an insect touches the hairs on its surface.

Butterworts
These small plants have sticky leaves. Small flies are attracted to their smell and get stuck. The leaves slowly roll up, and the insects are digested by juices that ooze out of the leaf.

Common butterwort

Leaf

Sundew flowers develop at the end of a long stalk.

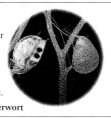

A fly stuck to the hairs on a sundew leaf

Cape sundew

Active traps

Any trap with moving parts is called an active trap. These include plants such as sundews and butterworts, and the Venus flytrap.

Sundews
The upper surface of a sundew leaf is covered with red hairs that secrete drops of clear, sticky liquid. Insects get stuck, then the edges of the leaf slowly roll inward enclosing the insect, and the plant secretes juices that digest it.

Sticky leaf

Bladderworts
These are rootless water plants. Their leaves and stems bear tiny bladders with a lid covered in sensitive hairs. If a creature brushes the hairs, the lid of the bladder flips open. Water rushes in, carrying the victim with it.

Greater bladderwort

Closed trap

Stimulation of at least three trigger hairs sets off the mechanism that closes the trap.

Surface of the trap

Venus flytrap

Magnified view of a trigger hair

How a Venus flytrap works

1 An insect lands on a leaf, touching the sensitive trigger hairs.

Trigger hair

Trap is fringed with long spines.

2 The leaf closes, and the spines interlock, trapping the insect.

3 The trap is fully closed in 30 minutes, and digestion begins.

Insect is trapped in one-fifth of a second.

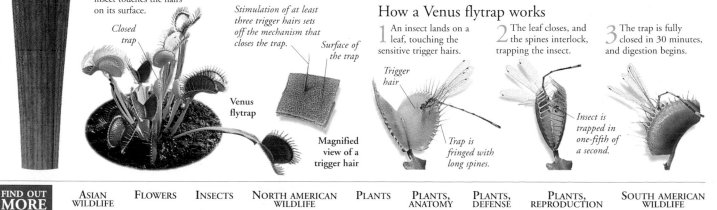

FIND OUT MORE | ASIAN WILDLIFE | FLOWERS | INSECTS | NORTH AMERICAN WILDLIFE | PLANTS | PLANTS, ANATOMY | PLANTS, DEFENSE | PLANTS, REPRODUCTION | SOUTH AMERICAN WILDLIFE

CARS AND TRUCKS

OF ALL THE DIFFERENT FORMS of transportation, cars have the biggest effect on our lives. Cars give people the freedom to go where they like, when they like – with some types of car you don't even need a road. Trucks are used for long-distance haulage and for performing many specialized tasks, such as fire-fighting. In parts of the world where there are no railroads, trucks offer the only way of transporting goods. But cars and trucks create pollution. Because there are now so many of them on the roads, the world's cities have become clogged with traffic, and the air that many of us breathe is poisoned with traffic fumes.

A Benz Motor Wagen of 1886

Early cars

Early cars were called "horseless carriages." They were made by manufacturers of horse-drawn carriages and coaches, and had the same large wheels, high driver's seat, and suspension. They were powered by a single-cylinder gasoline engine, which could reach a top speed of 9 mph (15 kmh).

Modern cars

Efficiency, safety, and comfort are the most important features of a modern car, as well as minimal air pollution from exhaust fumes. To be efficient, cars need engines that use as little fuel as possible, and a streamlined shape to reduce air resistance. In some cars, electronics help efficiency and safety. Modern cars are built with the help of computers and robots in high-tech, automated car plants.

Henry Ford

American engineer Henry Ford (1863–1947) formed the Ford Motor Company in 1903. In 1908 Ford launched the Model T. It was made cheaply on a factory assembly line and sold by the million.

Stiff body is made from thin sheets of steel pressed into shape and welded together. It is chemically treated and painted to protect against rusting.

Windshield of toughened glass protects driver and passengers from wind and rain. If hit by a stone, the windshield cracks but does not shatter.

Side windows can be lowered.

Padded seats

Engine burns fuel and uses the energy stored within the fuel to propel the car along.

Hood is raised to examine engine.

Radiator circulates water around the engine to cool it.

Luggage is stored in trunk.

Rear bumper

Exhaust pipe carries waste gases away from the engine and expels them at the rear of the car.

Hub-cap covers the center of the wheel.

Suspension spring allows the wheel to move up and down as the car travels over bumps in the road, protecting passengers against uncomfortable jolting.

Driveshaft connects the transmission to the rear wheels, which are driven around by the engine.

Transmission contains intermeshing gear wheels which allow the engine to drive the road wheels at different speeds.

Pneumatic (air-filled) tires grip the road and help give a smooth ride.

Front bumper

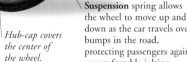

Car has plenty of room for luggage.

Family sedan

Waterproof roof can be folded down in good weather.

Convertible sports car

Minivan/MPV

Three rows of detachable seats

Formula 1 racer

Wing

Driver's cockpit

Types of cars

The most popular car is the sedan, which has an enclosed passenger compartment and a separate rear space for luggage. Hatchbacks are sedans with a large rear door and a folding back seat for extra luggage space.

Sports cars

Sports cars are designed to be stylish, fast, and fun. Some sports cars are convertibles, which have a flexible roof that can be folded down so that passengers can enjoy driving in the open air. Luxury convertibles have roofs that open and close automatically.

Minivan

One of the latest types of car is the minivan, or multi-purpose vehicle (MPV). This vehicle is a cross between a sedan car and a van. People carriers are very versatile, with at least six seats and plenty of space for luggage. They are perfect for outings or vacations.

Racing car

Some cars are custom-built for racing. They have a very powerful engine, wide tires, and a low, wide body for stability around fast corners. An aerodynamic "wing" on the back helps keep the car on the road at high speeds. Sedans can be converted into racing or rallying cars.

Trucks

Trucks are used for carrying cargo along roads. Their journeys can range from a few miles on local deliveries to thousands of miles across continents. The first trucks were built in the 1890s, and were driven by steam engines. Since then, trucks have grown ever larger. In Australia, trucks called road trains tow hundreds of tons of cargo across long distances in several full-sized trailers. Some trucks are "rigid," which means, built in one piece. Articulated trucks are built in two sections: a tractor unit and a semitrailer, which is designed to carry specialized loads. Great skill is required to drive an articulated truck.

Modern trucks

At the heart of most modern trucks is a powerful diesel engine, using diesel oil, a type of gasoline. Some diesel engines are turbocharged for extra power. The engine powers the truck, and operates any hydraulic parts, such as the lifting arms of a dumper. Some trucks, such as military vehicles, have chunky tires and strong suspensions, to enable them to travel off-road in rough terrain.

Some trucks have up to 20 forward and 10 reverse gears.

A tractor unit and semitrailer

Inside a truck cab

Long-distance truck drivers spend many hours in the cabs of their trucks. Cabs are designed for comfort, and some of the controls, such as the steering and brakes, are power-assisted to make them easy to use. Many cabs have a small rear room, with a bunk, washing facilities, and television. To help prevent accidents, some countries have introduced tachometers to record how many hours the truck is on the road. It is illegal for the driver to go beyond a certain number of hours.

Heating controls (temperature selector and fan speed selector) keep cab at a comfortable temperature in hot or cold weather.

Cassette, radio, and **CB** (citizens' band) radio provide entertainment on the road. Drivers may use CB to warn each other of traffic jams.

Adjustable nozzles allow fresh air into the cab.

Warning indicators light up if anything goes wrong with the truck.

Gauges, such as the speedometer, show speed, engine temperature, and the amount of fuel left.

Large diameter steering wheel is easy to turn with power assistance. This is known as power steering.

Gear selector | *Clutch pedal controls gears.* | *Brake pedal* | *Accelerator pedal*

Karl Benz

In 1886, German engineer Karl Benz (1844–1929) patented his first car, using an internal combustion engine. The car had electric ignition, three wheels, differential gears, and was water-cooled. In 1926, his company merged with Daimler to become one of the leading car and truck producers in the world.

Research and development

Modern research aims at improving car economy, safety, and ecology. Because gasoline reserves are limited and its use is environmentally unsound, research is taking place into new fuels from sustainable sources, such as plant oils. Researchers are also experimenting with new materials for car parts, including plastics for car bodies. Car manufacturers are aware that making cars cleaner and safer is likely to improve sales.

Crash test dummy

Catalytic converter

Cars and trucks are gradually becoming "cleaner," which means they create less pollution. Most new cars have a catalytic converter that removes carbon monoxide, nitrogen oxides, and other poisonous chemicals from the exhaust gases.

Catalytic converter from car exhaust

Testing airbag inflation

Safety features

Manufacturers are constantly developing new safety features, such as airbags that inflate automatically in the event of an accident. They are also working on new ways of preventing accidents, such as antilock brakes.

Types of truck

Most trucks start life as a standard chassis and cab. Car manufacturers can then add the body, which determines the function of the truck. Common specialized trucks include garbage trucks, flat trailers to transport large items such as cars, tankers, fire engines, and vehicles modified to carry animals, such as horse trailers.

Garbage truck

This truck has a closed container for garbage and a garbage-can elevator that empties a pail into the body through a protective shield.

Car transporter

A car transporter is used to convey cars to showrooms. There are ramps at the back that fold down at the rear so that the cars can be driven on and off. The trailer of a car transporter can carry up to 18 vehicles.

Storage space above the cab.

Horse trailer

This truck carries horses to shows. The horse enters the truck via a door at the rear that folds down to make a loading ramp.

 FIND OUT MORE   BICYCLES AND MOTORCYCLES   ENGINES AND MOTORS   FORCE AND MOTION   OIL   POLLUTION   ROADS   TRANSPORT HISTORY OF   TRAVEL   UNITED STATES, HISTORY OF

Cars

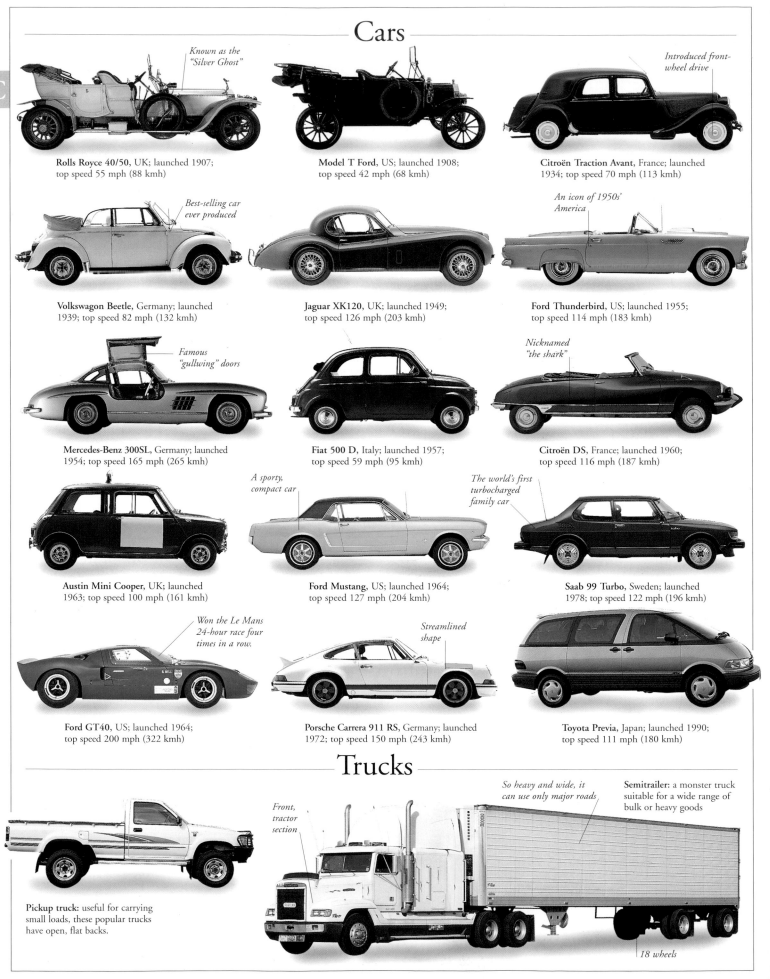

Known as the "Silver Ghost"

Rolls Royce 40/50, UK; launched 1907; top speed 55 mph (88 kmh)

Model T Ford, US; launched 1908; top speed 42 mph (68 kmh)

Introduced front-wheel drive

Citroën Traction Avant, France; launched 1934; top speed 70 mph (113 kmh)

Best-selling car ever produced

Volkswagon Beetle, Germany; launched 1939; top speed 82 mph (132 kmh)

Jaguar XK120, UK; launched 1949; top speed 126 mph (203 kmh)

An icon of 1950s' America

Ford Thunderbird, US; launched 1955; top speed 114 mph (183 kmh)

Famous "gullwing" doors

Mercedes-Benz 300SL, Germany; launched 1954; top speed 165 mph (265 kmh)

Fiat 500 D, Italy; launched 1957; top speed 59 mph (95 kmh)

Nicknamed "the shark"

Citroën DS, France; launched 1960; top speed 116 mph (187 kmh)

A sporty, compact car

Austin Mini Cooper, UK; launched 1963; top speed 100 mph (161 kmh)

Ford Mustang, US; launched 1964; top speed 127 mph (204 kmh)

The world's first turbocharged family car

Saab 99 Turbo, Sweden; launched 1978; top speed 122 mph (196 kmh)

Won the Le Mans 24-hour race four times in a row.

Ford GT40, US; launched 1964; top speed 200 mph (322 kmh)

Streamlined shape

Porsche Carrera 911 RS, Germany; launched 1972; top speed 150 mph (243 kmh)

Toyota Previa, Japan; launched 1990; top speed 111 mph (180 kmh)

Trucks

So heavy and wide, it can use only major roads

Semitrailer: a monster truck suitable for a wide range of bulk or heavy goods

Front, tractor section

Pickup truck: useful for carrying small loads, these popular trucks have open, flat backs.

18 wheels

CARTOONS AND ANIMATION

CARTOONS, OR ANIMATED FILMS, are movies in which drawings or models seem to come to life; the effect is achieved by slight changes to the drawing or model between each frame of film. Animated films first appeared in the 1900s, and the art has developed with motion pictures; today, computer animation is used to create amazing special effects in the movies. Cartoons usually have a comic theme, although animation can also be a thought-provoking medium for a serious message.

Hanna-Barbera
The US animators Bill Hanna (b.1910) and Joe Barbera (b.1911) created many of the most popular TV cartoon characters. Their first film, called *Puss Gets the Boot*, was released in 1940 and starred Tom and Jerry, the cat and mouse rivals. Other Hanna-Barbera characters include Yogi Bear and the Flintstones.

Tom and Jerry

The first drawings are very rough outlines.

More details added

Line tests use no color.

Squirrel features

To make the squirrel jump twice, technicians film the same sequence of cels again.

The animator tries to make the drawing "move" like a real squirrel.

The finished cels are placed in front of a background drawing.

Cel animation

In cel animation, animators produce at least 12 drawings for each second of action. The background, which usually does not move, is drawn on paper. The animator draws the moving characters on layers of cel (clear plastic film), so there is no need to redraw the parts that do not move between frames. The background shows through the clear areas of cel.

Starting off
Simple pencil sketches of each character are first photographed to check that all the movements look natural. An assistant then copies the lines in ink onto layers of cel.

Registration
A registration system is an arrangement of pegs that slot through holes punched in every sheet of cel. The system holds the cels securely so the animator can check how smoothly a character moves by laying cels on top of each other.

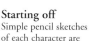

The layers of cels show how far the squirrel has moved.

Coloring in
Once the drawing on the front of a cel is finished, the colors are painted in on the reverse side. The technicians take care not to change the colors between frames. Large amounts of paints are mixed at the same time, so the colors last through the production.

Direct animation
With this method the animator creates characters from clay or other media. The characters are slightly repositioned before the camera between each frame of film, creating the effect of movement.

Clay model

Expression altered between frames

A Close Shave

Other techniques

Traditional cel animation is slow and expensive and can look crude. Many animators explore other methods that may be quicker or produce a more detailed image. For example, sculpting characters in modeling clay or putty allows the animator to reposition them easily.

Computer animation
Animators use computers to draw the images between the start and end of an action, or to improve or alter hand-drawn images, as in *Aladdin* (1992). Computers can now generate an entire film, as in *Toy Story* (1996).

Scene from Aladdin © Disney

Chuck Jones
US animator Chuck Jones (b. 1912) drew the rabbit Bugs Bunny and many other famous characters in Warner Brothers' "Looney Tunes" cartoons. He directed his first animated film in 1938 and has made 300 films since, winning three Academy Awards.

FIND OUT MORE   CAMERAS   DISNEY, WALT   FILMS AND FILMMAKING   NEWSPAPERS AND MAGAZINES   PAINTING AND DRAWING

CASTLES

IN MEDIEVAL EUROPE, castles acted as both home and military stronghold. They were occupied by a lord, his family, servants, and sometimes an army of professional soldiers. They provided refuge for local people in times of war. Local lords could control the surrounding land from their castles, which meant they were a very important part of feudalism. Castles were built to be defended, with walls strong enough to keep out an enemy while allowing the occupants to shoot at any attackers. Designs changed as builders invented better methods of defense, or adapted new ideas from castles in the Islamic world.

The Chapel
Every castle had its own chapel. It was usually in an upper room in one of the towers. This is the chancel of the chapel at Conwy. The altar would have been beneath the windows, and there would have been enough room for everyone in the castle to gather together.

Northwest Tower

Outer Ward

The Great Hall was the center of activity. There was a high table for the lord and lady, and lower tables for everyone else.

The Kitchen was where food for the whole castle was prepared. There were wood fires, oak tables, and alcoves.

The Stockhouse Tower got its name when stocks for prisoners were made here in the 1500s.

The Inner Ward was the last refuge in time of attack.

Machicolations, or overhanging parapets, allowed defenders to pour boiling water on their opponents.

Chapel Tower

The King's Tower
This room on the first floor close to the royal apartments has a stone fireplace and a recessed window. The recess means a person looking out remains safe from any enemy fire. The original floors have been removed.

The Prison Tower had a deep, dark dungeon.

Bakehouse Tower

King's Tower

Conwy Castle, Wales, in the 13th century

The East Barbican was the first line of defense against attack by sea, and was also a good position from which to fire. Defenders could isolate the enemy in this area.

Lookout Tower

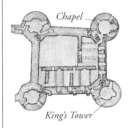

Parts of a castle

Early castles had a keep, which contained the lord's rooms, hall, chapel, storerooms, and a well-defended gatehouse. Later castles abandoned the keep and replaced it with a Great Hall, which was built against the castle walls. The lord's rooms were sometimes built into the gatehouse, but in Conwy they are in the Inner Ward, which was the heart of the castle, and most easily defended.

Chapel

King's Tower

Timeline

1066 The Normans erect wooden motte-and-bailey castles during the conquest of England. These are quick to build, and the motte, or tower on top of a mound, is easy to defend. Most buildings are in the bailey, or courtyard.

Krak des Chevaliers, Syria

1142 Krak des Chevaliers in Syria, one of the most easy-to-defend Crusader castles, has concentric stone walls.

1127 Rochester Castle has a great hall, chapel, and storerooms. The entrance is well protected, and defenders can shoot at attackers.

Great Tower, Rochester, England

1150 Many French lords build castles along the Loire River. Examples built (or enlarged) during this period include Loches, Chinon, and Montreuil-Bellay.

1200 The German lords of Liechtenstein build their castle on a high crag for extra defense.

1238 The Muslim rulers of medieval Spain begin the castle-palace of the Alhambra.

1271 Concentric castles, such as Caerphilly, become popular. They have rings of walls and sometimes water defenses (moats).

Caerphilly, Wales

How castles were built

Building a castle required many skilled workers. A master mason drew up plans and supervised the work, and senior masons carried out the building. Carpenters did the woodwork, and metalworkers made hinges and door fasteners. In a large castle, some specialists stayed on permanently to do the maintenance work.

Wood and earthwork

The Normans chose a site where there was a water supply, built a mound and a wooden castle on top, and surrounded the structure with a wooden fence, or palisade. Most were replaced with stone constructions.

Motte-and-bailey

Stonework

Building a stone castle took decades, but the result was a strong castle that would withstand attack well. The important structures, such as the outer walls, mural towers, and keep, were all made of stone. Buildings in the castle courtyard were still made of timber and had thatched roofs.

Windows

Most castle windows were narrow or cross-shaped slits. They usually had a large alcove on the inside of the wall. This alcove allowed an archer to stand aside and avoid missiles while preparing to shoot.

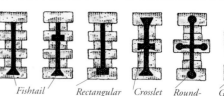
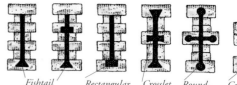

Fishtail bottoms   *Rectangular opening*   *Crosslet*   *Round-ended cross*   *Gun loop*

Arrow slits developed that were large enough for a defender to shoot an arrow out, but too small for an attacker's missiles. Later, the gun loop developed, with a circular hole to fit a gun barrel.

Edward I

In the early years of his reign, Edward I (r.1272–1307) conquered Wales and built an "iron ring" of castles in strategic Welsh towns to keep the country under his control. Many of these Welsh castles, such as Harlech and Beaumaris, were built on the concentric plan, which meant they had both inner and outer walls for defense. Concentric castles were very difficult to attack successfully.

Attack and defense

Attackers could fire arrows, hurl missiles using catapults, break down doors or walls with battering rams, climb the walls using ladders, or try to demolish the walls by tunneling under them (mining). In addition to defense features, such as thick walls and doors, moats, and machicolations, a castle also needed plenty of storage space for food so that the stronghold could withstand a long siege.

Sling pouch   *Arm*   *Rope to pull arm down again*

Ropes to pull arm down   *Wooden cup for missile*   *Handle to turn ropes*   *Throwing arm*   *Hauling rope*

Crossbow

Crossbows were powerful but slow to reload. Despite this they could be useful in defending castles, where they could be reloaded behind the safety of the stone walls.

Catapult

The soldiers used a handle attached to a rope (made from a skein of twisted rope) to pull the throwing arm down. They then released it, and the arm flew up, releasing its missile, usually a rock, from a wooden cup.

Traction trebuchet

This siege engine was like a giant catapult. When soldiers pulled down on the ropes, the end of the arm flew upward, and the sling opened to release a missile, which usually weighed about 100–200 lb (45–90 kg).

Asian and African castles

Castles have been built in many different places. There was a strong tradition of castle-building in the Islamic world, and medieval soldiers took Muslim ideas about fortification to western Europe when they returned from the Crusades.

Himeji Castle, Japan

Seventeenth-century Japan had a feudal system similar to that of medieval Europe, and Japanese lords also lived in castles. Tall towers with pagodalike roofs had narrow window openings through which soldiers could shoot. The towers were surrounded by courtyards and walls.

Fasilidas Castle, Ethiopia

The central stronghold shows many features in common with western castles,

including thick walls of stone, round corner towers, and battlements. The remains of the outer curtain wall can be seen in the foreground to the right.

Van Castle, Turkey

Built on a rocky outcrop, Van Castle was begun in 750. It was later enlarged, and was occupied by the Seljuk and Ottoman Turks before being taken over by Armenian Christians.

Pfalzgrafenstein, Germany

1338 Many German castles are built on the Rhine because of the river's importance as a trade route.

Bodiam, England

1385 Bodiam Castle has a curtain wall around a court-yard, which contains the hall and chapel.

Real de Manzanares, Spain

1416 By this time many French castles, such as Saumur on the Loire River, have conical towers, strong defensive walls, and luxurious rooms.

1435 The elaborate Real de Manzanares is built.

1642 In Traquair, a Scottish tower-house, turrets, and battlements are more for decoration than defense.

Traquair House, Scotland

1600s Many castles were built by local lords in Japan, like Himeji.

FIND OUT MORE   ARCHITECTURE   EUROPE, HISTORY OF   FEUDALISM   MEDIEVAL EUROPE   NORMANS

CATS

DOMESTIC CATS are related to wild cats such as lions and tigers, and they are able to fend well for themselves. They are excellent hunters and their eyes, ears, nose, and whiskers are well adapted to their natural preference for hunting at night. Cats are affectionate and respond well to humans. They were domesticated about 4,000 years ago to keep people company and to kill pests.

Kittens

Cats have an average of four or five kittens in a litter. Kittens love to stalk, chase, and pounce on things. This playful behavior helps make them strong and develops the skills they will need as adults.

Domestic cats

There are more than 100 recognized breeds of domestic cats. They are distinguished mainly by their body shape. People started to breed cats for their looks between 100 and 150 years ago.

White | Lilac | Red | Blue | Chocolate

Fur

Cats can be divided into long- and shorthaired breeds. The texture of their fur varies. Common coat colors are gray-blue, black, brown, white, red, and mixtures of these, such as silver and lilac.

Siamese | British shorthair | Persian longhair | Devon Rex

Head shapes

Cat head shapes range from large and round, like that of the British shorthair, to wedge-shaped, like that of the Siamese. Some breeds have special characteristics. The Scottish fold has ear tips that bend forward.

Games enable kittens to practice hunting skills, such as stalking and catching.

Loose-fitting skin gives freedom of movement.

Flexible spine allows the cat to twist its body.

1 If a cat suddenly falls, balance organs in its ears tell it which way is up.

Balance

A cat's long, flexible tail helps it balance. Cats will almost always land on their feet, even when falling from a great height. They have very quick reflexes and can twist and turn their body the right way up in a fraction of a second.

Grooming

Cats are very clean animals and spend at least an hour a day grooming, using their tongue as a "comb." The tongue has tiny hard spines called papillae on its surface. The licking helps keep the fur clean and waterproof, and also spreads the cat's scent all over its body.

Papillae

2 The cat turns its head around first so that it can see where it is falling, and where it is going to land.

3 Then the cat turns the rest of its body. By the time it reaches the ground, it will land on its feet.

Back paws are brought forward.

Senses

Cats can see well in low light and can focus on small objects at a distance. Their super-sensitive hearing picks up sounds that we cannot hear and can also take in two sounds at once, such as a mouse in a thunderstorm. Whiskers are sensitive to touch. Cats use them to feel their way in the dark and to measure whether spaces are wide enough for them to fit through.

Ears are funnel-shaped to draw sounds inside the ear.

Long, flexible ears can turn toward sounds.

4 The cat stretches out its front legs to absorb the impact of landing.

Cats rely more on eyesight than smell when hunting. They have the largest eyes in relation to their size of any animal.

Cats use their sense of smell to identify objects, other cats and animals, and food.

Sense of taste is important for distinguishing any food that may be harmful.

Claws

Cats use their claws to defend themselves and to climb. At other times, the claws are drawn in, or retracted, for protection. They are covered by a bony sheath that is an extension of the last bone of each toe and fit inside pockets in the skin.

Changing pupils

A cat's pupils expand enormously in the dark to let in as much light as possible. A layer of cells at the back of the eyes called the tapetum reflects light back into the eye and helps cats see in the dark.

Narrow pupils in the light

Large pupils in the dark

FIND OUT MORE | ANIMAL BEHAVIOR | EYES AND VISION | LIONS AND OTHER WILDCATS | MAMMALS | MOUNTAIN WILDLIFE

Cats

Longhaired

Turkish van (auburn) has a chalky white coat.

Persian longhair (blue) has a short, bushy tail.

Birman (seal tabby point) has pure white paws.

M-shaped tabby marking

Somali (sorrel) was bred from the Abyssinian.

Matching mittens

Ragdoll (blue mitted) goes limp when it is stroked.

Tufted ears

Turkish angora (blue-cream) has fine, silky fur.

Long, silky fur

Flattish, round face

Balinese (blue tabby point) has a long, well-plumed tail.

Javanese (cinnamon) is graceful and lithe – a typical Oriental cat.

Longer fur forms a ruff.

Somali (silver) has ticking (bands of color) on each hair.

Maine coon (brown classic tabby) is a large, hardy cat.

Color pointed longhair (chocolate point) has thick fur.

Shorthaired

Crimped coarse fur feels like lamb's wool.

American wirehair (brown mackerel tabby) is active.

Burmese (chocolate) has glossy fur with a satin feel.

Ears are folded forward and downward.

Scottish fold (tortie and white) has folded ears.

Massive round head on a thick neck

Exotic (blue) is playful and affectionate.

Thick undercoat with longer top coat

Manx (red classic tabby) is bred to have no tail.

Widely spaced ears with rounded tips

American shorthair (silver classic tabby) has thick fur.

Muscular body

Korat (blue) is a playful cat. It has close-lying fur.

4-in (10 cm) long inflexible tail

Japanese bobtail (red and white) is usually patterned.

Dorsal stripe

Egyptian mau (silver) has a spotted coat.

Color gets darker with age.

Siamese (seal point) has an angular face and large ears.

California spangled (gold) has well-defined spots.

Small rounded ears and rounded head

Color pointed British shorthair (cream point).

Oriental shorthair (foreign red) is a sleek, slender cat with fine, glossy fur.

British shorthair (chocolate) has a solid build with a round face and short nose.

Flat skull and large ears

Cornish rex (cinnamon silver) has a short wavy coat, patterned over the whole body.

Chartreux (blue-gray) is an old French breed. All Chartreux are this color.

Tonkinese (cream) is a Burmese and Siamese cross. It is active and affectionate.

Large, pricked ears

Abyssinian (usual) is an elegant cat and looks like the cats of ancient Egypt.

Coat has a silvery sheen.

Russian shorthair (blue) has a graceful, long body with abundant, fine fur.

Oriental shorthair (Havana) was developed from a chocolate point Siamese.

C

185

CAUCASUS REPUBLICS

THE COUNTRIES of Georgia, Armenia, and Azerbaijan lie just within Asia, on a narrow plateau sandwiched between the Greater and Lesser Caucasus Mountains. They are often collectively called Transcaucasia or the Caucasus Republics. To the west of the region lies the Black Sea, and to the east, the landlocked Caspian Sea. All three countries were part of the former Soviet Union and gained their independence in 1991. Since the end of communist rule, growing ethnic and religious tensions have caused civil unrest throughout much of the region.

79°F (26°C)   32°F (0°C)

15 in (375 mm)

Regional climate
The varied landscape of this region gives rise to a wide range of climates. Georgia's Black Sea coast is warm and humid, while Armenia is generally dry with long, cold winters. The lowland areas of Azerbaijan have long, hot summers and cool winters. Winters in the mountains are bitterly cold.

Physical features
Much of the land is mountainous and rugged, with large expanses of semidesert in the Armenian uplands. The Kura is the longest river, flowing 848 miles (1,364 km) from central Georgia, through the fertile lowlands of Azerbaijan, to the Caspian Sea. The low Black Sea coastal area in western Georgia is lush and green. The area suffers earthquakes.

Greater Caucasus Mountains
The Greater Caucasus stretch for about 745 miles (1,200 km) from the Black Sea to the Caspian Sea, effectively separating Europe from Asia. Rich in copper, iron, and lead, the mountains also shelter the Caucasus Republics from the icy winds that blow down from Russia in the north. The highest mountain is Mount El'brus at 18,481 ft (5,633 m), just over the Russian border.

Ararat Plains
Most of Armenia is a high plateau with large expanses of semidesert. In the southwest, the land drops toward the Aras River, which forms the border with Turkey and drains most of Armenia. Known as the Ararat Plains, this fertile, sheltered strip is used for growing vegetables and vines.

Lake Sevan
Once valued for its pure waters and stunning setting, Armenia's Lake Sevan is at the center of an ecological crisis. Tragically, irrigation and hydroelectric projects begun in the 1970s have caused the water level to drop by up to 53 ft (16 m).

People
More than 50 ethnic groups live in the Caucasus Republics. Most people speak the first language of their country but retain their local customs and culture. Communist efforts to end ethnic differences failed, and racial tension is a major problem in the region.

Refugees of the war over Nagorno-Karabakh

Georgia

Georgia is the westernmost of the three republics. About 70 percent of the people are ethnic Georgians, most of whom belong to the Christian Georgian Orthodox Church. In recent years, the economy has suffered as a result of civil wars and ethnic disputes in the regions of Abkhazia and South Ossetia, which are trying to break away. War has damaged the Black Sea tourist industry.

Gold threads enhance bright patterns.

Textiles
Georgia produces fine silk cloth and grows mulberry bushes, used to feed silkworms. Bright cotton fabrics are used to make the scarves worn by Georgian women.

GEORGIA FACTS

CAPITAL CITY	Tbilisi
AREA	26,911 sq miles (69,700 sq km)
POPULATION	5,478,000
MAIN LANGUAGE	Georgian
MAJOR RELIGION	Christian
CURRENCY	Lari

People
More Georgians claim to live for over 100 years than any other nationality in the world. Contributing factors are thought to be a healthy diet, regular exercise, a clean environment – and a genetic predisposition to longevity. Claims for ages over 120 have not yet been proved.

Tbilisi
Situated on the banks of the Kura River, Tbilisi, Georgia's capital since the 5th century, is a multicultural city of 1,200,000. Home to most of Georgia's Armenian minority, it has places of worship for many religions.

Tea and wine
More than 90 percent of the tea sold in Russia is grown in Georgia, which produces about 250,000 tons each year. Georgia also has extensive vineyards and produces excellent red wines.

Armenia

Landlocked and isolated from its neighbors, Armenia is the smallest of the Caucasus Republics. The only way out of the country is by difficult road and rail routes over the mountains to Georgia. The people, mostly ethnic Armenians, speak a unique language. The country exports fruit, brandy, and minerals such as copper.

ARMENIA FACTS

CAPITAL CITY	Yerevan
AREA	11,197 sq miles (29,000 sq km)
POPULATION	3,816,000
MAIN LANGUAGE	Armenian
MAJOR RELIGION	Christian
CURRENCY	Dram

Cubes of meat are separated by peppers and onions for flavor.

Metal skewer allows cooking meat to be turned.

Food
Lamb is the main meat, often served as kabobs, with a variety of vegetables. Cooks use pine nuts and almonds for flavoring. Local cheeses and rich desserts are specialties.

Yerevan
Armenia's capital, Yerevan, is also its largest city. Situated on the Razdan River, it is a major cultural and industrial center. Market traders sell fruit, vegetables, and rich, colorful rugs woven locally from silk and wool.

Farming
Agriculture, mainly in the Aras River valley, employs 30 percent of the work-force and is the country's main source of wealth. Crops include grains and fruit such as apricots, grapes, olives, and peaches.

Azerbaijan

The largest of the Caucasus Republics, Azerbaijan also has the most extensive area of farmland. More than four-fifths of the population are Muslims. Most other people are Christian Armenian and Russian. Naẓçivan, a separate part of Azerbaijan, lies within Armenian territory.

Oil industry
Natural gas and oil are extracted from the Caspian Sea. Pipelines link Baku, which is the center of the industry, with Iran, Russia, Kazakhstan, and Turkmenistan. Other oil-related industries include the production of chemicals and oil-drilling equipment.

AZERBAIJAN FACTS

CAPITAL CITY	Baku
AREA	33,436 sq miles (86,600 sq km)
POPULATION	7,507,000
MAIN LANGUAGE	Azerbaijani
MAJOR RELIGION	Muslim
CURRENCY	Manat

Territorial conflict
Nagorno-Karabakh, an enclave in southern Azerbaijan, has been the subject of armed conflict with Armenia since 1988. Most of the people here are Armenians, and Armenia claims the territory. A ceasefire was negotiated in 1994, but the dispute continued.

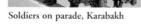

Soldiers on parade, Karabakh

People
Communal drinking of hot, sweet tea from tiny glasses is a typically male ceremony. As in neighboring Georgia, the Azerbaijanis have a reputation for longevity, and it is not uncommon for people to continue working into their eighties.

FIND OUT MORE   ASIA, HISTORY OF   CHRISTIANITY   ENERGY   FARMING   ISLAM   MOUNTAINS AND VALLEYS   OIL   SOVIET UNION   TEXTILES AND WEAVING   TRADE AND INDUSTRY

CAVES

BENEATH THE GROUND, there is a network of large holes, or caves. Caves are naturally occurring chambers formed out of rock. There are many different cave types, some housing hidden lakes and waterfalls; caverns are extensive networks of giant caves. Some caves are no bigger than a closet, but others are huge. The Sarawak Chamber in Malaysia is 2,296 ft (700 m) long and 164 ft (50 m) high; the world's biggest sports stadium, the Louisiana Superdome, could fit into it three times over. Damp and dark, caves have distinctive features, such as stalactites and stalagmites.

Types of caves

The biggest and most common cave systems are found in carbonate rocks such as dolomite and limestone, but small caves form in all kinds of rock. Caves are found in many terrains, from the sea to glaciers, and can have different formations.

Sea cave
Small caves form in sea cliffs; waves force water into cracks, blasting the rock apart. The hole may emerge as a blow-hole on the cliff-top.

Fissure cave
The movement and force of an earthquake can create deep fissures, long, narrow openings, and caves.

Ice cave
Greeny-blue tunnel caves form under glaciers after spring meltwater carves out passages under the ice.

Lava cave
Tunnellike caves form in lava – surface layers harden, and molten lava flows underneath.

Limestone cave
Most caves form in limestone. This rock has many joints and its calcium content is vulnerable to the acid in rainwater.

How a cave forms

Most of the world's biggest caves are formed by water trickling down through soluble rocks such as limestone. The water widens joints or cracks by dissolving the rock. Rainwater is dilute carbonic acid, and wears away the rock, creating a cave.

Stream emerges over waterfall

Sinkhole – point at which a stream disappears

Sparse vegetation

Ridges and grooves in the limestone surface are called clints and grykes.

Water seeps through rock joints; rock forms cracks that widen into potholes.

Icicle-like stalactites hang from the roof or walls.

Underground lake

Steep channel carved by stream

Later passage eroded by stream

Stalagmites grow up from cave floor.

Stream exits via cave mouth and flows along the valley bottom.

Groundwater fills a previously dry cavern to the level of the water table, which can rise and fall over time.

Cave features

Formed over thousands of years, stalactites and stalagmites are found in caves. Droplets of water partially evaporate to form calcium deposits (calcite); drips create hanging stalactites on the roof, and upright stalagmites where they fall to the floor. Spiraling drips form twisted helictites. Flowstone is solidified calcite on the cave floor or walls.

Merged stalactites

Stalactite

Stalactite with ring marks

Curtain stalactite

Stalagmite

Stalagmites and stalactites
Stalactites can form in different ways – a long, thin curtain stalactite is formed when water runs along the cave roof. When stalactites and stalagmites meet in the middle, they form a column. The biggest stalactite, 33 ft (10 m) long, is in Pruta do Janelão, Minas Gerais, Brazil; the biggest stalagmite is over 105 ft (32 m) tall in the Krasnohorska Cave in Slovakia.

Spelunking

Spelunks are the vertical pipes that lead down to many extensive cave networks. Today, spelunking is a popular but dangerous sport. Exploring and discovering caves can unearth historic treasures. The caves at Lascaux, France, for instance, which contain a wealth of prehistoric wall paintings and tools were discovered by spelunkers.

FIND OUT MORE   CAVE WILDLIFE   COAST   EARTHQUAKES   FOSSILS   PREHISTORIC PEOPLE   ROCKS AND MINERALS   SPORTS

CAVE WILDLIFE

A DEEP CAVE is a world of its own, with conditions far removed from those outside. Deep inside a cave there is no light. No day and night pass, and the temperature hardly changes with the seasons. Without light, plants cannot grow, yet animal life can exist in the dark. Some animals enter caves for shelter or to hunt for prey; others spend their entire lives in this environment and have adapted to moving around and sensing food in the dark.

Caves

Caves occur in sea cliffs, around volcanoes, and under glaciers, but the most spectacular are those formed when rainwater hollows out fissures in limestone rock. Limestone caves contain various habitats for wildlife, including narrow tunnels, chambers, streams, pools, and the partly lit entrance. Some caves, especially those in the tropics, are teeming with life. Bat colonies live in the roof, and an army of invertebrates consumes their droppings on the floor below.

Limestone cave

Plants

No plants can grow deep in a cave because there is no light. But the cave entrance is often framed by plants – such as liverworts, mosses, ferns, and algae – that have adapted to damp, shady conditions. Many plants grow without soil, sending out small roots that grip the bare rock.

Moss

Fern

Invertebrates

Caves are often full of invertebrate life. Beetles, spiders, snails, worms, and crayfish survive in large numbers in caves. They feed on debris brought in by running water or dropped by animals that feed outside.

Touch-sensitive spikes

Long antennae

Cave cricket

Scavenging cave crickets use their long, wiry antennae to feel their way past objects in the dark and toward food on the cave floor. Alert for the merest brush against them, they try to out-maneuver prey such as cave centipedes. Cave crickets, like cockroaches and other invertebrates, feed on debris dropped by bats and cave birds. They also eat the fallen carcasses of these animals when they die.

New Zealand glowworm

These glowworms are gnat larvae that live at the entrances to caves. They have evolved an ingenious method of catching food. The larvae spin dangling sticky threads that they illuminate with a light produced from their own bodies. In the darkness of a cave, the glowing threads lure and then snare small flying insects that the larvae haul up and devour.

Larvae hauling up an insect.

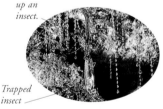

Trapped insect

Eyes

Transparent legs

Cave crab

Tropical caves are often home to some small species of crab that use their pincers to pick food debris from underground streams or the cave floor. Like many cave dwellers – among them millipedes, spiders, salamanders, and shrimps – cave crabs have lost their pigmentation and are almost colorless. Some animals also lose their sight because of the lack of natural light.

Birds

Some birds, such as barn owls and swifts, make nests inside caves. The oilbird of South America nests deep within caves and uses rapid tongue clicks to navigate by echolocation. Colonies of oilbirds fly outside the cave at night to feed on fruit in the surrounding forests. The birds' droppings litter the cave floor below the birds' roosting ledges, and bring nutrients into the cave from far and wide.

Oilbird

Mammals

Some mammals make temporary or permanent homes in caves. The American black bear sometimes takes shelter in caves during the winter months, as do some foxes. Many species of bats roost, rear their young, or hibernate in the security of caves, some forming colonies of thousands. Hanging from the roof by their hind feet, the bats are out of reach of almost all predators.

Lesser horseshoe bat

The lesser horseshoe bat is found in large numbers in caves all over Europe, Asia, and northern Africa, where it hibernates during the winter months. Like other bats, it navigates in the dark by using echolocation. It emits high-pitched calls and listens for echoes that bounce back from the cave walls, stalactites, and other obstructions.

Wings made of elastic skin supported by bones.

Fish

A number of fish species have adapted to living in subterranean streams that flow inside cave systems throughout the world. Most are sightless, with only remnants of eyes underneath their lids, because nothing can be seen underground.

Blind cave characin

Sightless cave animals compensate for their lack of vision with a highly refined sense of touch. Most fish have a lateral line along their sides – a row of sense organs containing nerve endings. The blind cave characin of Mexico has a very prominent lateral line with which it can sense vibrations from passing prey.

Row of dark scales is the lateral line.

FIND OUT MORE   BATS   BIRDS   CAVES   CRABS AND OTHER CRUSTACEANS   FERNS   FLIES   FISH   GRASSHOPPERS AND CRICKETS   HIBERNATION   MOSSES AND LIVERWORTS

CELLS

ALL LIVING ORGANISMS are made of self-contained units of life called cells. Some, such as the amoeba, consist of a single cell, while others, such as humans, are made up of billions of cells. Each cell has a nucleus, which contains the genetic material DNA; DNA provides the instructions the cell needs to maintain itself. Surrounding the nucleus is the cytoplasm, which contains the matter that makes the cell function. Forming a layer around the cytoplasm is the cell membrane which forms the cell's boundary.

Specialized cells

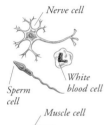

Nerve cell

Sperm cell

White blood cell

Muscle cell

Most plants and animals consist of many cell types, each specialized to perform a specific task. Neurones are long cells that carry nerve impulses around an animal's body; guard cells are rigid box-like structures filled with fluid. They open and close pores on the surface of plant leaves.

Palisade mesophyll cell

These cells are found in the upper layer of the middle part, or mesophyll, of plant leaves. They are packed with chloroplasts, which contain the green pigment chlorophyll which harnesses the energy in sunlight.

Palisade mesophyll cell

Liver cells

The human liver has over 500 functions related to controlling the chemical balance of the body. These functions are carried out by cells called hepatocytes. For instance, some liver cells remove poisons from blood.

Liver cell

Abnormal cells

When cells divide inside an organism they do so in a controlled way. Sometimes, cells become abnormal and start dividing uncontrollably, leading to the production of growths called tumors. The presence of these abnormal cells and tumors causes a number of different forms of a disease called cancer.

Cancer tumor cell (yellow) being attacked by a T-lymphocyte cell (green).

Marie François Bichat

French pathologist Marie François Bichat (1771–1802) showed that an organ, whether a leaf of a plant or a kidney of an animal, is made of different groups of cells. He called each group a tissue, and showed that the same tissues could appear in different organs. His research formed the basis of histology – the study of organs and tissues.

Cell structure

Most cells have similar structures. They consist of a fluid called cytoplasm, a surrounding cell membrane, and a nucleus. Cytoplasm contains structures known as organelles. Plant cells, unlike animal cells, have a tough outer wall and chloroplasts.

Model of an animal cell

Endoplasmic reticulum is a maze-like network of membranes that make and store chemicals.

Golgi apparatus sorts and stores proteins.

Nucleus is the cell's control center.

Vacuole is a small and temporary space where food and waste is stored.

Glycogen granules are food reserves or insoluble waste.

Pinocyte allows substances to filter in and out of cell.

Plasma membrane is the thin flexible layer surrounding the cytoplasm.

Mitochondrion generates energy from sugars and fatty acids.

Cytoplasm forms the bulk of the cell and gives it its shape.

Organelles are any structures that live in the cytoplasm and control special functions.

Model of a plant cell

Cellulose cell wall is a tough outer jacket mainly made of cellulose.

Plasma membrane is selectively permeable or semipermeable and receives stimuli.

Chloroplast is an organelle present in green plants; it converts light energy into food by photosynthesis.

Nucleolus, centre of nucleus

Cytoplasm

Vacuole is a clear space filled with fluid.

Cell division

Cells reproduce by dividing. During cell division, the nucleus divides first, followed by the cytoplasm. There are two kinds of cell division: mitosis and meiosis. Mitosis produces cells needed for growth and to replace dead cells. Meiosis produces sex cells for reproduction.

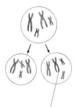

Mitosis

This produces two daughter cells that are identical to the parent cell. The cell's chromosomes (genetic material) make copies of themselves. These separate and move to opposite ends of the cell to form two new nuclei. The cytoplast splits, and two new cells are formed.

Mitosis

Meiosis

This takes place in sex organs and involves two cell divisions. It makes four sex cells that differ from the parent cells because they have half the normal number of chromosomes. These sex cells are called sperm in males and ova in females.

Meiosis

Studying cells

Cells are so small that they must be studied with a microscope. Both the light microscope and the electron microscope have revealed cells' external and internal structure. For this study, cells must be carefully prepared to see their details clearly.

Chemical dyes used for staining cells

Staining cells

When cells are seen under a microscope, they are often transparent, showing little detail. For that reason, they are colored with chemical stains to pick out details such as the nucleus.

FIND OUT MORE   BIOLOGY   GENETICS   HUMAN BODY   MICROSCOPES   MICROSCOPIC LIFE   PHOTOSYNTHESIS   PLANTS, REPRODUCTION   REPRODUCTION

C

CELTS

PROUD WARRIORS AND SKILLED METALWORKERS, the Celts were among Europe's oldest peoples. The first tribes lived in camps in central Europe, but by 400 BC, they also dominated the British Isles, Spain, Italy, and France, and had settled as far as western Asia. Unique and decorative Celtic arts spread, as did their mythology and religion, via trade routes, but the Celts showed no interest in building an empire by unifying all their territories. By 50 BC, the mighty Romans and Germanic peoples had squeezed the Celts into Europe's fringes, where they converted to Christianity. Today, Celtic culture and language survive in Ireland, Scotland, Wales, and parts of France and England.

Celtic world c.200 BC
The first phase of Celtic society probably developed around Hallstatt (now in Austria) between 1200 and 750 BC. From 500 to 50 BC, there was a second phase known as La Tène, after its center in modern France.

Celtic society

Celtic tribes were made up of three main classes: warriors, druids, and farmers. Warfare was an important part of life, so the warriors, armed with their sophisticated iron weaponry, formed an aristocracy. Druids were religious leaders who often held the power of life and death over other tribe members. Farmers, who reared cattle and cultivated crops using iron tools, kept the economy going. Celts lived in fortified camps called hillforts. Though built for defense, hillforts were also places of trade and religious worship – some even grew into towns. Each pagan Celtic tribe had its own king, and maybe even its own gods. Skilled metalworkers probably had high status.

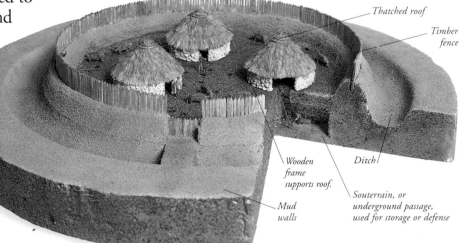

Thatched roof

Timber fence

Wooden frame supports roof.

Ditch

Mud walls

Souterrain, or underground passage, used for storage or defense

Celtic hillfort

Celtic horse
The horse played a major part in early Celtic warfare and religion. A horse-goddess called Peon was worshiped first by the Celts, but then also by cavalrymen in the Roman army. There are several chalk figures cut into the rock in former Celtic areas. Some resemble the horse figures that appear on surviving Celtic coins.

Chalk bedrock

Uffington horse, England

Druids

The druids were holy men in pagan Celtic society. The earliest record of them comes from Julius Caesar, who reported that they acted as judges, led rituals in forest clearings, and used golden sickles to cut mistletoe from sacred oak trees. Druids were skilled in herbalism and kept oral records of their tribe's history. Occasionally, they performed human and animal sacrifices. Those wanting to become druids had to study for up to 20 years.

Oak leaves

Ritual
The druids left no written records, so their rituals are shrouded in mystery. Celts worshiped many gods and spirits, particularly of trees, rocks, and mountains. One of the oldest gods, Cernunnos, is known as the lord of the beasts. He is often portrayed either wearing antlers or with horned animals, such as stags. He is also often shown wearing golden torques, and seems to represent fertility and abundance.

Stags are often shown with Cernunnos.

Horned animals symbolize aggression and vitality.

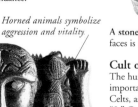

Detail from Gundestrup Cauldron

A stone head with three faces is called a triple head.

Cult of the head
The human head was very important to the pagan Celts, as was the number "3." One custom was to cut the head off a dead enemy, hang it from a horse bridle, then put it on public display. Druids may have believed that a person's soul was in his head, and it had to be defeated, too.

Boudicca
Boudicca (d.61 AD) was queen of the Iceni, one of Britain's Celtic tribes. When the Romans conquered Britain after 43 AD, the Iceni joined forces with them to defeat a rival tribe. However, the Romans then seized Iceni lands and flogged Boudicca. She led a huge revolt, destroying the Roman settlements at St. Albans, Colchester, and London. The Romans finally defeated the rebels, and Queen Boudicca killed herself by taking poison rather than risk being captured.

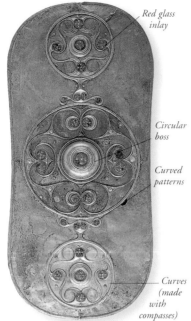

Red glass inlay

Circular boss

Curved patterns

Curves (made with compasses)

Battersea shield

Art and decoration

The Celts were a warlike people, but they were gifted craftworkers and artists, too. Celtic metalworkers excelled at decorative weapons, jewelry, vessels, and mirrors. After the conversion to Christianity, Celtic monks in the British Isles illustrated holy books with great detail. The Lindisfarne Gospels (c.700) feature 45 different colors – all made from finely ground minerals or vegetable dyes.

Battersea shield

Many of the most beautiful bronze Celtic shields were too lightweight to be used in battle and were purely ornamental. The Battersea shield was probably used only for military parades. It was found in the Thames River, London, in 1857.

Torque

According to the ancient Greek writer Strabo, Celts loved to dress in colorful clothes and wear jewelry in gold, silver, or electrum (an alloy of gold and silver): "They wear torques around their necks, and bracelets on their arms and wrists," he wrote. Many gold, bronze, and silver torques have been found in Celtic graves.

Electrum torque

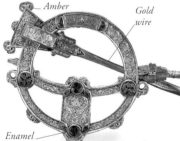

Amber

Gold wire

Enamel

Tara brooch

Tara brooch

Brooches, such as the Tara, date from the 8th century – the early Christian era in Celtic Ireland. Only 3.5 inches (9 cms) in diameter, the Tara brooch is a magnificently detailed piece of jewelry, featuring filigree, gilt chip-carvings, enameled glass, amber, and gold wire.

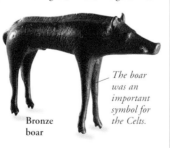

The boar was an important symbol for the Celts.

Bronze boar

Sculpture

Animals and birds often figured in Celtic art and decoration. Certain animals were sacred, such as pigs and boars, which often appear in Celtic legend. The legendary King Arthur himself was known as "the Boar of Cornwall."

Metalworking

As well as sophisticated iron weaponry and farming tools, skilled Celtic metalworkers produced elaborate goods for chieftains and highly decorated items for trade throughout Europe. In Gaul (modern France) the smiths even had their own god – a smith-god known as Sucellos.

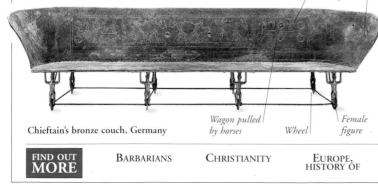

Sword and shield

Swirling abstract pattern

Chieftain's bronze couch, Germany

Wagon pulled by horses

Wheel

Female figure

Celtic cross

Christianity

During the Roman occupation, Christianity came to Britain – but failed to take hold among the people. However, one convert, St. Patrick, converted pagan Celtic Ireland in the 5th century. The Celts then adopted this religion with gusto, and Ireland became a Christian stronghold for the next three centuries.

Monks

Celtic Christianity was famous for the harshness of the monks' lives and the enthusiasm of its devotees. From c.500, monasteries ranged from simple cells for single monks to communities the size of towns.

Early Christian church, Ireland

Missionaries

After Irish Christians set up monasteries in Britain, France, and northern Italy, they started to convert the native peoples. The monks loved learning and helped keep culture alive in Europe during the chaos that followed the decline of the Roman Empire. Irish monks operating from the island of Iona, off western Scotland, produced the beautiful *Book of Kells*, c.800, with its extraordinary illuminated (decorative) lettering.

Monogram page, Gospel of St. Matthew, Book of Kells

XRI is short for "Christ."

Greek letter X

Greek R

Greek I

Myths

The pagan Celts had a rich oral tradition. Their stories included myths about mighty gods, such as the Welsh Bran the Blessed and the Irish Dagda (Father of All); legends about fearless warrior-heroes, such as Cuchulain and King Arthur; and tales of the "shape-changers" – magical creatures from the Underworld. Since the Celts had no written language, monks later wrote down the stories for future generations.

Merlin

The first written legends of the Welsh wizard Merlin said that he was a Celtic boy whose father was the devil. At an early age, he found he could predict the future. In later stories, he appeared as the wizard and mentor of King Arthur of England.

A still from the modern film, *Excalibur*

Languages

Two types of Celtic languages continue to be spoken and written today: Brythonic (Breton, Welsh, Cornish) and Gaelic (Irish, Scots Gaelic, Manx). They may all be traced back to a common, ancient Indo-European language.

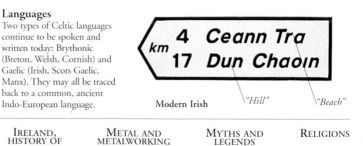

Modern Irish

"Hill"

"Beach"

FIND OUT MORE   BARBARIANS   CHRISTIANITY   EUROPE, HISTORY OF   IRELAND, HISTORY OF   METAL AND METALWORKING   MYTHS AND LEGENDS   RELIGIONS

CENTRAL AMERICA

SEVEN SMALL COUNTRIES make up Central America, a tapering neck of land that connects northern North America to South America. The Pacific Ocean lies to the west, and the Caribbean Sea, an arm of the Atlantic Ocean, lies to the east. The two oceans are connected by the Panama Canal, a shortcut that saves ships months of travel time. The original peoples of Central America were Native Americans, conquered by the Spaniards in the 1500s. Since gaining independence, these countries have had periods of turbulent politics and unstable economies.

Tropical rain forest
The hot, tropical climate and high rainfall of Central America's Caribbean coast supports vast areas of dense rain forest, particularly in Belize and Guatemala, and on Nicaragua's Mosquito Coast. Economic pressure is forcing people to cut and clear parts of the forest for crops.

Physical features

Central America has a backbone of rugged volcanic peaks and massive crater lakes that run from Guatemala down to Costa Rica. The Pacific coast is flat and fertile, and the eastern lowlands, stretching to the Caribbean Sea, are wild, empty swamps and rain forests, with little cultivation.

Sierra Madre
The Sierra Madre is the highland region of Guatemala and El Salvador and is a continuation of the Sierra Madre of Mexico. It includes Tajumulco, an extinct volcano, which, at 13,845 ft (4,220 m), is the highest peak in Central America. Most Guatemalans live in this cooler region.

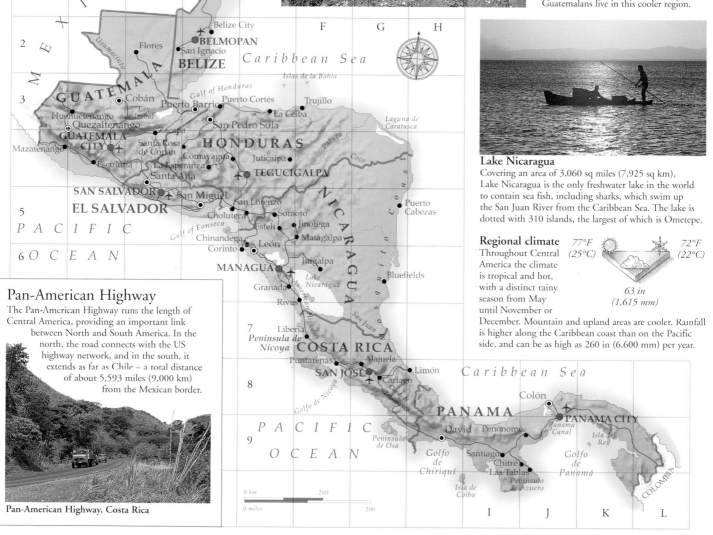

Lake Nicaragua
Covering an area of 3,060 sq miles (7,925 sq km), Lake Nicaragua is the only freshwater lake in the world to contain sea fish, including sharks, which swim up the San Juan River from the Caribbean Sea. The lake is dotted with 310 islands, the largest of which is Ometepe.

Regional climate   77°F (25°C)   72°F (22°C)
Throughout Central America the climate is tropical and hot, with a distinct rainy season from May until November or December. Mountain and upland areas are cooler. Rainfall is higher along the Caribbean coast than on the Pacific side, and can be as high as 260 in (6,600 mm) per year.   63 in (1,615 mm)

Pan-American Highway

The Pan-American Highway runs the length of Central America, providing an important link between North and South America. In the north, the road connects with the US highway network, and in the south, it extends as far as Chile – a total distance of about 5,593 miles (9,000 km) from the Mexican border.

Pan-American Highway, Costa Rica

Guatemala

Once the hub of the Mayan civilization, modern Guatemala is Central America's largest and most populated country and has the biggest manufacturing sector. Guatemalan factories produce foods, textiles, paper, pharmaceuticals, and rubber goods. Plantations in the south grow coffee, bananas, cotton, and sugarcane for export.

Farming

About half of Guatemala's people are of Mayan descent. Most live in the western highlands, growing crops and rearing animals, which they trade at local markets. People from distant hamlets use weekly markets as a chance to socialize and keep abreast of local news.

Tikal

Tourism is a growing industry in Guatemala, and each year about 500,000 people visit the country's Mayan ruins. Tikal, once a great Mayan city, was founded in about 600 BC and flourished until about AD 890, when it was suddenly deserted. The city once had about 40,000 inhabitants.

Honduras

A small, poor country, Honduras has relied for many years on bananas and hardwood timber as its main sources of income. About 40 percent of its people are unemployed. More than half live in small villages, growing just enough food for themselves. Plans are underway to cultivate flowers and new food crops.

People

About 90 percent of Hondurans are *mestizos*, of mixed European and Native American descent. Along the Caribbean coast are settlements of the Garifuna people, descendants of black slaves who swam ashore more than 350 years ago when ships from Nigeria were shipwrecked off the coast.

Bananas

Vast plantations in the northeast produce bananas for export. Bananas bring in 30 percent of the country's export income. Many plantations are owned by wealthy landowners and fruit companies who expect their workers to work long hours on low pay. Coffee is also grown on plantations.

El Salvador

The smallest country in Central America, El Salvador has a rugged landscape that includes more than 20 volcanoes. A thick layer of volcanic ash and lava on the highlands provides ideal conditions for growing coffee. Earthquakes sometimes shake the country. El Salvador is poor as a result of a civil war that raged from 1979–1992.

People

El Salvador is Central America's most densely populated country. There are now about 665 people per sq mile (257 per sq km) and the population is growing at about two-and-a-half percent a year. Almost 90 percent are *mestizos*, and three-quarters are Roman Catholics. More than half are farmers who scrape a living in the highlands.

Deforestation

Today, only about five percent of El Salvador is still forested. Vast tracts of forest, including cedar, oak, and mahogany, have been felled for export and to clear land for farming cash crops such as coffee.

Belize

Most of Belize is dense rain forest; most of its small population lives along the Caribbean coast. The two largest groups are the *mestizos* and Creoles, who also have African blood and are descended from black slaves who were marooned in Belize in the 17th century.

Barrier reef

Protecting Belize's swampy coastal plains from flooding is the world's second largest barrier reef, 190 miles (290 km) long. The reef supports a wide variety of colorful fish.

Belmopan

Belize City, the country's chief port, was the capital for many years. In 1960, a hurricane and tidal wave caused severe damage, so in 1970, a new capital, Belmopan, was built in the center of the country, far from coastal storms. Its population is only 4,000, mostly civil servants.

Nicaragua

Occasionally called the land of lakes and volcanoes, Nicaragua lies at the heart of Central America. Some volcanoes are active, and earthquakes frequently shake the country. In 1978, Nicaragua experienced a violent civil war between the left-wing Sandinista government and right-wing "contras," backed by the US. The war ended in 1990.

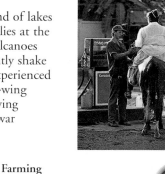

People

Mestizos make up 70 percent of Nicaraguans. The rest are whites or blacks, descended from Africans who were taken to Nicaragua as plantation workers in the 18th century. Three-quarters of the population is below the age of 30. Families are tight-knit and up to three generations may live together.

NICARAGUA FACTS

CAPITAL CITY Managua

AREA 50,193 sq miles (130,000 sq km)

POPULATION 4,100,000

MAIN LANGUAGES Spanish, English Creole, Miskito

MAJOR RELIGION Christian

CURRENCY Córdoba

Delivery of sugarcane

Farming

Agriculture employs about one-quarter of the workforce, growing cotton, coffee, sugar, bananas, and meat for export. The country has also developed related industries, such as sugar refineries and canning factories that process agricultural produce.

Chili pepper

Garlic

Black pepper

Onion

Scallions

Hot chili sauce

Food

Nicaraguans enjoy corn roasted on the cob. Meat and bean dishes are spiced with pepper and garlic and scooped up in thin pancakes called tortillas, made from corn flour. Food is often topped with hot chili sauce.

Costa Rica

Unlike its neighbors, Costa Rica is a stable and peaceful country with a democratically elected government. The army was abolished in 1949. Costa Ricans enjoy excellent schools and hospitals. Most people are *mestizos* of Spanish origin. In the Puerto Limón area on the east coast, one-third are English-speaking blacks, descended from plantation slaves.

COSTA RICA FACTS

CAPITAL CITY San José

AREA 19,730 sq miles (51,100 sq km)

POPULATION 3,300,000

MAIN LANGUAGES Spanish, English Creole, Bribri, Cabecar

MAJOR RELIGION Christian

CURRENCY Colón

Costa Rica has more than 750 species of birds – more than the whole of the US.

Dark-roasted coffee beans have a deep, rich taste.

San José

Founded in 1737, San José became Costa Rica's capital in 1823. With many parks and a mix of traditional and modern Spanish architecture, San José is a commercial center and has food processing factories. It has rail links with Pacific and Caribbean ports and lies on the Pan-American Highway.

Tourism

More than 20 percent of Costa Rica has been set aside to create a network of national parks, including volcanic peaks and undisturbed tropical forest rich in plant and animal species. Many ecotourists are attracted by the country's resident wildlife, such as jaguars, giant sea turtles, crocodiles, and armadillos.

Coffee

Costa Rican coffee is some of the world's finest and fetches a high price. It grows in the rich black volcanic soil near the capital, San José. Costa Rica was the first Central American country to grow the beans. Bananas are the other leading cash crop.

Panama

Occupying the southernmost and narrowest part of Central America, Panama is cut in two by the Panama Canal, which links the Atlantic and Pacific Oceans. A country of swamps, mountains, and grassy plains, Panama has some of Central America's wildest rain forest.

Some 14,000 ships pass through the canal every year, earning Panama valuable toll fees.

PANAMA FACTS

CAPITAL CITY Panama City

AREA 29,761 sq miles (77,080 sq km)

POPULATION 2,600,000

MAIN LANGUAGES Spanish, English Creole, Indian languages

MAJOR RELIGION Christian

CURRENCY Balboa

Financial centers

At opposite ends of the Panama Canal, Colón and Panama City are important business centers, providing banking, financial, and insurance services. A free trade zone in Colón enables goods to be imported and exported duty free.

Panama Canal

Linking the Caribbean Sea with the Pacific Ocean, the Panama Canal was built by the US and opened in 1914. It is more than 40 miles (65 km) long and passes through three sets of locks. The length, which is the distance between deep-water points of entry, is 51 miles (82 km).

Shrimp

Panama has a busy and important fishing fleet. The leading catch is shrimps, which form 11 percent of the country's exports. Anchovetas, small anchovies used for fish meal, make up three percent of exports. Other catches include herring and lobsters.

FIND OUT MORE CENTRAL AMERICA, HISTORY OF   COLUMBUS, CHRISTOPHER   CORAL REEFS   EARTHQUAKES   FARMING   FISHING INDUSTRY   FORESTS   MAYA   NATIVE AMERICANS   PORTS AND WATERWAYS   TRAVEL

CENTRAL AMERICA, HISTORY OF

RICHLY ENDOWED WITH natural resources, Central America has had a violent history, with civil wars, revolutions, and terrible repression. The area was home to the great Mayan civilization, but the Spanish arrived in the 16th century and began to conquer and settle Mexico and the lands to the southeast. As a Spanish colony, the area was called the Captaincy General of Guatemala and had its capital in Guatemala City. After gaining independence in the 1820s, the region split into separate nations ruled by a few rich families. During the 20th century, the United States often intervened in Central American politics with aid and arms.

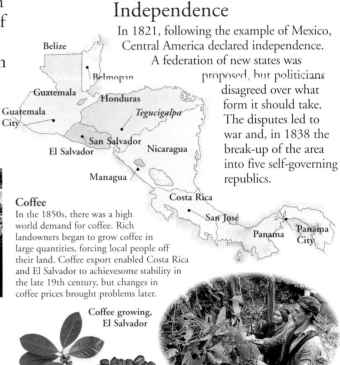

Maya
Mayan civilization was at its peak in the tropical forest lowland area of Guatemala from about AD 250 to 900. Here, the Maya built cities, with steep pyramids. Around AD 900, the Toltecs from the north conquered the Maya. The Maya revived around 1200, but were in decline by the time of the Spanish conquest.

Mayan pottery bowl

Independence
In 1821, following the example of Mexico, Central America declared independence. A federation of new states was proposed, but politicians disagreed over what form it should take. The disputes led to war and, in 1838 the break-up of the area into five self-governing republics.

The Captaincy General
A small group of wealthy Spanish merchants born in Central America dominated the rich trade in indigo dye, and also the political life of the colony. The area was ruled by a Captain General of Guatemala and his council at Guatemala City.

Panama Canal
With military support from the US, Panama separated from Colombia in 1903. US engineers built a great canal linking the Atlantic and the Pacific. The Panama Canal, which runs across the south of the country, opened in 1914. After this, the Panamanian economy came to depend almost entirely on the US.

Coffee
In the 1850s, there was a high world demand for coffee. Rich landowners began to grow coffee in large quantities, forcing local people off their land. Coffee export enabled Costa Rica and El Salvador to achieve some stability in the late 19th century, but changes in coffee prices brought problems later.

Coffee growing, El Salvador

Coffee beans

Modern Central America

Immense differences between rich and poor, combined with the strong economic, political, and cultural influence of the United States, made Central America a turbulent region in the 20th century. Many rulers were dictators and governments changed rapidly, giving little chance of political stability. There were many revolutions, which were often suppressed with huge loss of life.

US intervention
During the twentieth century, the United States was closely involved in the affairs of Central America. In 1909, the US supported a right-wing revolution in Nicaragua, and US marines occupied the country until 1933 when, after a guerrilla war, Augusto Sandino (1895–1934) forced them to withdraw. Later, the US intervened to stop left-wing revolutions and to prevent the spread of communism during the Cold War. More recently, the US supported the Contras (right-wing guerrillas) in Nicaragua and, in 1989, invaded Panama to oust corrupt ruler General Manuel Noriega.

Students in El Salvador erect a statue of Augusto Sandino.

Somoza family
Anastasio Somoza and his sons ruled Nicaragua from 1937–79. The economy grew under their rule, but there was widespread corruption. In 1979, an uprising led by the Sandinistas (a left-wing group named after the former socialist leader Augusto Sandino) ousted the Somozas from power.

Daniel Ortega
Socialist politician Daniel Ortega (b.1945) became the Nicaraguan head of state in 1981 and won free elections in 1984. He failed to free his country from the conflict between the right-wing politicians backed by the US and his own left-wing allies.

Oscar Romero
Archbishop Oscar Romero (1917–80) was head of the Catholic church in El Salvador. His reading of the Bible led him to demand better conditions for the poor. Many Catholics began to get involved in social activism in the 1970s. This annoyed the government, which employed death squads to kill priests. When Romero declared that armed struggle was the only option left, he, too, was shot dead.

FIND OUT MORE   AZTECS   CENTRAL AMERICA   CHRISTIANITY   EXPLORATION   MAYA   RELIGIONS   SOUTH AMERICA, HISTORY OF   SPAIN, HISTORY OF   UNITED STATES, HISTORY OF

CHARLEMAGNE

ON CHRISTMAS DAY, 800, a remarkable emperor was crowned in Europe. His name was Charles, and he was known as Charles the Great, or Charlemagne. He was king of the Franks of northern France and managed to create a large empire after the turmoil that followed the fall of Rome. Under Charlemagne, Europe enjoyed a period of peace and unity it had not had for 400 years. Yet the king was illiterate and brutal, and held his empire together only by force.

Early life
Charlemagne was born in Aachen in what is now Germany in about 742. He was the oldest son of Pepin, king of the Franks, and inherited his kingdom in 768 jointly with his brother, Carloman. When Carloman died in 771, Charlemagne became sole ruler of the Franks.

Carolingian Empire

In order to control his vast territory, Charlemagne installed bishops and counts in each district to run both the religious and the secular affairs of the empire. He supported an educational system based on the monasteries, and introduced a legal system that owed much to the Roman Empire.

The marches
In order to protect his vast empire, Charlemagne established marches, or buffer zones, along the southern border of Muslim Spain and the eastern border of the various Germanic tribes. Troops of armored horsemen patrolled the marches to protect the empire against raids across its lengthy borders.

Extent of the empire
By the time of his death in 814, Charlemagne controlled an empire that stretched from Hamburg in northern Germany to south of Rome, and from the Atlantic Ocean to the Danube River. He converted the warlike Saxons to Christianity, and subdued the Lombard kingdom of northern Italy.

Charlemagne's realm

Frankish lands, 714

Adjoining territories

— Empire of Charlemagne

Charlemagne used cavalrymen to protect the borders of his empire.

Double-edged blade

Socket to attach shaft

Carolingian spearhead

A new Roman emperor

In the 8th century, the Pope's security as head of the Christian church was threatened by the Lombards from northern Italy. In 773, Charlemagne conquered Lombardy. To recognize his support, the Pope gave Charlemagne the title of Emperor of the Romans.

Coin of Charlemagne

Coronation
Charlemagne visited Rome in 800, and Pope Leo III crowned him and paid him homage. For the first time since the Roman Empire, Christian Europe was united, and the idea of a Holy Roman Empire was born.

Dark Ages

For centuries, historians talked of the time after the fall of the Roman Empire as the Dark Ages. But we now know that the period was a time of great achievement in scholarship and the arts. This activity reached its height under Charlemagne.

Aachen
At his capital of Aachen (Aix-la-Chapelle), Charlemagne created a brilliant court where art flourished. He built a vast palace and chapel that some visitors thought of as a "second Rome."

Scholarship
Scholars came from all over Europe to Aachen to work for Charlemagne. They rescued classical Latin learning from oblivion, and ensured that future generations could learn about the Roman Empire.

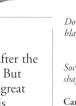

CHARLEMAGNE

c.742 Born in Aachen.

768 Succeeds to Frankish Empire with his brother Carloman.

771 Takes sole control of empire.

772 Begins conquest of Saxony in northern Germany.

773 Subdues Lombards in Italy.

778 Conquers Bavaria in southern Germany.

795 Establishes Spanish march to protect his kingdom from Muslim Spain.

800 Crowned Emperor of the Romans by Pope Leo III.

814 Dies and is buried at Aachen.

 FIND OUT MORE FEUDALISM • FRANCE, HISTORY OF • GERMANY, HISTORY OF • HOLY ROMAN EMPIRE • KNIGHTS AND HERALDRY • ROMAN EMPIRE • SPAIN, HISTORY OF • WRITING

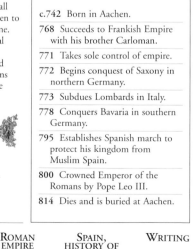

CHAVÍN

FROM THE 10TH to the 1st centuries BC, a brilliant civilization flourished in Peru. It is known today as Chavín, after the important town of Chavín de Huántar in central Peru. Its people produced large temples, fine textiles, and created religious art in a distinctive style. They were also the first people to unify the flat coastal region of Peru with the high Andes Mountains beyond. By doing this, they prepared the way for other important Peruvian civilizations such as the Inca.

Chimú
Huari
Tiahuanaco
Chimú and Huari

Civilizations
Other cultures, such as the Chimú, grew up in the Andes region after the Chavín declined.

Chavín de Huántar

The main city of the Chavín civilization was built at a natural transportation interchange. It lay on the Mosna River next to two passes into the mountains. The city was well placed for trade, with food such as chili and salt coming down to the city through the mountain passes.

Castillo
The people of Chavín de Huántar built stone temples at the center of their city. The famous Old Temple or Castillo was a complex stone structure containing many intricate passages. Some of these were probably drainage ducts, designed to channel away water from the temple. The adjoining rooms may have been storerooms for offerings and religious equipment.

Art

Chavín art was highly elaborate. Chavín artists made carved stone reliefs, statuettes in precious metals, and beautiful textiles, some of which have survived. Their favorite subjects were gods and goddesses, and the priests, birds, and animals that attended them. Many works of art, such as the textiles and gold statuettes, were small and easily portable. They were traded far and wide in South America, and later cultures copied their styles.

God carries shield with cross design in his left hand.

El Lanzón
This was probably the main god of the Old Temple. Its statue is found in one of the innermost rooms in the building. It was a human figure that had catlike teeth, suggesting that it was part-human, part-jaguar, like many ancient gods of South and Central America.

God carries staff in his right hand.

Religion

The Chavín people had several gods, including a creature called El Lanzón, or "the smiling god." His statue was placed in a central room in the temple at Chavín de Huántar. Above the statue was a hole. A hidden person could speak through this hole, giving the impression that the god himself was speaking.

The staff god
Another important Chavín deity is known as the staff god. This figure is shown in carved reliefs waving a long staff. He was often shown with crops such as cassava, gourds, and peppers, and was thought to be the provider and protector of these valuable foodstuffs.

Kennings
Chavín sculptors liked to use the kenning, a type of visual pun, to represent parts of the body. Instead of carving a person's face realistically, they made up their features using repeated elements such as eyes or snakes. Many Chavín carvings, like this stone relief of a god, are therefore intriguing but difficult to understand.

Jaguar vessel

Animal-figure bowl

Pottery vessel
Andean peoples such as the Chavín made highly decorated pottery with tall, curved handles. This example, from Chavín de Huántar, has the face of a jaguar god with a gold nose ornament and large, dangling earrings.

Ornate bowl
This bowl in the shape of an animal is another example of the skill of the Chavín potters' art. It may have been used in a religious ceremony, or adorned the table of a wealthy member of the Chavín nobility.

After the Chavín

Several civilizations dominated the Andes after Chavín declined. Tiahuanaco, another highland culture, and its neighbors the Huari, flourished from AD 500 to 900. On the coast, the Chimú were the dominant people from the 10th to 15th centuries until they were conquered by the Incas.

Vessel from Tiahuanaco

Tiahuanaco
This highland empire was a strong, centralized state based in a city on a high plain some 13,100 ft (4,000 m) above sea level. Its monuments included the Gateway of the Sun, which was carved out of a single block of stone.

Face of Sun god
Carved lintel
Typical square-headed opening

Gateway of the Sun

FIND OUT MORE

GODS AND GODDESSES | INCAS | POTTERY AND CERAMICS | SOUTH AMERICA, HISTORY OF

CHEMISTRY

THERE IS MORE TO CHEMISTRY than experiments in laboratories – doctors use it to fight disease, chefs use it to cook food, and farmers use it to increase the growth of their crops. Chemistry is the branch of science that studies the structure of different elements and compounds. It also investigates how they change and interact with each other during processes called chemical reactions.

Chemical change

When a pile of orange ammonium dichromate crystals is heated by a flame, a chemical reaction occurs. Heat, light, and gases are given off, and a mound of gray-green ash is left behind. The ash not only looks different from the crystals, but it also has a different chemical makeup – it has changed into the substance chromium oxide.

The reaction is so vigorous that a cloud of ash is hurled into the air.

Pile of crystals is lit by a flame.

Ash

Ammonium dichromate crystals

Antoine and Marie Lavoisier

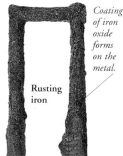

The French chemist Antoine Lavoisier (1743–94) showed that burning is a chemical reaction, that air is a mixture of gases, and that water is a compound of hydrogen and oxygen. His wife, Marie (1758–1836), translated and illustrated many of his scientific works.

$$2H_2 \quad + \quad O_2 \quad \longrightarrow \quad 2H_2O$$

Chemical equations

Scientists write equations to describe what happens during reactions. The equation above shows how hydrogen (H_2) and oxygen (O_2) react in the ratio of 2 to 1 to make water (H_2O).

Rates of reaction

Reactions can be sped up by making the reacting particles come into contact with each other more often. One way of doing this is by increasing a reactant's surface area. Sulfuric acid reacts more rapidly with powdered chalk than with chalk pieces because the powder has more surface area.

There is a gentle fizzing as carbon dioxide gas is given off.

Faster rate of reaction causes reactants to spill out of beaker.

Dilute sulfuric acid on powdered chalk

Dilute sulfuric acid on chalk pieces

Catalysts

Compounds called catalysts speed up a chemical reaction by helping substances react together. The catalysts are left unchanged by the reaction. Many cars are equipped with a catalytic converter to remove polluting gases from engine fumes. The converter forces the gases into close contact with catalysts. The catalysts make the gases react rapidly with each other, producing less harmful gases that escape out of the exhaust.

Chemical reactions

During a chemical reaction, substances called reactants break apart and new substances called products form. Energy is taken in to break the bonds between the reactants' atoms. As the atoms link up again in different combinations to make the products, new bonds form and energy is given out.

Exothermic reactions

In an exothermic reaction such as burning, more energy is given out than is taken in from the surroundings.

Endothermic reactions

Most of the reactions that occur in cooking are endothermic, meaning that more energy is taken in than is given out.

Oxidation and reduction

When iron rusts, a reaction occurs between the iron and oxygen in the air. The iron gains oxygen, and an orange-brown compound called iron oxide forms. A reaction in which a substance gains oxygen is called oxidation. When oxidation occurs, there is a simultaneous reaction called reduction, in which a substance loses oxygen. When iron oxidizes, the air is reduced as it loses oxygen to the iron.

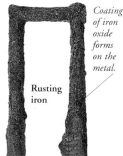

Coating of iron oxide forms on the metal.

Rusting iron

Reversible reactions

Many chemical reactions permanently change the reactants, but reversible reactions can go both forward and backward. For example, when nitrogen dioxide is heated, it breaks down into nitrogen monoxide and oxygen. Cooling this mixture makes the two gases react to form nitrogen dioxide again.

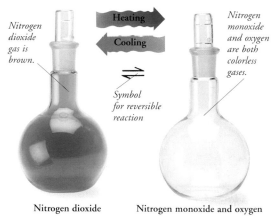

Nitrogen dioxide gas is brown.

Heating

Cooling

Symbol for reversible reaction

Nitrogen monoxide and oxygen are both colorless gases.

Nitrogen dioxide

Nitrogen monoxide and oxygen

Chemical industry

The chemical industry is one of the world's largest and most important industries. It involves taking raw materials – such as air, oil, water, coal, metal ores, limestone, and plants – and using chemical reactions to change them into useful products. These products include food, clothing, medicine, pesticides and fertilizers, paints and dyes, soaps and detergents, plastics, and glassware.

C

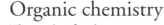

1 A container of whole milk is allowed to stand for a day or so. The curds are removed and then heated.

Organic chemistry

The study of carbon compounds is called organic chemistry, because all living organisms depend on carbon compounds for their existence. Today, chemists can also create synthetic carbon compounds. Natural and synthetic carbon compounds occur in a wide range of materials, such as food, fuel, paint, textiles, and plastics. This experiment shows how paint can be made from casein – an organic compound derived from milk.

Acetic acid

Casein forms in curds.

2 Acetic acid is added to the warm curds. A white, rubbery material called casein forms in the liquid.

3 The casein is removed by straining the liquid, It is kneaded in warm water and then dried.

Casein hardens as it dries.

4 Casein can then be mixed with other materials to form paint. The casein is used to bind the pigment to the surface.

Casein-based paint

Aliphatics

Organic compounds containing a chain of carbon atoms linked by single, double, or triple bonds are called aliphatics. The aliphatic ethane occurs in natural gas, and ethene is used to make plastics.

Ethane (C_2H_6)

Double bond

Single bond

Ethene (C_2H_4)

Aromatics

The strong-smelling organic compounds called aromatics contain a ring of six carbon atoms. Benzene, the simplest aromatic, is a colorless liquid obtained from coal, natural gas, and petroleum. Aromatics are used to make vivid dyes called anilines.

Carbon atoms (black)

Benzene (C_6H_6)

Hydrogen atoms (white)

Fats and oils

Liquid vegetable oil is an unsaturated fat – a type of fat in which some of the carbon atoms are linked by double bonds. When the oil reacts with hydrogen, the double bonds break and the carbon atoms link up with extra hydrogen atoms, forming a solid fat such as margarine. Solid fats contain only single bonds between their carbon atoms. These fats are said to be saturated because they cannot bond with more hydrogen atoms.

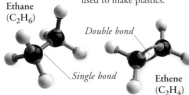

Liquid oil   Solid fat

Polymers

Plastics, such as polythene and PVC, are made up of polymers.

Polymers are giant molecules that consist of winding chains of thousands of small organic molecules called monomers. Fats, starches, and proteins are natural polymers; plastics and artificial fibers are made of synthetic polymers. Polythene contains polymers made of many ethene monomers joined together.

Plastic products

Electrochemistry

The study of the relationship between electricity and chemical substances is called electrochemistry. Many compounds consist of electrically charged particles called ions, which form when atoms lose or gain electrons. A battery uses a chemical reaction to generate an electric current.

Electrons flow toward copper plate.

Simple battery

As the zinc dissolves in the acid, the zinc atoms lose electrons and become ions.

Dilute sulfuric acid

Current lights bulb.

Electrons flow through wire as an electric current.

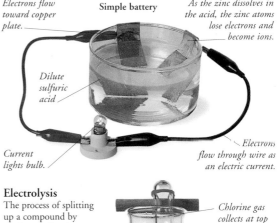

Electrolysis

The process of splitting up a compound by passing an electric current through it is known as electrolysis. Two metal or carbon rods called electrodes are placed in the compound and connected to a battery. As electricity flows through the compound, positive ions are attracted to the negative electrode (the cathode), and negative ions are attracted to the positive electrode (the anode), causing the compound to split.

Chlorine gas collects at top of tube.

Deposits of copper metal form as copper ions move to cathode.

Chlorine ions move to anode and form chlorine gas.

Electrolysis of copper chloride solution

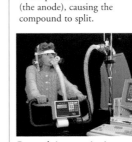

Research into respiration

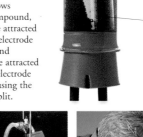

Geochemist examining rocks

Biochemistry

The study of the chemistry of living organisms and the chemical processes, such as respiration, that take place within them is called biochemistry. The discoveries of biochemists are used in industry, medicine, and agriculture.

Geochemistry

The Earth's composition and the chemical structure of rocks are studied in geochemistry. The findings of geochemists give us a greater knowledge of the Earth's history and help us find ores, minerals, and other resources.

Alfred Nobel

The Swedish chemist Alfred Nobel (1833–96) invented the explosives dynamite in 1867 and gelignite in 1875, which made him very rich. On his death, he left his vast wealth to pay for a series of annual awards – the Nobel Prizes – for achievements in science, art, and medicine.

Timeline

2 BC Egyptian alchemists try to change "base" metals such as lead into gold.

1661 Robert Boyle, an Irish scientist, realizes that chemical reactions can be explained by the existence of small particles.

1770s Antoine Lavoisier investigates compounds such as air and water.

1807 Englishman Humphry Davy uses electrolysis to discover the element sodium.

Davy's equipment

1808 English scientist John Dalton proposes that each element has its own unique type of atom.

1830s German chemists focus on studying carbon and its compounds.

1909 American Leo Baekeland makes the first fully synthetic plastic – Bakelite.

1939 Linus Pauling, an American chemist, explains the nature of chemical bonds between atoms and molecules.

Bakelite radio set

FIND OUT MORE   ACIDS AND ALKALIS   ATOMS AND MOLECULES   DYES AND PAINTS   ELECTRICITY   ELEMENTS   GLASS   MEDICINE   MIXTURES AND COMPOUNDS   PLASTICS

CHESS AND OTHER BOARD GAMES

BOTH CHILDREN AND ADULTS enjoy games, whether for the challenge of perfecting a skill, the excitement of competition, or simply for fun. Board games, in which competing players move pieces on a special board following rules agreed in advance, are particularly popular. They have a long history and exist in every culture. They range from demanding games of skill and strategy, such as the ancient game of chess, to more simple games of chance, like snakes and ladders, where a throw of the dice determines the winner.

Strategy games

Games of strategy are challenging, for superior skill, concentration, and tactics decide the winner. Chance plays no part. In most strategy games two players aim to cross the board, or to encircle or capture their opponent's pieces.

Go
Go, also known as *wei-ch'i*, is at least 4,300 years old. It is extremely popular in China, Japan, and Korea. Players capture areas of the board by surrounding them with their own pieces.

Chess

Chess is a war game. Two players aim to capture, or take, the other's pieces, ultimately trapping the opponent's king. This situation, known as checkmate, occurs when the king cannot be protected by his own pieces, and cannot move without being taken. The word checkmate comes from the Persian *shah-mat* (the king is dead). Chess can be enjoyed at all levels: by beginners, or by grandmasters in international competition.

The board has 64 squares.

Each player starts with 16 pieces.

Illumination from Persian treatise on chess, undated

Kasparov vs. the supercomputer

Computer chess
Computers can be programmed to play chess against humans. In 1997, the chess world was shocked when a supercomputer beat the Russian world champion Gary Kasparov (b.1963) in a match. A vast memory for the tactics of past games gives computers an edge.

History of chess
It is thought that chess originated in China or India more than 1,400 years ago. It spread to North Africa and was introduced to Europe after the Muslim conquest of Spain. Early pieces were based on an Asian army, with elephants, chariots, and foot soldiers.

Pieces
Chess pieces consist of eight pawns, two bishops, knights, and rooks (castles), a king, and a queen. Each piece has its distinctive moves: pawns, for instance, can only move one space forward, while the queen can move in any direction, as far as is needed.

Race games

Many board games are races, in which the winner is the first player to reach a certain part of the board or remove all their pieces. Some race games depend on luck, when a throw of the dice decides how quickly a player moves. This allows players of different ages or levels to compete fairly against each other.

Starting position for mancalah

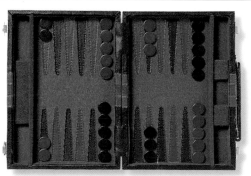

Starting position for backgammon

Men playing pachisi, India

Mancalah
There are many varieties of this ancient game of skill from Africa. Two or more players compete to clear their side of the board. Each takes turns to pick up a pile of pebbles, dropping them one by one in the hollows.

Pachisi
In India, pachisi is called the national game. Four players race counters around a cross-shaped board; they throw dice or shells to see how many spaces to move. Many other games, such as ludo, are based on pachisi.

Backgammon
Invented 5,000 years ago in Asia, backgammon is a fast-paced game for two players. It draws on both skill and chance, and is most popular around the Mediterranean. The first player to remove all his or her "men" from the board wins.

Playing cards
Card games do not need a special board, but must be played on a flat surface. Generally, games are for two or four players. Some games, such as bridge, require concentration and skill, and are played at international competition level; games such as poker, which rely more on luck are often played by gamblers for money.

A pack of cards contains 52 cards divided into four groups known as suits.

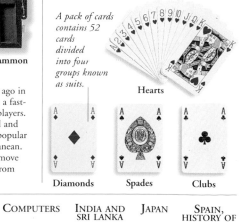

Hearts

Diamonds   Spades   Clubs

FIND OUT MORE   CHINA AND TAIWAN   COMPUTERS   INDIA AND SRI LANKA   JAPAN   SPAIN, HISTORY OF

C

Chess and other board games
Chess pieces

King moves one square at a time in any direction.

Bishop moves diagonally across the board.

Rook travels in straight lines but not diagonally.

Pawn moves forward one square at a time.

Knight can jump over other pieces to new position.

Queen can move in any direction, but cannot jump.

Board games

Game accessories

Checker piece

Pieces move around board collecting pies.

Checkers is a game of skill that was played in Ancient Egypt.

Trivial Pursuit, introduced in 1982, is available in a range of editions.

Players build up words from letter blocks.

Scrabble, originally known as Criss-Cross, is a word game that was devised in 1931.

Scrabble letters

Monopoly, patented in 1935, can be adapted to show streets of any major city in the world.

Players race each other around the board.

Peter Rabbit's Race Game, invented in 1910, is based on characters from Beatrix Potter stories.

Marbles are used as pieces.

Solitare is game of skill that is played by only one person.

Clue (or Cluedo), a detective game played around the world, was created in 1944.

Parcheesi, a game for two to four players, originated from an ancient Indian game called pachisi.

A compendium is a collection of different board games contained in one box.

Snakes and Ladders is a game of chance. Players move their pieces up ladders or down snakes.

CHILDREN'S LITERATURE

WRITTEN LITERATURE has existed for more than 3,000 years, but it is only in the past 300 years that literature has been created especially for children. Before then, children listened to oral fables and folktales. Early children's books were educational, but in the 19th century many new forms, or genres, developed such as adventure and fantasy stories, and picture books.

Finnish

French

German

Japanese

Russian

Swedish

Italian

Iranian

Books

Children's books are produced in more styles, shapes, and sizes than any other form of literature. They range from pop-up books to picture storybooks. Books for younger readers have large type, and use pictures to help explain the story. As readers get older, their books become longer and the stories more complex.

Fables

A short story that illustrates a moral or lesson is called a fable. Fables usually feature animals with human characteristics, such as wisdom or carelessness, and have traditionally been read or told to children in order to encourage good behavior. A fable may, therefore, end with a proverb such as "look before you leap."

Aesop's Fables

The most famous collection of fables are attributed to a Greek called Aesop who is thought to have lived in the 6th century BC. There are many stories about him; he is often described as a slave who gained freedom to become a royal adviser. The stories attributed to Aesop were first passed on orally, and then written down in the 4th century BC.

The *Tortoise and the Hare* is one of Aesop's fables.

Modern fables

Some modern children's stories have been strongly influenced by ancient fables. English author Beatrix Potter (1866–1943) wrote a story about a squirrel called Nutkin whose naughty behavior ended in punishment.

Uncle Remus

The *Uncle Remus* stories by American author Joel Chandler Harris (1848–1908) are fables based on the stories of plantation slaves in the United States. Told in African-American dialect, the tales are narrated by a wise, genial black man to the son of a plantation owner, and feature characters such as the trickster Brer Rabbit.

Brer Rabbit and Brer Fox

James Thurber (1894-1961)

In *Fables for Our Time* (1940), American author James Thurber reworked traditional stories, such as fairy tales, into fables that were relevant to the 20th century. For example, in Thurber's reworking of the tale of *Little Red Riding Hood*, the girl recognizes the wolf and shoots him dead.

Folk- and fairy tales

These are among the most popular types of stories, particularly for young children. All cultures have created their own stories about magical beings and events, and the same folk story may occur in many places. For instance, the tale of an orphaned girl with a wicked stepmother is found in most societies.

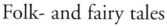

A scene from *Cinderella*, by the London City Ballet

Monkey King

The daring Monkey King is one of the best known folk heroes in Chinese literature. The Chinese writer Wu Cheng'en used many oral folktales as source material in his novel about the Monkey King's adventures, *Journey to the West* (1500s).

Monkey battles with the White-Bone Demon

An illustration from Andersen's *The Snow Queen*

Hans Christian Andersen

Danish writer Hans Christian Andersen (1805–75) was one of the first authors to write new fairy tales. His first collection, *Fairy Tales*, was published in 1835. By the time of his death, he had published more than 160 stories; most of them, such as *The Ugly Duckling*, are still read today.

Charles Perrault

Frenchman Charles Perrault (1628–1703) was the first person to write down oral folktales. His *Tales of Past Times* (1697) included *Cinderella*, but his version was less violent and bloody than the original.

Grimm Brothers

German brothers Jakob (1785–1863) and Wilhelm (1786–1859) Grimm were the editors of *Grimm's Fairy Tales*, which included *Snow White*, and *Hansel and Gretel*. Because of their scholarly approach to collecting folktales from Europe, their versions of these ancient stories are often regarded as definitive.

Wilhelm Grimm   Jakob Grimm

Fantasy stories

Until the mid-19th century, most of the stories written for children were concerned with the teaching of morals and good behavior. However, the enormous success of Hans Christian Andersen's fairy tales encouraged many writers to produce wild fantastic stories that celebrated the imagination above all else.

Alice in Wonderland
Written in 1865, English author Lewis Carroll's (1832–98) fantasy revolutionized children's literature with its fantastic plot, bizarre characters, and absence of any moral. The half-dream, half-nightmare world that Alice encounters when she plunges down the rabbit hole shows the limitless possibilities of the fantasy story.

Tenniel illustration of the Mad Hatter

Peter Pan
English author J. M. Barrie (1860–1937) originally wrote *Peter Pan* as a play in 1904. Peter, a motherless half-magical boy, takes the Darling children to Never Land.

The Wonderful Wizard of Oz
American author L. Frank Baum (1856–1919) wrote this fantasy in 1900. Dorothy is carried by a whirlwind out of Kansas to the magical Land of Oz, where she befriends the Scarecrow, Tin Woodman, and Cowardly Lion. In 1938, it was made into a popular movie, ensuring that people worldwide know the story, even if they have never read the book.

The Hobbit
J. R. R. Tolkien (1892–1973) published the tale of the Hobbit Bilbo Baggins in 1937. The trilogy that followed it, *The Lord of the Rings,* is one of the most popular stories ever published.

Peter Pan

Still from the 1938 film of *The Wizard of Oz*

The Hobbit

Adventure stories

The 19th century saw the beginning of great adventure stories for children. The books celebrated bravery, daring, and excitement, although the heroes were often boys rather than girls. Some books, such as *Treasure Island,* described imaginary lands, while others, such as *Huckleberry Finn,* were about adventures close to home.

Huck and Jim

Treasure Island
Scottish author Robert Louis Stevenson (1850–94) told a story of piracy. The tale is told by Jim Hawkins, who acquires a map showing hidden pirate gold. He has to defeat the pirates before he can claim the treasure.

Huckleberry Finn
American author Mark Twain (1835–1910) set his novel on the banks of the Mississippi River. One of its themes, black slavery, is illustrated by Huck's friendship with the runaway slave Jim.

A scene from the 1950 film of *Treasure Island*

Animal stories

Tales of talking beasts and fabulous creatures have always fascinated children. Many animal stories stress the bond between animals and children. Animals often display unquestioning devotion or instinctive wisdom.

Kes
English author Barry Hines wrote *Kes* in 1967. It tells the story of a boy who is bullied at school, and whose home life is violent and desperate. The boy finds a baby kestrel and teaches it to fly.

School stories

School is part of children's experience, and often features in literature. The first and most famous school story was called *Tom Brown's Schooldays* (1857) by Thomas Hughes (1822–96). It was based on the author's own time at boarding school in England. Today's school stories usually reflect the experiences of most children.

Roald Dahl
British author Roald Dahl (1916–90) is known for his fantasy stories, which include *James and the Giant Peach* (1961) and *Charlie and the Chocolate Factory* (1964). His popularity is partly due to his skill in describing adults' frightening peculiarities in such a way as to make them laughable.

Illustration from *Tom Brown's Schooldays*

Family stories

Children's literature often takes as its theme family life. Stories of family life date back to the 19th century; one of the first was *Little Women* (1869) by Louisa May Alcott. Today's family-based stories look at the difficulties that children may experience, such as divorcing parents, bereavement, or abuse.

Little Women
Louisa May Alcott's (1832–88) novel about life in a small town in New England, was one of the first books that presented children in a realistic fashion. The story of the March family, Meg, Jo, Beth, Amy, and their mother, Marmee, was in part autobiographical. It inspired many other American writers to produce stories about family life. Alcott wrote several sequels to *Little Women* including *Little Men* and *Good Wives.*

A scene from the 1949 movie of *Little Women*

C

Picture books

Children's picture books have a long history; from the *Orbis Pictus* in 1658 there have been picture books for children. Babies and young children can enjoy books in which pictures are just as important as words. The illustrations tell stories and help teach concepts such as colors, shapes, and the names of things. Many talented artists now make books for children.

Visible world

Even the earliest books included illustrations. However, the first picture book that was especially designed for children was called *Orbis Pictus,* or *Visible World* (1658), by John Amos Comenius. It used pictures in order to help the translation of German into Latin.

Merchandising

Successful children's books are now big business. Popular characters soon appear as toys, games, and even ceramics.The image of the characters can be found printed on clothing and books.

Pierre Lapin

Beatrix Potter books are printed in many languages.

Beatrix Potter

The first master of the picture storybook was Beatrix Potter (1866–1943). She was a lonely child who taught herself to draw and became skilled at painting animals. Her first book, *The Tale of Peter Rabbit,* was published in 1901. The books of Beatrix Potter are still popular throughout the world.

Cuddly Peter Rabbit toy

Beatrix Potter merchandise

Teapot

Jug

Mug

Board game

Where the Wild Things Are

When this book was published by the American writer Maurice Sendak (b.1928) in 1963, many people thought it was too scary for children. It tells the story of a boy called Max, who sails away to the land of the Wild Things, where after many adventures, he becomes their king.

Dr. Seuss

The American artist Dr. Seuss (Theodore Geisel 1904–90) created many classic picture books. Stories such as *The 500 Hats of Bartholomew Cubbins* (1938) are built around strange and improbable situations. Dr. Seuss was one of the first authors to make rhyming storybooks that helped teach children to read. In *The Cat in the Hat* (1958), a cat visits two children and creates rhyming chaos while their mother is away.

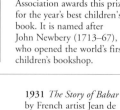

Children's poetry

Verse for children dates back to the songs and ballads of the oral tradition, and children still memorize rhymes and songs and pass them on among themselves. Children's poetry has been written in every style imaginable, from humoros fantasies and nonsense limericks to powerful social commentary.

Nursery rhymes

Spoken rhymes are found all over the world, and many are ancient. Little Bo Peep is linked to a hide-and-seek game called Bo-Pepe, which is more than 600 years old. Around the Rosey describes the symptoms of the plague, which left rose-like marks on its victims.

Limericks

The English artist Edward Lear (1812–88) wrote many nonsense rhymes. His limericks generally involve all sorts of people in very odd situations.

"There was an old man of Whitehaven, who danced a quadrille with a raven."

Prizes

Today, more children's books are being published than ever before. To encourage good writing and illustration, prizes are awarded for the best books. There are awards for everything from teenage fiction to picture books. Some prizes are nominated by children.

Newbery Medal

The American Library Association awards this prize for the year's best children's book. It is named after John Newbery (1713–67), who opened the world's first children's bookshop.

Carnegie Medal

This prize has been awarded by the British Library Association since 1936. It takes its name from American millionaire Andrew Carnegie (1835–1919), who founded libraries in Britain and the US.

Timeline

15th century Chapbooks (crime and miracle stories) published. Courtesy books tell children how to behave.

1745 John Newbery sells *Little Goody Two-Shoes* in the first children's bookshop.

Little Goody Two-shoes

1877 English author Anna Sewell publishes *Black Beauty.*

1883 *Pinochio* by Italian author Carlo Collodi (1826–90) published.

1894 *The Jungle Book* by Rudyard Kipling (1865–1936) published.

1908 Kenneth Grahame (1859–1932) publishes *The Wind in the Willows.*

1922 The first Newbery Medal for children's literature awarded.

1926 *Winnie-the-Pooh* by A. A. Milne (1882–1956) published.

1929 *Emil and the Detectives* by German author Eric Kästner (1899–1974) published.

1931 *The Story of Babar* by French artist Jean de Brunhoff published.

1952 E. B. White (1899–1985) publishes *Charlotte's Web.*

1968 *The Pigman* by Paul Zindel (b.1936) published.

1975 *Forever,* one of the first books for young adults, by American author Judy Blume (b.1938) published.

1977 *Fungus the Bogeyman* by Raymond Briggs (b.1934) published.

FIND OUT MORE   BOOKS   DRAMA   EDUCATION   LITERATURE   MYTHS AND LEGENDS   POETRY   PRINTING   WRITING

CHINA AND TAIWAN

THE WORLD'S THIRD LARGEST COUNTRY, after Russia and Canada, China covers a vast area of eastern Asia. It has, by far, the largest population in the world and contains about 36 percent of Asia's people. China has a long Pacific coastline to the southeast, but also borders 14 countries inland. Closely associated with China are Taiwan, an independent island, and the two former European colonies of Hong Kong and Macao. China is ruled by a communist government that is working to continue the country's economic boom of the 1990s.

Great Wall

More than 2,200 years ago, 300,000 slaves built the Great Wall of China to keep out invaders from the north. Stretching from Central Asia to the Yellow Sea, the wall's total length is 3,980 miles (6,400 km), and is the world's longest human-made structure.

Soldiers walking along the Great Wall

Physical features

China's vast land area includes rugged hills, subarctic regions, deserts, and tropical plains, and is watered by many river systems. High mountains, mainly in the north and west, dominate one-third of China's land.

Huang He

Two mighty rivers flow in eastern China, the Chang Jiang and the Huang He. At 3,395 miles (5,464 km), the Huang He is known in English as the Yellow River, or "China's Sorrow," after the yellow soil left behind by its devastating floods.

Guilin Hills

China's agricultural heartland is in the south and center of the country. The Li river is used to irrigate land that can be intensively farmed. Here at Guilin, the river supports fishermen and their families, who make a living from its rich waters. The steep Guilin Hills rise up behind the river.

Climate

China has two main climates. More than half of the country is arid or semiarid, and in the north and west, deserts and mountains experience extreme temperature variations. The winters are bitterly cold and summers are hot and dry. The summer monsoon brings rain from the Pacific to areas nearer the sea, particularly the south and east, where conditions are wet, warm, and often humid.

111°F (44°C) · -30°F (-34°C) · 79°F (26°C) · 24°F (-4°C) · 24 in (623 mm)

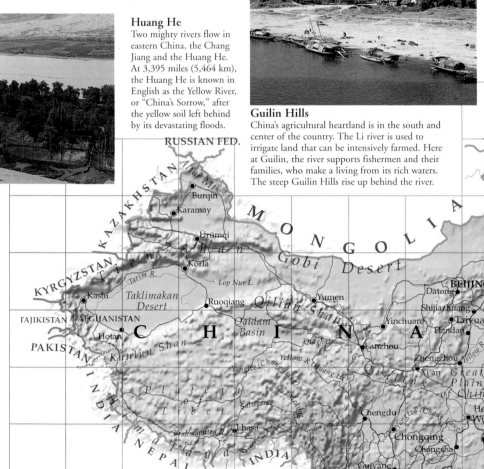

China

Ruled by the Communist Party since 1949, China is divided into 22 provinces, five autonomous regions and three special municipalities. Although technically governed from Beijing, many of these, are becoming increasingly independent. About 93 percent of China's people are Han Chinese, and more than 70 percent follow no religion because the communist rulers discourage religious beliefs. Although fertile land is in short supply, farming is often intensive and employs two-thirds of the workforce. Population growth has led to high unemployment.

Land use

The majority of China's farmland is in the east and south of the country. Much of the desert and mountain regions is uninhabitable. China has large mining areas in the Shaanxi and Sichuan basins, and is the world's largest coal producer.

Built-up 1.5%
Farming 36%
Wetland 2%
Barren 6.5%
Forest 9%
Desert 21%
Grassland 24%

CHINA FACTS

CAPITAL CITY Beijing

AREA 3,705,406 sq miles (9,596,961 sq km)

POPULATION 1,252,188,000

MAIN LANGUAGE Mandarin Chinese

MAJOR RELIGIONS Traditional beliefs, Buddhist

CURRENCY Yuan

LIFE EXPECTANCY 69 years

PEOPLE PER DOCTOR 730

GOVERNMENT One-party state

ADULT LITERACY 80%

Schoolchildren in Beijing

People

About 80 percent of Chinese live in less than half the country's land area, mostly in small villages. However, more than 30 of China's cities have more than one million inhabitants. China's population is growing by 15 million a year, so the government has asked families to have only one child, and fines those who have more. Known as "Little Emperors," single male children are often spoiled.

338 per sq mile (130 per sq km)

Urban 33%   Rural 67%

Food

Chinese food varies greatly from region to region. Rice is the basis of all dishes in the south, where it grows; in the north, wheat noodles are the staple food. Both noodles and rice are usually served with stir-fried vegetables and meat. Cantonese food is reputed to be the most exotic in China, using rare meats such as snake and turtle. Fish and duck are also served frequently. The Chinese eat with chopsticks held in one hand.

Chopsticks

Fried noodles

New Year

China's most important festival is the celebration of New Year, which begins in January or February at the second new Moon of winter. People celebrate with colorful processions and dragon dances and close all shops and offices. Each year is named after an animal.

Beijing

For more than 2,000 years, Beijing has been a capital city, either of all China or part of it. Built symmetrically within three rectangles, it is a bustling city of historical buildings, temples, and beautiful parks. The Forbidden City lies at its heart, home to the 15th-century emperor's Imperial Palace. Also from that period is the Temple of Heaven, designed in the Chinese pagoda style.

Temple of Heaven, Beijing

Leisure

City dwellers, who have no gardens, are encouraged to take exercise in the well-kept parks. On weekends and summer evenings, neighbors meet to play board games such as *mah jong*.

Shanghai

A leading center of trade and industry and a busy harbor, Shanghai is China's largest city and home to 8,760,000 people. The city has traditional pagodas and glittering skyscrapers alongside the Chang Jiang River.

Xi'an bicycle factory, Shaanxi

Handlebars

Industry

China has well-developed heavy industries such as iron and steel. Since the late 1970s, growth has been concentrated in Special Economic Zones in eastern China, where joint Chinese and foreign trade and enterprise are encouraged.

Rice farming

Many women work in flooded paddy fields in southern China. Rice is the main crop, and in a good year two yields can be harvested as is one of vegetables. When the crop is ready for harvesting, it turns golden. The women cut and tie the stalks into bundles for threshing, which separates the grain and its protective husk from the stalk.

Tibet

The mountainous region of Tibet became a part of China in 1965. Most Tibetans are devout Buddhists, but under Chinese rule their religious and civil liberties were taken away. Opponents of the government were exiled, and some Han Chinese were resettled in the area, causing tension. The monks still practice their faith and carry out ceremonies, such as offering beer to Buddha in a *hosar*, or New Year, ritual.

Tibetan monk pours Chang beer at hosar festival.

Taiwan

Often referred to as a "Little Dragon," Taiwan has one of Asia's most rapidly expanding economies. However, it is not recognized by the UN and lies at the center of a debate over ruling rights. China claims Taiwan to be a province of Beijing, although the Taiwanese have governed here since the communists took control of China in 1949. Despite this tension, Taiwan has established global trading markets and its people enjoy high living standards.

People

About 84 percent of Taiwanese are Han Chinese who moved to Taiwan when the communists took power in 1949. They live in extended family groups and follow traditional customs. Taiwan's native peoples of Indonesian origin now make up only two percent of the population. The Ami, of the eastern mountains, are the largest group. Expert potters and farmers, their women rule the household.

TAIWAN FACTS

CAPITAL CITY	Taipei
AREA	13,969 sq miles (36,179 sq km)
POPULATION	20,800,000
MAIN LANGUAGE	Mandarin Chinese
MAJOR RELIGIONS	Buddhist, traditional beliefs
CURRENCY	New Taiwan dollar
LIFE EXPECTANCY	75 years
PEOPLE PER DOCTOR	913
GOVERNMENT	Multiparty democracy
ADULT LITERACY	86%

Opera

Traditional Chinese opera was brought to the island with settlers from China. The operas are based on traditional stories. Stage sets are basic, but the costumes are elaborate, made from richly colored silks with delicate embroidery. Makeup is used to highlight emotions.

Fishermen unload their catch.

Sun Moon Lake

Taiwan's scenic Sun Moon Lake, known as *Jih-yüeh Tan,* is surrounded by the Central Mountains. The two parts of the lake, Sun Lake and Moon Lake, supply a hydroelectric plant that produces four percent of the country's power. The tranquil, forested area is known for its ornate buildings, including the Buddhist Wen Wu Temple.

Taipei

The high-tech capital in the north of the island is the fastest growing city in Asia, having expanded to four times its original size. Many of the three million inhabitants ride to work on motor scooters, causing pollution and jams.

Industry

A lack of natural resources forced Taiwan to develop highly specialized industry. Backed by an educated, ambitious workforce, the country exports electronic equipment, such as computers and television sets, machinery, textiles, sports equipment, toys, and watches. Profits are invested or used to buy oil for energy. Farming and fishing provide the nation's food.

Fishing

Taiwan's fishermen catch 1,290,793 tons (1,171,000 tonnes) of fish every year from the oceans that surround the island. Some Taiwanese fishermen have been accused of plundering Atlantic fishing grounds. Much of the catch goes to supply the huge Japanese market. Freshwater ponds are used for farming carp.

Hong Kong

Hong Kong is a territory in southeast China, made up of 236 islands and a mainland area. It has a busy port and is a leading financial center. Nearly six million people live in Hong Kong, making it the world's third most densely populated territory. A former British colony, Hong Kong was returned to China in 1997.

HONG KONG FACTS

CAPITAL CITY	Victoria
AREA	415 sq miles (1,076 sq km)
POPULATION	5,674,000
MAIN LANGUAGES	Chinese, English
MAJOR RELIGIONS	Buddhist, Christian
CURRENCY	Hong Kong dollar

Houseboats

Some Hong Kong fishing families live in houseboats called sampans, moored in the harbors. The fishermen are now facing increasing competition from more efficient deep-sea trawlers.

Macao

A tiny peninsula in southeastern China, Macao became a Portuguese colony nearly 450 years ago and will be returned to China in 1999. Located 40 miles (64 km) west of Hong Kong, Macao is a popular tourist destination, with fragrant woods and a sandy coastline on the South China Sea.

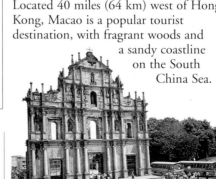

MACAO FACTS

CAPITAL CITY	Macao
AREA	7 sq miles (18 sq km)
POPULATION	355,700
MAIN LANGUAGES	Chinese, Portuguese
MAJOR RELIGIONS	Buddhist, Christian
CURRENCY	Pataca

Tourism

Macao has a thriving tourist industry. Visitors are attracted by historical Portuguese buildings like these ruins of St. Paul's Church, built in 1602. Macao's greatest tourist attractions, however, are the 24-hour casinos that bring the territory about one-third of its total income.

FIND OUT MORE: ASIA, HISTORY OF · BUDDHISM · CHESS AND OTHER BOARD GAMES · CHINA, HISTORY OF · FESTIVALS · FISHING INDUSTRY · GARDENS · OPERA · PORTS AND WATERWAYS · TRADE AND INDUSTRY

CHINA, HISTORY OF

CHINA IS THE WORLD'S oldest continuous civilization. For more than 2,000 years, from 221 BC to AD 1911, it was united as a single vast empire under a series of all powerful rulers. During this period, borders changed, capitals shifted, and the country was invaded by fierce tribes, including the Mongols. However, for most of its history, China led the world in art and technology, with inventions including paper, porcelain, and gunpowder. Despite its huge size, a unique system of government and a strong sense of national identity have helped to maintain a united China.

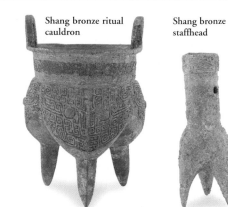

Shang bronze ritual cauldron

Shang bronze staffhead

Ancient China
The first known Chinese dynasty, the Shang, ruled from about 1500 to 1027 BC. The rulers of the Shang were believed to be semi-divine, and were called the Sons of Heaven. It was their duty to maintain good relations between earth and the heavenly realm.

Qin Shi Huangdi
When Zheng (258–210 BC), the leader of the victorious Qin army, took control of China in 221 BC, he took the title of First Sovereign Qin Emperor, or Qin Shi Huangdi. The First Emperor treated his subjects harshly, and his dynasty was overthrown by a peasant rebellion in 207 BC. The name China comes from Qin.

Each soldier has a different face and is modeled on a real soldier.

Hollow body

Unification

By 400 BC, central government had broken down, and many small kingdoms fought among themselves. In 221 BC, the state of Qin emerged victorious, uniting all the rival kingdoms under the rule of the First Emperor. The Great Wall was built at this time, using slave labor.

Chinese civil service exam paper

Han Dynasty

In 207 BC, a new dynasty took power. The Han emperors, who ruled until AD 220, set up a national civil service to run the country. Officials studied the teachings of the philosopher Confucius (551–479 BC), and were selected by a rigorous examination system. The structure of the civil service remained largely unchanged for 2,000 years. The Han reign marked a period of peace and prosperity.

Characters are read vertically.

Terra-cotta army
The First Emperor's tomb was guarded by thousands of life-size terra-cotta warriors with horses and chariots, whose job was to protect the emperor in the afterlife. This terracotta army was found in 1974 by men digging a well. The tomb lies near to the modern-day city of Xian.

The soldiers once carried real weapons made of bronze, but these were stolen by grave robbers.

Great Wall

First empire
Protected by the Great Wall, the Qin empire covered northern and eastern China. The Qin built the wall as a defence against hostile tribes from Central Asia.

Solid legs

Inventions

Throughout Chinese history, emperors encouraged the development of science and technology. Paper and printing, gunpowder, harnesses for animals, the magnetic compass and stern rudder, and the wheelbarrow were all invented in China.

15th-century gun

Shield protects soldier

Multiple gun fires a hail of bullets.

Gunpowder
Chinese scientists first produced gunpowder in the 9th century, and soon adapted their technology to make fireworks and weapons. Early Chinese rockets, fueled by gunpowder, were in use by the 13th century. The Chinese also invented the gun, the bomb, and the mine.

Chinese character, or symbol that translates to mean "happiness and good fortune"

Three perfections
The Chinese call calligraphy, poetry, and painting "the three perfections." From the Song dynasty (960–1279) onward, the combination of these three disciplines in a single work of art was considered to be the height of artistic expression, and to be skilled in them was seen as the greatest accomplishment of an educated person. Calligraphers spent many months practising the brushwork of just one or two characters.

Bronze "knife coins"

Paper money
The Chinese perfected papermaking in about AD 105, using pulped silk waste. In later years, hemp, bark, or bamboo were used. The development of printing followed, and paper money was first circulated in China in the 9th century. By this time, the Chinese were also printing books using carved wooden blocks.

C

Ming dynasty

Ming roof tile decorated with horse

In 1368, Hong Wu, a peasant who had led revolts against China's Mongol rulers, managed to drive the Mongols out and create a new dynasty, the Ming. He built a new capital at Beijing and established peace, prosperity, and good government. To make society more equal, he abolished slavery, confiscated big estates, gave land to the poor, and taxed the rich.

Tile would have decorated the ridge of a roof.

Admiral Zheng

As part of the policy of restoring Chinese prestige, the Ming emperors sent Admiral Zheng He (1371–1433) to visit foreign rulers. Zheng made seven voyages in Southeast Asia and the Indian Ocean, sailing as far west as East Africa. He was accompanied by a fleet of 317 oceangoing junks.

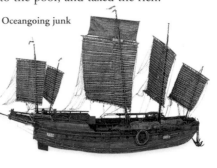
Oceangoing junk

Foot binding

The Chinese believed that tiny feet were a vital part of female beauty. Young girls from rich families had their feet tightly bound to prevent them from growing. This process was very painful. Adult women were also forced to wear platform shoes. In 1902, the emperor issued an order banning foot binding, although it continued for years.

Platform shoes made the wearer take tiny steps.

Decline of the empire

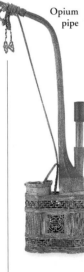
Opium pipe

During the last 250 years of the Chinese empire, the throne was occupied by the Manchus, a non-Chinese people from north of the Great Wall. The first Manchus were enlightened rulers, but later emperors feared that change might lead to rebellion and they clung to old traditions. In 1911, the Chinese overthrew the feeble Manchus, and established a republic.

Opium wars

In 1839, the Chinese tried to stop the British opium trade in Canton. The British went to war, forcing the Chinese to open ports to foreign trade and to cede Hong Kong to the British. France, Russia, and later Japan, made similar demands.

Boxer rebels

Boxer Rebellion

In 1900, a secret group called the Society of Harmonious Fists (Boxers) rose up in protest at European involvement in China. The rising was swiftly put down when an international force captured Beijing, but it weakened China's government.

Japanese troops in Manchuria

Japanese invasion

Civil war and a communist uprising weakened the new republican government. In 1931, the Japanese took advantage of the chaos to invade the northern province of Manchuria. Six years later they invaded the rest of China, capturing cities and ports.

Communist China

In 1949, the Communist party led by Mao Zedong (1893–1976) finally took control of China after years of civil war. The new government nationalized industry and the land, and began a series of five-year plans to transform the country into a major industrial power.

The red star, a Communist symbol from the Chinese flag

Modern China

After the death of Mao Zedong in 1976, the Chinese began to modernize their economy by introducing some western ideas and technology. Central government control over the economy relaxed, and this led to an economic boom as new industries were established.

Tiananmen Square

In 1989, students took to the streets of Beijing demanding democratic reform. Many students occupied Tiananmen Square, Beijing. On June 4, the army entered the square, killing more than 3,000 people. After this massacre, the pro-democracy movement was ruthlessly suppressed.

Troops in Tiananmen Square

Timeline

c.1650–1027 BC Shang dynasty rules northern China; bronzeworking and Chinese writing are developed.

221 BC First Emperor, Qin Shi Huangdi, founds the Qin dynasty and unites the country.

Shang bronze halberd (dagger)

221 BC–AD 618 Great Wall of China built.

589–618 Short-lived Sui dynasty builds the Grand Canal linking major rivers.

618–906 Tang dynasty brings great prosperity to China; art and trade flourish.

960–1279 Under the Song dynasty, advances in technology produce an industrial revolution.

1279 Mongols under Kublai Khan conquer China; trade with Europe flourishes along the Silk Road.

1368–1644 Ming dynasty establishes China as a major world power.

Mao Zedong

1644–1911 Manchu (Qing) dynasty.

1911 Chinese republic declared.

1949 Communists declare the People's Republic of China.

1966 Mao Zedong launches his Cultural Revolution.

1976 Chinese economy is modernized.

FIND OUT MORE   ASIA, HISTORY OF   CHINESE REVOLUTION   GUNS   INVENTIONS   MONGOL EMPIRE   POTTERY AND CERAMICS   WRITING

Chinese arts and crafts
Jewelry and adornment

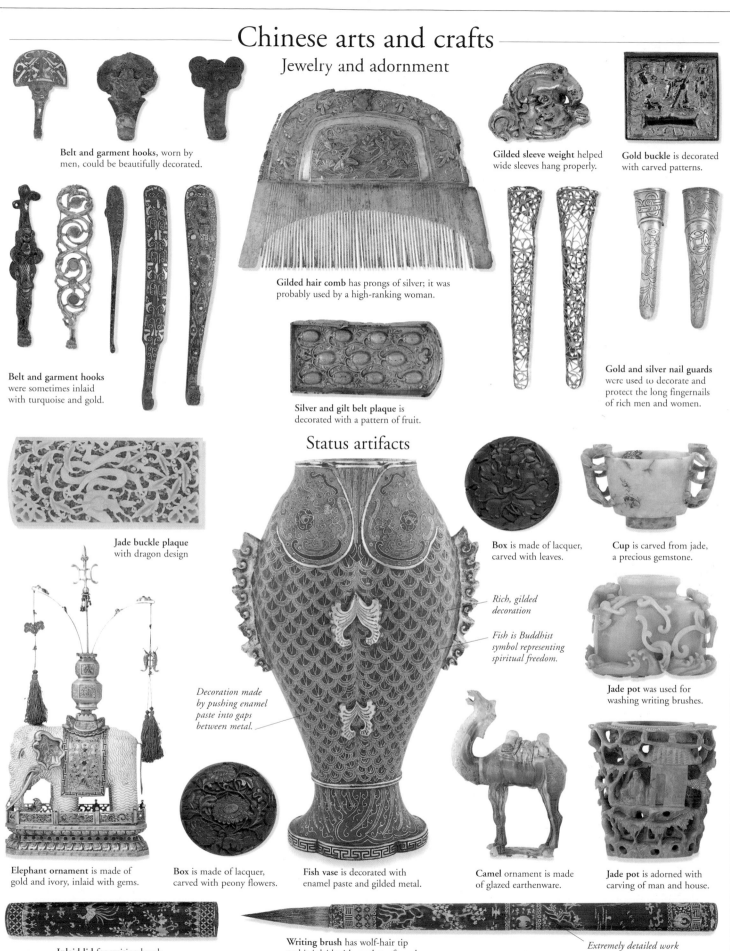

Belt and garment hooks, worn by men, could be beautifully decorated.

Gilded sleeve weight helped wide sleeves hang properly.

Gold buckle is decorated with carved patterns.

Gilded hair comb has prongs of silver; it was probably used by a high-ranking woman.

Belt and garment hooks were sometimes inlaid with turquoise and gold.

Silver and gilt belt plaque is decorated with a pattern of fruit.

Gold and silver nail guards were used to decorate and protect the long fingernails of rich men and women.

Status artifacts

Jade buckle plaque with dragon design

Box is made of lacquer, carved with leaves.

Cup is carved from jade, a precious gemstone.

Rich, gilded decoration

Fish is Buddhist symbol representing spiritual freedom.

Jade pot was used for washing writing brushes.

Decoration made by pushing enamel paste into gaps between metal.

Elephant ornament is made of gold and ivory, inlaid with gems.

Box is made of lacquer, carved with peony flowers.

Fish vase is decorated with enamel paste and gilded metal.

Camel ornament is made of glazed earthenware.

Jade pot is adorned with carving of man and house.

Inlaid lid for writing brush

Writing brush has wolf-hair tip and is inlaid with mother-of-pearl.

Extremely detailed work

CHINESE REVOLUTION

THE CHINESE REVOLUTION refers to the bitter struggle for control of China between the Kuomintang, or nationalists, led by Chiang Kai-shek, and the communists, led by Mao Zedong. The struggle began in the 1920s when the nationalists expelled the communists from their movement; it ended in 1949 when the communist party took power and Chairman Mao proclaimed that China was a People's Republic. Under Mao's leadership China was transformed from a backward peasant society into one of the most powerful nations in the world.

1911 Revolution

In 1911, a nationalist revolution overthrew the Manchu dynasty and created a republic in southern China. Sun Yat-sen (1866–1925) was elected provisional president of the republic, but the lives of the peasants did not improve and real power remained with warlords (military leaders).

Kuomintang

In 1926, a Kuomintang general named Chiang Kai-shek (1887–1975) defeated the warlords, helped by the communist party. Chiang set up a government in Nanking but, once in power, he threw the communists out of the government and massacred many communist leaders.

Long March

In 1931 Mao and a small band of communists set up China's first communist state in Jiangxi, southern China. The Kuomintang attacked them constantly, and in 1934 Mao was forced to withdraw. The following year he led 100,000 people, mostly peasants, over 6,000 miles (9,000 km) of some of the world's roughest terrain, to a new base in Shaanxi province in the north. The Long March crossed 18 mountain ranges, 24 rivers, and passed through 11 provinces and 62 cities.

Only 30,000 marchers out of the original 100,000 reached their destination.

Mao Zedong addressing followers at the Yan'an soviet during the early days of the revolution.

Liberation Army

Mao's Liberation (Red) Army was made up of peasant militia. It had an enormous amount of support; numbers rose from 150,000 in 1938 to 3 million in 1945.

Yan'an soviet

In 1935, Mao set up new headquarters in northern China – his Yan'an soviet, or base. He and his followers lived in caves around the city of Yan'an, and went into the countryside where they recruited a huge following among the peasantry.

Cap featuring red star

Epaulets show rank

Green wool pants

Red Army uniform

Little Red Book

Cultural Revolution

In 1966, in an attempt to introduce revolutionary zeal, Mao introduced a socialist cultural revolution to attack the four "olds": old ideas, old culture, old customs, and old habits. Those accused of "revisionism" (rejecting the revolution) were publicly humiliated in "struggle meetings." The Cultural Revolution ended in 1969, but its excesses nearly led to civil war.

Red Guard

Radical students, trained as Red Guards, were the main participants in the Cultural Revolution. Using the *Little Red Book* containing the thoughts of Chairman Mao, the Red Guard attacked anyone they believed guilty of betraying the revolution.

Mao Zedong

The son of a peasant, Mao (1893–1976) followed the nationalist ideals of Sun Yat-sen. In 1921, he helped found the Chinese communist party. Convinced that revolution should come from the peasants, not from the industrial workers, he built a massive following among them. After victory against Chiang Kai-shek, he became chairman of the new republic.

Timeline

1911 Nationalist revolution ends rule of the Manchu dynasty. A republic is formed.

1921 Chinese communist party formed.

1926 Northern Expedition: communists and nationalists unite to fight warlords.

1927 Kuomintang under General Chiang Kai-shek attacks and executes hundreds of communists.

Chairman Mao

1931 Japan invades Manchuria.

1934–5 Long March. Communists march to Shaanxi.

1937–45 Japan invades China. Communist guerilas harass Japanese and liberate most of northern China by 1945.

1945–48 Civil war between Kuomintang and Communists after Japanese surrender in World War II. Mao's communists gain control and set up government in Beijing (Peking). Nationalists and Chiang Kai-shek flee to Taiwan.

October 1, 1949 People's Republic of China is declared.

FIND OUT MORE

CHINA, HISTORY OF · COLD WAR · GOVERNMENTS AND POLITICS · JAPAN, HISTORY OF · RUSSIAN REVOLUTION · SOVIET UNION

CHRISTIANITY

CHRISTIANS BELIEVE that Jesus of Nazareth was the son of God, who came to Earth as promised in the Old Testament, and through whose life, death, and resurrection, believers are freed from their sinful state. Christianity began in the first century AD in the area now known as Israel and Palestine, which was then a part of the Roman Empire. The faith gradually spread throughout the Mediterranean, promoted by followers of Christ such as Saint Paul.

The cross symbolizes Christ's resurrection from the dead.

This elaborate gold cross is ornamented with precious stones.

The cross
Christ's death on the cross and his resurrection were the two key events in his life on Earth. The cross has therefore become the most important Christian symbol. Every church is marked by a cross, and crosses are placed on altars and in other prominent places in churches. During worship, Christians make the sign of the cross.

The Christian world
In the early years there were few Christians, and they were persecuted by the Romans because they refused to worship the Roman gods. But in AD 394, Christianity became the official religion of the Roman Empire after the conversion of the emperor Constantine. The faith spread quickly throughout the empire. Today's Catholic church is still based in Rome and claims to be the descendant of the early church in the Mediterranean. There are now nearly 1.6 billion Christians worldwide.

God the Father

The holy spirit is shown as a white dove, the symbol of peace.

Christ on the cross is a symbol of death and salvation.

Beneath Christ's feet is a globe representing the Earth.

Shading shows worldwide distribution of Christians.

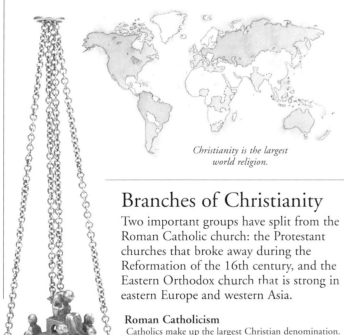

Christianity is the largest world religion.

Stained-glass window showing St. Luke and St. John teaching the gospel

Spreading the word
Jesus preached the coming of God's kingdom, but his message was rejected and he was put to death. On the third day after Christ's death, God brought him back to life. Christ met his followers and told them to spread the word. Since then, Christianity has been spread by preachers and missionaries. From Europe, colonists took the faith with them to Africa and the Americas.

The Holy Trinity
Christians believe that God exists as three persons: God the Father is the creator; God the Son is Jesus Christ; and God the Holy Spirit is the presence of God on Earth. It is the Holy Spirit that inspires prophets and acts as a means of divine revelation. Although there are three persons in the Holy Trinity, they exist as one substance, so Christians believe in one God.

Branches of Christianity
Two important groups have split from the Roman Catholic church: the Protestant churches that broke away during the Reformation of the 16th century, and the Eastern Orthodox church that is strong in eastern Europe and western Asia.

Roman Catholicism
Catholics make up the largest Christian denomination. They stress the importance of the church's role in interpreting the scriptures and the authority of the Pope as the leader of the church. They believe in the doctrine of transubstantiation – that the bread and wine used in the Mass are actually converted into the body and blood of Christ.

In Catholic churches, incense is burned to release scented smoke.

Charcoal is put into the censer and lit to heat the incense.

Medieval censer

A Protestant service in London, UK

Bare walls without paintings or statues

Protestantism
There are many different Protestant churches around the world, especially in North America. To a greater or lesser extent, they all stress the authority of scripture itself, rather than the clergy's interpretation of the text of the Bible. These branches do not believe in the doctrine of transubstantiation. Although there is great variation in their rituals, Protestants have simpler church buildings and less elaborate ceremonies than the Catholic and Orthodox churches.

Orthodox Christians pray to icons, such as this image of St. George.

Orthodoxy
Like the Roman church, the Eastern Orthodox church stresses the importance of the sacraments. Orthodox Christians do not recognize the authority of the Pope: the highest authority is the church's Ecumenical Council.

Ceremonies

The most important Christian ceremonies are the sacred rites known as sacraments. The Roman Catholic and Orthodox churches recognize seven sacraments: baptism (the rite of entry into the church), confirmation (a further initiation ceremony), the Eucharist (Mass), penance (turning to God after sin), extreme unction (preparation for death), ordination (becoming a priest), and marriage. The Protestant churches recognize baptism and the Eucharist.

Baptism

This ritual is an act of ceremonial cleansing before becoming a member of a church. In some cases, holy water is splashed on the head of the infant. In other cases, an adult entering the church is totally immersed in water.

Marriage

Christians believe that marriage symbolizes the relationship of Christ with his church. Marriage marks the beginning of a new family and a new generation.

Eucharist

At his last supper with his disciples, Christ identified the bread and wine as his body and blood. Christians remember this at the Eucharist (or Mass), at which a priest consecrates bread and wine and distributes it among the worshipers.

Head of saint

A priest blesses the wine in a chalice.

Sixteenth-century silver chalice

Festivals

The most important Christian festival is Easter when believers commemorate Christ's crucifixion and resurrection. The celebration of Christ's birth, Christmas, is an important festival. Ancient pagan festivals merged with Christian festivals so that old fertility rites are linked with Easter and winter festivals with Christmas.

An Amish couple in Pennsylvania travel in a horse-drawn carriage.

Amish

The Amish are a Protestant sect founded in the 17th century. Its followers live separately from the rest of society and believe that salvation can only be reached within the community. In the US, Amish communities follow a simple lifestyle with strict rules. They reject modern technology and wear traditional clothing, such as vests and hats and bonnets and capes.

In the Middle Ages, saints' relics were kept in reliquaries.

Reliquary of St. Eustace, an early Roman Christian martyr

The Adoration of the Magi, by Botticelli (1444–1510)

Saints' days

Christians who have lived outstanding lives or who were killed for their beliefs are revered as saints. Each saint has his or her own special day, and these are often marked with processions, celebrations, and church services. Festivals on saints' days are particularly popular in Catholic countries.

Easter

The celebration of Easter can involve many moods, from the solemn prayers of Good Friday, when the crucifixion is remembered, to joy at the resurrection three days later. A spring festival, Easter is a time when new life is celebrated. Christ's resurrection is reflected in the new growth of plants and crops, and is celebrated by children when they hunt for decorated eggs.

Christmas

Christ's nativity (birth) is traditionally celebrated in December. The Christmas story tells of his birth in a stable in Bethlehem. The many Christmas customs include giving presents, decorating trees, lighting candles, singing special hymns (or carols), and eating elaborate meals.

This nativity painting shows the worship of the Magi, the three Wise Men who came bearing gifts.

An Easter procession in Granada, Spain

Christians carry a statue to symbolize Christ carrying the cross.

The Bible

The sacred text of the Christian religion is the Bible. Its first part is the Old Testament, a group of books inherited from the Jews, among whom Christianity originally took root. Second comes the New Testament, which is made up of books dealing with the early history of Christianity. The New Testament includes the four gospels, the Acts and Epistles (giving details of the spread of Christianity), and the Book of Revelation (containing prophecies for the future).

The Dead Sea Scrolls

The gospels

The first four books of the New Testament are called the gospels, from a word meaning "good news." They tell the story of the life of Christ. Three of the four gospels (those of Matthew, Mark, and Luke) are very similar; they are known as the synoptic gospels. John's gospel is quite different from the others, and its author may not have known the other three texts.

The Dead Sea Scrolls

These scrolls of parchment were discovered in caves near Qumran on the Dead Sea in the 1940s and 1950s. They contain writings that include texts of parts of the Old Testament in versions earlier than any previously discovered. They were hidden in AD 68.

St. Paul

Originally opposed to Christianity, Paul converted when he had a vision of Christ. He began to preach Christianity and spread the faith on four arduous missionary journeys through Greece and Asia Minor. His role was central to the early development of the church. He wrote several of the New Testament books in the form of letters to the Christian communities he visited. He died c. AD 64-68.

FIND OUT MORE CHURCHES AND CATHEDRALS CRUSADES EUROPE, HISTORY OF FESTIVALS HOLY LAND JESUS CHRIST MONASTERIES MOTHER TERESA REFORMATION RELIGIONS

CHURCHES AND CATHEDRALS

CHURCHES AND CATHEDRALS are Christian places of worship. Early churches were small, with only enough room for an altar and a small congregation. As Christianity spread, larger churches, with separate areas for the clergy and the followers, were built. A cathedral is a church in which a bishop presides; he organizes the day-to-day running of local parishes.

The first churches

Christianity began in the Mediterranean during the time of the Roman Empire. Early churches were modeled on the public buildings of ancient Rome, especially basilicas, where meetings and law courts were held. The congregation sat in an area called the nave, and the altar was housed in a smaller area, the sanctuary.

St. Sabina, Rome
Founded in AD 422, this early church has a wide nave and small, semicircular sanctuary.

Parts of a cathedral

Many cathedrals and churches are designed in the shape of a cross. The "arms" of the cross, the transepts, contain small chapels. The altar lies to the east to face the rising sun; the nave lies toward the west.

404-ft (123-m) spire

Columns and vaults
The interior has decorative stone ceilings, called ribbed vaults, supported on columns of local Purbeck marble. Each column is surrounded by four shafts (smaller columns), which create a light, delicate effect.

Bell towers have openings to allow the sound of the bells to escape.

The large nave can accommodate big congregations.

Salisbury Cathedral
This 13th-century Gothic cathedral has slender walls and pointed arches and windows. These features help make it elegant and delicate in spite of its huge size. The 14th-century spire is the tallest in England and can be seen from far away.

Lady chapel — *High altar* — *Sanctuary* — *Eastern transept* — *Sacristy* — *Western transept* — *North aisle* — *Nave* — *South aisle* — *North porch* — *West front*

Floor plan
The cross shape symbolizes the wooden cross on which Christ died.

Cathedral interior
The great nave, with its high, vaulted ceiling, is made to appear larger still by aisles on either side. Light comes in through stained glass windows.

Intricately carved west front

Main entrance

Western transept *Eastern transept*

Sanctuary

Pointed arches are a typical feature of Gothic architecture.

Lady chapel

Buttresses (supports) help bear the weight of heavy vaults.

Church decoration

Many churches and cathedrals are richly decorated with symbols of the Christian religion, including images of Christ, angels, the saints, and crosses. Protestant churches tend to be less elaborately decorated than Roman Catholic and Eastern Orthodox churches.

Fan vaulting
This delicate fan vault can be found at Canterbury Cathedral, England.

Statuary
Representations of the Madonna and Child are found in Roman Catholic churches. This Renaissance-style statue, which was finished in 1896, is in the church of the Sacré-Coeur, Paris.

Mosaic
Mosaics were an early form of decoration in Mediterranean churches. This 9th-century mosaic is in the Santi Nereo e Achilleo, Rome.

Gargoyle
Devils and grotesques were carved on church exteriors during the Middle Ages to represent evil outside the church.

Triptych
The finest decoration of all is usually close to the altar, such as this triptych in St. Peter's Basilica, Rome.

Stained glass windows
Beautiful colored windows that decorate churches often illustrate Bible stories told by Jesus and his disciples.

Churchyards

Churchyards separate a church from noisy streets and provide land to bury the dead. Burials also take place in large cemeteries.

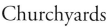

Celtic cross
This cross in Ireland combines two Christian symbols: the cross and the circle, a symbol of eternity.

Columbarium
A Columbarium houses the ashes of cremated people.

Burial tombs
Some tombs tell the lives of those buried inside. This tomb of much-imprisoned French revolutionary Raspail is in the form of a prison.

FIND OUT MORE ARCHITECTURE CHRISTIANITY FESTIVALS GLASS MEDIEVAL EUROPE RELIGIONS

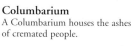

CITIES

C

LESS THAN 200 YEARS AGO, most people lived in villages. Today, about one-half of the world's population lives in cities. During the 19th century, towns and cities expanded as people moved away from rural areas to work in new industries. Cities have continued to grow haphazardly, in contrast to the carefully-planned cities of the ancient world.

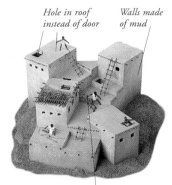

Hole in roof instead of door
Walls made of mud
Early cities had no streets.

Çatal Hüyük

First cities

Settlements in western Asia, such as Jericho (Israel), Çatal Hüyük (Turkey), and Ur (Iraq), started to expand around 4000 BC. At this time, craftsworkers began to trade goods outside their local areas, creating new wealth that was used to build palaces, large temples, and strong walls for defense. These towns grew in importance and emerged as the first cities.

Modern cities

The world's cities have grown rapidly in modern times but inadequate planning has contributed to poor living conditions and poverty in many urban centers. Poor areas, wealthy neighborhoods, and areas dominated by one particular ethnic group are all features of city life. Most cities offer many people a wide choice of jobs, houses, and recreational facilities.

Gardens, parks, and squares give people the chance to escape the bustle of city streets.

Entertainment is a feature of most cities. Cities are usually cultural centers with theaters, museums, galleries, and music venues, such as Sydney's striking Opera House.

Residential
There are different residential areas in cities. Older houses and apartments are close to the city center, while modern developments extend outwards, clustering around railroad lines and major roads.

Sydney, Australia

Roads, railroads, boats, and airlines bring people into the city center.

Business is always located close to the heart of the city. Nowadays, the business area is usually dominated by skyscrapers.

Manufacturing
Small factories and light industry were once at the heart of cities. Today, large industrial complexes are usually built farther out, reducing pollution.

Apartment building
Skyscraper
Converted loft
Brownstone
Underground
Services

New York
The city of New York contains some of the world's tallest skyscrapers. It also has large apartment buildings, low-rise commercial sites (some of which have been converted into homes called lofts), 19th-century brownstone (a type of sandstone) houses, and smaller, modern houses. Steps lead to underground subways and shops.

Villages

A traditional village is a small, rural settlement, often by a stream or river. In most parts of the world, people still live and work in villages, farming the surrounding countryside and trading with nearby settlements.

Masai village, Kenya
Many of the Masai people live in groups of thatched, mud houses surrounding a central cattle enclosure.

Stilt village, Sumatra
In many Southeast Asian villages, houses are raised on stilts to keep out unwanted animals, like snakes.

Gold rush town
Towns grew around 19th century gold mines. Abandoned as the gold ran out, some still stand as "ghost towns".

Forbidden City
The Forbidden City in Beijing, China, was built in the 15th century. Only the emperor, his family, and his officials were allowed in.

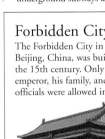

Timeline

8000 BC Strong walls and a stone tower are built at Jericho.

3500 BC City-states such as Ur develop in Mesopotamia (modern Iraq).

5th century BC Greeks plan and build the elegant city of Athens.

1st century BC The Roman Empire expands, and new European cities are built.

12th century AD Stone walls, such as those at Carcassonne, France, are built to protect medieval towns and cities.

1421 Construction starts on Forbidden City, Beijing, China.

15th century Renaissance architects lay out classical cities, such as Florence and Siena in Italy.

Siena, Italy

19th century Industrialization stimulates growth of towns and cities in Europe and America.

1950s Brasilia designed and constructed as new capital of Brazil.

1990s Skyscrapers dominate most city skylines.

| FIND OUT MORE | ARCHAEOLOGY | ARCHITECTURE | BUILDING AND CONSTRUCTION | INDUSTRIAL REVOLUTION | IRON AND STEEL | RENAISSANCE | SOCIETIES, HUMAN | TRAINS AND RAILROADS |